Praise for Steve Bogira's

COURTROOM 302

"Steve Bogira shines a blazing new light on America's criminal justice system. This book is filled with one revelatory insight after another about how that system really works. . . . Mr. Bogira shows that he is a masterful reporter not only of our country's criminal justice system but also of human beings caught up in its gears."
—Robert A. Caro

"Powerful and moving. . . . Bogira is more than a gifted writer. . . . [He] is an inspiring reminder of what investigative reporting can and should do to keep our national institutions cleaner and better than they are."
—*Los Angeles Times*

"A gripping, insightful book. . . . Required reading for anyone interested in the realities of the American justice system."
—*Newsday*

"Bogira writes with clarity, passion, and often lyrical beauty. . . . With a good eye for detail and a dramatist's attention to what motivates his characters, he reveals the common humanity of the rumpled and rank prisoners. . . . Those who consider it long overdue to shine a light on this branch of government might start by reading his book."
—*The Providence Journal*

"Riveting. . . . An immensely important book that exposes how America's criminal justice system really works. . . . Its steady stream of powerful insights inevitably apply to every big city court system in the nation."
—*Chicago Sun-Times*

"Brilliant. . . . A genuine eye-opener. Bogira . . . has produced a compelling narrative, that is often more entertaining than most of the cop shows which are so popular on American television." —*The Economist*

"Fascinating." —*Entertainment Weekly*

"An eye-opener. Bogira is a journalist who knows his trade as well as anyone I've encountered in recent years. A remarkable book." —Studs Terkel

STEVE BOGIRA

COURTROOM 302

Steve Bogira graduated from Northwestern University and has been a prizewinning writer for the *Chicago Reader* since 1981. He is a former Alicia Patterson Fellow. He lives with his wife in Evanston, Illinois.

COURTROOM 302

COURTROOM 302

A YEAR BEHIND THE SCENES IN AN
AMERICAN CRIMINAL COURTHOUSE

STEVE BOGIRA

VINTAGE BOOKS
A Division of Random House, Inc.
New York

FIRST VINTAGE BOOKS EDITION, FEBRUARY 2006

The Library of Congress has cataloged the Knopf edition as follows:
Bogira, Steve.
Courtroom 302 : a year behind the scenes in an American criminal courthouse /
Steve Bogira. —1st ed.
p. cm.
Includes index.
1. Criminal courts—Illinois—Chicago. 2. Criminal justice, Administration of—Illinois—
Chicago. 3. Criminal Justice personnel—Illinois—Chicago. 4. Criminals—Illinois—
Chicago. I. Title.
KFX1247.B64 2005
345.773'1101—dc22
2004057636

Vintage ISBN-10: 0-679-75206-4
Vintage ISBN-13: 978-0-679-75206-6

Author photograph © Jack Demuth
Book design by Iris Weinstein

www.vintagebooks.com

Printed in the United States of America
10 9 8 7 6 5 4 3 2

For Jane, my partner in crime

The horrible thing about all legal officials, even the best, about all judges, magistrates, barristers, detectives, and policemen, is not that they are wicked (some of them are good), not that they are stupid (several of them are quite intelligent), it is simply that they have got used to it. Strictly they do not see the prisoner in the dock; all they see is the usual man in the usual place. They do not see the awful court of judgment; they only see their own workshop.

—G. K. CHESTERTON
Tremendous Trifles

The lockups are always open and there are always new faces. . . . Where they all come from nobody knows and where they'll go from here nobody cares.

—NELSON ALGREN
Chicago: City on the Make

CONTENTS

COURTROOM 302

PROLOGUE

Welcome to County

EVERY DAY, Chicago police wagons swing onto the grounds of the Cook County Criminal Courthouse and deposit their cargo at a rear door.

The prisoners being unloaded on this particular evening—January 20, 1998—are here for the usual reasons. They sold cocaine rocks on a corner, until an unmarked car screeched up out of nowhere. They tried to buy heroin from an undercover cop. They pocketed a fifth of booze at a grocery and failed to outrun the security guard. They relieved a pickup truck of its tools and a nosy neighbor called 911.

At the district station, they pulled off their belts and pulled out their laces. They emptied their pockets of combs, cigarettes, matchbooks. They pressed their fingers onto the ink pad, frowned for the camera, and joined the rest of the day's catch in a frigid lockup. They curled up on a metal bench or a concrete floor and waited—midnight, four in the morning, noon—while computers checked their prints for outstanding warrants. They were treated to a baloney-on-white and coffee in a Styrofoam cup. Those with misdemeanor charges and no warrants were given a court date and released. The others were cuffed wrist to wrist and loaded into the large police wagon that swung by the station. The chain of prisoners in the wagon lengthened as the driver made pickups at other stations. The wagon bumped along toward the courthouse at 26th and California.

The Cook County Criminal Courthouse—the biggest and busiest felony courthouse in the nation—sits in a Mexican neighborhood on Chicago's southwest side. It's a boxy limestone structure, seven stories high and seven decades old, with Doric columns, Latin phrases carved into the limestone, and eight sculpted figures above the columns, representing law, justice, liberty, truth, might, love, wisdom, and peace. None of them is visible from the back of a police wagon.

A paunchy, balding white officer is behind the wheel of the first wagon to dip down a ramp and dock at the rear door this evening. He opens the wagon's tail, and a chain of fifteen men, a dozen black and three white, winds its way out. The prisoners are rumpled and rank—the wagon-tossed, wretched refuse of a major American city, arrested on Martin Luther King Day. The driver follows the prisoners to the door, balancing over one shoulder a clear bag holding fifteen smaller clear bags that contain keys, combs, lip salve, cigarettes, lighters, beepers, eyeglasses, belts, shoelaces. In his other hand is a sheaf of arrest reports and rap sheets.

A navy-shirted sheriff's deputy slides open the barred door, and the prisoners file into the courthouse basement. About fifteen hundred prisoners pass through this doorway weekly on their way to a bond hearing—78,000 men and women a year accused of violating the peace and dignity of the State of Illinois.

In thirty courtrooms on floors two through seven, plea deals are fashioned and hearings and trials conducted every weekday. But for most defendants, the first glimpse of the interior of the courthouse is of this cellar.

The cellar holds several dank chambers with cinder-block walls and metal benches bolted to concrete floors. The grimy walls have been decorated here and there by deputies who had a black marker or a tube of Preparation H and time on their hands. WELCOME TO COUNTY—GET SERVED WITH A SMILE reads the script next to a horned and goateed grinning devil on a wall near the entrance. Other greetings: THIS WAY TO THE DANCE, and HEAD FIRST—HIT HERE, and YOU WON'T BE HOME FOR CHRISTMAS.

Later tonight the prisoners will be escorted through a tunnel to the quivering elevator that will carry them up to Courtroom 100 for their bond hearings. At evening's end the lucky prisoners who can make bond or who get an "I-bond" (a no-money-down individual-recognizance bond) will walk out of the courthouse's front door. The rest of the prisoners—about two-thirds of them, if this is a typical night—will ride the elevator back downstairs and march through a longer tunnel to jail.

"Okay, fifteen desperate criminals," the paunchy officer tells the deputy at the entrance, one of twenty deputies working in the basement this evening. Yawning, the officer hands over the property bag and the paperwork.

The prisoners are directed to a bench in a bullpen down the hall, where they stand as they're told—silently, backs of their legs against the edge of the bench. A second police officer is already at the door, dropping off three bleary-eyed black women. A deputy points them to a nearby bench. They step warily past Blackjack, a German shepherd, and Harley, a Rottweiler, the dogs straining toward them, tugging on the leashes gripped by two deputies.

Meanwhile a deputy in the bullpen at the end of the hall makes his way down the line of fifteen men, unlocking and collecting the handcuffs for the first wagon driver.

"When the cuffs come off, your hands go behind your back," snaps the bull-necked, light-skinned African American deputy who's got the paperwork now. "All right, when you hear your last name, tell me your first name. Powell."

"Here."

Bullneck stalks over to Powell, a frail black youth in a neon-orange windbreaker. "Is your first name *Here*, motherfucker?" the deputy hollers in the startled youth's face.

The prisoners make it through the rest of roll call flawlessly, and then Bullneck directs them to sit. Another wagon arrives, and ten more disheveled males join the first fifteen in the back room. After they're uncuffed and checked in and have taken their seats on one of the benches that line three sides of the chamber, Bullneck welcomes them all to 26th Street.

"You don't scare me," he tells them. "You don't intimidate me. And you sure fucking don't impress me." He informs the prisoners that they'll be going to bond court, and that after that they'll be headed home or to jail. But there's a third place they can end up if they don't follow the rules here, Bullneck warns—the jail hospital.

The rules are simple and not to be questioned, he says—no food, no phone calls, no smoking. "I don't care if you haven't eaten all week or made a phone call all day. It's not my problem." And the cardinal rule: in the hallways, on the elevator, in the courtroom upstairs, a prisoner's hands must remain behind his back. "We don't know you. We don't know what the fuck is on your mind. You come out with your hands swinging, you're gonna get dropped," Bullneck says. "If you forget every other rule I tell you, don't forget the hands-behind-the-back rule."

Bullneck surveys his mute, expressionless subjects.

"Does everybody understand the fucking rules?"

A handful of mumbled *yessir*s.

"Let me hear that *again*."

"Yes *sir*!"

Next Bullneck announces "freebie time," inviting the prisoners to surrender any drugs they've managed to retain despite earlier searches by Chicago police. Nobody gets charged for what they give up now, he promises. But those who think they can sneak something by the deputies should know that Blackjack and Harley will be along presently. And if those dogs sniff a rock, a pinch of blow, or a roach, "you're gonna get bit, and you're gonna get charged." As usual, no one takes advantage of freebie time.

Now Bullneck has the men remove their coats and jackets and toss them onto the floor in the middle of the room. Four deputies wearing black gloves work through the heap of sports team jackets and Salvation Army specials, exploring pockets and kneading collars and waistbands. Meanwhile Bullneck directs the prisoners to pull off their laceless sneakers or workboots, tear out any liners, and hold the shoes upside down by the toes, arms outstretched. The men dutifully comply, and in a moment a ring of stocking-footed men are wordlessly offering up their soles to him.

"And when I tell you to, don't bang 'em like a buncha pussies," Bullneck says. "Bang 'em so anything inside falls out." He studies the group; all eyes are on him.

"Now—*bang* 'em!"

A host of arms are immediately pumping, *beating* those shoes and boots together, admirably unpussylike, the stampede echoing off the walls for a quarter of a minute, until Bullneck raises a hand. Nothing but lint has fallen to the concrete.

Next he has the men peel off their socks, extend their legs in front of them, and shake their socks while wiggling their toes. A yeasty odor rises in the room.

"All right, everybody stand up!" Bullneck bellows. "Turn around, grab some wall!" The four gloved deputies commence the pat-downs. It's not a penetrating search: anyone willing to tuck a cocaine rock up his butt will get away with it for now, but those who end up going to jail had better smoke up that rock in the jail bullpens before the strip-search there. Blackjack and Harley are mainly showpieces, Bullneck's warning about the dogs' impending sniff-search an empty threat. The deputies are checking for weapons now more than drugs. They don't trust the pat-downs of Chicago's finest; prisoners have arrived here with knives in their pockets, the deputies claim. (Chicago cops "couldn't find their ass with both hands," one deputy says.)

A skinny Hispanic man awaiting his search foolishly peeks over his shoulder. The boss here tonight, the white-shirted Sergeant London Thomas, who's been watching the pat-downs from just outside the bullpen, is at the skinny man's side in an instant. "What the *fuck*'re you staring at *me* for?" Thomas roars in the man's ear. "Face the fucking wall!

"*Everybody* should be staring at the wall," Thomas growls. "Ain't nothing behind you but an ass-kicking."

"This guy's got a ring on that don't come off," a deputy says. "Guess we'll just have to lop off a finger."

"What's with you?" asks another deputy, of the trembling middle-aged man he's searching.

"I have MS," the man mumbles.

"Oh, he has *PMS*," the deputy announces, to his comrades' snickers.

There's a method to the deputies' malice, Sergeant Thomas says later: it's to let the prisoners know immediately who's in charge in the court-house. "Control is something we cannot relinquish," the sergeant says. "If we did that, we'd be fucked up right away. Extremely." The twenty or so deputies who work a bond court shift are watching at least sixty and some-times more than a hundred prisoners. The deputies carry no weapons, to eliminate the risk of a prisoner seizing one. "We're armed with gloves, handcuffs, and attitude," Thomas says.

But the deputies' tone also expresses their sentiments about the prison-ers. Those marched into the basement are cloaked in the presumption of innocence—in theory. The prevailing wisdom down here, however, is: if they're so innocent, why'd they arrive in handcuffs?

"We get the dregs of humanity here," says Lieutenant John Hopkins, tonight's watch commander in the courthouse. "If these people moved in next door to you, your lawn would die."

Hopkins believes in the golden rule. Treat the prisoners respectfully, he instructs his deputies, and don't get rough if you're not provoked. But some of his deputies are a little too eager to do unto others, he concedes, believ-ing "that the only justice is at the end of a good right cross." Hopkins doesn't spend much time in the basement, allowing Sergeant Thomas to run the show down here most evenings. Hopkins says an occupational haz-ard of his job as watch commander is "the stiff neck you can get from looking the other way."

Sergeant Thomas, a tall, muscular African American, says the depu-ties threaten violence a lot more than they deliver it. Every now and then, though, certain prisoners require "a little—*positive reinforcement*," he says with a chuckle.

When the deputies have finished their pat-downs and the prisoners have been allowed to retrieve their coats from the pile, Thomas strides to the center of the group—the head coach with the final pregame chat, now that his assistant has warmed up the team. "I want to have a nice, quiet night," he tells the prisoners. "I want to get done, have a drink, and go home. Gen-tlemen, your situation's fucked up enough as it is. You don't need it any more fucked up."

It's time to move these first twenty-five men to a bullpen around the corner to make room for another batch at the door. Bullneck instructs his prisoners to follow another deputy down the hall—single file, hands behind their backs, of course. Shoves and shouts from Bullneck and his colleagues chase the line of prisoners on their way: "Get the *fuck* going!" "Keep moving, *dick*head!"

A different deputy gives the welcoming speech to the second bedraggled collection, reminding these men "what a fucked-up bunch of smelly motherfuckers" they are. There's never a lack of volunteers among the deputies for the honor of delivering the welcoming talk, with each succeeding speaker trying to outbadass the last one. "Some of 'em get off on it more than others," Sergeant Thomas says.

A prisoner at the entrance complains of dizziness. He fell and hit his head shortly before his arrest, he tells Thomas. Thomas surveys the man's head for cuts or swelling, finds none. Almost every night the sergeant has to do a diagnosis such as this. Anyone who insists he needs medical care will be taken to nearby St. Anthony Hospital—Holy Tony's, as the deputies call it. But Thomas discourages the trips when he's not convinced of the need. He knows some of the prisoners are merely trying to postpone their date with jail. The regulations require two deputies to accompany each prisoner who goes to the hospital, so Thomas would be shorthanded fast if he granted every request. There's paperwork involved as well. The prisoners aren't likely to expire in court, and in a couple of hours they'll either be the jail hospital's concern or, if they bond out, not the county's problem at all. Thus Thomas is often like the detective who persuades a suspect he doesn't really need a lawyer. For tonight's dizzy prisoner, he invokes one of his standard fabrications: "I can send you to the hospital if you *want*. But the officer who drove you here? He's got to drive you to the hospital. And then you got to ride *all* the way back here with him." Dizzy or not, the prisoner gets Thomas's hint about the peril of being alone in the custody of an aggravated cop, and he decides to forgo medical aid.

The initial group of prisoners is occupying one of three bullpens down another hallway. The benches are full, the overflow on the floor. Soon the second group comes marching single file down the corridor and fills the middle bullpen. Thomas tells everybody that standing isn't allowed. Fights in the bullpens were common when Thomas began working bond court three years ago—there were more "gangbangers" (gang members) being arrested then, he says. The fights led to the rule against standing, the idea being that it's harder to throw a punch while sitting. The prohibition probably isn't needed anymore, Thomas says, because the prisoners these days are mostly a docile bunch of addicts and small-time dealers. But rules are rules, and so when Thomas spots a man standing in bullpen two, he strides immediately over to him and booms, "What the *fuck* you doing standing in my bullpen? Do I have to *chain* you to the floor to get you to sit down?" The man quickly drops to the floor.

When more prisoners come down the hall, Thomas splits them between bullpens one and two, jamming those chambers, the men shoulder to shoulder on the benches and the floor. The female prisoners are being held in an anteroom near the basement entrance. Thomas wishes he could put some of the men in bullpen three, but it's occupied by the juveniles—the kiddie criminals, as the deputies call them. Most juveniles charged with delinquency are tried at the juvenile court two miles northeast of here. But thirteen- to sixteen-year-olds facing adult charges—murder, rape, armed robbery, drug dealing near a school—are bused here from the detention center next to the juvenile court for their court dates. A dozen of them who had court appearances here earlier today are on the benches of bullpen three, chatting quietly, waiting for the bus to return them to the detention center. The bus, as usual, is late. Thomas will be happier when the juveniles are gone, not just because it'll free up another bullpen but also because of what pests the kiddie criminals can be, with their godawful whining. "It's 'What time's the *bus* coming?'" Thomas says. "'Can I get something to *eat*?'"

Thomas calls his adult prisoners out to the hallway one at a time and with a black marker prints a three-digit number on the back of each prisoner's hand, and the same number on each prisoner's property bag. Many of the prisoners already have a number scrawled on one arm, a memento from the district station. Those who end up going to jail tonight will get further markings on their hands or arms as they're assigned to a division, a tier, and a cell. The bullpens are quiet while Thomas does his numbering. Some of the prisoners are dozing; others are studying the floor or the back of the head of the prisoner in front of them. Most of the adult prisoners have been through this before, and those who haven't catch on quickly, understanding that remaining silent is not a right now but an expectation.

There's always a slow learner, however. Tonight it's a balding white man, who hails a deputy passing in the hallway, telling him he's got a question. Thomas overhears, drops the hand of the prisoner he's numbering, rushes into the bullpen, and sticks his nose menacingly in the balding man's ruddy face: "Ex*cuse* me—why am I about to beat the *piss* outta you?" The prisoner averts his eyes and says nothing more. Thomas returns to the hallway.

The sergeant is never surprised when the pain-in-the-ass is a white guy. White prisoners tend to be either too dumb or too smart to do jail well, Thomas says. The white guys, like the kiddie criminals, seem compelled to broadcast that they know their rights, he says. Female prisoners aggravate Thomas even more. White, black, or Hispanic, the women wail about everything, he says, often in grating voices. Give me fifty male prisoners instead of five females any day, he likes to say.

After he's numbered the men, Thomas skims through their arrest reports to see if he needs to keep a special eye on anyone. Out of curiosity, too. Tonight it's mostly the standard crowd of accused drug offenders. The only arrest report catching his attention is the one for Chester G., a twenty-eight-year-old white man charged with aggravated battery against police officers. Chester G. walked into a northwest-side station yelling obscenities, the report says, then struck one officer in the arm and another in the face.

Kevin O'Hara, a cherub-faced deputy, reads the report on Chester over Thomas's shoulder. When Bullneck appears in the hallway, O'Hara excitedly informs him, "This guy walked into the Twenty-fifth District swinging at cops."

"Which one?" Bullneck asks.

O'Hara peers into bullpen two and makes an intelligent guess. "The guy with the bandage around his head, whaddya think?"

Chester, olive-skinned and broad-shouldered, is sitting on the floor in bullpen two. Below the wide bandage that covers his forehead, and beneath his bushy eyebrows, one eye is blackened and swollen shut. His lips are swollen as well, and his gray turtleneck is blood-spattered. O'Hara studies Chester's battered face from the hallway and chuckles. "I fought the law, and the law won."

Bullneck searches the paperwork for Chester's rap sheet, but apparently this is the twenty-eight-year-old's first arrest. Bullneck considers himself an expert on human nature, at least on the nature of the humans brought into this basement. He wonders aloud what would prompt a guy who's stayed out of trouble this long to walk into a police station swinging. "I think Chester's got something wrong with him," he tells O'Hara. "I think there's some psych meds that Chester forgot to take. Well, let's just ask him." He calls Chester out to the hallway.

"So you were swinging at cops," Bullneck says.

"I would never do it. I never did it," Chester says.

You been seeing a doctor? Bullneck asks. Uh-huh, Chester says. Taking any medicine? Nuh-unh, Chester says with a shake of his head; nothing besides the Haldol, the Ritalin, and the Cogentin. Bullneck and O'Hara exchange looks. Hearing any voices? Bullneck asks. "Not all the time," Chester says. Hear any voices in the police station last night? Chester nods.

"Well, you're gonna have to stay calm tonight," Bullneck says. "You hear any voices, tell us."

"Yeah, don't swing at us, just tell us," O'Hara adds.

Chester nods and returns to his spot on the floor in bullpen two.

The bus for the kiddie criminals finally arrives, and they're escorted out of the basement. Blackjack and Harley, apparently as fond of the youths as Thomas is, snarl and snap as they walk by.

Thomas moves some of his prisoners into the vacated bullpen, easing the crowding in bullpens one and two. A glassy-eyed young black man walking from one lockup to the next has forgotten the First Commandment; his hands are in the pockets of his windbreaker. Thomas positively reinforces him, slamming an open palm into the man's chest. "Where the *fuck*'re your hands s'posed to go?" The man grunts from the blow, his hands jerking out of the windbreaker to their proper place.

When the bars at the entryway are slid shut for the evening at six-thirty, the basement chambers hold seventy-seven prisoners—sixty-five men and twelve women. Those are typical numbers for night bond court. (In 1998 bond court sessions were held twice a day on weekdays and once a day on weekends and holidays. Court officials have since switched to a once-a-day schedule, but the typical weekday total of 150 prisoners hasn't changed. About 350 prisoners are processed on each weekend day.) The racial breakdown tonight is typical, too: fifty African Americans, fourteen Hispanics, thirteen whites. Most are in their teens or twenties, according to their arrest reports, and most are unemployed.

At seven P.M. the deputies prepare to move the prisoners up to the first-floor lockups behind Courtroom 100. Thomas barks out the directions, and the prisoners pair up and link arms—like first-graders, except for the handcuffs the sergeant clicks on. They follow a deputy through the tunnel to the elevator.

The caboose on this train, a prisoner without a partner—a skinny black man in a tattered jacket and dirty pants—manages to keep up with the line, no easy trick for a man with one leg, one stump, and one crutch. He hops behind the others, rebalancing himself with the crutch every half-dozen hops.

His name is Walter Williams, and he turned thirty-four just three days ago. He lost the leg as a child. One afternoon when he was nine, he climbed into a slow-moving boxcar near his home on the south side. When he fell from the car, the train crushed his left leg. But he didn't wallow in self-pity afterward, his brother Henry tells me later. He learned to swim, play basketball, and ice skate—the TV program *That's Incredible!* showed him skating as a teen in the early 1980s. He also learned to fix cars. But repair shops weren't looking for a one-legged asthmatic mechanic, so he worked only sporadically, on the cars of relatives and friends. In his late twenties he took to snorting heroin, then to stealing hubcaps and batteries to pay for it. The flabbiest cop could catch a one-legged thief, and so he'd been arrested a half-dozen times, though no judge had ever given him more than court supervision. Yesterday afternoon he and a cousin were caught in a stolen van. The deputies in this basement know nothing about Williams's life, of course. To them he's just another scumbag, with three limbs instead of four.

The elevator doors rattle open. "Face the back, shut up, and let's go," a deputy commands. The weary elevator gradually transports its load to the first floor, ten prisoners and two deputies at a time.

Upstairs the prisoners are parceled out into three lockups behind Courtroom 100—one for the twelve women, one for the thirty-six males accused of felonies, the third for the twenty-nine males charged with misdemeanors or who have outstanding warrants. This last lockup is fetid before the prisoners arrive because of the toilet that backed up earlier today.

A prisoner in the felony lockup calls through the bars to a deputy in the hallway, asking when the public defender will be by. "Number one, I don't know," the deputy responds. "Number two, I don't care. Number three, you're guilty."

The judge won't be arriving for an hour or so. Some of the deputies huddle over a desk in an anteroom, studying carry-out menus. They settle on Chinese.

Private attorneys are on the way for three of tonight's prisoners, who reached them through a phone call from the district station. The other seventy-four prisoners will be represented by two public defenders.

One of the PDs, Fred DeBartolo, arrives at seven-thirty, and begins interviewing his clients through the lockup bars. He trots through a series of rote questions about work, school, family, and financial means, recording the answers on a clipboard. Each client gets about two minutes. The prisoners all want only one thing from DeBartolo: they want him to keep them out of jail. "This is no easy cup of tea," DeBartolo says. "A guy's got a warrant, nothing I can do about that. They want me to get them out, but I am not a miracle worker." DeBartolo wants out, too. Bond court is not a preferred assignment, and he's anxious for his "ticket out of this toilet," he says.

Walter Williams, the one-legged prisoner, hops to the bars at the front of his bullpen and calls to Sergeant Thomas. He's having trouble breathing, he tells Thomas; he needs a whiff from an inhaler. Thomas says he can be taken to the hospital if he really wants to go. But he reminds Williams that if he does go, he'll have to wait at least until tomorrow for his bond hearing. Williams purses his lips and considers. The central question for a heroin addict at this juncture on the road to justice is, What's the fastest route to my next blow? Williams should know an I-bond isn't in the cards tonight, considering that he was already on bond for another car theft when the cops arrested him yesterday. But appetite sometimes overwhelms reason. Perhaps Williams is thinking the judge might err, or God might intervene, granting him his freedom tonight, and maybe even a bag of heroin before dawn. He tells Thomas he'll do without the asthma meds.

A moment later a prisoner in the women's bullpen begins shouting that another prisoner needs help. A deputy finds a white woman slumped in a corner of the bullpen. Her name is Cecilia, the women say. The deputy grasps Cecilia by the shoulders of her red-and-black Bulls jacket and shakes her gently. "Ce'lia! Wake up, Ce'lia!" No response.

Her full name is Cecilia Diaz, according to her arrest report. At least tonight it is; it's also been Janet Long, Debra Gartner, Debra Bascaglia, Debra Berman, Debra Grandeau, and Andria Patterson. She has four felony convictions—two for drugs, two for theft. Tonight she's in for attempted drug possession, a misdemeanor; the arrest report says she tried to buy two bags of heroin from an undercover police officer. Names change, but fingerprints don't; the police computer found an outstanding warrant on another possession case, depriving her of an I-bond at the station.

The paperwork also indicates she's a diabetic, so one deputy worries aloud that she may have slipped into a diabetic coma. The consensus among the deputies, though, is that she's just dope-sick. Which merits no sympathy.

In the lockup Bullneck and two other deputies are still trying vainly to rouse Diaz, standing over her and hollering. The women in the lockup urge the deputies to call a doctor. Bullneck pivots and lets the women know the regard he has for their advice. "When we ask about doing drugs, selling drugs, or selling pussy, you can talk. Until then, shut the *fuck* up."

Two other deputies, lured by the shouting, stand at the door of the lockup scooping fried rice out of cardboard boxes as they appraise the situation.

"You walk in there with a bag a blow, she's gonna jump through those bars to get it," the first one says between gulps.

"Tell her she's got an I-bond, she'll be all right," the second one agrees, stabbing the air with his plastic fork.

Sergeant Thomas summons his boss, Lieutenant Hopkins. Hopkins, too, doubts that Diaz is suffering from any condition a bag of heroin wouldn't cure. But to be on the safe side, he gets on his radio and calls for fire department paramedics. Two of them arrive twenty minutes later, toting a litter.

"I think this is gonna be a false alarm," Thomas tells them apologetically.

The paramedics enter the bullpen and lean over Diaz. "Okay, wuzza matter, Ce'lia?" the taller one says solicitously. "What hurts, Ce'lia?" Diaz, eyes clamped shut, just groans.

The two paramedics gingerly stand her up, leaning her against the dirty beige wall. The moment they release her, she slides right back down the wall to a sitting position.

"You wanna juice her now?" the shorter paramedic says.

Soon the taller one has stuck a needle in above her wrist, plunging a dose of glucose into a vein. A deputy standing nearby edges uneasily away. "Don't wanna get no blood from her on me," he mutters.

The glucose fails to invigorate Diaz; her blood sugar is apparently not the problem. "C'mon, open your eyes," the taller paramedic says. "What's going on? What doesn't feel good?"

Diaz mumbles something about her chest.

"Oh, now your *chest* hurts," the paramedic says, looking up at the deputies.

"She's playing it off," Bullneck says.

"There's a sub joint on Sacramento where you can get her a rock and a sub," Deputy O'Hara says.

"You do know an ambulance ride is not a get-out-of-jail-free card?" Sergeant Thomas says.

Then Bullneck hears a comment from one of the other women in the lockup, a leather-faced African American. Whatever she's said has clearly annoyed him. He darts over to her, grabs her arms, spins her around, and butts her head into the wall. She groans, and her fellow prisoners murmur a meek protest. Over his shoulder Bullneck shoots back: "That's all right. Those of you who're going to jail? You're not eating. Those of you who got someone coming to bond you out? We'll kick 'em outta the building."

"I don't feel good," Diaz moans softly, folding over to the floor. The taller paramedic props her back up against the wall. Diaz moans again, clutching her stomach.

"Watch she don't puke on you," a deputy advises the paramedics.

"Does she need to go to the hospital?" Thomas asks.

The taller paramedic shrugs, then shakes his head.

"All right, she's dope-sick," Thomas renders his verdict. "She goes to court, she goes to jail."

"THEY ACT LIKE slave masters," one of tonight's prisoners, Terrance Evans, says later of the deputies. But at least they don't play favorites,

Evans says. "You could be black or white, crippled or mental—they still treat you like a dog."

The prisoners are too dangerous to be treated any other way, the deputies insist. "We get people who cut people, who shoot people—we get the *worst*," says Deputy Fred Holcomb. "Things you read about in the paper, see on TV—it all comes here."

But nobody here this evening is accused of cutting or shooting anyone. Defendants charged with murder or rape usually have their bonds set in an afternoon "violence court." Of the forty-three prisoners with felony charges tonight, thirty-seven are accused of drug crimes. Most are charged with buying, holding, or trying to sell a tiny white rock of cocaine, or a thumbnail-sized foil packet of brown powder heroin—not a kilo, not an ounce, but in most cases a gram or less.

Four of the accused felons are charged with burglaries, one with a firearms offense. That leaves one prisoner charged with a violent felony—the bandaged and bruised Chester G., accused of that aggravated battery in the police station.

Most of tonight's allegedly violent offenders—the nine men here for domestic battery—are sitting in the misdemeanor lockup, it being a graver offense in Illinois to possess a minute amount of cocaine or heroin than to beat a wife, a girlfriend, or a sister.

Among the other misdemeanor defendants, Linda L. is accused of pocketing two bottles of E & J Brandy, Tyrone S., two remote controls, Duane P., a bottle of Downy fabric softener. The oldest of tonight's prisoners, Carlos O., fifty-nine, purportedly tried to liberate two cases of Miller High Life from a grocery store. Stefahn J. got caught peddling watches on a train. The misdemeanor defendants will have their bonds set here, but their cases will be handled in branch courtrooms elsewhere in the county.

In an office around the corner from the bullpens, Ralph Ferro and three other clerks hunch over old desks, recording information from the arrest reports onto forms.

Ferro lifts an arrest report from the pile in front of him. The cop responsible for this particular bust estimated the street value of the drugs involved at $18.75. Ferro wonders aloud about the final tab for catching, prosecuting, and perhaps punishing the defendant for his $18.75 felony.

A heavy-set man who peers at the paperwork through thick plastic glasses, Ferro, at thirty-eight, has already worked bond court for two decades. At eighteen, he had the kind of credentials that merits a clerical post at 26th Street: a bigwig uncle in the front office. The evening work complements his day job as a bricklayer, providing him comp days, sick days, and health insurance. A sense of satisfaction from his labor isn't among the benefits. "We probably don't accomplish nothing here," he says. "It's just jobs for people. We're just pushing papers around."

COURTROOM 100 has bare beige walls and a grimy tile floor. A U.S. flag stands behind the judge's bench. The bench, and the pews in the gallery, are a dark oak. The backs of the pews are engraved with such sentiments as "Fuck All Police" and "Fuck All Police 1000 Times." By eight-fifteen, most of the pews are filled with relatives and friends of the prisoners, some with money in their pockets, others merely with I-bond hopes in their hearts. They wait quietly in the pews. Deputies appear at the front of the courtroom periodically, gabbing and laughing.

At 8:40 P.M. the Honorable Lambros Kutrubis takes the bench. He's got short black hair, thick eyebrows, and a studious face. A judge for eight years now, Kutrubis, fifty-four, is assigned to the division that hears pretrial matters. He gets night bond court duty one month a year. His job here is "to keep things moving as fast as I can," he says.

The deputies like Kutrubis. He's got all the attributes of an exceptional bond court judge, they say—meaning he's fast and doesn't dispense too many I-bonds, or set too many low bonds. It takes only a few minutes to escort prisoners to the jail, whereas completing the paperwork required for prisoners who bond out can keep the deputies from getting off early.

Kutrubis typically deals with the male defendants first, working his way through the warrants and misdemeanors to the felonies, then finishing with the females. The twelve defendants with warrants earned them by missing court dates. Kutrubis declares "warrant to stand" when each of these defendants is marched before him; they'll spend the night in jail, then be taken tomorrow morning to the courtroom from which the warrant was issued.

With the other defendants, Kutrubis has two matters to resolve. The first is the Gerstein hearing. No one can be detained for long after arrest without a determination that there's probable cause to believe he's committed the crime he's charged with. The stakes are too high to relegate the decision to jail a person to the officer who makes the arrest or the prosecutor who files the charge, the U.S. Supreme Court ruled in 1975 in *Gerstein v. Pugh.* "The detached judgment of a neutral magistrate" is required, the high court said.

At 26th Street, though, as in many criminal courthouses, nothing is heard in a Gerstein hearing; the judge skims the arrest report and almost instantly seconds the officer's decision. Kutrubis throws out far fewer than one case in a hundred, he says. Usually the defendant has barely reached the bench before Kutrubis has made his detached judgment that there is "probable cause to detain."

The second matter is the bond. Illinois law directs the judge to consider a host of factors before setting bond: the nature and circumstances of the offense charged, the weight of the evidence against the defendant, the likelihood of conviction, the sentence applicable upon conviction, whether there's motivation or ability to flee, the defendant's family ties in the community and how long he's lived there, his employment, financial resources, character, mental condition, and past conduct, whether he's given consent to periodic drug testing, his criminal history, his record of appearances or failures to appear at previous court proceedings, whether he tried to flee from police before his arrest, whether he refused to identify himself or to be fingerprinted, any uses of aliases or false dates of birth.

The bond decision is of course a critical one for the defendant, often determining whether he'll be sleeping in the jail or at home for the weeks or months until his case is resolved. A defendant can ask his trial judge to lower his bond when his case makes it to a trial court, but judges don't often do so.

At 26th Street the lawyers and the judge polish off bond hearings almost as rapidly as the judge does the Gersteins. The assistant state's attorney takes fifteen seconds or so to inform the judge of any blemishes in the defendant's background—convictions, failures to appear in court. The PD then takes his quarter-minute to summarize the defendant's pluses—a job, a family, a stable address. The lawyers speak at an auctioneer's pace, knowing that any dallying will subject them to the grumbles and eye-rolls of the deputies. And usually without pause, the judge announces the defendant's bond. As Kutrubis puts it: "Once you get the man's criminal background and his bond forfeitures, and you hear any mitigation, I mean, what else is there to know?" For the felony defendants, the bond hearing serves a second purpose, whether intended or not: it prepares them for what they'll likely experience in a trial court upstairs. The time devoted to considering whether they actually did what they're accused of and, if so, what should be done about it will be dwarfed in most instances by the time spent on procedural matters, such as determining what sentence might induce their guilty plea.

The bond is an amount and a letter—five thousand–D or five thousand–I, for instance. D, for "deposit," means the defendant has to post 10 percent of the amount to stay out of jail; I, for "individual recognizance," means the defendant will be out the door as soon as the paperwork's done. (The amount of the I-bond is the money the defendant will owe if he doesn't show for court, although the county rarely tries to collect.) A defendant with no felony convictions charged with possessing a small amount of drugs will get an I-bond from Kutrubis; a convicted felon with a history of bond forfeitures will get a D-bond. For defendants with D-bonds, freedom boils down to money: the haves can post and leave; the have-nots will be making that long walk through the tunnel. A study of the Cook County Jail and the courthouse published in 1922 denounced this blatant economic discrimination, noting that it relegated to jail mostly the "poor and friend-less." That hasn't changed.

Bond court is slickly choreographed. The deputies line up the defen-dants in the hallway between the lockups and the courtroom in the order in which they're going to be called, positioning the first defendant just inside the courtroom. A clerk calls a name; as the first defendant approaches the bench, the deputies replace him with the next defendant from the hallway. At the bench Kutrubis chirps, "Probable cause to detain, background?" The lawyers rush through their spiels; Kutrubis declares the bond; a deputy slips a folded copy of the charge into the behind-the-back hands of the defendant and nudges him back toward the door to the hallway. There's a rustle of paper, the snap of staplers. The whole transaction usually takes about a minute. The clerk calls another name.

A private attorney steps forward when the bandaged Chester G. is called to the bench. The attorney softly informs Kutrubis of his client's mental health problems and his immaculate record. He promises that Chester will take his medicine if he's released. Chester gets an I-bond.

A month from now a prosecutor will dangle in front of Chester misde-meanor battery and one-year conditional discharge (nonreporting proba-tion). Chester's lawyer will tell me he thinks the police likely overreacted to whatever Chester did in the station, but that the deal will allow Chester to get the case behind him "without a drawn-out battle that we have no guarantee of winning." The officers involved will endorse the deal—Chester's admission of guilt relieves them of the threat of a lawsuit or bru-tality complaint.

Walter Williams, the one-legged asthmatic, is the on-deck defendant at nine P.M. A deputy to one side of the judge's bench surveys him from the waist down as Williams awaits his turn at the front of the courtroom. "You try and run, I'm gonna take that other one," he says, laughing. Williams looks away.

"Walter Williams."

Williams crutches his way over to the bench. "Probable cause to detain, background?" Kutrubis says. The state's attorney informs the judge of the car theft case Williams had pending before yesterday's arrest. DeBartolo tells the judge Williams is a high school graduate and the father of three, and that he's on disability. Seventy-five-hundred–D, Kutrubis decides. Williams's head drops. Seven hundred fifty to walk; 750 more than he has. There'll be no blow tonight—just cramps, diarrhea, and wheezing in a county cell.

Four days from now Williams will collapse in a jail dorm—and there, exactly one week after his thirty-fourth birthday, he'll die. A medical examiner will attribute the death to "massive gastric dilatation" (stomach swelling) and bronchial asthma, with narcotics withdrawal a significant contributor. Inmates in Williams's dorm will tell the medical examiner that on the day he died Williams complained of stomach pain, vomited all day, and asked for medical attention—but that the sergeant on duty told them Williams was merely dope-sick and if they kept banging on the door to get the officers' attention, the officers would tear the dorm up. The Cook County medical examiner will close his investigation into Williams's death with no finding of negligence by the Cook County Jail. Ten days after Williams's death, he'll be indicted posthumously for stealing the van—news of his passing not having caught up with the state, which will seek and get the indictment from the grand jury. At a court date two weeks later a prosecutor will inform the judge of Williams's demise. "Death suggested, cause abated," the judge will declare for the record, before he moves on to the next case.

At nine-thirty, Cecilia Diaz wobbles into the courtroom, blinking against the glare. Kutrubis gives her an I-bond on the attempted possession charge. Her outstanding warrant will keep her in jail for now anyway, Kutrubis notes.

A week from today a judge will toss out the older drug case that was the basis of the warrant. Diaz will be released from jail on the I-bond Kutrubis issued tonight on her latest case. Five weeks later she'll fail to show in court for that case, earning her a fresh warrant.

Kutrubis sets bond for the final defendant at 9:52 P.M. Subtracting the ten-minute recess he'd taken between the misdemeanor and felony cases, he's disposed of the seventy-seven defendants in sixty-two minutes on the bench.

In his turns in night bond court, Kutrubis has noticed the prevalence of small drug cases, but it's not something he dwells on. "I'm more concerned with getting people in and out as fast as I can," he says. The prevalence of minorities among defendants isn't something he thinks about either. "It really doesn't faze me. It's just a fact of life."

Back in the lockups, the deputies have soon divided the prisoners into those being released—the usual one-third—and those bound for jail.

They cuff the jail group in pairs again and return the prisoners to the basement via the elevator. Then four of the deputies hustle the prisoners down the dank tunnel into the jail. Their workday almost over, the deputies are as gleeful as their captives are gloomy. A black deputy sings cadence, his voice echoing merrily off the walls: "Left, left, left-right, left; left-right, left-right, left-right, left . . . Halt! That means stop, motherfuckers!"

He parks the prisoners in front of the doors to the Division 5 basement, where all new jail prisoners are processed. A colleague walks through the doors and hands the paperwork to a jail guard. A moment later the jail guard waves the troop in, directing them to a bench bolted to the floor. "All right, when I call your number, give me your name," the guard says gruffly. Three hours of processing await the prisoners: fingerprinting, photographing, a terse consultation with a mental health aide, hurried examinations by a paramedic and a "dick doctor," as he's known here, more numbering and lettering on their arms, and finally a group strip-search.

While these prisoners await the start of their processing, the luckier defendants—those bonding out—are sitting in the jury box of a courtroom down the hall from Courtroom 100, eager for their release. It's almost 11:20 P.M. Sergeant Thomas hopes to be finished by 11:30. He's on the witness stand, scratching away at the last of the paperwork. He's been calling the prisoners over to him one by one. They sign their bond slips, he gives them a copy, and then he directs them to the gallery benches. After Chester G. signs his slip, he mistakenly heads back toward the jury box. "Hey, *brain-dead*," Deputy O'Hara calls after him, pointing him toward the gallery benches.

"That's no joke, he *is* brain-dead," another deputy says.

"He'd have to be, to go into a police station and start swinging at cops," says another.

Bullneck has been bickering with one of the prisoners in the jury box, a white woman in her thirties charged with drug possession. The arrest report says she left her kids at home, went to a drug spot, and bought a rock. Now she's annoying Bullneck no end, daring to carp about how long it's taking for her and the others to be released.

"Why are you whining?" Bullneck is asking her. "You're getting on my nerves."

"Well, we're all *tired*, for Chrissakes," the woman says. "I've never been through this before. *Jee*sus."

Sergeant Thomas overhears and looks up from the bond slip he's completing. "Ex*cuse* me—where did you see the sign that says that we have to care about you?"

The woman ignores Thomas, focusing on Bullneck. "I just wanna know why you're picking on me."

Bullneck's eyes widen. "Because you're a crazy-ass fucking hype who can't take care of her own *kids*. *That's* why."

"We ain't required to be concerned about your situation," Thomas pipes in. "So if I'm not bleeding fucking tears for you, *fuck* that. Fuck *you.* Shut the *fuck* up and sit there until we fucking say you can go."

"You got ten minutes till you can get outta here and suck your way to another rock," Bullneck adds.

"I ain't goin' back there," the woman says softly.

"Your life's over anyway," another deputy says. "You may not wanna hear that, but it's true."

WHETHER THEY'RE bonding out or going to jail, these defendants are beginning a journey. They are setting off into America's criminal justice system.

This is the story of that system, as shown through one year in one busy Chicago courtroom.

The men and women toiling in this courtroom work hard—but ultimately they are gears in a machine. More than a century ago, observers were already noting that criminal justice in America was a vast, expensive, relentless system. "No man can examine the great penal system of this country without being astounded at its magnitude, its cost, and its unsatisfactory results," John Altgeld said in 1890. Altgeld had been a Cook County judge, and he later was elected governor of Illinois. In an 1884 pamphlet, *Our Penal Machinery and Its Victims,* Altgeld condemned criminal justice in this nation, noting its end product: the imprisonment of fifty thousand citizens. He called the criminal justice system a "maelstrom which draws from the outside, and then keeps its victims moving in a circle until swallowed in the vortex."

One might describe it similarly today. Except its yield—the number of people in prison—is now nearly 1.5 million.

The system is run by people, but, as with many systems, it often seems the other way around. The courtroom staff works as it must, reflexively, not reflectively. The workers have no time to give much thought to any but the most extraordinary case, or to examine what they are doing.

What the system looks like depends, of course, on who's doing the looking. So this story is told from myriad perspectives: those of the judge, the lawyers, the deputies, the jurors. And it is told also from the perspective of those snagged on the gears—the defendants.

From city to city, from courtroom to courtroom, one thing about most defendants varies little: their poverty. It has ever been thus. As historian Samuel Walker wrote in 1998 in his book *Popular Justice:* "At every point in the history of criminal justice, the people arrested, prosecuted, and punished have been mainly the poor and the powerless." One hundred fifty years ago most defendants were European immigrants, Walker observed; today they are blacks and Hispanics.

This is largely the story of those defendants.

Recent reporting about criminal justice has focused heavily on two important issues: the death penalty, and the conviction of defendants later proven innocent. Death penalty cases are rare, however, and, even though DNA technology has proven that innocent defendants are convicted more often than once believed, such blatant miscarriages of justice are also unusual. This book intends to show more of what's typical about a courtroom. It is about how justice miscarries every day, by doing precisely what we ask it to.

ONE

White Sales

LARRY BATES pauses on the sidewalk long enough to fish his cigarettes out of a coat pocket and light one. Then he trudges on down California toward the courthouse.

The sidewalk is damp, the trees and rooftops dusted with yesterday's snow. It's not especially cold for a January morning, and so Bates has chosen to walk the two and a half miles from his west-side apartment to the courthouse and save the dollar-eighty bus fare. He doesn't have a steady job at the moment.

He'd considered not going to court at all today. Go, and you might get locked up, he'd thought. But staying home wouldn't mean staying free forever; they'll put a warrant on your ass, he'd reminded himself, and when they catch up to you, they'll lock you up for sure. Better to go, he'd decided, and just hope Locallo's in a good mood.

Locallo being Daniel Locallo, the judge whose probation terms Bates hasn't met—the reason for the letter summoning him to court this morning. In March 1997 Bates pled guilty to selling half a gram of heroin, and Locallo sentenced him to probation and twenty days' community service. He picked litter off of vacant lots and railroad tracks several times since, as part of the sheriff's orange-vest brigade. But he stopped showing up last fall, four days short of the twenty. He couldn't explain why he'd been so foolish, though he knew deep down that the pipe had something to do with it.

He passes a winking FLATS FIXED sign under the El tracks near 21st Street. South of the El, the neighborhood becomes distinctly Hispanic—

he passes *frutería y carnicería* markets, cafés offering tacos, tortas, and burritos.

I'm too old for this, Bates tells himself as he walks along, too old to be sweating jail all the time. Besides, this ain't me, I'm a working man. He delivered papers in grade school, flipped burgers in high school, filled orders in a warehouse for years after that. But he also drank heavily and developed a cocaine addiction along the way. He was forty-two when he picked up his first criminal case, in 1996. The police caught him buying one rock on a street corner, for five dollars. The prosecutor offered him probation for his plea, and he grabbed it; who'd turn down "paper" when a trip downstate was an option? He stayed clean briefly after that. But he could hardly walk a block in his neighborhood without hearing the call of "rocks and blows"; soon he was backsliding, and busted, again.

The judge the second time had been Locallo. That was lucky for Bates, because unlike many judges at 26th Street, Locallo was willing to give paper on paper—that is, to give a two-time loser a second shot at probation. And so Bates copped out again. The twenty days of grunt work Locallo tacked on wasn't any big thing—except for someone stuck on stupid, as Bates has chided himself since.

At 24th Street, California widens into a boulevard, with a parkway between the northbound and southbound lanes. Heavier traffic swishes by Bates. He passes the 1-800-NOTGLTY billboard at 25th Street and an *abogados'* office a few doors down. Two black men are beckoning cars into the lot next to the *abogados'* office—COURT PARKING $7, ALL DAY—while other workers in the lot wriggle the cars into bumper-to-bumper columns from the sidewalk back to the rat-baited alley.

Across 26th Street the sidewalk in front of the gray courthouse is thick with men and women in sports team jackets and hooded sweatshirts and coats, heading toward the plaza that leads to the entrance. Some of the women clutch babies or tow toddlers. A bus squeals to a stop and spits out a dozen more 26th Street customers. Others climb out of cars pulling up at the curb.

Bates mounts the steps to the plaza, and, off to one side, lights another smoke. It's nine A.M., and court isn't scheduled to start until nine-thirty. He leans on a railing and checks out the crowd converging on the plaza. On the east side of California, facing the courthouse, is the five-story parking garage for the courthouse employees, the cops here to testify, and the jurors. They're rushing across California now, men and women clutching folded newspapers and briefcases, their ties and trench coats flapping in the wind. Most of those coming from the garage are white; most of those arriving on foot or by bus or getting dropped off are black or brown. It's more or less a racket, Bates thinks to himself, as he often has—all these people fattening up on us.

Bates takes a final drag, flicks the butt to the concrete, and makes for the entrance—the windowed lobby that connects the courthouse on the right with its younger and taller sibling on the left, the fifteen-story copper and glass administration building that houses the offices of the prosecutors, the public defenders, the clerks, the court reporters, and the probation officers.

Inside the revolving doors, the courthouse employees and police officers sweep past Bates, flashing their IDs at a deputy or tapping the badge attached to their belts and walking right in. Bates joins a long line at a metal detector. A scowling deputy warns those in line to remove belts and to empty pockets. The hyperactive metal detectors frequently chirp out accusations usually refuted by pat-downs.

The employees and the prospective jurors head toward the administration building elevators on the left. Bates turns to the right, along with the defendants, fellow probationers with court dates, and any of their relatives or friends who've come along. They stream through the lobby and into the courthouse.

Stapled to an immense bulletin board around a corner is today's docket—printouts listing the eleven hundred felony cases scheduled for the building's thirty trial courtrooms. It's a sea of drug cases—possession, delivery, possession with intent to deliver—with islets of murder, criminal sexual assault, aggravated battery, and burglary. Defendants and their relatives and friends huddle around the bulletin board, scanning the alphabetical list. A few timidly ask strangers for help finding a name. Bates doesn't need to look; he knows he's headed for Courtroom 302.

Next to the bulletin board is the entrance to a stand-up coffee shop patronized mostly by the building's visitors—the Gangbanger Café, as the courthouse employees call it. Customers lean on counters and fuel up on junk cuisine—doughnuts, chips, candy bars, juice, pop, coffee. Bates has breakfasted here on other court dates—a Snickers washed down with a Pepsi and chased with a smoke. But he's squeezing his nickels this morning—he isn't going to feed a vending machine or himself. He continues down the hall, heading straight to a stairwell, avoiding the crowd at the elevators. Bates has never liked bumping into acquaintances in the courthouse. ("What *you* here for, Larry?") It's embarrassing enough exchanging glances with people he doesn't know, especially with the blacks who work here. He's sure he sees disapproval in their eyes, a look intended to remind him that he's shaming not only himself but his brothers and sisters. "Hey, I ain't really about this," he wants to tell them.

On the third floor he walks to the end of a hallway, then eases open the door to Courtroom 302 and peeks in. The courtroom is empty. The clock above the jury box says 9:10. Okay, he thinks, I got here in time, I ain't gonna piss off the judge by being late—at least I did this right. He slips into a back bench. Just hope Locallo is in a good mood today.

TO PLEAD OR NOT to plead: that's Tony Cameron's dilemma on this same January morning.

He's downing a bowl of bland oatmeal and a soggy piece of toast in a Division 2 cafeteria as he once again considers his options, at four-fifteen A.M. If you want breakfast in the Cook County Jail, this is when it's served.

Cameron is tired and not just because of the hour. He hasn't been sleeping well. The housing in Division 2 is dormitory style: fifty men in one large room, sleeping on metal cots topped with flimsy foam mattresses. Cameron tends to distrust people to begin with, and this open arrangement has kept him on constant guard. You never know when someone's going to go off on you, or when you might get caught in the middle of some other brothers' beef. Hefty and broad-shouldered, he's been in more than his share of fights; but he'd just as soon avoid them here, so he's been sleeping with one eye open and one eye closed, as he likes to say. He worries about thievery, too. Inmates keep their possessions in a basket under their cots. When something turns up missing, there are only forty-nine possible culprits. Cameron is protective of his basket even though it currently holds only a toothbrush, a tube of toothpaste, and a bar of soap. He's not one of the lucky inmates who's getting money from home for the commissary.

Cameron has been in the jail five months now, since his arrest last August for armed robbery. The judge had set his bond at fifty thousand dollars. Five thousand to walk—about five thousand more than his family had.

He wanted to go to trial, he told his public defender every time he was in court. But nothing much had happened on his first five trips, as far as he could tell. He suspected the PD and the state's attorney were ganging up on him, trying to squeeze out his guilty plea. Go to trial, and you could get thirty years, the PD had told him; cop out, and the state will recommend the minimum six. If the plan was to wear him out, it was working; he was so sick of the jail that he'd pretty well decided to take the deal today and go ahead on downstate, do his bit, and get it over with.

After he finishes eating, he returns to his dorm. Like the cafeteria, it's on the first floor of the three-story building. Most of the other prisoners are still in their cots, having skipped breakfast or gone back to bed after eating. Cameron takes a seat at the front of the dorm and watches the news on the TV.

He isn't fond of these court days. Some of the younger prisoners look forward to the chance of meeting up with friends in one of the bullpens on the way to the courthouse or in the courtroom lockup. Court days also provide a rare opportunity to see prisoners of the opposite sex. The male and female lockups behind most courtrooms are only a few feet apart; often the younger men and women stand at the front of the cells, chatting through the bars. Cameron is thirty-four, though, and for prisoners of his age, going to court is often just a nuisance. A prisoner gets bumped along from one bullpen to the next on the way to the courthouse and back. If he were in the jail, he could at least be watching TV; in the courtroom lockups, there's just a camera watching him. The PD is likely to tell him she's too busy to discuss his case, that she'll catch him next time. He'll be strip-searched before he's returned to his division. He goes through all the fuss for maybe two minutes in front of the judge; when he gets back to his dorm later in the day, what he's learned about his case is his next court date.

At five forty-five A.M. Cameron and three dozen other Division 2 inmates with court dates today are lined up in a hallway. They're all in their jail uniforms—the tan shirt and pants with the big black DOC (Department of Corrections) across the back, an XL or an XXL or an XXXL over the breast pocket. A guard distributes jail IDs and courtroom passes. Each prisoner also gets a navy jacket to zip on over his shirt for the walk to Division 5, the first stop on the way to the courthouse.

At six A.M. sharp this bleary-eyed, yawning platoon is marched in pairs out the door into the chilly predawn darkness. Court isn't scheduled to start for three and a half hours, and the courthouse is five minutes away. But it's no small task to deliver six hundred prisoners to thirty-four courtrooms (thirty trial and four preliminary hearing courtrooms). And the judges want their prisoners in their courtroom lockups early, no matter if the judges themselves are late. The divisions on the periphery of the jail grounds start shipping their prisoners even earlier. Most of the divisions are linked to the jail's tunnel system; between five-thirty and six-fifteen each weekday morning there's a pulsing of tan uniforms through the tunnels toward Division 5. An hour later a blue procession begins from the female divisions. A yellow line is painted on the tunnel floor; the prisoners walk on the narrow side, the guards on the other.

But Division 2 isn't linked to the tunnels, so its prisoners take this short walk outside first. Cameron and his cohorts traipse quietly past a damp basketball court, two guards behind them. They round a corner and then descend stairs into the tunnel, where they pause to slip off their jackets, which a prisoner collects in a sack. Then it's onward through the tunnel to the Division 5 bullpens.

Those bullpens are already swarming and noisy when the Division 2 prisoners arrive. They're quickly parceled out to three large lockups based on the floor of the courthouse they're bound for. Cameron threads his way to a spot near the back of the bullpen he's assigned to. His main goal in a bullpen is to stay out of any mess. He tends not to talk to anyone he doesn't know and tries not to crowd anyone, though that's not easy in here. Prisoners are often on edge on their court days, as he well understands; saying the wrong thing or stepping on someone's foot by accident can lead to a whole lot of drama.

A few minutes later Cameron is called out to the hallway, where a nurse gives him his meds—two antipsychotic tablets and one for his manic symptoms. He's been taking psychotropics since he was sixteen.

Soon Cameron and his cellmates are on their way once more, heading north through the dank tunnel, then east. The guards dock them at a string of bullpens just short of the courthouse basement.

In his lockup here, Cameron mulls his options again. He realizes no one can deny him a trial if he insists on one. But he's also been around long enough to know that the judges here don't play. They don't appreciate defendants who won't bend over and cop, he reminds himself. If I go to trial, I better win—because if I don't, the judge is gonna bang me, he thinks. And the PD ain't gonna do nothing to stop it. His PD seemed nice enough, but he's sure she doesn't really care about his case. How can she, when she has so many of them? Besides, he thinks, *her* ass ain't on the line, *she* ain't looking at prison; don't matter if I go home, get six or thirty, she's gonna get paid tomorrow.

Cameron committed the robbery he's accused of, he admits to me later. But on his way to court this morning, that's not what he's thinking about. He's thinking he could beat this case if only he could afford a real lawyer.

At seven-thirty the prisoners going to third-floor courtrooms are summoned out of the pens. Two guards sitting at a podium call out names from a printout, and the prisoners step forward one at a time, displaying their jail IDs. Another guard hands them each a plastic juice bottle and a plastic-wrapped cardboard tray with a baloney-on-white and crackers.

Cameron and ten other prisoners headed for Courtroom 302 are buzzed through a door to the "bridge," the main tunnel in the courthouse basement. This is where the jail guards hand off custody of the prisoners to the courthouse deputies.

"Step right up, step right up, the greatest show on earth!" a deputy on the bridge blares at the prisoners. "Spread out, empty your pockets! Drop your lunches on the yellow line! Take off your shoes and pull out the insoles! Turn around, grab some wall!"

The prisoners fan out in the tunnel, a half-dozen gloved deputies behind them. Matchbooks, sugar packets, jail IDs, courtroom passes, scraps of toilet paper drop to the concrete. Deputies scoop the matchbooks off the floor and set them ablaze, to mask the odor budding as the prisoners slip off their shoes.

Cameron presses his palms against the brown brick wall in front of him and leans forward while a deputy paws him, shoulders to ankles, with a token swipe at his crotch.

Some of the deputies assigned to courtrooms work the bridge first each morning, helping with the pat-downs until their prisoners arrive, then shepherding them upstairs to their courtroom. The deputy for 302, Gil Guerrero, is here now, doing pat-downs and chiming in with the repartee.

"Can I have my comb back?" a young Hispanic prisoner a few feet down from Cameron beseeches a deputy after he's been searched.

"No, you can't have your comb back," the deputy sneers.

"I need my comb," the prisoner says meekly.

"Use your fingers. You remember *Happy Days*?"

"He *needs* his *comb*," another deputy whimpers.

"I need my fucking *comb*," Guerrero says.

The Hispanic youth doesn't respond. Cameron can imagine what he's thinking. At home and in the streets, Cameron isn't shy about running his mouth. But he knows that the smartest plan here is to go along with the program. He's seen prisoners slapped silly for answering back.

"Let's *go*!" a deputy hollers. "Get your motherfucking shoes on and get outta here!"

Cameron and the others rush to comply, jamming insoles back into shoes and yanking on the shoes, grabbing lunches and IDs off the floor and hurrying down the tunnel toward the elevators, under the constant encouragement of the deputies: "Move, move, move! Get the fuck outta here!"

At the end of the tunnel Guerrero handcuffs his ten prisoners for the elevator ride. Another deputy joins him for the trip. The prisoners—seven blacks, two Hispanics, and one white—are silent while the elevator shudders upward.

The elevator opens at the 302 bullpens. Guerrero unlocks the men's cell with a large brass skeleton key. He uncuffs each prisoner, and they hand him their IDs and head in.

"Can you tell my lawyer I wanna speak to him before we go in court?" a prisoner asks Guerrero.

"I don't know who your lawyer is—it's not my problem," Guerrero snaps over his shoulder. He drops the handcuffs, the IDs, and the key with a clang onto a metal desk in an anteroom around the corner.

Although he's been wearing gloves, Guerrero heads straight for the jury room washroom now, as he always does after a stint on the bridge. "Gotta wash my hands," he says on the way. "Been touching DOC all morning."

Meanwhile, Cameron has found a spot on a bench and has started peeling the plastic from his lunch tray. He's not hungry yet—it's only eight A.M. But he'd rather eat his lunch before one of his bullpen mates tries snatching it from him. The other prisoners are unwrapping their lunches, too. *Ain't no way I'm gonna win on this case*, Cameron thinks as he bites into his sandwich. *It's gonna go like everything else in my life.*

LARRY BATES glances at the clock on the wall above the jury box: 9:25. Six black women and two black men have joined him in the gallery. Like Bates, they're stiff, silent, and grim on the benches. The gallery has six wooden pews, three on either side of an aisle, all of them carved with gang insignia—pitchforks, stars, and crowns. The gallery is separated from the front of the courtroom by tinted Plexiglas and a glass double door.

The benches rapidly fill, and the courtroom staff begin arriving as well, marching through the gallery and on into the well of the courtroom. Bates recognizes some of them from his previous visits and guesses at the rest of the cast. He remembers that the chubby balding man in the short-sleeved shirt and tie is the clerk. The man lugging a steno machine in one hand and a laptop in the other is obviously the court reporter. The two young men with the closely shaven chins, the dark pin-striped suits, and button-down shirts have prosecutor written all over them. That means the two young women in business suits, cradling file folders, must be the PDs. Bates can tell that someone works here as soon as he or she enters the door at the back of the gallery, and not just by how they're dressed. The workers move with the comfort of those who belong, and they greet each other amiably as they pass through the gallery, like one big happy family. Not to mention that they're all white.

Bates checks the clock again. Nine thirty-five; still no judge. Sure, *he* can come late, Bates thinks; *we* do, and it's a warrant.

AT HIS KITCHEN TABLE, Dan Locallo sips tea, munches on toast, and scans the morning's *Chicago Tribune*. His wife, Jean, and his twelve-year-old son, Kevin, are elsewhere in the house, dressing for their day at a Catholic grammar school, where Kevin is a seventh-grader and Jean a teacher's aide. His seventeen-year-old daughter, Lauren, has already left for her Catholic high school. By eight-thirty A.M. he's out the door as well.

The Locallos live on the outskirts of Chicago, in Norwood Park, one of the city's more affluent neighborhoods, an area of brick homes and quiet streets whose residents fear property tax hikes more than crime or unemployment. Polish, German, Italian, and Irish ancestries predominate. There are virtually no blacks. Locallo grew up not far away.

The reassuring drone of an AM news station fills his 1992 Lumina as he cruises south on Austin Boulevard—traffic and weather, sports, business. The overnight crime reports always interest him. They're like coming attractions—the first accounts of the mayhem wrought by future 26th Street customers, any one of whom could end up in his courtroom. His ears are tuned especially for the potential heaters, the crimes with a special twist that are likely to captivate the press; those he *hopes* end up in his courtroom. The heaters can burn a judge, and many of his colleagues would just as soon keep their distance. Locallo likes the challenge.

No future heaters on this morning's radio, though. Certainly nothing rivaling the Bridgeport case. Three white teens from the south-side Bridgeport neighborhood were charged last year with attempted murder, having allegedly beaten a thirteen-year-old black boy nearly to death for bicycling through their neighborhood. One of the defendants, Frank Caruso Jr., is the son of a reputed mobster. Locallo can't imagine a hotter heater: President Clinton decried the attack in his weekly radio address, and Mayor Daley demanded the culprits be brought to justice. Reporters surely will flock to the trial. And Locallo is still pinching himself: the Randomizer—the computer program that parcels out 26th Street's cases among its thirty trial court judges—kicked the case into his courtroom. The upcoming trial alone is reason to look forward to this year—and not just because of the certain publicity. No, the Bridgeport case is more than a heater; in Locallo's mind, it is a pivotal case, a chance to show African Americans that the system isn't really stacked against them.

He's always known he'd do something momentous. When he was three, his mother sewed him a Superman cape, and he wore it constantly. A flight from a bedroom dresser one afternoon that resulted in stitches under his chin didn't shake his faith in his endowments.

At age ten, he saw *To Kill a Mockingbird* in a Little Rock, Arkansas, theater. Little Rock was his mother's hometown, and his family was visiting relatives. He watched the handsome country lawyer, Atticus Finch, argue passionately on behalf of Tom Robinson, the black man wrongly accused of rape. He listened intently as Finch told the white jury and the packed courtroom how the courts were "the great levelers," how in the courts "all men are created equal." No matter that Finch and Robinson lost; Finch had done the honorable thing, and the ten-year-old boy could picture himself in that dashing three-piece suit, arguing bravely in that crowded courtroom.

He got his chance in 1978, though as a prosecutor instead of as a defense lawyer. It took him less than nine years to win appointment to the bench, at age thirty-three. The bar associations have praised his intelligence, diligence, fairness, and integrity as a judge.

When he reaches Jackson Boulevard this morning, he turns east. The road curves through Columbus Park and then straightens, slicing through a neighborhood markedly different from his own. Small frame houses with sagging porches are mixed in with boarded-up buildings and weedy vacant lots. A sign in one of the vacant lots promises "$10 for Good Used Radiators." Discount food and liquor stores advertise the Lotto in their front windows. This is the Austin neighborhood, part of the city's sprawling, poor, black west side—a fertile pasture for defendants. He finds the shift in landscape unremarkable; he's driven this route or similar ones to the courthouse for years. He follows the sweep of the boulevards—Jackson to Independence to Douglas. He happens to cross the route Larry Bates hiked earlier this morning.

He'd never have recognized Bates on the street, though. Hundreds of defendants pass through his courtroom each year; he couldn't remember each one. The heater defendants, for sure, but they're few and far between. The vast majority of 26th Street cases don't attract the eye of an alderman, let alone the mayor or the president. Car thefts. Possession cases involving sneeze-and-it's-gone amounts of cocaine or heroin. No reporters watch these; often the defendant's relatives don't even show.

The judges in TV dramas and movies are always presiding over heart-stopping jury trials, with riveting testimony and passionate arguments—action punctuated by a banging gavel and calls for order by the judge. About the only use a gavel gets at 26th Street is holding down papers in chambers. As for jury trials, judges here might do one a month. Locallo and his colleagues spend most of their days prodding defendants toward the finish line—toward pleas of guilty that spare the county the burden of trials. A judge could tire of this mundane work, could wonder what he was accomplishing as he hurried defendants out the back door while ever more streamed in the front. And many judges did tire of it, requesting transfers to the civil courts downtown. But eleven years on the bench, most of them at 26th Street, have yet to sour Locallo; he still awakens eager to get to the courthouse, even on mornings like this, with no trial scheduled. He prides himself on his management skills, especially in how nimbly he sheds the fat from his docket, how quickly he disposes of the "bullshit cases," as he calls them, saving the court's time for the cases that merit it. The Bridge-port case, for instance.

Douglas Boulevard bends into Sacramento Boulevard, Sacramento into California. He cruises by the 1-800-NOTGLTY billboard and the parking lot beyond it. Just past 26th and California, he swings onto the courthouse grounds at the "Shipping/Receiving" sign, waving to the deputy in the small brick outpost nearby. He parks his Lumina in the lot for judges behind the courthouse and enters a rear door.

His first stop today, as usual, is the office of the presiding judge at 26th Street, Thomas Fitzgerald. A half-dozen judges are drinking coffee and chatting in the first-floor suite already. Fitzgerald has let his judges know they can drop by any morning before they head upstairs. Locallo looks forward to these few minutes of fraternizing before taking the bench. He tends to gab about his golf game or his kids' athletic achievements. Sometimes he'll solicit a veteran judge's advice on a thorny issue developing in a case in his courtroom. In recent years, judges more often have sought *his* counsel, aware of his grasp of case law. This morning, after coffee and twenty minutes of small talk, Locallo leaves Fitzgerald's office and walks down a corridor toward the judges' elevator. It's nine forty-five, time to get the call going.

BATES IS HEMMED IN on the back pew between a skinny young man in a Dallas Cowboys jacket and an older woman in a Fila coat when Locallo materializes at the front of the courtroom, in the doorway to the left of the judicial bench, at 9:50. He's still zipping on the black robe over his white shirt and tie as he heads to the bench.

When the judge appears in some courtrooms at 26th Street, the clerk or a deputy commands everyone to rise, declaring that the Circuit Court of Cook County is now in session, the Honorable So-and-So presiding, and informing the spectators that talking and newspaper reading are forbidden. Locallo finds such pomp embarrassing and the prohibitions silly, especially in a courtroom with a sealed-off gallery. Court starts without ceremony once he settles into his high-backed leather swivel chair, and he or his clerk calls the first case.

Locallo has brown eyes and a fair complexion that pinks up in the golf season. Well-developed jaw muscles broaden his face below the ears. His hair is wavy black and full but graying on the sides. He keeps it medium length and feathered back on top, but short on the sides and in back. He stays closely shaven. He often wears a bemused expression, as if he knows the joke but is above laughing at it.

He played baseball and football in high school and still has an athlete's cocky carriage—shoulders back, chest out. But he's forty-five now, and he doesn't burn many calories swiveling and rocking behind the bench. As with many judges, the robe hides an expanding belly.

His long, curved bench is cluttered with law books, file folders in precarious heaps, and transcripts in black binders. More files and binders litter the floor beneath the bench. A desk calendar from Notre Dame High School, the judge's alma mater, occupies the eye of the turmoil, the area on the bench he leans over from his leather chair. In the calendar's squares Locallo records, in black ink, the dates of upcoming trials and hearings on motions and, in red, the dates of his son's and daughter's cross-country meets, volleyball matches, baseball and basketball games. Trials and hearings frequently extend into early evenings, so whenever possible he schedules them for dates other than the ones containing red ink. His clerk, Duane Sundberg, is lining up files at the end of the bench to the judge's right; today's court reporter, Paul Marzano, sits poised before his steno at the bench's other end, adjacent to the witness stand.

Twenty-sixth Street's original courtrooms, spacious and trimmed in oak, are on floors four through seven. These cramped courtrooms on the second and third floors were added a half century later. Prosecutors and defense lawyers may have polar views about their cases, but in 302 they make their pitches from tables a yard apart. A drab gray carpet covers the floor, and a chintzy fabric is peeling from the walls. The lack of any windows in the courtroom proper accentuates the claustrophobic feel. In the old courtrooms upstairs, with their rows of tall windows, the sun occasionally registers its own opinion at a trial's pivotal moment, casting a lawyer in brightness or a defendant in shadows during closing argument. The immutable fluorescent lights in 302 free the proceedings of such bias and drama. The majestic courtrooms upstairs were built when jury trials were more common. For taking a plea, a broom closet will do.

The courtroom's only windows are in the gallery, three narrow ones on the right. On sunny mornings the reflection on the Plexiglas makes it hard to see into the courtroom from the gallery. The courtroom proceedings are transmitted to the spectators via ceiling speakers. From time to time during a typical day, a lawyer will have a bit of news to share privately with the judge—an update on a prosecutor's recovery from gallbladder surgery or on a defense attorney's case before a disciplinary committee. Locallo will lean forward confidentially and flip a switch on the underside of the bench; the spectators in the gallery will hear only their own breathing. Locallo is better than many judges at remembering to turn the sound back on after

the social sidebar, but he too forgets sometimes. When he does, the spectators usually sit in meek silence at first; then glance quizzically at one
another; then start analyzing their predicament. ("He need to cut that mike
back on.") Before one of them risks an act so bold as tapping on the Plexiglas or gesturing to a deputy or clerk, a courthouse regular is likely to happen into the gallery from the hallway, grasp the problem, and come to the
rescue, approaching the glass doors with a hand cupped behind an ear, and
Locallo will lean forward and restore the audio.

A "Do *Not* Use This Door!" warning is taped on the left side of the glass
double door to the courtroom proper. Lawyers often ignore it, barreling
mindlessly through the door, which then screeches in protest. The door
sticks open as the attorney hurries on into the courtroom. The job of shov-
ing the door closed, with another irritating screech, belongs to a person of
lesser rank, usually one of the deputies. When Deputy Guerrero does it,
he's likely to be muttering something about law school graduates not being
able to read a damn sign. The door has been out of whack for as long as
anyone can remember. When the sign becomes too tattered, the deputies
replace it with a fresh one.

THE MAIN JOB in the courthouse has always been sorting. The judges
and lawyers sift through the raw material dropped off by police and determine who gets to walk out of the courthouse and who must leave on a bus
with barred windows. About three-quarters of the defendants are convicted. Of these, just over half are sentenced to prison, with most of the
remainder getting probation. Clerks write the shipping orders for the
prison-bound, judges sign them, and jail guards fill them.

Twenty defendants are scheduled to appear before the bench on this
Thursday in mid-January. Their cases are various distances from comple-
tion. Lawyers will update Locallo on a case's status, and in most instances,
after a couple of minutes, he'll give the defendant another court date. But
with luck at least a few cases will cross the finish line today.

Prosecutor Joe Alesia tenders "discovery" to defense attorneys in one of
the day's first cases, in which two young men are charged with relieving
two other young men of their Air Jordans at gunpoint. As usual, this "discovery" consists mostly of police reports regarding the alleged robbery.
Before the next court date, the defense lawyers will study the reports for
inconsistencies and omissions. A glaring error can cause a lawyer to
advise his client to gamble on a trial; a minor flaw can at least be brought
up in plea discussions when trying to extract a markdown from the state.
Even an airtight police report helps the defense lawyer: he can use it to per-

suade his client to wave the white flag and grab the state's best offer. Locallo continues the robbery case to February.

Clerk Sundberg calls Leslie McGee. A seventeen-year-old female from the lockup is ushered before the bench. She blows a kiss to a relative in the gallery on her way. McGee is charged with shooting a cabbie to death. Her public defender tells Locallo she's involved in "negotiations" with the state. Locallo continues the case for a month.

Soon the judge starts running through the VOPs—the violation of probation cases. Larry Bates is the first probationer summoned before the judge. His stomach flutters when Sundberg calls his name, but he rises quickly in his pew and strides purposefully to the bench. In front of the bench, he parks himself next to a tall, olive-skinned woman with long dark hair, assuming she's the PD who's representing him today. Actually the woman, Rhonda Schullo, is a liaison for the probation department.

Schullo informs the judge of Bates's failure to complete his community service. Locallo glances down at Bates.

"Do you wanna be able to leave this courtroom?" Locallo's voice is a strong, sure tenor, with the authentic twang and *dis-an-dat*s of a white Chicago product. He slightly slurs his *s*'s.

"Yes, sir," Bates says. He tries to catch Locallo's eyes, but they've already shifted back to the paperwork in front of him on the bench.

"Do you wanna be able to be on the street?"

"Yes, sir."

Locallo gives him another court date—March 25—and a warning that he complete the last four days of community service by then. If his docket were less bloated, the judge wouldn't grant Bates two months to finish up four days' work. Bates glides out of the courtroom to the hallway. Smoking isn't allowed in the corridors, but many people do, and Bates is craving a cigarette. The urge to leave the building, however, is stronger right now. He hustles down the stairs, past the docket board, the Gangbanger Café, and the sour deputies at the metal detectors, and out the revolving door. He lights his cigarette on the plaza, promising himself he'll take care of that community service really soon.

Two other probationers who are called before Locallo aren't as lucky as Bates. One has gone AWOL from a stretch of home confinement mandated as a condition of his probation; the other hasn't done any of his required forty hours of community service in the six months since he was sentenced. Locallo orders both men into custody. Deputy Guerrero escorts one and then the other back to the lockup. After lunch, however, Locallo will give the two men firm warnings and fresh court dates and free them. The jail is crammed enough without judges locking up every probation violator. The judge is hoping the few hours in the lockup will scare some future compliance out of them.

Locallo signs an arrest warrant for a defendant on bond who hasn't shown this morning and continues several more cases. Then Sundberg calls Jermaine Tidmore, and a skinny youth, charged with car theft, steps forward from the gallery. Amy Campanelli, the courtroom's senior public defender, tells Locallo that Tidmore wants a 402.

That's the number of the Illinois Supreme Court rule governing plea-bargain conferences. More than four of every five cases here are disposed of in 402s.

In a 402 the judge must issue a long series of admonishments to ensure that the defendant's plea is "knowing and voluntary"—or at least looks that way in the record. When he was a novice on the bench, Locallo, like most new judges, plodded through these warnings. But soon he could dash them off from memory. As usual, he's sprinting through them now. It's a testament to the dancing fingers of court reporter Marzano that he can keep pace; many of his colleagues turn on their cassette recorders when Locallo starts a 402.

"Mr. Tidmore, your attorney's requesting a conference to discuss the possible disposition of your matter, are you asking to have that conference, sir?" Locallo says in a breath.

"Yes," Tidmore murmurs.

"D'ya understand at the conference we'd be discussing facts about you, about this case, and about your background, some of the information that might be brought to my attention would normally not be admitted at trial, d'ya understand?"

"Yes."

"If you do not wish to plead guilty, nothing said or done during the conference can be used against you, d'ya understand?"

"Yes."

"D'ya still wish to have that conference?"

"Yes."

There's little conferring in a 402 conference. Usually the sale has already been made; this is just the closing. The lawyers have come to terms, and often they've also checked with the judge to make sure he'll approve the deal. In Locallo's courtroom, when the parties can't agree on a sentence, the courtroom PD will frequently ask Locallo for a 402 anyway, knowing the clearance-sale offers he makes to dispose of his "bullshit" cases. In these instances, Locallo and the lawyers will indeed confer during the 402—for perhaps two minutes. The prosecutor will inform Locallo of the defendant's criminal background. The PD will counter with some commendable nugget about the defendant she's managed to mine from a brisk interview with him through the bars of the courtroom lockup—his recent job at a Burger King, his work on a GED. Then Locallo will announce his offer, the defendant and his lawyer will whisper briefly, and the defendant will usually accept. Prosecutors aren't required to go along with the judge's offer; in fact, prosecutors, not the judge, are the ones who are supposed to be making the offer. But as Locallo well knows, the assistant state's attorneys aren't often going to fight him on the smaller cases, because they want his help in the bigger ones.

The defense lawyer sometimes serves as floor salesperson before the 402, softening up the defendant by stressing the maximum he might get if he insists on trial—even when the lawyer knows the judge would never go that high. Next to the sticker price, the wholesale offer is attractive.

Not many defendants would plead, of course, if they had nothing to lose by going to trial. But a jury trial usually takes two days to a week, and if the jury convicts, there will be post-trial motions and a sentencing hearing as well. A guilty plea can usually be wrapped up in twenty minutes. The jail behind the courthouse—the most populated single-site jail in the nation, with more than nine thousand inmates in 1998—has always been overcrowded. But its eleven divisions couldn't possibly contain all the defendants if even a tenth of them insisted on a jury trial, instead of the one percent who do.

The simple solution: make the defendant pay for a trial. Not with money, of course, but with a stiffer sentence if he rolls the dice and loses. The trial tax is as much a part of the courthouse as its limestone columns. The markup for a jury trial is higher than for a quicker "bench" trial, in which the judge decides the case. Lawyers trade scouting reports on particular judges' standard assessments. Inmates do likewise in the courtroom lockups and on the jail grapevine. The book on Locallo says his taxes are modest but that he'll bluff about sizable tariffs to get a defendant to fold.

Since it's unconstitutional to coerce a defendant into surrendering his Sixth Amendment right to a jury trial, the most that judges will admit is that some other judges do it. ("I have heard about it," Locallo says of the trial tax.) And the subtext to every 402 never is spoken, never makes it into the record: *In return for the favor of your guilty plea and the time it'll save us, I've agreed not to bang ya, d'ya understand?* Everyone understands.

Perusing a police report, assistant state's attorney Alesia gives Locallo the alleged facts of the Tidmore case. The arresting officers observed a 1996 Buick Century being driven erratically, ran the car's plates, and discovered it was stolen. When they gave chase, Tidmore jumped from the car and fled, and the officers caught him under a porch. The Buick's driver's-side window was broken, the steering column peeled, and a screwdriver was on the floor of the car.

Tidmore has no felony convictions, Alesia says. (He turned seventeen—majority age under criminal law in Illinois—just eleven days before his arrest.) Public defender Campanelli tells Locallo that Tidmore lives with his grandmother and is a high school student.

"Suggest he consider eighteen months' conditional discharge, with a condition he obtain his high school or GED degree," Locallo says.

If probation is a tap on the wrist, conditional discharge is a tickle. Tidmore won't even have to report to a probation officer. But the plea will give him a felony conviction. And if he commits another offense during the next eighteen months, he could be sentenced to prison on this case. On the other hand, Campanelli has already told the youth that if he goes to trial and is convicted, he could get as many as seven years. Tidmore nods to Campanelli: he'll cop to the judge's offer.

"Before I accept your plea of guilty, d'ya understand by pleading guilty that you're giving up your right to trial by jury?" Locallo asks.

"Yeah."

Locallo has given these admonishments too many times to be anything but mechanical in his delivery. In the preceding year, he presided over fifteen jury trials and eighty-eight benches. And he took 805 guilty pleas.

He races through the remaining admonishments. Tidmore says yes, no, and at the correct time, guilty. Fifteen minutes after his case was called, the young man is on his way, and Locallo has his first "dispo" of the morning.

The judges here get weekly printouts from the presiding judge listing the disposition totals for the week, the month, and the year, for each judge in the building. When a judge is up for retention—as Locallo is this November—his disposition totals will be published and disseminated before the election by the Chicago Crime Commission. Dispo totals have been important for judges since at least 1920, a year after the crime commission was formed. The commission began sending its clerks into courtrooms to tally judges' dispositions, in accordance with the group's belief that swift punishment was the key to cutting crime. Judicial efficiency was prized in Cook County long before that, however. In 1885 historian A. T. Andreas, writing about the Cook County Circuit Court, observed that a trial court judge who hesitates, "trying to decide every case exactly right and beyond cavil is not a good judge nor well fitted for his position. . . . Business must go forward, or the courts will get immediately clogged."

Locallo ranked below average in dispos in his first few years in a trial courtroom. But last year he surged to tenth among the building's thirty trial judges, cracking the one-thousand mark for the first time, with 1,058 dispos.

(That includes 150 pretrial dismissals by the state.) He says the spike in his dispos as his retention election nears is coincidental—he's just gotten faster with experience.

WHEN LOCALLO BEGAN his criminal justice career as a Cook County prosecutor in 1978, the primary lesson he was taught from the beginning was "how to move cases." And he was an eager learner.

After six months in traffic court, he was transferred to the municipal division, where he handled misdemeanor cases in police station branch courtrooms. Misdemeanor arrests were soaring in the late 1970s, and so the branches were even busier than usual, making efficiency all the more important. In a grimy courtroom in the police headquarters building downtown—"whore court," as Locallo and most lawyers and judges called it—Locallo helped the judge rush hookers and shoplifters past the bench. "Defendant pleads guilty, found guilty, two days' time served," the judge would say over and over. Locallo soon moved on to a south-side branch, where he helped process waves of accused wife-beaters, barroom brawlers, and window-breakers—defendants who paused at the bench long enough to have their cases tossed because the complaining witness hadn't shown, or to grab conditional discharge or probation.

After prosecuting drug cases in various 26th Street courtrooms for a year, Locallo graduated to a regular assignment as a third-chair prosecutor in a courtroom. While the stakes were higher in the felony courtrooms than in the branches, the essential task was the same: moving cases quickly. Locallo was blessed with an incomparable tutor in one of the first courtrooms he was assigned—Judge James Bailey, the courthouse's perennial dispo champ for twenty years. "What's next, what's next?" Bailey would bark at his prosecutors as soon as a case was disposed of. The judge offered unbeatable deals to petty offenders, reminding his prosecutors that time spent on a theft case was time taken from a murder. Defendants charged with violent crimes, on the other hand, got no breaks from Bailey.

This philosophy made sense to Locallo. He had a chance to apply what he learned when he was transferred to the courtroom of Judge William Cousins Jr. as a second chair. Locallo would come to admire Cousins more than any other judge. But efficiency wasn't Cousins's forte; when Locallo arrived in 1981, Cousins's call was hopelessly clogged. After Locallo was promoted to first chair, he began wheeling and dealing, making tantalizing offers to defense lawyers in lesser cases. "Counsel? What can we do for *you* today?" Locallo would greet the lawyers. "It was like white sales," Locallo recalls now with a laugh. The backup cleared.

"In Cousins's courtroom, we were trying the murders, rapes, and robberies," Locallo says. "And the rest of the stuff? I couldn't care less. If it wasn't a violent offense, I'm sorry, I admit it, I plead guilty—I gave away the store. But I got rid of a case, defense counsel got rid of a case." He made it a practice to check with the arresting officer and the victim before finalizing a deal. "Most police officers tell you, 'I don't give a shit. All I get credit for is the arrest.' And most victims say, 'You mean I don't have to come back to court?'"

Plea bargaining has been a staple in criminal courthouses throughout the nation since at least the late nineteenth century. The practice used to have many ardent critics. Conservatives said it let criminals off too easily; liberals said it promoted mindless, routinized sentencing of defendants. In 1973 the National Advisory Commission on Criminal Justice Standards and Goals called for the abolition of plea bargaining within five years. Under plea bargaining, the commission said, the focus wasn't on rehabilitation or even deterrence but merely on the disposal of cases, the quicker the better. The commission imagined sentencing hearings in which judges paid more attention to the offender than the offense; in which they considered not just an offender's criminal background but his upbringing, skills, and deficits; and in which a plan was devised for actually changing him into a law-abiding citizen—a plan whose implementation would be monitored by the judge.

The number of felony cases has risen dramatically throughout the country since the commission made its recommendation three decades ago, so instead of being abolished, plea bargaining has been relied on all the more, and the critics have largely disappeared. The concept of studying an offender and devising a rehabilitation plan isn't frowned upon so much as not looked upon at all; the proper sentence is whatever both sides can agree on to belch out one defendant and make space for the next. Locallo, like many judges here, has little regard for the ivory tower notions of yesterday's commissions. "We don't live in a theoretical world," he says. "Under ideal circumstances, you'd get a complete analysis of the defendant you were going to sentence. But you're not gonna have that. So you take the realistic approach."

JERMAINE TIDMORE'S PLEA is a dispo for Locallo, a conviction for the prosecutors, and one less case for the public defenders to fret. The conveyor is humming along this particular morning—until Tony Cameron manages to gum things up.

It happens after Campanelli's partner, public defender Diana Bidawid, informs Locallo that Cameron wants a 402. (Like most courtrooms at 26th Street, 302 has two public defenders and three assistant state's attorneys assigned to it.) Cameron is in front of the bench with Bidawid at his side, and prosecutor Alesia is next to Bidawid.

"Mr. Cameron, your attorney is requesting a conference to discuss the possible disposition of your matter, are you asking to have a conference?" Locallo begins.

"Yes," Cameron says.

Locallo sails through the first part of the 402 without a stoplight. Alesia, surveying a police report, tells the judge that the robbery occurred outside a currency exchange on Chicago's south side. According to the arresting officers, Cameron got into the victim's car, sat in her lap, put a gun to her head, and told her, "Give me your money or I'll blow your ass away." She handed over $260. Cameron fled, Alesia says—but he returned to the scene, and the victim identified him, as did her sister, who'd also been in the car.

Cameron has one other conviction, Alesia tells the judge: in 1986 he was found guilty but mentally ill in another robbery case, for which he got six years.

Public defender Bidawid takes a half minute to summarize Cameron for Locallo: thirty-four, lives with his mother on the south side, does odd jobs, has an eighth-grade education, learning disabled, a long history of mental disorders, taking an antipsychotic in the jail.

"All right. We did have a fitness hearing on December fourth," Locallo says, scrutinizing the court file in front of him.

"Correct. He was found fit," Bidawid says.

A defendant can be mentally ill, or even insane, and still be deemed fit for trial. He's fit if he understands the nature of the charges against him and the basics of the court proceedings, and if he can cooperate with his lawyer's efforts on his behalf. At the December hearing, a county psychiatrist testified that based on his interview of Cameron and his review of some of his mental health records, Cameron was "fit to stand trial, with medications." Cameron has been in psychiatric hospitals sixteen times, and he's received treatment from outpatient clinics throughout his adult life as well; yet the psychiatrist made his determination without reviewing any of Cameron's treatment records from the last twelve years, other than notes on the medicine he'd been prescribed in the jail. Following the psychiatrist's testimony, Locallo declared Cameron fit. The hearing had taken less than ten minutes.

Now Locallo glances down at Cameron. He sees a dark-skinned African American with wide-set eyes, a pencil mustache, and a wispy goatee. The judge asks him if he understands what's going on; Cameron says he does. Locallo then explains that armed robbery carries six to thirty, and that in return for his guilty plea, Cameron would get the minimum six. With day-for-day credit and other credits Cameron can compile in prison, minus the five months he's already spent in jail, he'll likely have to serve only another two years. (In 1998 convicts in Illinois get a day off their sentence for each day served. This is called a "good-conduct" credit—but inmates usually get it regardless of their behavior because the prisons are so overcrowded. A "truth-in-sentencing" law that will go into effect later in 1998 will require those convicted of murder to serve 100 percent of their time, and those convicted of many other violent offenses to do 85 percent of their time.)

"I'll accept that," Cameron says.

Cameron's 1986 conviction came in a bench trial. His public defender had sought a verdict of not guilty by reason of insanity, a finding that would have committed Cameron to a mental hospital. The judge's rejection of that verdict in favor of a finding of guilty but mentally ill had sent Cameron to prison instead. In that sentencing hearing, his PD had told the judge that if the aim was to steer Cameron from further crime, he needed psychiatric treatment. The PD urged the judge not to "turn the clock back here maybe a century or so and punish someone such as Tony by sending him to prison for being psychotic." But prison it was, though the judge did tell Cameron, "I hope you'll solve your mental difficulties" before sending him away. (It's up to prison officials what treatment, if any, to give a prisoner who's been found guilty but mentally ill. Cameron says he mainly got pills.)

Bidawid opted not to attempt an insanity defense in Cameron's present case. The county psychiatrist had concluded not only that Cameron was fit but that he'd been sane at the time of the offense. That opinion would have been hard to overcome. Bidawid didn't think it would be worth seeking another guilty-but-mentally-ill finding for Cameron, given the lack of benefit for such convicts.

In 1986 Cameron's mental status at least merited prolonged consideration. But in today's plea conference, the only real issue is whether he'll take the six.

Bidawid tells Locallo that Cameron is addicted to crack and asks the judge to include a recommendation in his sentencing order that Cameron be assigned to the Graham Correctional Center, a prison with a drug treatment program. Locallo quickly assents. He's always happy to make such a recommendation. He knows that prison officials don't necessarily follow such a suggestion from a judge, and he normally cautions defendants of this (though he neglects to advise Cameron of the possibility). But such recommendations are helpful to Locallo if not to the defendant; they're another extra he can offer to ice a deal. Locallo is adept at closing 402s, throwing in contact visits with family in the courtroom on the day of the plea and recommendations to particular prisons as if they're power windows and CD players.

Locallo asks Cameron if anyone is forcing him to plead guilty instead of taking his case to trial.

"I'm just tired—I'm really tired," Cameron says. His voice is deep and scratchy. "I just wanna get this over with."

Red alert. The defendant has departed from his lines. A 402 is a tightly scripted exercise, and when the defendant starts ad-libbing, it ruffles everyone. Locallo seems to sense Cameron wavering. Time to sweeten the pot.

"How long has he been in custody?" the judge asks Bidawid. One hundred forty-five days, she says. "I'll give him credit for 145 days," Locallo says, glancing benevolently at Cameron. It's like telling him if he buys the car, he'll get the tires for free; Cameron has that 145-day credit coming by law.

"Mr. Cameron, I'm going to ask you some questions," Locallo says. "If there's anything that you don't understand, I want you to tell me. I'll try to explain. All right, sir?"

"Yes, sir," Cameron says.

"All right. Is his mother here?"

"Yes, Judge," Bidawid says, peering into the gallery.

"She can come in."

A short woman in a Fila coat, sweatpants, and sneakers steps meekly through the glass doors, stopping a dozen feet behind Cameron.

"He's also asking for a contact visit," Bidawid says.

"Sure," Locallo says. "Good morning—thank you for coming to court," he tells Cameron's mother. "If there's anything you don't understand, tell me, and I'll try to explain, all right?"

"Yes," the mother says, looking blankly at the judge.

Locallo again advises Cameron of the charge against him and of the six-to-thirty-year term he is subject to. "Knowing the nature of the charges and the possible penalties, how do you plead to the charge of armed robbery, guilty or not guilty?"

"I plead guilty," Cameron says.

"Has anybody forced you, threatened you, or made any promise to you to get you to do this?"

"No, I just did it because I'm tired," Cameron says again. "I mean, I feel that no matter what I'm saying, it's not gonna go in my favor."

Clerk Sundberg looks up from an arrest warrant he's been filling out and studies Cameron.

"Well, you're entitled to have your trial," Locallo says.

"Yeah, but I was here twelve years ago in the same type of case like that," Cameron says. "It was purse-snatching instead of robbery. I didn't get no say-so on my behalf. So that's why I said, 'Well, okay,' because I'll never be heard, okay?"

"You will have an opportunity to say something before I sentence you," Locallo assures him.

"I understand, but nothing will happen for me," Cameron says. "It just never do."

Cameron's father abandoned the family when Cameron was small. The family lived off the disability check his mother got for her own mental disorder. Cameron later describes his mother to me as "sweet" but "slow, like a real little kid." Various aunts and uncles lived in the household, several of them with alcohol and drug addictions. (One uncle has a drug case pending on this floor.) School was a mystery to Cameron, perhaps because he had an IQ of 62 and hearing loss in one ear. He was barely a teen when he began hanging on corners with a forty-ounce bottle of beer, his pills, and marijuana joints. His mother brought him to a mental hospital when he was sixteen. He'd been hearing voices, and whenever the doorbell rang, he'd hide in a closet, she reported; he refused to go outside and did little inside but sit and stare into space. The psychiatrists said he was schizophrenic and retarded. He was hospitalized almost two years. During one psychological test, when he was shown a certain picture, he said the character in the picture was happy because he jumped out the window and died. Before he was released, a psychologist observed that Cameron had "the unfortunate combination of a handsome, well-developed body of an adolescent with the mind of a ten-year-old and the emotional development of a four-year-old." Some of his problems likely were organic, the psychologist said, but they were also probably due to Cameron's having been "vastly deprived intellectually, socially, and emotionally" at home and in school.

Cameron says he did get guidance as a youngster from one of his uncles. "Uncle Poochie" would gather Tony and his two brothers and their cousins in a bedroom, lock the door, match the boys up by size, and direct them to fight until blood was drawn. Cameron got his nose broken once, and he recalls losing most of the fights; but he appreciates Uncle Poochie's attempts to "teach us how to be a man." Cameron absorbed numerous beatings from an older brother as well. Cameron's two brothers have been arrested repeatedly for battery and assault. But such troubles aren't due to a lack of discipline in the household, according to Cameron; when he and his siblings were kids, several of the adults in the home were willing to administer the necessary whuppings. Uncle Poochie was feared the most; he'd order his target to strip, then lash him with an extension cord "on your legs, arms, your ass, didn't make no difference." Cameron's mother was gentler, he says, though she whupped him with "extension cords, bottles, shoes." Cameron isn't squawking about how he was punished. "When you bad kids, that's what you get."

Locallo isn't familiar with any of these details about Cameron. The judge has more than three hundred cases involving more than 350 defendants on his call; how could he be expected to delve into such minutiae? Besides, it isn't relevant to the matter at hand, which still is whether Cameron will go through with his plea.

When a defendant hesitates in the middle of a plea, some judges rush to wrap things up, lest the defendant back out. Locallo responds instead with patience. It isn't that he wants to learn more about Cameron; it's that he not only wants to get the plea, he also wants it to stick. He's dropped well below the speed limit in his delivery of the admonishments, and he'll explain everything three times if he must, to make it clear in the record that Cameron knew what he was doing when he pled—so Cameron would have a hard time claiming on an appeal that he didn't. (The watchdog group that publishes judges' dispo records tracks their record of appellate reversals as well.) "A bad plea is like a vampire—it can always come back," Locallo often tells younger judges. He urges them to take the extra few minutes sometimes needed "to kill a case—to put that stake in the vampire's heart."

So Locallo now tells Cameron: "Well, you understand that if you wanted to have a trial, I would give you a trial. You know that."

"Yeah, but I mean, you would still—I've been looking at six to thirty years."

"That's if you're found guilty," Locallo says.

"That could be the maximum, you know, or whatever you could find."

"Oh no, you can't be penalized for taking a trial," Locallo responds, grasping Cameron's allusion to a tax. "What I'm saying to you, I can't force you to plead guilty. I can't force you to plead not guilty. You understand?"

"Right," Cameron says. "But if I take the trial, I mean, would I get thirty years? That's what I'm scared of. That's what I'm looking at."

"The range is six to thirty, but I can't tell you what your sentence would be," Locallo says.

"That's what I'm saying. I got no choice."

"I realize that," Locallo says. "But I'd have to hear the facts and I'd have to make the decision as to what your background is."

"There ain't no kinda way that I'm gonna win on this case at all," Cameron says with a shake of his head. "Ain't nothing gonna go in my favor. It never have, you know."

"All right," Locallo says. "Now, do you understand that by pleading guilty, there's not going to be a trial?"

"Yes, I understand all of that," Cameron says.

"You understand by pleading guilty you're giving up your right to see, to confront, and question any of the witnesses who'd testify against you?"

"I understand all that," Cameron says. "I mean, you know, that's why I have a problem, because I always been rejected from society. I never had a chance in life."

"Other than the promise that in return for your plea of guilty your sentence would be six years—which is the minimum—other than that promise, have there been any other promises made to you to get you to plead guilty?"

"I ain't gonna win," Cameron says.

"Well, is anybody promising you anything other than the six years?"

"Ain't nobody promising no freedom," Cameron says. Deputy Guerrero, standing a few feet behind Cameron, shakes his head and chuckles softly.

"All right," Locallo says. "But I'm asking you, has anybody promised you anything other than the six years?"

"Nobody did promise me anything. Nobody told me nothing. I don't know nothing. I've been stuck here, going back and forth to court. I don't know what I'm here for or what I'm supposed to have done. I'm just up against something I don't know nothing about."

"Well—"

"I don't understand nothing whatsoever, but I'm just taking something that I don't even understand myself," Cameron says.

"Do you understand what the charges are?" Locallo tries again.

"I understand clearly what the charges were, you know what I'm saying, all of that—but I wasn't the person."

"Well, the law does recognize that an individual can plead guilty if he wishes to," Locallo says. Locallo knows that the U.S. Supreme Court has even condoned the taking of guilty pleas, under certain circumstances, from defendants who insist they're innocent. Critics of this holding say it makes it easier for courts to convict the truly innocent. But Supreme Court justices have been more concerned with the backlog in the criminal courts, and the need to keep the line moving.

"The law also recognizes if you want a trial, you can get a trial," Locallo goes on. "Do you want a trial?"

"No, I'm gonna take this because I'm not gonna win," Cameron says. "Ain't no way I'm gonna win. I can't beat this system, your honor."

"You have to answer his questions," Bidawid says.

Locallo asks him once more if he still wants to plead.

"Yeah, I still wish to do that."

Locallo finds his plea to be "knowing and voluntary."

Bidawid has Cameron sign a waiver of his right to a presentence investigation. The PSI, prepared by a probation officer, is designed to acquaint a judge more thoroughly with the defendant's background—his upbringing, family, education, work history—so the sentencing decision will be an informed one. All that information is moot, though, in a 402, since the sentence has already been agreed upon.

IN THE PREDAWN HOURS a week later, Cameron is loaded onto a bus with barred windows that takes him down Interstate 55 to Joliet, where he's processed into the state's prison system. Two weeks later another bus takes him farther southwest, not to the Graham Correctional Center—the one with the drug treatment program Locallo mentioned—but to the Illinois River Correctional Center in the town of Canton. "These people trick you," Cameron says, of ending up in Illinois River instead of Graham.

Cameron says he spoke up during the plea conference because "I wanted someone to understand where I was coming from. We all got a story to tell. And some people had a rough life and some people didn't. I think they should find out why people do the things they do. And see who the person really is. And see what you could do to make him *not* do the things they do, instead of always just locking 'em up."

TWO

A Growth Industry

THE COURTHOUSE has survived seven decades of hard wear and neglect largely because of the foresight of its designers. "Lamentable but true, most civic and public buildings do not receive the best of care either from the occupants or from the caretakers," Ralph Hammet, the building's chief designer, wrote in an architectural magazine shortly after the building opened in 1929. "Special concern was taken to select good wearing materials, and floors, walls and trimmings that would not require expensive janitorial service."

Expensive janitorial service isn't provided, as visitors to the building's public washrooms quickly learn. In the rusted and filthy sinks the water runs nonstop or not at all. Toilet stalls lack doors, and some lack toilets as well. Paper towel dispensers and toilet paper holders commonly dispense and hold nothing. The mirrors are cracked in the few washrooms that still have them. Floors are sticky, ceilings drip, and the insulation is frayed on the overhead pipes. The norm is expressed by the sign that appears one day on a wall in a first-floor washroom: HAND BLOWER IS WORKING.

The building's water fountains function only as oversize ashtrays. Ceiling tiles are missing in some corridors, revealing the pipes above.

But the halls are mopped and the courtrooms vacuumed frequently. Except for the washrooms, the building isn't particularly decrepit. More noticeable is the unwelcoming tenor of the hallways. There are no benches or chairs. Security cameras peep down from the ceilings. The walls are bare, save for the fire extinguishers and the many prohibition signs—forbidding smoking, hat-wearing, "unapproved group congregating," and the "causing of a disturbance or nuisance."

QUIET—NO SMOKING, EATING, CHILDREN, TALKING plaques hang next to the doors of most courtrooms. The view out the east windows is of the parking garage across California Boulevard; the west windows stare into the brick face of Division 1, the jail's oldest building.

People congregate in the hallways despite the posted ban. Family members with worried faces talk in low voices, and defense lawyers inform clients of the prosecutor's latest offer. A wet-eyed, middle-aged black woman may step into a hallway from a courtroom at any moment. Cops waiting to testify lean against walls, trading jokes. The officers in their navy sweaters and powder-blue shirts and the small clusters of dark-skinned youths in sports team jackets pretend to ignore one another. But perhaps they're conversing on the washroom walls, where scrawled greetings such as FUCK THE POLICE adjoin salutations such as ALL GANG-BANGERS SUCK THEIR DEAD DADDIES DICK.

From the outside the courthouse looks misplaced in this humble neighborhood. With its broad columns and Greco-Roman flourishes, the building resembles a museum—but no tour buses, and few cabs, ever venture to this location, six miles southwest of downtown. The eight allegorical figures in tunics and togas adorning the courthouse's seventh story now seem a wasted effort. Each centered above one of the eight columns that stretch from floors three through six, they stare straight ahead, like police-lineup subjects ordered to face forward. They were carved by German-born sculptor Peter Toneman. In December 1997 Chicago artist Lynn Toneman, the wife of Peter Toneman's great-grandson, had jury duty at 26th Street and saw the sculptures for the first time. She found them "impressive and intriguing" but was more struck by the "depressing chemistry" inside the courthouse, the "heartbreaking sight of these people in the hallways—people in trouble and their mothers and siblings." Toneman and her fellow jurors voted to convict, after which she left the building "hoping I'd never have to return."

On the boulevard in front of the courthouse, workers begin constructing a decorative fountain in early 1998, one of three being added to the city's boulevards with federal funds. The fountain will "blend Beaux Arts and Prairie Style," a city press release says. It will have handmade ceramic tile accents, and lights in the pool and bowl will illuminate the cascading water at night. Benches, shade trees, and flowering shrubs will surround the fountain. A defense lawyer visiting Courtroom 302 one afternoon suggests it be christened the Bond Pond, in honor of the relatives of defendants he expects will loot it of its coins on their way to bond court. Andrew Dalkin, one of the prosecutors in 302, thinks the $280,000 to be spent on the fountain is money down the drain. "They're trying to add beauty to a place that's beyond beautification," Dalkin says.

COOK COUNTY was founded in 1831, after soldiers had pushed most of the local Indians westward. That same year state legislators, recognizing the need for an organized system of law if justice were to prevail in the land taken from the Potawatomi, established the Circuit Court of Cook County.

Hearings and trials at first were conducted in taverns, stores, and churches. But the growth of the county seat, Chicago—from 350 residents in 1833, when it was incorporated as a town, to 3,300 two years later—led to the building of the county's first courthouse in 1835, on Chicago's public square, at Clark and Randolph. Civil cases predominated initially. As Chicago's population swelled, however, so did crime. The original courthouse was torn down and a larger one built on the public square in 1853.

The Chicago Fire destroyed that courthouse in 1871. In 1873 the county for the first time opened a courthouse exclusively for criminal cases, just north of downtown at Dearborn and Hubbard. Officials predicted it would suffice for fifty years. But the city's population continued to increase, as did crime, and in twenty years that courthouse came down and a larger one went up on the spot. "No other city of its size on earth goes often deeper or more wisely into its pockets to down crime," the *Chicago Herald* boasted on the eve of the opening of the latest courthouse in 1893. "This big clearinghouse for crime will prove a mighty impregnable thing for evildoers to run against." Evildoers continued to run against it, though, and soon that courthouse, too, was awash in cases, the jail overflowing with defendants. County officials responded in their usual way, asking taxpayers for yet another bigger courthouse and jail. But this time taxpayers balked, rejecting four bond appeals from 1915 through 1921.

In 1922 the county hired criminologist George Kirchwey to study its dilemma. Kirchwey—former dean of the Columbia University Law School and former warden of New York's Sing Sing prison—recommended that the county quit trying to build its way out of its crime problem and instead focus on stemming the tide of defendants. This would entail examining what led people to commit crime, and what could be done to change that, Kirchwey said—a tall order, he allowed, but in his mind the only real long-term solution. County officials weren't interested in such a fanciful idea, but Kirchwey's report helped them nonetheless, because he acknowledged that the present courthouse and jail were in such bad shape that new ones had to be built. The officials rallied civic leaders and the city's newspapers behind that recommendation, and taxpayers finally approved a bond appeal in 1925.

Kirchwey's larger point, about the need to study the causes of crime, was soon forgotten. The county's power brokers had little incentive to do anything that might reduce the number of defendants; by the 1920s ward bosses were already hopelessly hooked on courthouse and jail patronage. Judges, prosecutors, bailiffs, clerks, probation officers, and jail guards owed their jobs to the ward bosses—and showed their thanks by knocking on doors on election day.

In anticipation of the expected approval of the 1925 bond appeal, a committee was formed in 1924 to recommend a site for the new courthouse and jail. The first sites considered were all downtown, out of regard for the convenience of those who would use the courthouse. But then a committee member proposed a large parcel of land at 26th and California. The land was vacant, except for the city's House of Corrections, a jail for ordinance violators who couldn't afford to pay their fines. Because the land was owned by the city, it could be obtained cheaply through a city-county swap. Committee members allowed that the location was far less accessible than the downtown sites being considered, but argued that accessibility had its drawbacks. A downtown jail hurt a city's spirit, committee members maintained, as well as the values of nearby businesses.

And so the committee settled on 26th and California. Politics may have also influenced the decision. Most of the committee members owed their allegiance to county board president Anton Cermak, in whose ward the chosen site happened to be. So what if for decades judges, lawyers, jurors, witnesses, and relatives and friends of defendants would have to struggle to reach the remote location; the important thing was that members of Cermak's ward organization, to whom the county board president could dole out courthouse and jail jobs, would have a pleasantly short commute. And if a host of lawyers did indeed establish offices up 26th Street and down California, it wouldn't hurt Cermak's real estate holdings in the area.

THE COURTHOUSE OPENED on April Fools' Day, 1929. Chicago was battered with its worst spring storm in years that day, fierce winds and sleet damaging lakefront property and forcing the closing of the Outer Drive (now known as Lake Shore Drive).

The courthouse's facade impressed reporters. They were charmed as well by the look of the building's fourteen courtrooms, with their marble walls, oak benches trimmed with bronze rosettes, and brass light fixtures. But those who worked in the courthouse reached a quick negative verdict on the building. "Chicago's worst April Fools' joke," one judge called it.

From their towering thronelike perches, judges could barely hear the proceedings below—especially with a fan whirring in the wall behind them. When they turned off the fans, the judges heard lawyers and witnesses distinctly—the lawyers and witnesses in the courtroom above, whose voices would drift in through the vents. Then there were the freight trains that regularly roared by on the tracks along 26th Street. A bailiff told a reporter that the courthouse's designers must have "meant to keep the judges fair and impartial by preventing them from hearing." One judge had so much trouble following testimony in the kidnapping trial he was presiding over that he angrily recessed it and resumed it in a courtroom downtown.

The acoustics weren't the only target of criticism. Deputies who escorted prisoners between the jail and the courthouse via a tunnel griped about the icy rain dripping from the tunnel's ceiling. The courthouse's elevators quit at week's end, trapping sixty people between floors for forty minutes, and the heat soon failed. Adding insult to injury, there was an appalling dearth of spittoons. The object of the courthouse staffers' wrath, county board president Cermak, was vacationing in Florida.

Workers fixed the elevators and improved the acoustics, and the county board appropriated money to rectify the heat problem. A custodian gathered up the old courthouse's spittoons and installed them in the new building. Judges with courtrooms on the 26th Street side of the building dealt with the noise from the freight trains by keeping their windows closed, although this made their courtrooms broil in the summer. (The county board wouldn't fund air-conditioning for the building until 1973.)

But the main trouble with the courthouse—its location—wasn't so easily corrected. Only a handful of lawyers ever set up shop nearby, and the courthouse failed to attract restaurants or other businesses to the area. Young lawyers torn between practicing civil or criminal law tended to opt for the convenience of the downtown civil courts, diminishing the pool of private defense attorneys and increasing the load on public defenders.

The Chicago Bar Association campaigned repeatedly to move the criminal court back downtown—always in vain. In 1960 a huge civic center was on the drawing board for the Loop, with plans for it to house the county's civil courtrooms. Bar associations, civic groups, and the city's newspapers agreed: the criminal court ought to be in the civic center, too. But an officer of the Chicago Real Estate Board warned that having the criminal court downtown, with its "certain elements," might create a "real hazard" for the Loop. The *Chicago Daily News* called the resistance to the criminal court in the Loop by the "well-heeled tenants of the city's skyscrapers" part of a "wider inclination to hide away somewhere as many unpleasant facts as possible" about crime and criminal justice in Chicago.

Mayor Richard J. Daley—for whom the new civic center would be named—was not about to have the unseemly criminal court in it. Like the realtors, he considered the remote site at 26th and California the ideal one—and his was the opinion that mattered.

Still today, citizens summoned to 26th Street for jury duty often beg to be assigned to another courthouse, saying the one on the southwest side is just too hard to reach. It's a difficult trip by car for many county residents and not well served by public transportation.

AT THE CORNERSTONE ceremony for the new courthouse, in September 1927, the dignitaries who spoke "expressed the hope that crime in Chicago would soon be under such control that the [new] jail would never be overcrowded or even uncomfortably filled," the journal of the Chicago Crime Commission reported that year. When the courthouse opened a year and a half later, it had five more trial courtrooms than its predecessor, and the new jail behind the courthouse could hold four times as many inmates as the previous jail. But with crime escalating during Prohibition, the new jail was overbooked on opening day, with a capacity of 1,302, and 1,341 prisoners. The jail and the courthouse became even more glutted when the stock market crashed later that year. Prohibition's repeal in 1933, however, along with the waning of the Depression in the late 1930s, led to a quarter century of relative calm at 26th Street.

That calm ended in the 1960s. Blacks escaping southern racism had been streaming into northern cities, where they were confined to dilapidated ghettoes and limited to the lowest-paying jobs. The deepening poverty in these areas, combined with the large proportion of inhabitants in their teens and twenties, resulted in a vast escalation in street crime.

"Crime flourishes where the conditions of life are the worst," President Lyndon Johnson's Commission on Law Enforcement and Administration of Justice observed in 1967. The criminal justice system could deal with "individual instances of crime," but it was "not designed to eliminate the conditions in which most crime breeds"—namely poverty and racism. The best way to attack crime was "to eliminate slums and ghettoes, to improve education, to provide jobs, to make sure that every American is given the opportunities and the freedoms that will enable him to assume his responsibilities." The following year the National Advisory Commission on Civil Disorders said that urban slums were making their youthful residents "better candidates for crime and civil disorder than for jobs," and it called for sustained attempts to end segregation and "unprecedented levels of funding" to eradicate slums.

In 1973 the National Advisory Commission on Criminal Justice Standards and Goals—the commission that called for an end to plea bargaining—asserted that the nation had come to lean mindlessly on prison to reduce crime, and that the failure of this approach was "incontestable." The time had come to question this strategy, the commission said: "If New York has 31 times as many armed robberies as London, if Philadelphia has 44 times as many criminal homicides as Vienna, if Chicago has more burglaries than all of Japan, if Los Angeles has more drug addiction than all of Western Europe, than we must concentrate on the social and economic ills of New York, Philadelphia, Chicago, Los Angeles, and America." These social and economic ills "form the freshets that make the streams that form the rivers that flood our criminal justice system and ultimately its correctional institutions." A more just society would protect the public more than prison ever would, the commission said. The prison was "obsolete, cannot be reformed . . . and should be repudiated as useless for any purpose other than locking away persons who are too dangerous to be allowed at large in free society. For the latter purpose we already have more prison space than we need." The commission urged that no new prisons be built in the foreseeable future.

But an all-out attack on the nation's social ills never happened—not with the Vietnam War distracting the nation and draining its budget. The closing of factories in central cities throughout the 1960s and 1970s only worsened things. Street crime kept climbing, and the public wearied of the idea of addressing root causes, yearning for a quick fix instead.

The new prevailing sentiment was expressed in 1981 by Illinois governor James Thompson, chair of the Attorney General's Task Force on Violent Crime. "We have to lock up more violent offenders and we have to keep them locked up," Thompson declared. While "unfortunate social conditions, unemployment, and inadequate education undoubtedly contribute to crime," he conceded, the task force wanted to bring about "an immediate impact" on the crime problem. Its main recommendation: two billion federal dollars for the construction of state prisons.

"Unprecedented levels of funding" were indeed dispensed—but not to fight poverty. The 1980s and 1990s saw the opening of more than six hundred state and fifty federal prisons in the United States, with huge expenditures for building and running them. The total number of inmates in the nation's prisons and jails has quadrupled, from half a million in 1980 to almost 2.1 million in 2003.

It's not clear that this imprisonment binge has had the intended effect. Since 1980, the violent crime rate has waxed and waned, while the incarceration rate has risen every year. Criminologists have linked the rises and falls in violent crime to such factors as the persistence of poverty, the proportion of young males in the population, the prevalence of guns, and the emergence of certain drugs in society—notably crack cocaine in the 1980s. But no consensus has emerged.

There's no question, though, about what the get-tough approach has meant for felony courts. Since the late 1970s the pace at 26th Street has been more frenzied than ever.

In 1978, Cook County erected the fifteen-story administration building that's joined to the courthouse by the first-floor lobby. The transfer of offices out of the courthouse opened space for sixteen new courtrooms on the second and third floors of the old building. County board secretary Michael Igoe called the administration building a worthy investment of $32 million, observing that "the biggest growth industry we've got going right now is crime."

And the sunniest days for the industry lay ahead. From 1977 to 1985 the caseload in the courthouse more than doubled, from 6,900 cases annually to 15,000. From 1985 to 1990 it doubled again, thanks mainly to the horde of drug addicts and small-time dealers being dropped off at the courthouse basement. The caseload has since leveled off at about thirty thousand a year.

The principal job in the courthouse still is sorting; the sorting is just done even faster now. The 1973 National Advisory Commission on Criminal Justice Standards and Goals urged judges and lawyers to put more thought into their actions, but there's no chance of that today. "There is not sufficient time to be introspective," says Thomas Fitzgerald, the presiding judge at 26th Street in 1998. "Thinking time doesn't show up on a cost-benefit analysis."

For decades the jail consisted of a single division directly behind the courthouse, with a population around two thousand. Starting in the 1970s building after building went up on the jail grounds adjoining the courthouse. By the early 1990s the inmate population had surpassed seven thousand, and the jail "campus," as jail officials now call it, was five blocks long and two blocks wide. The more than nine thousand inmates in the jail as 1998 dawned were costing taxpayers a half-million dollars a day in room and board. (The jail population has since surpassed eleven thousand.)

The jail's most expensive addition—the $97 million maximum-security Division 11—opened for business in 1995 at 31st and California, on the former site of International Harvester's Tractor Works plant. For decades Tractor Works had thrived down the street from the courthouse, its workers building crawler tractors, bulldozers, and graders, equipment that was shipped nationwide and around the world. In 1960 Tractor Works employed five thousand. But in 1969 International Harvester closed the plant and fled for the suburbs. At 31st and California, where laborers once forged steel on presses, machined parts, welded, assembled, and painted, today men and women in navy uniforms watch men in tan uniforms watch TV.

In 1978 Illinois spent $100 million on its prison system; now it spends more than a billion. Most of that goes for warehousing the commodities rolling out of 26th Street; Cook County furnishes two-thirds of the state's prison inmates, sixteen thousand new ones a year. Eighty percent of those inmates are black, though only 26 percent of Cook County's population is. The exportables are loaded before dawn onto the sheriff's buses. Most of them couldn't support families at home, but they put food on the table for the families of prison workers in Danville and Dixon, Vandalia and Vienna, Jacksonville and Taylorville, and the Land of Lincoln's eighteen other prison-dependent towns.

Not that crime doesn't pay for Cook County as well. The multitudes brought to 26th Street in handcuffs, whether they're eventually deemed exportable or not, help cover mortgages, car payments, and tuition bills for jail guards, prosecutors, public defenders, private lawyers, judges, clerks, court reporters, deputies, probation officers, police officers, psychiatrists, social workers, translaters, cooks, janitors. Jail guards here sometimes greet batches of new prisoners by saying, "We'd like to thank you for committing your crimes in Cook County."

THREE

Baggage

AUGUST LOCALLO was a frequent visitor to the witness stands at 26th Street in the 1950s and 1960s, most of those years as a robbery detective. He became a Chicago police officer in December 1952, two months after his son Daniel was born.

For many police officers, coming to the courthouse to testify is an aggravation barely offset by the time and a half. They wait in hallways or empty jury rooms, sometimes for hours, for the privilege of squaring off with a defense lawyer bent on demonstrating their carelessness or deceit. But Detective Locallo relished the challenge. While he waited, he thought about the traps the defense lawyer would likely set for him on cross, and how he could evade them. As a result, he usually was an effective witness for the state. But he wouldn't stretch his testimony to help prosecutors win—unlike some officers, he says. "I used to take great pride in putting someone in the penitentiary," he says. "But I think I took greater pride in keeping someone out who didn't deserve to go."

August Locallo regaled his wife and children at the dinner table with stories of his courtroom experiences. Dan Locallo listened with pride.

After the younger Locallo graduated from Chicago's John Marshall Law School in 1977, he hoped for a job as a Cook County prosecutor. And he soon had one, thanks to his father's police work.

For six months in 1977 state police were unable to solve the $120,000 robbery of a toll collection driver near O'Hare Airport. Late that year August Locallo, then a north-side commander of robbery detectives, pried a confession from a suspect, as well as information leading to the indictment of his coconspirators: two Chicago cops and two state transportation department workers. At the press conference announcing the indictments, the elder Locallo sat next to Cook County state's attorney Bernard Carey. "I mentioned the fact that my son was an attorney who would like to become an assistant state's attorney," August Locallo says. A month later his son was one.

DAN LOCALLO says that when he started out as a prosecutor, he was "kind of an asshole" to defense lawyers. One day he had a heated exchange with a defense lawyer named Roosevelt Thomas. He doesn't remember the substance of the dispute, but the episode troubled him. "Something just clicked. I realized that I have my job to do, and defense counsel has his job to do, and it's nothing personal."

He speaks highly of all the judges in whose courtrooms he served as an assistant state's attorney. But it is Judge William Cousins whose photo now hangs in Locallo's chambers.

Cousins later was elected to the appellate bench and is now retired. Locallo admired his independence. Before he became a judge, Cousins was an alderman—one of the few who dared oppose Mayor Richard J. Daley. He retained that independence while he was on the bench. In many courtrooms prosecutors would "back-door" the judge, Locallo says— they'd discuss upcoming cases with the judge in his chambers, hinting broadly at how the judge should rule on certain key issues. There was no back-dooring Cousins; he wouldn't discuss a case off the bench with either side. Locallo respected this even though it made his job harder.

Locallo didn't want to win by manipulating the judge, anyway—but he certainly wanted to win. He was "very intense and very competitive" as a prosecutor, says Richard Schwind, who was one of Locallo's partners in Cousins's courtroom. "He'd prepare and prepare and prepare, and cover every angle. And he'd get very upset when something happened that he didn't anticipate. He was very focused, almost to the point of having tunnel vision."

Locallo hadn't been a prosecutor long before he decided he wanted to be a judge. "The power to influence was a great attraction," he says. "But it was never a power-trip type thing, like being able to order people around. For me, what was attractive was the ability to make decisions, to do justice."

He left the state's attorney's office in 1983, reasoning that he'd improve his chances of getting to the bench by broadening his résumé and contacts. He did labor law for the Teamsters, then personal injury work. But he couldn't get excited about slip-and-falls after prosecuting rapes and murders at 26th Street.

Cook County has two levels of judges: circuit judges, who are elected by the public, and associate judges, who are picked by the circuit judges to fill vacancies between elections. In 1986 court officials announced they'd be filling nine vacancies with associates. Locallo was among the 150 lawyers to apply. He'd been a lawyer less than nine years. But he had connections: the head of the committee selecting the eighteen finalists was a friend of Locallo's father. Locallo was named a finalist.

After the finalists for associate judgeships are announced, political heavyweights contact the sitting circuit judges and let them know whom they'd like to be elected. Judge Cousins called a longtime friend on Locallo's behalf—Mayor Harold Washington. Locallo's name went on the list of candidates the mayor backed.

Locallo didn't rest on his clout, however. He traversed the county, shaking hands with the circuit judges and soliciting their support. He personally contacted 175 of the 177 circuit judges—two were out of town. When the nine winners were announced, Locallo was among them. He was sworn in on June 13, 1986—a judge at thirty-three.

His first assignment was in the northwest suburbs, where he handled drunk-driving cases, misdemeanors, and an occasional felony preliminary hearing. It was hard for a judge to distinguish himself with such a docket, but Locallo managed to. He boned up on recent DUI case law to prepare himself for those cases, summarizing on paper the rulings he was reading. It occurred to him that his colleagues could benefit from these summaries, and he started photocopying and distributing them. He began to be thought of as a judge who went the extra mile.

After eighteen months he was on the verge of advancing to a felony courtroom in the suburbs. But then Locallo got into a dispute with an elderly colleague and, within earshot of numerous other judges, informed him he was "full of shit."

Instead of being promoted to a felony courtroom, Locallo was transferred to the branch courts in Chicago—a demotion, in effect, since it relegated him to small matters still longer. "I did the right thing, but I paid the price," he says. The episode taught him that "you have to show some finesse. You can't go around telling judges they're full of shit."

For the next few years he sat in the dismal branches, conducting bond hearings and presiding over preliminary hearings in drug cases. Even in this lowly setting, he continued to make a name for himself. He began publishing and distributing summaries of Illinois Supreme Court decisions in death penalty cases. Periodically, after a preliminary hearing in a drug case, he'd give the lawyers a written ruling, replete with case citations. Even trial court judges at 26th Street rarely do that, and written opinions in the branch courts were unheard of. During one preliminary hearing Locallo told the parties he couldn't make an informed decision without visiting the scene of the crime; soon Locallo, the lawyers, the defendant, the court reporter, and the deputies were on their way. Nobody had ever heard of a branch court judge doing that, either.

In 1990 a candidate for president of the Cook County Board, R. Eugene Pincham, was blasted by his opponent for having been "predisposed toward criminals" when he was on the appellate court. Locallo sent a letter to the *Chicago Tribune* backing Pincham. "It is essential that our judiciary be free and courageous enough to take unpopular positions," Locallo wrote. "We should all remember: 'What is right is not always popular, and what is popular is not always right.'" The letter didn't win Locallo any points with prosecutors.

In 1992 Locallo ran for circuit judge in a northwest-side subcircuit. Circuit judges earn slightly more than associate judges, their jobs are more secure, and they get better assignments. With the rave reviews of bar groups and the endorsements of both of Chicago's major dailies, he won the Democratic primary, then coasted to victory on November 3, 1992. This boosted his pay from $81,000 to $87,000. He worked as a "floater" at 26th Street, filling in for vacationing judges, until a permanent spot opened in a trial courtroom in December 1994. That was when he moved into Courtroom 302.

HUGE ART PHOTOS of John F. Kennedy dominate Locallo's windowless chambers. On election night in 1960 Locallo, then eight, stayed up after his bedtime cheering Kennedy's victory over Richard Nixon. The Kennedy charm and eloquence awed him. He'd watch a Kennedy speech on TV, listen to the applause, and imagine himself president. When did that fantasy end? "I still want to be president," Locallo says with a smile.

His desktop is usually suffocating under files, mail, faxes, transcripts, and legal newspapers. More newspapers are heaped in corners and piled on a couch and two chairs. Judges at 26th Street have no personal secretaries or law clerks. Locallo has slept on the couch on occasion after a late night's work. There's a shower upstairs in the chambers of one of the old courtrooms that he'll use after such a night; his wife will bring him fresh clothes from home.

Long after other courtrooms have been vacuumed and dead-bolted, Locallo is often still on the bench or at his desk in his chambers. His off-bench judicial activities are extensive, including work for a state bar council and a judges' group, the annual updating of his DUI and death penalty summaries, addresses to law groups, and occasional articles for legal journals.

Sam Adam, a defense lawyer who's been trying cases in the courthouse since 1961, considers Locallo a "throwback to the old days at 26th Street, when judges took the intellectual side of their job more seriously." Adam says that in years past, "You could go to a judge's chambers at eight in the morning and find him reading recent decisions from the Supreme Court, or looking up some law. You almost never see that today. Locallo's an exception."

"He has a built-in sense of fairness," says Charles Ingles, another veteran defense lawyer. In Ingles's opinion, police officers lie routinely at 26th Street, and judges rarely call them on it. "But if Locallo thinks a case is bad, he'll pitch it."

Prosecutors are less fond of Locallo. "He's thought of by prosecutors as somebody who wants to be on the appellate court and is gonna kowtow to the defense bar to get that to happen," says one prosecutor who's worked in Locallo's courtroom. (Defense lawyers outnumber prosecutors in the bar groups that publish ratings of judicial candidates before elections, and it's therefore believed they have more influence on a judge's future.) "He knows the law better than most judges in the building, and he'll give you a fair trial," this prosecutor says. "But day to day, he gives real softball sentences."

"Sometimes Dan Locallo does things to benefit Dan Locallo," says Mark Ostrowski, the lead prosecutor in 302 as 1998 begins. "He'll do things to make himself look good. I see him as a guy who can play it both ways, who will do what's politically correct." Locallo will sentence defendants stiffly in heater cases, with the press watching, Ostrowski says. But in the vast majority of lesser cases, he hands out conditional discharge, probation, and boot-camp terms much too easily, in Ostrowski's opinion.

Locallo dislikes formality. He dreads the idea of appearing pretentious, especially to a jury. After a panel of prospective jurors has been seated in his courtroom, he'll ask its members to "please put out of your mind anything you've seen about those goofy judges on TV." He breaks up the tedium of jury-picking with frequent canned one-liners. To the man who mentions bowling as a hobby: "Oh, you got a lotta time to spare?" To the woman who works in a bakery: "I hear they make a lotta dough in that business."

Locallo does indeed have his sights on the appellate court and, ultimately, the Illinois Supreme Court. In November 1997 he appeared before a Democratic Party subcommittee in the Bismarck Hotel downtown, seeking slating for one of two appellate vacancies. He took it in stride when he wasn't anointed. At forty-five, he was still relatively young, he told himself; his day would come. He needed to maintain his reputation with the bar groups. And it wouldn't hurt to get his name in the newspapers now and then. He's never shrunk from publicity. When he was a prosecutor in Judge Cousins's courtroom, he used to call reporters to try to interest them in the cases he was prosecuting. "I subscribe to the proposition that any publicity is good publicity," he says.

The Bridgeport case—the racial-beating trial that he'll preside over later this year—promises plenty of that.

ON A MARCH AFTERNOON in 1997 two eighth-grade classmates decided to take advantage of the unseasonable warmth with a bike ride after school. The boys, Lenard Clark and Clevan Nicholson, both thirteen, lived in Stateway Gardens, a high-rise public housing project on Chicago's south side. The tires of Lenard's bike were low on air. The gas stations near Stateway charged a quarter for air, whereas the air was free at the gas stations in Bridgeport, the neighborhood to the west. So Lenard and Clevan pedaled west down 35th Street, across the bridge that spans the Dan Ryan Expressway, and into Bridgeport.

Bridgeport's tidy redbrick bungalows are occupied mainly by whites, many of them city workers. The neighborhood was home to the first Mayor Daley—Chicago's mayor from 1955 until his death in 1976—the two mayors before him, and the mayor after him. The present Mayor Daley, Richard J.'s son Richard M., lived in Bridgeport until 1993, when he moved to a neighborhood near the Loop. African Americans shop and work in Bridgeport, but most don't linger after dark.

Lenard filled his tires at a gas station on Halsted Street, in the heart of Bridgeport, and then he and Clevan pedaled back east. They stopped at a playground and played football with three Mexican American boys. Then they resumed their homeward trip, accompanied by one of the Mexican American youths, eighteen-year-old William Jaramillo, who walked between Lenard and Clevan as they pedaled along. It had gotten dark. At the corner of 33rd and Shields—two blocks north of Comiskey Park, home of the White Sox—a white youth confronted the three boys. As Clevan and Jaramillo would later tell it, the youth called Clevan a nigger and punched him in the head, knocking him off his bike, then punched Lenard in the head, knocking him off his bike, too. Lenard's head snapped back into the aluminum-sided wall behind him—Jaramillo heard a *crunch*—and Lenard slid down the wall to the ground.

Lenard managed to push himself to his feet, and he took off, running and screaming, east on 33rd, his attacker in pursuit. (Clevan fled in a different direction; Jaramillo righted the bikes and wheeled them from the scene.) Lenard raced around a corner and into the street, but three white youths caught up with him and he was knocked to the ground. His attackers then kicked him in the side and stomped his head into the pavement. They fled when a neighbor who was walking by warned them he was calling the police on his cell phone. The police officers who responded found Lenard facedown in the street and unconscious. An ambulance took him to Cook County Hospital.

Mayor Daley, no doubt recognizing the potential for racial unrest, was quick to condemn the beating and to assure the public that the police would soon be making arrests. Sure enough, in less than forty-eight hours three Bridgeport youths were charged with the attempted murder of Lenard, with the aggravated battery of both Lenard and Clevan, and with a hate crime. At their bond hearing, a prosecutor informed the judge that Lenard was in a coma. The judge fixed bond for high school seniors Frank Caruso, eighteen, and Victor Jasas, seventeen, at $100,000, and set a seven P.M. to seven A.M. curfew if they made bond. The third defendant, nineteen-year-old Michael Kwidzinski, had already graduated high school and sometimes worked nights, so the judge gave him no curfew but set his bond at $150,000. All three defendants posted the required 10 percent and were released shortly after the hearing.

Daley called the defendants a "bunch of thugs" and decried their bonds as too low. In a letter published on the front page of the *Chicago Sun-Times* six days after the beating, he called on Chicagoans "to join together to denounce this mindless act of violence and hatred." He visited the comatose Lenard at the hospital, as did Reverend Jesse Jackson, Nation of Islam leader minister Louis Farrakhan, Catholic archbishop Francis George, and a stream of celebrities. Daley also hosted a VIP breakfast that raised $100,000 for Lenard's family.

For some African Americans in Chicago, the beating of Lenard was a painful reminder of the lynching forty-two years earlier of another southside black youth, fourteen-year-old Emmett Till. In August 1955, Till had taken a train to Mississippi to pick cotton with his cousins. While there he apparently made the mistake of whistling at or "talking fresh" to a white woman. His mutilated body came back north in a coffin. An all-white jury hurriedly acquitted the two men charged with his killing. Shielded from retrial by the constitutional protection against double jeopardy, the two men then confessed to the lynching in a story they sold to *Look* magazine.

"We African-Americans will not tolerate another Emmett Till situation," warned a letter published in the *Chicago Defender,* the city's African American daily, after Lenard's beating. "No justice, no peace!" chanted the band of African Americans who marched into Bridgeport several times in the days after the attack.

Newspapers and magazines from coast to coast wagged a finger at Chicago's "race chasm" and "ugly side." "Will a savage crime help the city face its hate?" *Time* magazine asked.

In his weekly radio speech eight days after the beating, President Clinton deplored the "savage, senseless" assault and urged Americans to fight "the divide of race . . . America's constant curse." The president later extended his best wishes to Lenard's mother on the phone.

Lenard emerged from his coma six days after the beating. Two days later, at a crowded Easter weekend meeting of the PUSH/Rainbow Coalition on the south side, Reverend Jackson likened the attack on Lenard and his recovery to Jesus's crucifixion and resurrection.

After a month in a rehabilitation center, Lenard was sent home. He'd had to relearn how to feed and dress himself. He still had difficulties with memory, abstract learning, and impulsivity—problems typical for a young person who'd suffered severe head trauma, his doctor said. He reportedly had no memory of the beating. He'd need daily physical, occupational, and speech therapy, and it likely would be years before he recovered fully, if he ever did. A host of cameras were trained on him as he left the center and as he climbed into a van loaded with donated toys, clothes, and flowers. Then he went home—but not to his Stateway Gardens housing project. City officials had found a place for Lenard, his mother, and his three siblings in a middle-class south-side neighborhood, in a four-bedroom home furnished with new appliances and furniture contributed by merchants. Back at Stateway, some of Lenard's neighbors admitted they were jealous; they said Lenard might be better off than they were, even with his brain injury, since he was able to leave the project. "Many kids are saying . . . 'I wish it was me that got hurt,'" one Stateway resident told a *Chicago Tribune* reporter.

The grand jury indictments of the three defendants were announced in a 26th Street courtroom on an April morning. Afterward deputies hustled Caruso, Jasas, Kwidzinski, and their families down the courthouse steps through a media crowd and African American protesters. "Hang those white boys!" some of the protesters shouted.

Once the defendants and their families were whisked away, the protesters joined hands on the courthouse plaza, and led by Reverend Paul Jakes, president of the west-side NAACP, they prayed: "We ask that this court system will be just and will be fair."

BLACKS IN CHICAGO might pray for justice, but they wouldn't bet on it. Years of experience with Chicago police and the Cook County courts have taught them to be wary.

There was the race riot of 1919, touched off by the drowning of a black youth in Lake Michigan after he'd been stoned. The youth had drifted into waters that whites considered their own; the riot began after police refused to arrest the white man seen stoning him. Whites committed the vast majority of the violence in the riot, but most of those jailed and prosecuted were blacks. There were the decades of beatings and stonings of blacks who tried moving into white neighborhoods, and the torching and bombing of their homes—and the cops who rarely caught anyone, and the prosecutors who found the evidence insufficient when they did. There were the innumerable beatings and shootings of blacks by white cops—beatings and shootings almost invariably deemed justified by police officials and prosecutors.

There was the raid on a west-side apartment in 1969 by fourteen police officers assigned to the state's attorney's office, in which Black Panther leaders Fred Hampton and Mark Clark were shot to death and four other occupants wounded. The seven surviving occupants, including the four who'd been wounded, were charged with attempted murder. State's attorney Edward Hanrahan assured reporters the police officers had been defending themselves from a Panther barrage and lauded the officers' "considerable restraint." A federal grand jury later determined that the Panther barrage had consisted of a single shot, while the officers' considerable restraint consisted of eighty-two to ninety-nine shots, half of them from a submachine gun. (Under intense media pressure, county prosecutors dropped the charges against the seven survivors. None of the police officers was found criminally accountable for the shootings of the Panthers.)

In the 1980s, there was a profusion of allegations of detectives torturing suspects—white detectives torturing black suspects in almost every instance. Detectives in one south-side station were accused of electrically shocking suspects, suffocating them with typewriter covers and plastic bags, putting guns in their mouths, and hanging them by their handcuffs. When the allegations were made in hearings and trials at 26th Street during that decade, prosecutors and judges belittled them, and they continued to belittle them during hearings and retrials in the 1990s, even after an internal Chicago police investigation concluded that abuse of suspects at the station had been "systematic."

In the courts, there has been the Cook County prosecutors' tradition of cleansing juries of blacks. The criminal court judges commented on this custom in 1920, when they were interviewed by a commission investigating the previous year's riot. The judges said the standard all-white juries tended to disbelieve black witnesses testifying against white defendants, were apt to convict blacks and acquit whites on similar evidence, and would convict whites on lesser charges when they convicted them at all. "Where a white man will be found guilty of manslaughter, a colored man will be found guilty of murder," Judge Hugo Pam said. Pam added: "In the more serious crimes, where a holdup is committed or guns are used, I think there is great prejudice. . . . I see colored men . . . very often feeling that most people are not interested in them. They come and take their medicine, and go away."

As late as the 1950s, a black defendant in Illinois could ask the judge to remind the jurors that they were to consider his case "as if he were a white man." In 1953 and 1955 the Illinois Supreme Court reversed two Cook County cases in which judges had declined to give that instruction, first used in Illinois in 1854. The state supreme court observed in the 1955 case, *People v. Crump,* that while Negroes no longer should have to ask for equal consideration, "we must recognize that our American system of justice and equality before the law is still administered by human beings."

In 1955—while Chicago officials were clucking their tongues about the all-white Mississippi jury that had acquitted Emmett Till's accused killers—juries here were still typically snow white as well, thanks mainly to prosecutors' continued use of peremptory challenges to routinely dismiss blacks. That practice continued into the 1980s; an Illinois Supreme Court justice noted in 1983 that in Cook County, blacks were still being stricken from juries because of their race in "case after case." And the practice has endured, in spite of a U.S. Supreme Court decision in 1986 forbidding it. Illinois reviewing courts have found that Cook County prosecutors have tried to skirt that decision.

Cases at 26th Street today still are often handled by an all-white cast. Eighty-four percent of the lawyers in the state's attorney's office, 69 percent of the public defenders, and 74 percent of the trial court judges are white.

AND MANY BLACKS here believe that white defendants have the ultimate advantage: if worse comes to worst, they can always buy their way out of trouble.

From before the days of Al Capone, Cook County residents have suspected that justice was for sale here. Such suspicions remained unproven for decades, as county prosecutors were unwilling to investigate the judges with whom they needed to work. After changes in federal law led to probes by federal agents in the early 1980s, it became apparent that judges here were in fact fixing everything from parking tickets to murder cases. Since 1984 U.S. prosecutors have convicted eighteen Cook County judges and fifty-two lawyers on corruption-related charges. The federal investigations showed that the defendants who got cases fixed—syndicate gangsters, defendants with political connections, defendants who could afford the judges' rate—usually were white. The typical poor and cloutless defendant, meanwhile, may have been punished for his inability to pay. Federal prosecutors have contended that some crooked judges sentenced nonbribing defendants harshly as part of their corruption scheme—to divert doubts about their propriety, and to warn other defendants what they risked if they didn't ante up.

So when reporters disclosed that the alleged ringleader in the Bridgeport attack, Frank Caruso Jr., came from a family with roots in organized crime, it didn't raise the confidence of blacks that justice was forthcoming for Lenard Clark.

It was all the more reason for blacks to scrutinize the Bridgeport case as it proceeded, some African Americans maintained. As one letter writer put it in the *Chicago Defender:* "This case will be closely monitored. The eyes of the nation will be on the Chicago judicial system. . . . If the system works, let it be demonstrated here."

LOCALLO DOESN'T THINK racism is really a problem at 26th Street. "When I worked in the system as a prosecutor, we didn't look at the defendant and say, 'Well, because he's black, we're gonna push harder,' or 'Because the victim's white, we're gonna work the case up more.' I didn't care what color they were. And as a judge, I don't care whether the person is white or black or Latino."

But he's well aware that there's a perception of racism in the courthouse, and he's anxious to dispel it. Whatever the outcome of the Bridgeport case, he wants blacks to feel that the judge handled it without bias.

How suitable is Locallo for that task?

Like most white Chicago natives, Locallo is the product of a white neighborhood and a white grammar school. His suburban Catholic high school had a few imported blacks, most of them athletes. In his formative years, what he heard about blacks from his father—and from his uncle Joe, also a police officer—wasn't always flattering. "They had their certain, you know, feelings," Locallo says. What kind of feelings? "I would say that they probably had a low opinion of blacks. But as police officers, they were dealing with the lowest elements of that race." As his father and uncle encountered blacks of a higher "element"—fellow officers, the occasional black lawyer or judge—their views modified, he says. "So when you start out, you have some baggage from your environment. And hopefully you expand."

As a prosecutor, Locallo's experience with blacks was skewed, as his father's had been. Day in and day out he dealt with accused criminals, the vast majority of them black. The colleagues with whom he was laboring to convict these blacks were, with rare exception, white.

The state's attorney's office, moreover, has not been known through the years as a citadel of racial enlightenment. Consider the contest prosecutors once competed in when they reached the felony trial courts. The goal was to be the first prosecutor in one's class to convict four thousand pounds of defendants. When a defendant pled guilty or was found guilty after a trial, the prosecutor would tally the defendant's weight from the arrest report. This was known as the "Two-Ton Contest." But since most defendants were black, some prosecutors called the competition "Niggers by the Pound." Locallo says he learned of the contest from veteran prosecutors, but that it had ceased before he reached the trial courts. He found it amusing, however. From what he'd heard, "a lot of fat guys [defendants] were getting great deals," he says with a laugh. "Let's say a prosecutor's got a guy who's 350 pounds. Where the guy normally would have gotten ten years, the prosecutor might offer him a year"—to get a quick and certain conviction. "Skinny guys wouldn't get offered anything," Locallo says. Did it sound like a racist contest to him? "Not necessarily," he says. He considered the Niggers by the Pound title "very offensive." But the contest itself was harmless "gallows humor."

Ethnic jesting was common in the state's attorney's office when he was there, Locallo says. Because he was Italian American, one prosecutor called him a trunk-stuffer. And because that prosecutor was a Greek American, when an arson case would come into the office, Locallo would ask him, "Is there a Greek involved here?" (Foundering Greek-owned apartment buildings and businesses used to burn down with suspicious frequency here, according to Locallo. He says the Greek American prosecutor he used to joke with defined spontaneous combustion as a Greek landlord rubbing two leases together.) On the office softball team, Locallo showed such speed that prosecutors dubbed him "the fastest white man alive." It was all in good fun, Locallo says.

Locallo expected that some African Americans would have an ethnic bias against *him* regarding his ability to preside fairly in the Bridgeport case. They'd realize from his last name that he was not just white but Italian American; and they'd assume he'd therefore be partial to Caruso. (While the judge's mother was Irish American, his father's ancestors were from Sicily, as were Caruso's ancestors.)

Something in Locallo's background likely would have caused blacks even more concern, had it been publicized after Locallo got the Bridgeport case.

On December 16, 1967, the *Chicago Tribune* reported the FBI arrests of eight mob bookies after a four-year investigation. Federal authorities had charged the bookies with running a racetrack communications network, the only one of its kind in the country and "the lifeblood of syndicate controlled gambling" in five midwestern states. One of the accused was Victor Locallo—August Locallo's oldest brother. Victor Locallo was described as a "close associate of Ross Prio, north-side gambling overseer." (Victor Locallo pled guilty in 1969 and was sentenced to five years' probation.)

Dan Locallo's late uncle Victor was indeed, he says, a close associate of Prio. And Victor wasn't the only relative to work as a bookie. So had his uncle Joe, Dan says, before he became a police officer. And so had his father.

Bookmaking used to be a misdemeanor. When it became a felony about 1950, the judge says, his father and his uncle Joe decided to quit the gambling business. Not long after that they joined the police force. His uncle Victor didn't quit.

Locallo was aware of the Caruso family's mob roots, and he presumed the Carusos were aware of his family tree as well. "I would imagine that when they first heard that I had the case, they assumed, 'Okay, we're in,' " he was to tell me after the trial.

But there was something about Locallo that the Carusos likely didn't know—something that might have given *them* pause.

Despite the negative comments about blacks he'd heard when he was small, Locallo seemed to have developed an affinity for African Americans. When he was a teen, what had most impressed him about JFK had been his fight for civil rights for blacks. The judge that Locallo most revered, William Cousins, is African American. Roosevelt Thomas, the defense lawyer he'd had the run-in with that had convinced him not to be such a strident prosecutor, is African American. R. Eugene Pincham, the former appellate justice whom Locallo had supported when he was being disparaged, is African American.

Then there's the striking impact that *To Kill a Mockingbird* has had on Locallo.

He's hardly the only lawyer of his generation for whom that movie, or book, was an early inspiration. Locallo, however, has watched the film repeatedly. And one particular scene still brings on tears. Once when we were in a crowded downtown restaurant, he got choked up just *talking* about the scene. "It's where Gregory Peck [playing lawyer Atticus Finch] is walking out of the courtroom," Locallo said, his voice beginning to crack and soften. "The blacks stand up." Here Locallo's eyes flooded and his face reddened. A hand flew to his brow to shield his eyes. His head shook. A half-minute passed before he regained his composure. I asked him why that particular scene affected him so deeply. "I just thought that was *so great*—here's the community standing up out of great respect for someone who fought for them. That's the thing you have to do—stand by what you believe in. And that's the only way you'll *get* respect, is if you *don't* compromise your beliefs. It was sad that the judge in *To Kill a Mockingbird* couldn't see the injustices there. Atticus Finch saw the injustices."

FOUR

Good Facts, Bad Facts

THE THREE REPORTERS assigned full-time to the building descend on 302 whenever the Bridgeport case is on the schedule for a pretrial matter, large or small. Often a handful of other reporters show up as well. Ever accommodating to the media, Locallo usually beckons the reporters to sit in the jury box instead of the gallery, so they can more easily follow the proceedings.

The three beat reporters have to be highly selective about what they cover, given the more than one thousand cases on the courthouse's menu every day. A crime needs a special twist to win their attention—a mother suffocating her children, a teen beating his father to death, a congressman having sex with a minor. Almost any killing of or by a police officer makes the cut.

But the trial of one young black male for slaying another rarely does. So the reporters are elsewhere on the morning late in January when the De'Angelo Harris jury trial begins.

The case concerns a shooting in front of Rockwell Gardens, a public housing project on Chicago's west side, on a May evening in 1995. Harris, then seventeen, allegedly fired three times into the parked car of twenty-year-old Bennie Williams. Williams was hit twice in the back, the lethal bullet piercing his aorta and his main pulmonary artery.

Harris was a member of the Gangster Disciples. The prosecutors believe he assumed that Williams was a member of the rival Traveling Vice Lords because he was wearing a Texas Rangers baseball cap, with a *T* on it. But Williams wasn't a gang member and didn't even live in the neighborhood. He was a University of Arkansas student home for the summer, who'd driven to the west side from his parents' suburban Oak Park home to visit his baby daughter. Williams's mother says her son liked the cap with the *T* because his middle name was Terrell.

Harris is represented by Amy Campanelli, the senior public defender assigned to 302, and Cynthia Brown, a member of the PD's Homicide Task Force, an elite unit whose members represent only homicide defendants.

Every case has its "good facts and bad facts," Campanelli says. The lawyer's job is to highlight the good facts and play down the bad ones. A bad fact for Harris is the eyewitness who says he did the shooting; a worse fact is that Harris confessed to it. A good fact for Harris is that the eyewitness initially identified a different young man as the shooter. Another good fact is Harris's youth when he confessed. Campanelli and Brown will try to convince the jury that veteran homicide detectives coerced their naïve young client into confessing to a crime he didn't commit.

Locallo is anxious to dispose of the case because it's one of the oldest on his call. Every Thursday a legal newspaper, the *Chicago Daily Law Bulletin,* lists each criminal court judge's "priority cases"—his or her five oldest. It's a public prod from the chief judge to dispose of those cases. Locallo has two cases from 1996 and three from 1995, one of them being *Harris.* It's not Locallo's fault that the case has been around so long. Public defender Brown has made pretrial motions contending there hadn't been probable cause for Harris's arrest and challenging the admissibility of his confession and of testimony regarding the lineup ID made by the eyewitness. These motions have required three separate hearings, all of which Harris lost. The case has also been delayed twice by the rotation of prosecutors from 302 to other courtrooms.

Illinois's speedy trial act gives the state 120 days to bring defendants to trial—160 days for defendants on bond. But cases often take far longer. No days are tolled against the time limit while pretrial motions initiated by the defendant are pending. And the clock runs only if the defendant formally demands trial instead of agreeing with the state on continuances, which is what defense lawyers usually do. Harris's final pretrial motion was disposed of three months ago, but Campanelli and Brown still haven't demanded trial on their client's behalf. When the evidence is strong against a defendant, his lawyers are happy to let the case age, since it sometimes weakens as it does—the state's witnesses disappear, or get cold feet, or get arrested themselves, hurting their credibility. If the defendant is in jail, prosecutors often don't feel much urgency about getting to trial either.

Defense lawyers who demand trial risk alienating the prosecutors, who couldn't possibly adhere to the time limits if every defendant in their courtroom demanded trial. Prosecutors sometimes consider trial demands to be inconsiderate if not a personal affront, Locallo says, and so work extra hard to convict defendants who demand trial. "You know the old adage, 'Don't wake up a sleeping tiger,'" Locallo says.

Of course, the defense lawyers themselves, the PDs especially, have their own caseload problems, and that's often the real reason they agree to continuances—though they're likely to tell their clients it's purely for tactical purposes that they're not pushing the case to trial.

PROSECUTOR MARK OSTROWSKI begins the state's case with his "life-and-death" witness, Bennie Williams's mother, Diane Smith. In a murder case, the life-and-death witness establishes that the victim did indeed die. The defense would gladly stipulate to this fact; but in a jury trial, prosecutors favor presenting it through the anguished testimony of one of the bereaved. Like many prosecutors, Ostrowski says that in murder cases, he hopes to ease the pain of the victim's survivors by bringing them a conviction. But from a strategic point of view, the more the life-and-death witness suffers in front of the jury, the better.

Diane Smith is dressed sedately in a navy pin-striped pantsuit and a dark broad-brimmed hat. Though she attended all the pretrial hearings, she hasn't grown any more comfortable with the courthouse; the visits still make her queasy, she says later, reminding her of Bennie's death. The prospect of testifying has been worrying her, and the tension is written across her face as she takes the stand.

She tells the jury she last saw her son alive on the morning of May 25, 1995—and that the next time she saw him, it was at the medical examiner's office. Several jurors lean forward, brows knitted.

"What was his condition when you saw him at the medical examiner's office?" Ostrowski asks.

"He was *dead*!" Smith wails. She cradles her face with her hands and sobs. Ostrowski cocks his head sympathetically and offers her his handkerchief.

After Smith is excused, she joins her husband and several other family members in the front row of the gallery. Smith is hoping Harris gets convicted and sentenced to the maximum sixty years. She also hopes to learn from the trial why Harris shot her son.

Across the aisle from Smith and her family sits a stout woman with red streaks in her black hair—the defendant's mother, Karen Harris. Next to her is her bright-eyed seven-year-old daughter, Tiara. Tiara's hair is festooned with orange and white barrettes. Her sneakers swing freely above the tile floor. Through the tinted glass she can see her brother's back. He's in a suit, sitting at a table with two white women. Two white men are at another table. The lady police officer sitting just inside the glass doors is also white. So is the man in the black robe behind the big desk. So are all the people in the two rows of chairs at the side of the courtroom, except for one black lady.

Tiara has three older brothers. De'Angelo, now nineteen, has been in the jail here for two years and eight months. Tiara's seventeen-year-old brother is in a boot camp because of a drug conviction, and her sixteen-year-old brother is in a juvenile home because of a gun case.

The eyewitness to the shooting, Mary Armstrong, testifies next. The grandmother of Bennie Williams's baby daughter, Armstrong was standing just outside the passenger door of his car when he was shot. She tells the jury that Williams had gotten into the car and was leaning over to open the passenger door for her when a young man approached the rear of the car, pulled a gun from his pants, crouched slightly, and fired through the back window.

Armstrong fled to a security shack in a nearby parking lot. She heard two more shots as she ran. A guard in the shack called 911. Williams was slumped backward in the car, unconscious, when police arrived.

Armstrong acknowledges on direct examination that she originally "picked out the wrong gentleman" from a lineup as the shooter. But then she identified Harris in a second lineup, and now she's positive he was the shooter. On cross-examination, Campanelli asks her if she hadn't also been positive after the first lineup that the young black male she'd picked had been the shooter. "At that time, I was," Armstrong concedes.

DETECTIVES' SUSPICIONS after the shooting had quickly settled on a twenty-year-old named Dante Johnson. He fit the rough description Armstrong gave (male black, six feet, 180 pounds), and one witness said he'd been in the center of an argument between the Gangster Disciples and the Traveling Vice Lords an hour before the shooting. Johnson admitted being in the argument but said he'd left the scene soon afterward, going to his girlfriend's on the south side. After Armstrong picked him out of a lineup, however, he was charged with murder and jailed with a $1 million bond.

Four days later a man named Anthony Perkins told police they had the wrong man in the Williams slaying. Perkins said the real culprit was his stepson, De'Angelo Harris.

Ten days after that detectives showed Armstrong an array of photos that included one of Harris but none of Dante Johnson. According to a police report, as soon as she saw Harris's photo she realized she'd erred in identifying Johnson. Police arrested Harris and put him in a lineup. Johnson and Harris were both six foot one, but Harris was three years younger, twenty-five pounds lighter, and much fairer-skinned than Johnson. Armstrong picked Harris. Harris signed his confession not long after the lineup. It was a full week after Armstrong told police she had been wrong about Dante Johnson before prosecutors dropped the charges against him. In all, he spent three weeks in jail for the Williams murder.

AFTER THE LUNCH BREAK Susan Butera, the assistant state's attorney who wrote up Harris's confession at the police station, reads it to the jury.

"De'Angelo Harris states that he is a member of the Gangster Disciples and has been a member for the past four years," Butera begins. "De'Angelo Harris states that the Traveling Vice Lords is a rival gang of the Gangster Disciples, and these two gangs were at war on May 25, 1995."

In the gallery, the boredom is wearing on seven-year-old Tiara. She stretches out across one of the benches and closes her eyes—but they soon pop open. She whispers something to her mother; but her mother is trying to hear De'Angelo's confession. "Shut *up*," Karen Harris says sternly. "*Sit* up." Tiara grudgingly pushes herself upright. She peers through the glass a moment; then sighs, lets her head drop backward to the top of the back of the bench, and studies the ceiling. Soon she winces and rubs her neck, then tries cushioning her head with her hands. The fidgeting is annoying her mother. "I'm gonna take you in the back and whup your butt, you understand me?"

"De'Angelo Harris states that . . . on May 25, 1995, some members of the Traveling Vice Lords were throwing rocks" at a Gangster Disciple's car, assistant state's attorney Butera continues. This led to an argument with the TVLs. According to the confession, Harris heard gunfire as he and his fellow GDs were heading back to Rockwell Gardens after the argument. In the high-rise at 340 South Western, he armed himself with an automatic gun that the gang kept in a "spot." He left the building about an hour later with the gun tucked in his pants. On Western Avenue he came upon a parked car with someone in the driver's seat. He didn't see who the person was, according to the confession, because he approached the car from the rear.

"De'Angelo Harris states he saw the person in the car lean over toward the passenger side of the car," Butera reads. "De'Angelo Harris states when he saw this person lean over, De'Angelo pulled out the loaded gun from his pants, pointed it towards the person that he saw in the car, and pulled the trigger. De'Angelo Harris states he heard the gun go pow, pow, pow."

Harris raced back across Western, discarding the gun as he ran, and into the 340 South Western high-rise, according to the confession. When he heard sirens, he left the building and watched the paramedics "pull the person he shot out of the car on Western," Butera reads.

"De'Angelo Harris states that he has been treated well by the police," Butera goes on. "De'Angelo Harris states that he was given two baloney sandwiches to eat and an Orange Crush to drink. . . . De'Angelo Harris states that he is giving this statement because it's the truth and he wanted to get it off of his conscience."

De'Angelo's mother, Karen Harris, is as still as a stone in the gallery. It's the first time she's heard exactly what De'Angelo allegedly told authorities about the shooting. She doubts he gave the confession without any pressure from detectives. But an awareness is surfacing: De'Angelo did it.

There's no answer in the confession, however, to her chief remaining question: *Why?*

That's also what Bennie Williams's mother, Diane Smith, is pondering across the aisle.

Smith had come to the trial "wanting to hate" De'Angelo Harris, she says later. But hate isn't exactly what she's feeling now. For one thing, her son Bennie was such a compassionate person that she doubts he'd have been bent on vengeance. Smith has also noticed Karen Harris's stern manner toward the little girl in the barrettes. To Smith's surprise, she's feeling a stirring of sympathy for De'Angelo. But she still wishes she knew what prompted him to shoot her son.

On cross, public defender Cynthia Brown asks Butera if she asked Harris why he'd done the shooting. Butera doesn't recall doing so.

"You never asked him why he did this?"

"I don't remember specifically asking that question or not asking that question," Butera says.

Prosecutor Ostrowski and his partner on this case, Andrew Dalkin, would have preferred a clear motive in the confession—such confessions are more persuasive to a jury. But a motive isn't essential. The prosecutors don't have to show why Harris pulled the trigger; they only have to show that he did (and that it wasn't in self-defense). Ostrowski says later that he has no idea why Harris didn't acknowledge in his confession that he'd seen the *T* on Williams's cap, as Ostrowski believes he did. Dalkin guesses that Harris felt the crime would sound less heinous if he didn't admit that he believed he was shooting a rival gangbanger.

Neither prosecutor has given much thought to why Harris would respond to a rock-throwing incident with lethal violence. Their job is to convict defendants, not to try to understand them. In his opening statement, Ostrowski has called the trial "a case about senseless violence"— and that's how he sees it. "I'm not sure that we can ever figure out why these people do the things they do," he says. Dalkin likewise shrugs and says, "Some people are just violent."

• • •

DE'ANGELO HARRIS WAS BORN into a world of bad facts. His mother, Karen, was fourteen when she got pregnant with him in 1977. She raised him and her three subsequent children in the west-side Garfield Park neighborhood—then and now an area of abandoned factories, collapsing frame homes, burned-out apartment buildings, and empty lots sparkling with broken glass. She relied on welfare. When her kids were young, she got arrested for allegedly: striking a woman in the chest and head during an argument; threatening to hit her mother with a portable TV; menacing two people with a stick and threatening to kill them; and promising to tear down her apartment building and kill its owners. All the cases were dismissed. De'Angelo says his mother would sometimes punish him by hitting him in the head or punching him in the chest—"wasn't nothing way unexpected."

The first time De'Angelo caught his mother sucking on a crack pipe was when she was pregnant with Tiara, he says. De'Angelo was only eleven, but he knew that a pregnant woman, especially, shouldn't be doing that, and he made his mother promise to quit. He thinks she did for a time. But when Tiara was two, Karen Harris's own mother lodged a child-neglect charge against her, alleging that Karen had been leaving Tiara with her for days on end without providing any food or money, while Karen went out and spent her aid check on cocaine. Karen pled guilty to the neglect charge and was sentenced to one year of court supervision.

At an early age De'Angelo began running away. He'd often stay with a friend of his mother's. Karen Harris says she didn't mind him staying with this woman because "I knew he was safe with her." The woman, Lorraine Butts, has been arrested for allegedly: striking a woman with a baseball bat; punching and biting other women; smashing a windshield with a bat; and keeping a loaded, unregistered semiautomatic in her apartment. All the cases were dismissed.

Butts lived in a Rockwell Gardens high-rise. Rockwell Gardens was one of the score of vertical slums that Chicago erected in the 1950s and 1960s, when city officials dealt with housing shortages for the poor by planting high-rises in ghettoes rather than forcing white Chicagoans to live with blacks nearby. The concentration of poverty made the projects dreadful places to raise children and incubators for the state's penitentiaries. For decades, young black males would graduate from teeming projects to teeming prisons, pausing at 26th Street to pick up their diplomas.

De'Angelo joined the Gangster Disciples before he was a teen. "I can't even explain why," he says. "I was twelve then." Soon he had a steady job—

peddling marijuana in a Rockwell breezeway every weekday after school, from five in the evening to midnight. He enjoyed an earning power he couldn't imagine equaling in any legitimate job as an adult. He wore gold chains, Pelle Pelle sweaters, Guess jeans, and Nikes or Air Jordans. Lorraine Butts gave him the benefit of her advice, he says. "She was like, 'Don't get caught.'" (Butts says she suspected De'Angelo was dealing and did indeed give him that advice.)

In 1990, at his paternal grandfather's funeral, De'Angelo, then twelve, saw his father for the first time in nine years. "Everything gonna be all right, Dad," De'Angelo consoled his father. "Don't call me 'Dad,'" his father responded.

When De'Angelo was living in Butts's Rockwell Gardens apartment, he developed a bond with her boyfriend, a man named Anthony Perkins who was sixteen years older than he was. "I'm talking about like father and son," De'Angelo says. Perkins has been arrested repeatedly; by 2000 he would have three felony drug convictions. De'Angelo says Perkins helped his marijuana business in Rockwell by referring customers to him in exchange for samples. It was Perkins who told police that he believed De'Angelo had shot Williams.

In the two years and eight months that De'Angelo was in jail awaiting trial, his mother rarely visited him. It hurt too much to see him locked up, she says. But she had her own legal worries as well. In 1995, two months before De'Angelo was charged with shooting Williams, Karen Harris had picked up her first felony charge, for allegedly selling two rocks of cocaine to an undercover officer. She soon pled guilty for probation, a hundred hours of community service, and $200 in fines. Sixteen months later a probation officer told a judge that Harris hadn't completed a single hour of community service or paid a dollar of her fines. Harris pled guilty to violating her probation and was sentenced to two months in jail.

ON THE EVENING of the Harris trial's first day, after the proceedings have been recessed, an investigator for the state's attorney's office gets a call from a woman who says she witnessed the Williams shooting.

The investigator talked with this woman, Evelyn Cruz, the day before the trial. Cruz said then that on the night of the shooting, she'd gotten off a Western Avenue bus, in front of Rockwell Gardens, and had walked to her building in the project. While waiting for the elevator, she'd heard gunfire.

Now she tells the investigator she actually saw the shooting—and Harris doing it. She knew Harris from the project—they'd lived in the same building for a time—and so she was sure it was him. She says she was afraid to tell the whole truth before, but she's reconsidered.

The prosecutors had Harris himself to thank for this witness. Harris had given Cruz's name to his lawyers before the trial as a possible alibi witness. The PDs had sent an investigator to talk with her, but she'd told him what she later told the state's investigator—that she'd only heard the shooting and hadn't seen Harris until afterward. The PDs decided they probably wouldn't call her as a witness, but they included her name on the list of potential witnesses they gave the state.

Prosecutors Ostrowski and Dalkin can hardly believe their ears the following morning when their investigator tells them about the call from Cruz. It's like one of those far-fetched scenarios that happen weekly in courtroom dramas on TV. It looks like a great fact for the state and an awful one for Harris. But there is a problem for the prosecutors: they rested their case the day before.

With the jury waiting in the jury room, Ostrowski and Dalkin ask Locallo to allow them to reopen so they can put Cruz on the stand. Campanelli and Brown strenuously object. Cruz's testimony would be suspect, Campanelli contends—she's given conflicting statements about what she actually witnessed, and it's taken her more than two and a half years to incriminate Harris. "All right, she has some baggage," Locallo concedes. But it should be up to the jury, he says, to evaluate her credibility. Locallo retires to his chambers and calls his boss, Presiding Judge Thomas Fitzgerald, to get his opinion. Then, back in the courtroom, he says that since a trial's mission is to seek the truth, he'll allow the state to reopen. He tells Campanelli and Brown they can interview Cruz before she takes the stand. She's waiting in the prosecutor's office.

After Campanelli's talk with Cruz convinces her she'd be a devastating witness against Harris, the PDs see the writing on the wall. This extra ace for the state makes it foolish for Harris to stay in the game, they decide. It's time for him to cut his losses if he can by pleading.

But Ostrowski isn't eager to bargain now that he holds all the cards. So the PDs decide to haggle directly with Locallo.

Harris can't expect a huge discount for folding in the middle of his trial. Including the day spent picking the jury, he's already eaten up two court days. But his plea right now would save the full day the remainder of the trial would likely consume. That ought to be worth *some*thing, the PDs figure.

After broaching the plea possibility with Locallo, all the lawyers meet in his chambers. Harris is present, too. Brown reminds Locallo that Harris was barely seventeen at the time of the shooting. He'd done well in school before he'd given in to neighborhood pressures and joined a gang, she says. He'd been abandoned by his father. But he has a supportive family, Brown says, including his mother and a woman he regards as his stepmother (Butts), both of whom are in court today.

Locallo always factors the victim's background into his sentencing calculation. Had Bennie Williams indeed been a gangbanger, Locallo would have offered Harris a shorter term. "When a victim is productive and going to school and has potential, that's a greater loss to society than if he's some goof who's involved in gangs," the judge says later. Williams "was a solid kid, a college kid—there was no reason for that student to be killed."

Campanelli thinks it's wrong for a judge to decide "that one victim's life is worth more than another" when he's contemplating a sentence. Ostrowski likewise thinks judges shouldn't consider the victim's background—for a different reason. Most victims of violent crimes tried at 26th Street aren't college students from the suburbs; they tend to be from the same slum as the defendant, with their own gang affiliations and criminal records. So judges who weigh the victim's background in the manner Locallo does are apt to sentence most defendants more lightly.

In a murder case, Locallo also factors in the interest shown by the surviving family. If they come to court regularly—as Williams's survivors have—he's likely to give the defendant a longer term. "Sometimes you take into consideration who weeps for the deceased," he says. Campanelli thinks this, too, is improper. "But judges are human, and it's hard not to be influenced" by the survivors in the gallery, she says.

The sentencing range is twenty to sixty years. (None of the aggravating circumstances exist that would allow an even stiffer penalty.)

Locallo offers Harris forty years for his plea today.

Ostrowski would like to push Locallo for a longer term—in part because of all the time his office has expended on Harris, what with the three hearings his pretrial motions necessitated and these two days of a jury trial. "He put us through a lot," the prosecutor says later. But since Locallo just sided with the state on a key issue—the motion to reopen—Ostrowski thinks he owes it to Locallo not to quibble with him about his plea proposal.

Ostrowski's partner, Dalkin, is ambivalent about the prospects of the trial ending early. It makes sense to him to secure the conviction. But a guilty plea would leave him feeling deprived. After six months as a third-chair prosecutor, this is his first murder-jury. When he was in law school, imagining himself as a lawyer, he saw himself trying cases in front of a jury—not standing in front of the bench day after day, pushing through plea deals in car thefts and two-bit drug cases. He stayed up late last night crafting his closing argument, and he was looking forward to delivering it today. Now it appears that that was a wasted effort. Dalkin also worries that if the trial is truncated with a plea, it may not count as one of the six jury trials he needs to advance to second chair.

In a small conference room off the courtroom, Campanelli and Brown urge Harris to take Locallo's offer. They remind him that with the day-for-day good-conduct credit he'd really need to do only twenty years. The PDs also remind Harris that he's already served almost three years in the jail, so he'd only be locked up another seventeen. Insist on the trial continuing, and he could end up with a sixty-year sentence, they warn him. "This offer is guaranteed," Campanelli tells Harris. "But nothing is guaranteed after trial."

Harris, however, declines. He's not going to cop to a crime he didn't commit, he tells his lawyers. And if the jury does convict him, he says, at least he can appeal—whereas if he pleads, there's no turning back.

Campanelli and Brown turn to Karen Harris for help. After convincing her that De'Angelo is being foolish, they arrange for her to talk to him in the conference room.

She returns to the gallery sniffly and wet-eyed after her meeting with De'Angelo. "I told him, 'It look like you got to take this cop-out,'" she says to Lorraine Butts. "He say, 'Mama, I didn't do it.' He say he wouldn't get no appeal if he copped out, so he just gonna take the sixty." She sobs, then inhales deeply and dries her eyes with the base of her hand.

In the early afternoon, Locallo sends the jury home, telling the panel that "certain matters" have to be resolved before the trial can proceed.

The judge and the lawyers reconvene in Locallo's chambers. Locallo bumps his bid down to thirty-eight, but says that's his final offer. Campanelli and Brown march to the lockup to tell Harris. Harris says he doesn't know what to do. The PDs leave him alone to think it over. When they return twenty minutes later, Harris reluctantly says he'll take the thirty-eight.

In the courtroom, Locallo quickly gets the plea on record. He defers formal sentencing until the following afternoon so Williams's family can submit a "victim-impact" statement.

"SIXTEEN YEARS," Karen Harris says to Butts in the gallery, after the plea has been recorded and De'Angelo has been ushered back to the lockup. That's how many years De'Angelo will have left to serve, the PDs have explained to her. "That's still a long time," she tells Butts.

"Well, might be for the best," Butts says.

Karen Harris brightens. "That's what I thought. I said, 'God did this for a reason.'"

"If he didn't get locked up, he might be dead," Butts says.

Karen Harris starts listing friends in her neighborhood whose children have been killed. "When my kids is out somewhere, and I hear bullet shots?" She rises from her bench, steps up to the Plexiglas, and peers through it. "I'm right away in the window, looking out in the street. I get my clothes on, go out there and find 'em." She settles back down on the bench. "I'm glad my kids is locked up," she says. "'Cause if they be out there in the street, that could be one of them gets killed."

Maybe prison will even make a better man out of De'Angelo, she tells me. She's been hoping lately that her second-oldest son might be straightened up by the no-nonsense boot camp he's now in. "They teach you to be more mannerable, more respectful," she says. "And if you ain't, they spit in your face and everything."

In his chambers, Locallo is personally calling the twelve jurors and two alternates, letting them know they won't need to return, and why, telling them their checks (for three days' work, at $17.20 a day) will be mailed to them, and thanking them for their service. Most judges would let a deputy handle this chore, but Locallo always goes out of his way to make jurors feel appreciated. He wants them to spread the word that jury service isn't so bad after all. Jurors also represent a potential political benefit for a judge, he says. "That's fourteen people that, assuming you don't act like an asshole, are going to be your supporters" come retention time or when he runs for a higher judicial post.

The judge is almost giddy about the plea. Anything can happen when a case goes to the jury, he says. The jury might have decided that Harris's confession was coerced from him, that Armstrong's ID couldn't be trusted because of her original mistake, and that Cruz's testimony was suspect because it took so long for her to come forward. This was unlikely, but "you never know what those twelve great citizens are going to do," the judge says. "They come back with a not guilty, and then the Williams family would have been further disappointed—they've lost their loved one, and the person who they believe committed the act walks out the door."

So rather than trust what those twelve citizens might do, he brokered the plea. It was in the interests of the Harris family as well, he says; had the trial continued and had Harris been convicted, he could have gotten a sentence so long that his family "would never see him free again." Locallo insists this wouldn't have been a tax, much as it sounds like one. Had the trial proceeded, he would have learned more about the crime, he says, and maybe it would have seemed more heinous than he'd realized. This is the standard rationalization cited by judges for giving a longer term to a defendant after a trial.

The deal provided "closure" for everyone, Locallo says, himself included. "It's one less day with the jury. We can move on to the next case."

IN THE GALLERY the following afternoon, while waiting for De'Angelo to be formally sentenced, Karen Harris has her hands twice as full. She has to mind not only Tiara but also De'Angelo's toddler son, Tyreece. The twenty-three-month-old Tyreece is dressed in a striped shirt and blue corduroys. He's wearing a bright red-and-blue backpack with TIME FOR SCHOOL! in big letters over a clock. De'Angelo was already in jail when Tyreece was born, so although they've seen each other through a Plexiglas window in a jail visiting area, he and his son have never touched. Karen Harris is hoping Locallo will allow that to happen today in a contact visit. She figures that De'Angelo and Tyreece may not have a similar chance until De'Angelo is back from downstate, when Tyreece is eighteen.

Karen Harris sometimes wonders whether she has other grandchildren through De'Angelo. (De'Angelo tells me later he's also got a three-year-old daughter.)

The afternoon session in 302 hasn't begun yet, but already Tyreece is trying his grandmother's patience. "Grandma gonna whup you," Karen Harris warns him as he crawls across a bench. Tyreece stops and studies her, then pushes himself into a sitting position. Tiara, who's been standing at the Plexiglas, tapping on a ledge, decides to park herself on the bench as well.

"I'm just very relieved that it's all out in the open," Karen Harris tells me. She feels bad for Bennie Williams's mother, she says, "because her son is no longer here and my son is." Her voice drops. "I'm sorry that my son took her son's life. I still would like to know what was the motive for him to do that."

Gazing at Tyreece, she describes De'Angelo when he was small. He was a cheerful little boy who liked sports and music and got A's in grammar school, she says. She brightens as she recalls how De'Angelo would don leather pants and a white glove and mimic Michael Jackson. ("That wasn't even me," De'Angelo says later. "That was my little brother.")

Tyreece, who's been chewing on his fingers and wriggling in his seat, suddenly collapses to the floor, sobbing. "Sit *down*," Karen Harris commands, but he continues wailing. She raises a hand menacingly. Tyreece's eyes follow the hand, but his crying persists. Harris angrily scoops him off the tile floor and lugs him out to the hallway.

A few minutes later she's back on a bench in the courtroom, with Tyreece and Tiara glum and silent on either side of her, when Diane Smith and her family enter. After they've settled into a bench across the aisle, Karen Harris takes a deep breath, pushes herself to her feet, and steps hesitantly over to the aisle. She catches Diane Smith's attention, then quickly averts her eyes.

"I'm sorry about what my son did to your son," Harris says softly.

Smith tilts her head subtly in Harris's direction, nods, and says, "Thank you."

The sentencing hearing begins with Ostrowski reading the victim-impact statement that Theodis Smith, Bennie Williams's stepfather, wrote on behalf of the Smiths. It describes Williams as a "kind, compassionate" person who would run errands for seniors and sometimes bring homeless people home with him for a meal.

"The news of our son's death was devastating," Ostrowski reads. "We were thinking, 'How could this happen?' We were an average, law-abiding family." The killing had harmed the family "mentally, emotionally, physically, and financially." After Bennie was slain, Diane Smith began to frequently visit and call the school her eight-year-old son attended to check on his safety. She asked her husband to phone her several times a day to assure her he was all right. Bennie's younger brother likewise was tormented with fears of another sudden loss. He couldn't sleep, his grades declined. Now, almost three years after the murder, the brother has yet to utter Bennie's name or visit his grave.

"Nineteen years seems a very cheap amount of time for our son's life," Ostrowski reads. The family blames not only Harris but also his parents "for their lack of guidance for their son.

"Our son will never have the opportunity to fulfill his dreams," Ostrowski continues. "He will never be able to marry. He has a daughter who will never know her father. . . . However, we do know that a higher court will someday convene, and justice will truly be served when they judge De'Angelo Harris."

Harris declines Locallo's offer to say anything before he's sentenced.

Locallo calls it "tragic" for "a man in college" to be gunned down when he wasn't doing any wrong. Then he issues the thirty-eight-year term. He says he'll give Harris a contact visit with his family before he's returned to the jail.

Diane Smith appreciated Karen Harris's apology. Though she wanted a longer sentence, that's not what Smith is thinking about as De'Angelo Harris is led away. She's not feeling anger so much as sorrow—not only for the loss of her son, but for the loss of Harris, too. Another life wasted, she says to herself.

HARRIS IS SOON SHIPPED to the Illinois River Correctional Center, in the town of Canton, 155 miles southwest of Chicago. The prison, which

opened in 1989, is the second-leading employer in Canton, a town of fifteen thousand. Inside the prison the population is 64 percent black; outside
the prison the town is 98 percent white. The prison is designed to house
1,211 inmates; Harris is one of 1,900.

After a year in Illinois River, Harris gives up on the prospect of ever
receiving a visit from a friend or a relative. His friends are all locked up. As
for his family, "If they don't wanna think about me, they don't need to
think about me," he says bitterly. "I don't try to think about nobody. I blank
all my problems out."

The minimum $380,000 that taxpayers will spend to keep Harris locked
up until 2014 is far more than ever was invested in him before, or that ever
will be spent on either of his children, probably, unless they too end up in
prison.

WHEN THE PUBLIC DEFENDERS were lobbying Locallo for a shorter
term for Harris during the plea negotiations in the judge's chambers, they
didn't mention Harris's poverty-stricken background. That fact is taken for
granted about defendants here and thus is usually ignored.

Prosecutor Dalkin worked in juvenile court for two years before he was
assigned to 26th Street. That stint exposed him to rampant neglect and
physical abuse of children in poor neighborhoods. He doesn't doubt that
maltreated kids are more likely to themselves become violent. But Dalkin,
the son of a real estate developer and the product of an affluent North
Shore suburb, thinks such kids ought to overcome their disadvantages.
"Maybe it's closed-minded or unsympathetic, but I don't feel sorry for
people who can't handle something like that, because I know there are
people who can."

Locallo, likewise, considers poverty no excuse for crime. "No way I'm
gonna buy this, 'I'm poor, therefore I had no choice,'" he says. His mentor,
Judge William Cousins, "came out of poverty. He came out of some small
town in Mississippi. His parents didn't graduate from grammar school, but
they showed him the right way. *My* dad was poor. My mom was poor. Why
did they make that jump and get out of that situation? Because they
wanted to."

But what about kids who *don't* have parents showing them the right
way? "Yeah, some people have a bad start," Locallo concedes. "If you don't
have parents who stress hard work, and getting an education, and being a
productive citizen, it might be harder to go down the right road. But at
some point—assuming there are no mental problems—you make a choice.
You take the high road, or you take the low road."

Campanelli has heard many judges and prosecutors at 26th Street recite this view. "It just helps them do what they're going to do," she says. "They're sending people to prison for years and years. They have to convince themselves that the person deserves it so they can sleep at night."

Locallo is less critical of his uncle Victor, the one who spent his life working for the mob. He didn't freely choose to take the low road, Locallo says; there were circumstances that compelled his illicit career. The judge explains that his dad's and his uncle Victor's parents divorced, after which their father didn't contribute financially to the family. "My uncle Vic was the oldest child, and he got into bookmaking to support my dad, his brother, and their mother. Maybe it's because I loved my uncle Vic, but I never looked down on him because of what he was involved in. You do what you have to do sometimes."

FIVE

Luck

ON WEEKDAY MORNINGS a clerk named Marcus Ferguson can be found in front of an old IBM computer in a dingy first-floor office. An assistant state's attorney standing near him pulls a manila folder from a stack on a desk and calls out a case number and a court date. Ferguson's meaty fingers then race over the keyboard, the two hefty gold rings on his right hand glinting. He's proud of how quickly he can enter the data—in eight seconds or less. When he jabs the enter key with his middle finger, the name of a judge appears on his monitor. He announces the name to the state's attorney, who prints it in black marker on the folder.

Thus are new cases parceled out to judges here by a computer program called the Randomizer. With that poke of Ferguson's middle finger, the Randomizer blesses a defendant with a benevolent judge or consigns him to a banger; it sends him to a courtroom with reasonable prosecutors or cut-throats, with energetic PDs or mopes.

The thirty trial courtrooms at 26th Street "are like thirty different countries," Locallo says. Sentencing standards can vary markedly from courtroom to courtroom. He's given probation to defendants who likely would have gotten double-digit prison terms from other judges, he says.

None of the sculpted figures on the courthouse's front wall is squeezing a rabbit's foot or spinning a roulette wheel. But luck often seems the deciding factor here, and not only because of the Randomizer. A defendant's fate may hinge on a judge's mood, or who's in the jury pool on a given morning, or whether a lawyer is in top form and nails a key cross-examination or is hungover and blows it.

• • •

BUT FOR THE WAY a bullet was deflected in 1989, Deputy Gil Guerrero might have been one of those victims whose death is lamented in a murder trial here, he's often thought. And yet if he hadn't been shot at all, he's also thought, he might have ended up like one of those gangbangers he ushers into the lockup every morning.

Guerrero, twenty-seven, grew up in McKinley Park, a predominantly white, working-class neighborhood not far from the courthouse. As a youngster, Guerrero, a Mexican American, had to steer clear of white gangs such as the Popes (Protect Our People, Eliminate Spics) and the Heads (Help Eliminate And Destroy Spics). Slurs and swastikas were sometimes spray-painted on the family's garage door.

Guerrero never formally joined a gang, but he hung out with gangbangers in his high school years. One summer night after he graduated, he and friends were driving around when they encountered some rivals on a corner. Threats were shouted by both sides, hand signs were flashed, and then something shattered the side window behind Guerrero, who was riding in the front passenger seat. When the driver pulled over a few blocks down to check the damage to his car, Guerrero's friends noticed the bullet hole in the back of the front seat, and the bloody hole in the back of Guerrero's shirt.

He was treated at a hospital and released. But if the metal in the seat hadn't redirected the bullet, he says, he could have been crippled or killed.

His distressed mother told him she had no interest in burying her son at an early age. She urged him to leave Chicago, suggesting he either move in with an uncle in Mexico or join the army. Guerrero pictured himself in a primitive shack with an outhouse behind it and opted to enlist.

He'd felt adrift since graduating high school. In basic training in Georgia, he was given challenges he felt were beyond him, like walking fifteen miles with a hefty rucksack on his back. "I'd think, 'That's impossible.' And then I'd do it, and say, 'Oh, I guess it's not.'"

After two years in Germany and two in California, he left the army and returned to Chicago. An army buddy suggested he apply for a job with the sheriff's department. Guerrero thought that might be a good fit. "You get your badge, you get your gun. I was used to wearing a uniform." He worked a factory job for a year until he got the call from the sheriff's department offering him a position. He began working in the courthouse in 1995, substituting for other courtroom deputies, until he got his first permanent assignment, in April 1997, to Courtroom 302.

Guerrero has dark bushy eyebrows and a broad expressive face. It's often expressing the aggravation he suffers in his job. Every morning he has to field the same questions from the lockup: *Is my lawyer here? Are my people out there?* "I don't know who your lawyer is," he'll tell them. "I don't know who your people are." *Is the judge in a good mood?* "I don't hang out with the man, I don't know what kind of a mood he's in."

Defendants also ask him, during breaks in their trials, if he thinks they're winning or losing. "They're looking for reassurance," he says. "But I'm not gonna tell nobody I think it's gonna be not guilty, and it turns around and it's guilty. But they don't wanna hear 'I don't know.' They're like, 'Well, you been here a long time.' Yeah, well, what does that mean, though? What I say don't mean nothing."

Guerrero believes the prisoners are always watching him for signs of weakness. He isn't really a tough guy, he says, but he feels compelled to act like one. Whenever he's at all lenient with the prisoners, they take advantage. That's been his experience with the one regular concession he makes—the smoking he allows in the lockups. The prisoners aren't even supposed to have cigarettes, but they always do. Guerrero just asks them to restrict their smoking to the rear of the lockups, out of the eye of the security cameras, so his bosses won't see it on their monitors downstairs. But someone frequently disappoints him by stepping into a camera's view. The prisoners' behavior in the lockups doesn't worry him as much as their behavior in the courtroom, though. "Just don't make me look bad when you go before the judge," he often tells them.

Guerrero and his partner, Deputy Laura Rhodes, are usually in a cramped anteroom near the lockups when they're not out in the courtroom. The audiovisual unit resting on a metal desk in the middle of the anteroom allows Guerrero and Rhodes to monitor the inaction in the lockups around the corner. (The prisoners spend most of the time dozing on the benches or staring into space.) The unit also has controls to the intercom that lets defendants in the lockups hear the court proceedings. The deputies leave the intercom on except in special circumstances. If a defendant is accused of sexually abusing a child, for instance, Locallo or the defendant's lawyer may ask Guerrero or Rhodes to cut the feed to the lockups, to spare the defendant the beating he'd likely receive in the jail if word got out about the nature of his alleged crime.

Guerrero and Rhodes work well together despite contrasting personalities. Rhodes, twenty-nine—the taller of the two deputies by several inches—doesn't subscribe to her partner's "not my problem" maxim and doesn't feel compelled to act tough in front of the prisoners. Female deputies can get away with treating prisoners with respect, she says. The problem with male deputies doing so is not that prisoners take advantage, she says, but that other deputies are likely to brand them sissies.

The disdain that many deputies show prisoners is more than posturing, she says. It's a genuine contempt, a belief that the prisoners are "monsters in brown suits, that they're scum, they're worthless." She hears deputies brag about striking prisoners in the lockups or in the basement, and when they do, "nobody ever asks anything about how it happened or why it was necessary. They just say, 'Oh, did you get him good?'"

She grew up in Marengo, a small semirural town northwest of Chicago. After graduating high school in 1986, she worked days as a salesclerk and studied photography in the evenings at Columbia College downtown. Sometimes she toured the Loop with her camera, asking "thuggish-looking types" if she could photograph them. She was fascinated by such characters, particularly by their faces. She felt she could see beyond the anger in their eyes to the child they'd been, "wanting to be like every other kid, to have a house and a mom and dad that's living with them." She thought about doing a photo book one day of jail inmates.

After she got a BA from Columbia in 1992, she taught a city college literacy class for adults. Her boyfriend, a jail guard, told her that the jail had openings for teachers. She first applied with the sheriff's department in 1992, but by the time the department hired her in 1994, teachers in the jail weren't needed; instead, she was given the task of taking the mug shots of the new prisoners. Soon she was transferred to the courthouse. She was assigned to 302 in 1997, a few months after Guerrero.

Rhodes and Guerrero spend much of their day ushering prisoners between the lockup and the courtroom. In the courtroom they stand behind the prisoner while the judge and the lawyers transact their business. It's often boring, Guerrero says. He expected to see more trials. "Instead everybody just makes deals, like it's a garage sale or something."

"It's all just a game, to everyone involved," Rhodes says. "For the defendants, it's 'I can beat this case,' or 'I can get this deal.' For the judges, it's the big dispo race. I don't think they really care whether the defendant is innocent or guilty—it's how many defendants they can get to plead out. For the state's attorneys, it's 'I can get this death sentence or this natural life sentence.' For the private defense attorneys, it's mainly about getting paid. You got some who truly care and a lot who think it's just a case." She thinks jurors are usually the only ones interested in what really happened. A few are in a hurry to go home, but most take their job seriously, she says. Rhodes has applied for work with the probation department for two years now but with no luck. She pictures herself prodding her probationers into getting their GEDs and helping them find work. She could make a real difference as a probation officer, she says, which is more than she feels she can do as a deputy.

GUERRERO FACES a challenge early one February morning, on the day jury-picking is set to begin in the murder trial of a defendant named Kevin Betts.

The incident occurs in the courthouse basement. The batch of prisoners bound for 302 this particular morning includes six convicts brought here from penitentiaries throughout Illinois to testify for Betts. Guerrero is patting down one of them when the man suddenly jerks an arm backward at him. No contact is made, but Guerrero sees it as a test of his authority—a test calling for a response. He slams the prisoner's arm back against the wall and begins barking at him: "You got a fucking problem? You don't like being searched? You think you're special?" The prisoner scowls over his shoulder at Guerrero—a scowl Guerrero interprets as, Watch out—we're all from the *state pen*. Guerrero scowls back.

The elevator ride up to 302 is tense, this prisoner and his cohorts eyeing Guerrero menacingly. Whenever Guerrero walks near the lockup this morning, he gets more glares from the Betts contingent, and when he is around the corner, he hears muttered threats about the ass-kicking they are planning for him. But Guerrero is proud he's let them know he won't be intimidated. "If I show them I'm scared, they're gonna eat me up," he says. It does unnerve him, though, when the prosecutors inform him later that all six of these inmates have been convicted of murder.

The Betts case concerns the stabbing of an inmate in a jail barbershop with a shank (a homemade knife). Like his witnesses, Betts already has one murder conviction. But so did the victim.

Prosecutors wish they were always fighting for angels—that every victim was a Lenard Clark or a Bennie Williams. But the victims are more likely to be an Insane Vice Lord shot by a Spanish Cobra, a pimp slashed by his hooker, or a cocaine dealer beaten by the customer who paid for a rock and got a piece of drywall. Bernard Carter, the victim in this case, was convicted in 1993 of killing a gas station clerk during a robbery. Since winning posthumous justice for a killer isn't much of a motivator, prosecutors Mark Ostrowski and Joe Alesia instead are simply focusing on making Betts pay. "Just because he was in the jail," Alesia says, "why should he get a free murder?"

It wasn't a murder at first, because Carter didn't die until almost two years after he was stabbed. He was working as a barber in the Division 1 barbershop the morning of the attack, in March 1993. He was still in the jail because he was awaiting sentencing for the gas station murder. Someone plunged a shank into his neck, and he fell to the floor. The shank punctured his spinal cord, paralyzing him from the shoulders down. Betts had been the last inmate whose hair Carter had cut. According to police who visited Carter in the hospital the next day, he nodded at a photo of Betts when asked to identify his attacker. Betts was charged with attempted murder.

A month later Betts was convicted in the case that had brought him to the jail—the fatal shooting of one man and the wounding of another during an argument in a south-side home. In June 1993 Betts, then twenty-four, was sentenced to sixty-five years for those crimes.

And he still had the barbershop case looming over him, as well as another jail shanking he'd been charged with in August 1992. These two attempted murder cases each carried six to thirty years. Under Illinois law, moreover, sentences for crimes committed in custody are supposed to run consecutively to other sentences.

But then prosecutors made him an offer he couldn't resist: two twenty-year terms that would run concurrent with each other *and* with his sixty-five-year sentence, in exchange for his guilty pleas to both shankings. Prosecutors would be getting two tough cases off the books. (Jail crimes are hard cases to prosecute because the key witnesses usually are inmates, who tend to be reluctant to testify and easy to discredit when they do.) Since the sentences for the shankings would be concurrent, they wouldn't increase the time Betts owed beyond his sixty-five-year term. With day-for-day credit, he'd still be getting out at age fifty-eight. "I couldn't beat that with a baseball bat," Betts says. "I wouldn't do an extra day." He grabbed the deal in April 1994.

Meantime, though, Bernard Carter's health continued to decline. He lay in a prison infirmary bed, a quadriplegic, his breathing assisted by one tube, his urine draining through another, his body shrinking and sprouting bedsores, until he died in December 1994. A coroner's jury attributed his death to acute bronchial pneumonia, resulting from his quadriplegia, which in turn had been caused by the shanking. It ruled the death a homicide.

Case law is clear that a charge can be upgraded to murder if the victim's death is directly attributable to the injuries allegedly caused by the defendant, even if the victim doesn't die until years later—and even if the alleged offender has already pled guilty to a lesser charge. Betts had one murder conviction; a second would make him eligible for the death penalty. In June 1995 the state indicted Betts for Carter's murder, and the Randomizer kicked his case to Locallo.

In his four years as a trial judge, Locallo has had about ten cases in which the state has sought the death penalty, but he's yet to impose it. Ostrowski and Alesia find this ironic, given the praise the judge has received for the summaries of death penalty cases he publishes. If he really wants to be an expert on the death penalty, the prosecutors say, he ought to at least give it once.

Locallo chafes at such criticism. He says he'll impose death when he gets a case that merits it. He points to other respected 26th Street judges—William Cousins, for one—who never sent anyone to death row. "You don't judge a judge by how many times he gives death," Locallo says. "If that's the criterion, I guess I'll be on the low end. But I'll be with judges I've always admired who never gave it either."

In Illinois a defendant convicted in a capital case can opt to have either the jury or judge decide whether to impose the death penalty. On the advice of his lawyers, Betts has already agreed to have Locallo decide his fate if the jury finds him guilty. Since it would be his second murder conviction, the minimum sentence would be natural life.

The curious course of events since the barbershop shanking has put Betts in the position of asserting his innocence of an attack he has already pled guilty to. The jury won't be informed of the plea, however, Locallo precluding mention of it as prejudicial.

"THIS CASE, LADIES AND GENTLEMEN, is about a violent act committed by a violent person, Kevin Betts," prosecutor Joe Alesia tells the jury in his opening statement. He sketches the shanking of Bernard Carter in the barbershop and his slow demise in an infirmary bed. "The last thing he felt was that shank going into his neck," Alesia says.

Betts's lawyer, public defender Tony Eben, begins his opening statement by standing behind Betts at the defense table, resting a hand warmly on one of Betts's shoulders, and introducing "Kevin" to the jury, displaying a palpable fondness between lawyer and client.

The fondness is an act, however; there's no love lost between Eben and Betts. Betts thinks he got a bad break when Eben was dealt to him by the public defenders' Homicide Task Force. The fifty-four-year-old Eben has been a lawyer for twenty-four years, a member of the task force for thirteen. Colleagues laud his courtroom skills. But Betts says Eben hasn't given his case the time of day. In a November 1997 letter to Eben, Betts noted that in the more than two years since he'd been back in the Cook County Jail after being indicted for the Carter murder, Eben had visited him only once to discuss his case and that consequently, Betts was firing him. Betts then also wrote Locallo asking for a new lawyer, and he wrote a letter of complaint against Eben to Illinois's attorney disciplinary committee. (That complaint was ultimately dismissed.)

Eben says that although he may not have visited Betts much in the jail, he spoke privately with him in the jury room or the conference room of 302 on numerous pretrial court dates, and he also sent an investigator to the jail several times to get information from Betts.

After Betts wrote the letter saying he was firing Eben, the lawyer visited his client in the jail, and the two men had a heated exchange. Betts admits making not-so-veiled threats during this meeting regarding Eben's well-being if Eben didn't devote more time to the case.

"They trying to give me the death penalty or natural life—and he [Eben] taking it all nonchalant, casual, like it's nothing," Betts says later. He thought the PD assisting Eben, Amy Campanelli, was more interested in helping him but unable to because she was the junior lawyer.

Locallo denied Betts's petition for a new lawyer. A judge can't grant such a request lightly, Locallo says, or soon many of the defendants with PDs will be asking for a different one. If he'd heard of other complaints about Eben, he'd have given Betts's request more consideration, the judge says. Betts considers the denial an example of how judges and lawyers protect each other at the expense of defendants.

Eben regards Betts as a bright if unreasonable client. He says their differences won't affect how hard he works for Betts. "Sometimes clients are hard to deal with. It's the nature of the business. You just have to do a professional job."

Eben now tells the jury that jail authorities botched their investigation and ended up charging the wrong inmate. The defense will present five witnesses who were in or near the barbershop at the time of the shanking who will testify that an inmate named Angelo Roberts did it.

Betts looks like an up-and-coming accountant at the defense table—a bright-eyed young man with rounded shoulders, at home in his fine brown suit, suspenders, crisp white shirt, paisley tie, and shiny shoes. It's his brother's suit, but his brother can't use it; he's doing twelve at Stateville for armed violence and aggravated kidnapping. The clothes hide the skeleton and tombstone tattooed on Betts's chest, the "Sir Kevin" and the "4" on his right forearm (signifying his gang, the Four Corner Hustlers). He's clean-shaven, and his hair is trimmed to the scalp, thanks to another visit to the jail barbershop.

During opening statements the jurors size up Betts, their eyes straying from the lawyers. Betts had already sized up the jury, and it has him worried. Half of the jurors are over forty, and seven are men. He thinks a younger jury with more women would be more sympathetic. There are ten whites, one Hispanic, and only one black. Most disturbing to Betts is the fact that six of the jurors are from the suburbs, and none of the city residents live anywhere near the west-side slum where he was raised. "A jury of my peers would've been a bunch of people from the city sleeping under them viaducts," he says. Betts believes that middle-class people tend to trust the authorities, whereas poor people know from experience that law enforcement officers will lie to make a case.

The life-and-death witness is Bernard Carter's grandmother, Ora Lee Carter. Bernard was her only grandchild, and she visited him regularly when he was in the jail here. She saw him on the morning of March 18, 1993, before he was shanked. He seemed healthy that morning, she tells the jury. She also visited him twice a week in the infirmary in Dixon, Illinois. "Some days I would go and he would know who I was," she says. The only part of his body he could move was his head. She saw him in the infirmary the day before he died, and then she saw him at the funeral home.

After Ora Lee Carter the prosecutors call James Jackson, the officer on duty in the barbershop at the time of the shanking. Jackson looks to be in his sixties, and he's now retired. He says there were five barber chairs in the shop, and a desk, at which he was sitting. Carter was cutting Betts's hair in chair number one, right next to the desk. After Carter finished the haircut, he turned to the table behind him to get a brush to clean off Betts. Betts then jumped out of the chair, pulled off the cape he was wearing, and punched Carter in the back of the neck—or at least it looked to Jackson as if he'd merely punched him. Carter collapsed to the floor, and Betts ran out of the shop. Jackson phoned the security post down the hall, alerting the officer there to stop the man running toward him.

Johnnie Debergh, the officer who answered that call, tells the jury he stopped an inmate headed his way and escorted him back to the barbershop. Asked by prosecutor Alesia if he sees the individual in the courtroom, Debergh points to Betts at the defense table. Debergh says he noticed red droplets on the shoulder of Betts's jail shirt. In a search of the hallway after the attack, Debergh found a seven-inch spike behind a radiator just outside the barbershop.

Investigator Robert Sullivan describes how Carter was shown an array of photos in the hospital and nodded at the one of Betts.

The state's case is compelling, but it's not without weaknesses, which Eben and Campanelli highlight on their cross-examinations. While questioning Jackson, Eben refers to a log indicating there may have been as many as fourteen inmates in the barbershop, not counting the barbers, at the time of the shanking. He wants the jury to picture a barbershop that was more chaotic at the time of the crime than Jackson made it seem on direct. Campanelli confronts Officer Debergh with a memo he wrote for an investigator on the day of the attack, in which he says he stopped two inmates who were leaving the barbershop, not one, and that he returned both of them to the shop. Debergh acknowledges that he encountered a second inmate just outside the barbershop door. He also acknowledges he made no mention in his memo of any red droplets on Betts's shirt; nor did he make sure the shirt was inventoried.

The jury has seen the spike that Debergh found behind the radiator outside the barbershop. But in her cross of Debergh, Campanelli focuses attention on a second shank that was discovered after the attack, this one in a towel bin inside the barbershop. Campanelli knows that the authorities say they now can't locate this shank—the state only has a photocopy of it. It's a good fact for the defense. Campanelli asks Debergh what he did with this second shank. Debergh says he put it in a brown envelope and gave it to an investigator.

"Where is the shank today?" Campanelli asks.

"I have no idea," Debergh says.

WHEN THE BETTS JURORS entered the courtroom for opening statements, they may have presumed that this was a case of exceptional public interest—the gallery was packed with young white spectators. But these were students from a suburban religious college on a field trip. They filed out after opening statements, returning the gallery to its usual desolate state during a trial. A few defendants on bond stroll in and out, alternating between naps on the benches and cigarette breaks in the hallway. Locallo will deal briefly with their cases during recesses. The only spectator with a personal interest in the trial to watch it for an extended period is the victim's grandmother, Ora Lee Carter, who watches the whole thing.

The seventy-year-old Carter has lavender lipstick and nails, and several of her teeth are gold. The first day of the trial, she's wearing gold bracelets on one wrist, a gold-banded watch on the other, and sequined earrings. A large velvet handbag leans against her on her gallery bench. A retired factory worker, recently widowed a second time, she spends much of her days reading the Bible. She grew up in Yazoo City, Mississippi. She was raised by a sister from the time she was twelve, after her father went to prison for killing her mother. She married at fifteen, a year after giving birth to her first child—Bernard Carter's mother, Catherine. Catherine died of cancer in 1993, at age fifty-two, two months before Bernard was shanked. Ora Carter then felt a greater responsibility toward her grandson, and in his last months in the prison infirmary she was his sole regular visitor, driving the hundred miles to Dixon from her home on the near west side. "Four tolls there and four back, and I went there twice a week," she says during the lunch break on the trial's first day.

She isn't looking for retribution from the trial. She's just curious about exactly how and why her grandson was attacked. "Vengeance is not mine," she says. "I never want to judge right from wrong—God's the only one can do that. To tell you the truth, I don't really care [what happens]. Whatever they do it ain't gonna bring him back." She feels only pity for Betts.

Betts's mother lives in Chicago, as do various aunts, uncles, and other relatives, none of whom have shown for the trial. "This ain't nothing new," he says.

He's closest to his only sibling, Shawn, the brother who's in prison. Shawn is thirty, a year and a half older than Kevin. He was convicted of snatching a purse shortly after his seventeenth birthday, and he's been in and out of jail ever since. During a 1996 presentence interview by a probation officer, Shawn described his childhood as "fucked up." He said he'd been physically abused by the relatives and friends who'd raised him.

Kevin Betts's early years were also marked by trouble with the law— trips to the juvenile detention center for stealing, arrests as a young adult for theft, drug possession, unlawful use of a weapon, and aggravated assault—charges that were dropped or tossed out. At nineteen he pled guilty to car theft, drug possession, and violation of bail bond and was shipped to prison with a six-year term. Soon after his release, he was charged with the murder he was convicted of in 1993—but he fled to Tennessee before he could be arrested. When he picked up charges there of aggravated kidnapping, aggravated sexual battery, and aggravated robbery, he fled back to Chicago. An informant tipped police to his whereabouts, and he was arrested shortly after his return.

An evaluation by a school psychologist when he was sixteen and living in a shelter said he needed a strongly structured environment. "It is evident that his dependency needs have never been met," the psychologist wrote. "He is suspicious of others and has strong hostile impulses."

Betts says his parents broke up around the time he was born. His father moved to California, leaving his mother to raise him and Shawn. She's strong-willed and strict, he says, a devoutly religious teetotaler. She worked steadily to support the family, first as a security guard, then as a nurse after she went back to school and earned a nursing degree. "We got some of the best genes, some of the best equipment, as far as thinking and being able to persevere through all types of trials and tribulations," he says.

But his mother also had a fierce temper, he says. "The dumbest things would set her off. A kid would get what I call brain-lock and just do something that an average ordinary kid would do, and—she ain't going for it. A lot of the things she done, man, there wasn't cause for." He and Shawn ran away from home when they were eleven and twelve. "It was either stay there and deal with her, or go out there and deal with the world. I guess we felt braver dealing with the world." They lived "house to house, with friends, in vacant apartments—just basically waking up wherever we laid down at. Wasn't no set place.

"I put no fault on her, though," he says of his mother. "I haven't been an angel, and I've done some wrong things, and I hope and I pray I'll get a chance to even things out."

IN THE AFTERNOON and on the following morning, the defense puts on five of the convicted killers who've been waiting in the lockup to testify for Betts. They each come to the stand in a white dress shirt and black trousers they've been issued by prison officials for their courtroom appearance.

The first four of these witnesses tell the jury they were in the barbershop when the shanking occurred. The shop was crowded with inmates, they say. Betts walked out of the shop after his haircut, they all remember—and then the inmate who'd been in the chair *next* to Betts, Angelo Roberts, got out of his chair and hugged Carter, with Carter then falling to the ground. One of the four witnesses recalls seeing a knife in Roberts's hand. The public defenders have the witnesses disclose on direct examination the murder sentences they're serving—otherwise the state will bring it out on cross, and it'll look as if the defense were hiding the fact. The four witnesses are serving terms of forty, seventy, eighty, and a hundred years. Eben and Campanelli save their choirboy for last—a young man doing a mere twenty for murder. He was sweeping and mopping the hallway outside the barbershop on the morning in question and saw Betts leave the shop, followed by Roberts. He says Roberts put something behind the radiator outside the shop.

Ora Lee Carter listens impassively in the gallery, her folded hands resting in her lap. At one point she leans over and says, "Sound to me like they all rehearsed it, and they rehearsed it good."

The mother of one of the defense witnesses shows up in the gallery on the trial's second morning. She's heard of Locallo's generosity with contact visits, and came hoping for a brief visit with her son, who's been in a downstate prison for five years. Locallo later accommodates her. A young man appears in the gallery as well on the second day—a fellow Four Corner Hustler, Betts later says. Betts appreciates this show of support, the only one he gets.

During their cross-examinations of the defense witnesses, the prosecutors point out that they all declined to offer any information to investigators right after the shanking; and that the assertions about Angelo Roberts are convenient ones, since Roberts himself is now dead.

Nicknamed "Baby Locust," Roberts was a rising star in the Four Corner Hustlers. At the time of the barbershop shanking—March 1993—he was awaiting trial on two separate cases, one for murder and one for a weapons offense. He was acquitted of the murder and convicted of the gun charge, for which he was sentenced to five years. Seven months after he was released from prison, police found his body in the trunk of a Chevy on the south side, riddled with bullet holes and stab wounds. He was twenty-four. His murder remains unsolved.

IN HIS CLOSING ARGUMENT, public defender Eben focuses on the purported bedside identification of Betts by Bernard Carter. It wasn't surprising that Carter picked Betts out of the photo array, he says, since Betts was the only inmate who'd been in the barbershop who was in the array. He says investigators didn't show Carter a photo of Angelo Roberts or any of the other inmates in the shop because they "wanted to reach a certain end." He wonders how Carter could have seen who shanked him anyway if, as Officer Jackson testified, he was attacked from behind. He wonders why investigators didn't visit Carter again in the hospital after he was able to talk, to make sure nothing had been lost in translation in the nodding ID. "Why don't they respect you enough to present you with a complete picture of what happened here?" Eben asks. He maintains that the defense witnesses were simply "coming forward at this time to do justice."

In rebuttal, prosecutor Alesia stresses that Betts is on trial, not Officer Jackson, or Officer Debergh, or investigator Sullivan, or Angelo Roberts. Jackson, Debergh, and Sullivan had no reason to pin the crime on Betts, Alesia says. They simply did their jobs, and the reason the evidence pointed directly at Betts was because he was the offender. Betts "would want you to believe that anybody and everybody is responsible except him," Alesia says. "Right now that spotlight's shining down on that head of his and he's sweating because this is the day he feared."

Betts's frustration has been mounting. He feels certain he's going to get convicted. He thinks the jurors have paid much closer attention to the state's attorneys. He's noticed the younger women on the jury brightening whenever one of the two young prosecutors is speaking. He wrote numerous reminders to Eben on the lawyer's yellow pads about points to stress in the closing argument, but in his view Eben ignored most of them. He wanted to testify, but Eben and Campanelli persuaded him not to, reminding him that the jury would learn about his criminal background if he did. (A defendant's criminal background is normally inadmissible. But it becomes admissible if he testifies, because the jury is allowed to take it into account in assessing his credibility.) At his first murder trial, too, his lawyers convinced him not to take the stand, and he's always believed he'd have been acquitted if he'd only been able to tell the jury his side.

Now, as Alesia is winding up, saying the only sensible conclusion is that Betts was Carter's assailant, Betts can restrain himself no longer.

"Why you ain't bringing nobody on the witness stand to say that?" he blurts out from the defense table. "This the only person, this the only— Officer Jackson the only person you brought in here on the witness stand to say that." Alesia allows Betts to have the floor, figuring the outburst is only showing the jury Betts's volatility. Campanelli puts a hand on Betts's shoulder, imploring him in a loud whisper to desist. But it's as though Betts doesn't notice her. "It's seventeen people in the barbershop. Out of seventeen people, you can't get nobody else to say that—"

Locallo instructs the startled jurors to retire to the jury room. Their eyes shift from Betts to the judge and back to Betts as they push themselves up from their chairs and begin edging out of the box.

"—out of seventeen people, you can't get nobody to say that?"

"Disregard," Locallo says.

As soon as the jurors are out of the courtroom, Locallo asks Betts to approach the bench.

The judge could banish Betts to the lockup for the last bit of the trial. But Betts's absence at the defense table certainly might weigh against him in the jurors' minds. A reviewing court could one day find such a remedy an overreaction, Locallo thinks, and the whole trial could go down the drain. Better to see if he can calm Betts down and have him remain.

"I understand your frustration," he tells Betts. "But you have to let your lawyers do their job, and let me conduct a trial." He warns Betts that if he interrupts again, he may have to be removed from the courtroom.

When the jury is back in the box, Alesia finishes up. "The inhumanity of prisons is not a result of the institution, of the system, of the officers, of others," he says. "It's a result of inmates, and in this case, Kevin Betts." Then, as prosecutors here often do, Alesia paraphrases a maxim of British statesman Edmund Burke to end his argument: "All it takes for evil to thrive, Kevin Betts to thrive, is for good men and women to do nothing. He asks you to do that today. Do not do that. Do something. Find him guilty of first-degree murder."

JURIES ARE GENERALLY considered the biggest wild card of all at 26th Street. The lawyers' influence over a jury's makeup is limited. They use their peremptory challenges (seven a side in most cases, fourteen in a capital case such as this one) to craft a panel to their liking. But with only superficial information about prospective jurors, the lawyers base their choices on stereotypes and gut reactions. "Juries are the one thing you can't control," Alesia says. "You control what witnesses you call and your trial strategy. But when the jurors start deliberating, it's up to them."

Which can be particularly disturbing for prosecutors. The state wins most trials, and so winning is an expectation. (Between 1996 and 2003 felony defendants in Cook County were convicted of at least one charge in 74 percent of the jury trials that ended in a verdict.) It takes just one wayward juror to force a retrial, a result the prosecutor may view as an undeserved embarrassment. Thus prosecutors frequently grumble to one another about the wisdom of a process that consumes so much time and money, and in which the decision is then entrusted to a batch of $17.20 day laborers. Juries trouble Alesia more than anything else at 26th Street. "You just can't trust 'em," he says.

Like most jury rooms at 26th Street, the one in 302 is dreary. Ceiling tiles are missing and broken. The beige walls are grimy and bare. The view from the two narrow north windows is of a parking lot and a Popeyes. There's a washroom on either end of the room, an empty water cooler in a corner, and foil ashtrays on the conference table. The plastic backs and cushions of most of the chairs are torn.

It's nearly two o'clock on a Wednesday afternoon when the jury gets the Betts case. John Hillebrand, a sixty-seven-year-old semiretired school administrator from the suburbs, is selected foreperson. The first vote he conducts is oral: three guilty, four not, five undecided.

There's a consensus in the room that the investigation could have been more carefully conducted, Hillebrand and other jurors tell me later. In particular, it's felt that someone should have revisited Carter after he was able to speak to verify his identification of Betts. But there's also agreement that the defense witnesses can't be trusted.

Dinner arrives at six: bland, soggy-crusted pizza in Styrofoam cartons. Hillebrand conducts a second poll, also oral. The undecided are asked to take a stand. Seven guilty, five not.

At nine P.M., with no word yet from the jury, prosecutor Alesia is growing anxious. He's sitting in the deputies' anteroom down the hall from the jury room. "You can never tell what twelve idiots are gonna do," he says with a shake of his head.

At ten P.M. Locallo directs Deputy Laura Rhodes to sequester the jury for the evening. When Rhodes informs the jurors of the imminent bus trip to a hotel, the news, as always, is greeted with protests. Rhodes volleys back with promises of a real dinner at the hotel and two drinks on the county.

Deputy Guerrero escorts Betts downstairs. Betts wonders which way the jury seems to be leaning. Guerrero says he has no idea. But Betts is heartened nonetheless by the realization that at least someone on the jury must be in his corner. When he tells his tiermates about the jury being sequestered, they congratulate him and give him thumbs-up. "It was like a sign of hope for the other guys," Betts says. Inmates may clash from time to time, he says, "but nobody wants to see nobody else get found guilty."

RHODES AND GUERRERO look exhausted the next morning in 302. They've taken turns sitting in the hotel corridor overnight, safeguarding the jury according to regulations. Juries are sequestered only about once or twice a year per courtroom. Even though it's taxing, Rhodes and Guerrero wish it happened more often. Rhodes enjoys chatting with the jurors. Guerrero likes the hotel's cable TV and twice-baked potatoes. Both deputies appreciate the time and a half.

Locallo takes the bench shortly after ten and starts working through other cases on the day's schedule. Meanwhile, deliberations resume in the jury room over coffee and doughnuts. Foreperson Hillebrand tallies a midmorning vote, this time by paper ballot. Ten guilty, two not.

It's obvious from the ensuing discussion who the holdouts are: a black woman—the lone black on the jury—and a white man. By lunchtime the black woman has joined the fold.

This leaves only Bill Massey, a sixty-three-year-old mailroom clerk, in the way of a guilty verdict. Some of Massey's fellow jurors ask him impatiently how he can take the word of convicted killers over that of guards and an investigator. Massey responds that he doesn't necessarily believe the defense witnesses, but that the issue is whether Betts has been proven guilty beyond a reasonable doubt. The missing shank, the shirt that never was inventoried, the dubious identification at the hospital, all bother him.

Massey is a movie buff, and his situation reminds him of one of his favorite films, *Twelve Angry Men,* the classic story of a jury anxious to convict in a murder case that's stalled by one stubbornly ethical juror, played by Henry Fonda. Fonda ultimately persuades the other eleven to acquit. But Massey can tell there'll be no persuading these eleven. Throughout the afternoon he feels the pressure on him mounting. A juror announces he has tickets to a play this evening, tickets that will go wasted if a verdict isn't reached soon. Massey recalls the juror in *Twelve Angry Men* who wanted a verdict because he had tickets to a ball game. Another time Hillebrand lays an arm on Massey's back while making a point. Massey recoils, and Hillebrand pulls the arm away. A little later Hillebrand rests a hand on Massey's arm. Massey curtly directs the foreperson to stop all this touching. Hillebrand testily promises never to touch Massey again. Later Hillebrand realizes he hasn't put his arm similarly on any other juror and chastises himself for trying to be manipulative.

At four-thirty P.M. Rhodes delivers a note from the jury to Locallo, informing the judge the panel is stuck eleven to one, but without saying which way. Locallo reads the note to the lawyers.

Betts has spent a good deal of his time in jail and prison hunched over books in the law library. He knows he could direct his lawyers to ask Locallo to declare a mistrial, arguing that the jury is hopelessly deadlocked. But Eben counsels patience. The eleven votes could be for acquittal, he says. Betts agrees to wait, but he's skeptical of Eben's advice. With just one black on the jury, he doubts he's got eleven jurors siding with him. He notes that the prosecutors are strongly in favor of the jury deliberating further. He suspects Eben would prefer a guilty verdict over having to retry the case.

After consulting with the lawyers, Locallo directs the jury to continue deliberating.

Dinner arrives in the jury room shortly thereafter. Pizza again. Most of the jurors leave the cartons unopened. The room is hot and stuffy. The smokers on the jury have agreed to confine their smoking to the washrooms, but this means the washrooms reek. Tempers are wearing thin. One juror reaches for a pizza carton, annoying the man next to him: "How can you *eat* that crap?" Occasionally Rhodes and Guerrero, waiting in the anteroom around the corner, hear raised voices through the jury room walls. "They've got the shank in there, you know," Rhodes tells her partner. "Maybe that's not a good idea."

In the courtroom Locallo asks the lawyers how they'd like to proceed. Eben suggests the jurors be sent home for the night instead of to a hotel, with directions that they return in the morning to resume deliberations. Locallo likes the idea. Ostrowski wonders whether it's legally permissible to allow a jury to separate once it's begun deliberating. Locallo leaves the bench to consult the law books in his chambers.

Betts now feels certain the eleven-to-one vote is against him. He imagines how weary the lone dissenter must be getting. "People give in because it's the easiest thing to do," Betts tells me later. "You got a lotta people in jail right now because of that." And so while the judge is gone, Betts tells Eben he wants him to make the motion for a mistrial.

When Locallo resumes the bench, Eben makes the motion. The judge can't hide his disappointment. He's found a case that says he can indeed allow the jurors to go home for the night and resume deliberations tomorrow. He denies the mistrial motion. He says he'll inform the jurors of his preference to let them go home tonight instead of to a hotel before resuming tomorrow. If the jurors say it won't help them reach a verdict, he'll reconsider the motion.

At seven-fifteen in the evening, after the jurors tell Locallo they'll never reach a verdict no matter where they spend the night, Locallo declares a mistrial.

"I'M FRUSTRATED, because we didn't do our job," Hillebrand says later. "Now somebody else will have to do it." He describes Massey as "stubborn as a mule."

Massey says, "I understood that it was my job to make the state prove its case."

He assumes investigators didn't visit Carter in the hospital again after he could talk because they were afraid he might not identify Betts. But "justice is being sure of things, not going in and trying to slip something in quickly," Massey says.

Some jurors seemed to side with the authorities just because they were the authorities, he says. This didn't surprise him. "You see similar things every day—people listening to the news and accepting what they're hearing at face value without ever questioning it." He was bothered that several jurors appeared to be in such a hurry to decide so serious a matter. Some of the jurors had speculated that it was a death penalty case even though the lawyers hadn't said anything about that. "But the attitude was 'So it's the guy's life. So what? I've gotta be home by six.'"

Betts is relieved he'll get a second chance and amazed about who made it possible. He'd tried to guess before Locallo declared the mistrial who his lone supporter was. Massey never came to mind. "Here I am, complaining about a race issue," he says, "and it was a white guy that held out for me."

He marvels at Massey's fortitude. "I know the judge was mad. I know the state's attorney was mad. I know my lawyer was mad. I know the other jurors was mad. Anybody that don't conform to the rules of these people here or to this system, they're not gonna like him. For a person to stick to his beliefs regardless of what everybody else is thinking—you definitely admire a person like that."

Alesia has a different view. "I wanted to kick him in the face," he says of Massey. "I wanted to grab him by the neck and say, 'What were you thinking?'"

Hung juries aren't common at 26th Street. Locallo says this was the fourth or fifth he's had in more than a hundred jury trials. In his chambers the day after the trial, the judge says he'd have preferred a verdict either way to the mistrial just so he could have gotten the case off his call. But "it's not something I'm going to get an ulcer about. Instead of throwing my hands in the air, shaking my head and groaning, I'll just set it for another date." He hopes to retry the case in the spring.

Though he doesn't get a dispo, the trial has benefited the judge in another way. Foreperson Hillebrand's first opinion of Locallo was that he was "pompous—a know-it-all maybe." But he was impressed by the way the judge ran the trial and by his graciousness afterward in the jury room. The judge made everyone feel their efforts were worth it despite the mistrial, Hillebrand says. So Hillebrand asked the judge when his next retention election was, and how the jurors might help. When Hillebrand called later to reiterate the offer, Locallo said it might be inappropriate for him to use former jurors to promote his retention. But at Hillebrand's prodding, the judge sent the foreperson a list of the names and addresses of the jurors, Hillebrand promising to send each a note urging them to push for the judge's retention.

Eben says he considers the mistrial a victory because the state didn't convict his client. He'd hoped for a "finality" to the case, though, and his pleasure in the "victory" is tempered by his understanding that the case will require yet more work. He didn't push for a mistrial earlier because he genuinely felt the eleven jurors might be favoring acquittal, he says. He dismisses Betts's suggestion that he'd have preferred a loss. "We don't go into these cases callously just wanting to put them on and get rid of them," he says.

The case's twists and turns thus far haven't really surprised him. He's been at 26th Street long enough to know how things work. "The stars come together, and you never know what's gonna happen."

SIX

Busted Again

LARRY BATES, the forty-four-year-old probationer Locallo had warned in January to finish up his community service, did indeed quickly take care of that business. He picked up litter with the sheriff's neon-vest crew in February, and the four remaining days he owed were history. This street-cleaning didn't cure him of his crack addiction, though.

On March 15 police caught Bates selling drugs on a west-side corner. Since he was on probation, the bond court judge wouldn't give him a recognizance bond. The judge set his bail at $10,000. Bates didn't have anything near the $1,000 he needed to walk, and so he was jailed. But eight days later, on March 23, jail officials gave him a recognizance bond. Prisoners with low bonds are often released this way to ease overcrowding as part of the jail's AMF program—Administrative Mandatory Furlough, or as jail guards call it, "Adios, Mother Fucker."

Bates was due back in Locallo's courtroom on March 25, the deadline Locallo had previously set for him to complete his community service. And so on that morning Bates again takes the stairs to the third floor, hoping not to be seen by anyone he knows.

Bates is superstitious. Before he sells drugs on a street corner, he'll look for wood to knock on—a tree trunk will do—asking Lady Luck to keep the police away. As he steps into Courtroom 302 at 9:20 A.M., fingers on both hands are crossed.

Locallo isn't here yet. Bates, wearing a thin blue jacket and tattered black jeans, slides onto a bench and watches the gallery fill.

Not long after his arrival, a tall, olive-skinned woman enters the gallery from the front of the courtroom. "Larry Bates?" she asks, scanning the benches. Bates raises his hand and says, "Right here," and the woman sits down next to him. She glances at a file, then tells Bates he'll probably be jailed again today—it's Locallo's usual practice when a probationer is arrested for another felony. Bates purses his lips and nods. The woman heads to the hallway in search of another probationer. Bates remembers her from his last visit to 302—she'd stood next to him in front of the bench. Bates had assumed she was his public defender. When I tell him now that she works for probation, Bates frowns. "They don't explain nothing to people here—they think we're all psychic," he says. Then he laughs. "If I was psychic, I wouldn't be here."

Locallo assumes the bench a few minutes later. No private lawyers are here yet, so the judge begins with his probation cases, which are presented to him by probation liaison Rhonda Schullo, the woman who had talked briefly with Bates.

The first probationer, Anthony Coleman—a forty-six-year-old African American in a dark suit—pled guilty fourteen months ago to his third DUI. In Illinois, drunk driving becomes a felony upon the third conviction. (In Illinois as in most states, possession of a minuscule amount of cocaine or heroin is a more serious offense than drunk driving. Bates's first conviction, in 1996, for possession of 0.08 grams of crack cocaine, was a Class 4 felony, as was a third drunk-driving conviction.) Locallo had given Coleman probation and two hundred hours of community service. Coleman's probation officer had him called before the judge last October, because he'd been terminated from his community service work site—he kept arriving drunk. He'd done only thirty-nine of the two hundred hours at that point. Locallo had warned Coleman he'd send him to jail if he didn't make significant progress on the community service by his next court date. Now, six months later, Coleman has done only eighteen hours more. But the jail is too crowded to view this as anything but significant progress. "All right, good work," Locallo says. The judge tells Coleman to return to court in six months for another progress report.

Coleman hurries out of the courtroom. This appearance before Locallo worried him greatly, he says in the hallway; he feared that the judge would indeed jail him. He gave up on sleep and got out of bed at four this morning, he says. He reeks of booze.

The next probationer has completed only half of his two hundred community service hours in three years. There are limits to Locallo's permissiveness with his probationers. Locallo instructs deputy Guerrero to take the man into custody. A third probationer has complied with all of his requirements; Locallo congratulates him and formally ends his probation.

Schullo tells the judge that's it for her probation cases today. It's only after she steps into the gallery and sees Bates that she remembers his case. But Locallo has already moved on—he's doling out continuances hurriedly now, because he's got a jury in the jury room waiting to hear closing arguments in a trial that began yesterday. Schullo tells Bates he'll have to sit tight now until the trial finishes. Bates sighs and heads to the hallway for a cigarette.

He lights it near a window in the grimy hallway. It worried him to see a probationer taken into custody. "But that guy didn't finish his community service, and I have," Bates says. He's hoping Locallo will let him stay on house arrest while his new case is pending, but his expression betrays his doubts. He gazes out the window down at the traffic on California. He says he feels foolish waiting here for them to possibly jail him when he could walk out of the courthouse right now. But he knows he'd be digging himself a deeper hole if he left.

Bates allows that he hasn't often acted in his long-term interests lately. Locallo gave him probation almost a year ago today. He's reminded himself frequently since to keep on walking when he passes one of the innumerable drug spots in his neighborhood. He's already gotten probation twice; catch another case and I'm definitely going to prison, he's told himself again and again. But "the thought of that taste"—crack cocaine—is overwhelming, he says.

The easiest way to get drugs when you're broke, unemployed, and a convicted felon, he says, is to work at a drug spot. The spots always need help, and they don't do criminal background checks. He worked as a lookout at first, watching for police, then began slinging the drugs himself, serving the walk-up and drive-up customers. A supervisor would give him a "jab" to sell—thirteen tiny tinfoil packets of brown heroin, or a like number of white rocks in thumbnail-size Ziplocs. These "blows" of heroin and rocks of cocaine went for $10 each; a "server" turned in $100 and got to keep the other $30. Bates could sell a jab in half an hour—faster when whites came to buy. Whites tended to buy in quantity, sometimes purchasing a whole jab. He'd have turned a decent profit if his earnings hadn't always gone up in smoke.

The arrest earlier this month came after he sold two rocks, for $20, to an undercover officer. Anyone who works on a corner knows he'll sell to an undercover sooner or later; as Bates puts it, the police have plenty of black officers willing to go unshaven and dress raggedy just to catch a brother in the act. "You ain't no police?" he sometimes asked a customer, while recognizing the futility of the question. Like the person was going to say, "Yeah, I'm a cop, don't serve me."

They didn't arrest him immediately after the sale—that's not how the "buy-busts" work. Different officers swoop in to make the arrest so the phony buyer doesn't blow his cover. A young woman cautioned Bates that the "five-ohs" (police) were in the area, but as he later realized, he'd already made the fateful sale. He had five rocks left in his jab, but after the woman's warning he headed over to a nearby apartment building to alert the teens who ran the operation.

He was inside an apartment in the building, talking to the teen "supervisors," when there was a rap on the front door of the apartment. One of the youths opened the door, even as Bates warned him not to. The police rushed in, guns drawn. "We all scattered like roaches," Bates says. He scrambled into a bathroom and deposited his five unsold rocks inside the bathtub. He walked out of the bathroom when ordered to and was handcuffed. An officer surveyed the bathroom quickly but didn't seem to find the rocks Bates left in the tub. It didn't much matter. One officer slapped him in the head, he says. "I'm thinking, 'I'm already handcuffed—why you got to give me this abuse?'"

After a night in a district lockup, a police wagon took Bates and the other prisoners to 26th Street, where they received the standard welcome from the guards in the courthouse basement. "They was cussing and going on, calling us dogs and all that, threatening, 'If you do this and that, we gonna beat your ass,'" Bates says. As he sat in a bullpen awaiting his bond hearing, "I kept saying to myself, 'Why'd you act stupid and bring yourself back in here, knowing how they talk to you and treat you?'"

He drops his cigarette butt to the tile floor now, flattens it with the sole of his shoe, and returns to the courtroom, fingers crossed.

Prosecutor Joe Alesia is in the middle of his closing argument in the jury trial. He's talking about the "face of evil" at the defense table, pointing at the eighteen-year-old African American accused of a carjacking. "Today is the day he's held responsible for what he did," Alesia is telling the jury. Bates resumes his seat on a rear bench. Soon his breathing deepens and his eyelids flicker shut. They spring open periodically with the swellings in Alesia's delivery, then flutter closed again.

LARRY BATES LOOKS HARMLESS, dozing on that gallery bench, but he's really Public Enemy Number One—he and his fellow drug offenders.

They must be a real menace, considering how much is spent trying to thwart them. Nationally, more than 320,000 drug offenders are in prison, and it costs well over $7 billion to keep them there. That's on top of the cost for police officers to arrest alleged drug offenders, for courts to process them, and for jails to house them while their cases are pending. It also doesn't include the cost for the probation officers who monitor the nearly one million drug probationers like Bates who hover near the prison door.

The drug war has tightened the criminal justice grip on blacks in particular. Blacks are incarcerated for drug crimes at a rate fourteen times that of whites. While the imprisonment rate for white drug offenders doubled between 1986 and 1996, it quintupled for blacks. Bates is one of 133 drug defendants on Locallo's docket in March 1998. Five are white, fifteen Hispanic. Bates is among the 113 who are black.

The current drug war is a rerun of a 1950s campaign, with racial overtones.

With heroin use climbing in northern ghettoes after World War II, white elected officials and civic leaders demanded action, fearful that the scourge could spread to their neighborhoods. The ghettoes were swelling in these cities—it wasn't only heroin that whites feared moving in next door. Police began sweeping addicts into jail, and lawmakers greatly toughened drug laws. Officials acknowledged that whites were the main drug profiteers, but those caught and prosecuted were almost always minority users and street dealers. The dealers were equated with murderers. In 1951 Frank Lopez was tried at 26th Street for selling marijuana to a person under twenty-one. Lopez was a "vicious, contemptible man," the prosecutor told the jury in his closing argument. "He doesn't have to have horns on his head. He doesn't have to be carrying a pitchfork. He doesn't have to wear a dark and sinister look. . . . Right before you today you see a dope seller. You see a man . . . who tears the living soul out of human beings." Lopez was convicted and sentenced to twenty-five years to life.

In the 1960s a kinder attitude toward illicit drug use developed, a change of heart that coincided with more illicit drug use by whites. Sentences were eased. Treatment centers sprouted thanks to federal funding. At 26th Street judges began tossing out more and more drug cases in preliminary hearings. This happened especially when the defendants were "white kids from the suburbs" whom the judges didn't want to jail, Chicago police sergeant John Killacky recalled in a 1986 interview with a University of Chicago researcher.

But in 1979 the use of illicit drugs by whites began falling, and as it did, so did support for a compassionate approach to drug abuse.

In 1980, with the economy in recession, Bates, then twenty-six, was laid off of the warehouse job he'd held for five years. His drinking increased, and he was smoking marijuana frequently. He thinks a regular full-time job would have gotten him back on track, but all he could find on the west side were "little old jive-time jobs"—day labor, drywall, part-time gas station attendant. He was still without a regular job in 1982—and he wasn't alone. The national unemployment rate for blacks that year was 19 percent, more than twice the rate for whites. As joblessness soared in urban slums, so did drug use. President Ronald Reagan responded with the current war on drugs. The heavy reliance on law enforcement ultimately brightened the unemployment picture: it increased the need for cops, lawyers, judges, clerks, prison guards, and construction workers; and it moved many of the jobless into jails and prisons and thus out of the unemployment totals.

Even with severe mandatory minimum drug sentences at the federal level, and in New York and several other states, the vast majority of drug offenders don't receive the draconian terms often recounted in the media. Nationally, a third of state drug offenders are sentenced to probation, and, for those who are incarcerated, the average term is two and a half years. Those harsh mandatory minimums induce drug defendants to plead guilty to lesser charges, making felony convictions quicker and easier. In courthouses like the one at 26th Street, addicts like Bates often do indeed make progress: they work their way up from probation to a short prison sentence, to longer and longer ones.

AFTER THE JURY RETIRES to deliberate in the carjacking trial, Locallo says he'll handle one more case before releasing his hungry staff for lunch. "I'm just gonna take this Nelson Mandela plea," the judge says.

"Miranda," prosecutor Mark Ostrowski corrects him.

Locallo's slips of the tongue tend toward the grandiose—it's not the first time he's elevated Miranda from accused car thief to Nobel Peace Prize winner. Ushered before the bench now by Deputy Guerrero, Miranda is a broad-shouldered, goateed Puerto Rican. He was caught in a stolen 1984 Buick Riviera last June. That case was still pending, with Miranda out on bond, when he was caught a few months later in another stolen car—this one an '85 Riviera.

In a January appearance in 302, Neil Cohen, the private lawyer Miranda's family had managed to retain, told Locallo his client was a drug addict who needed treatment. Under Illinois law, addicts accused of nonviolent crimes can be sentenced to probation and treatment under certain circumstances, even for nondrug offenses. But Locallo pointed out that Miranda wasn't eligible for that because more than one case was pending against him. And prosecutor Alesia interjected that Miranda already had three felony convictions—for two car thefts and one other theft. He'd been to prison once and he'd gotten probation twice, once with drug treatment. He was still on probation when he was arrested for the Buick thefts.

Miranda had already been given "every opportunity" to reform and hadn't, Alesia said, and so now it was time he received "severe sentencing."

Miranda has worked as a carpet layer and a mechanic, but all his earnings "go in his veins," lawyer Cohen says later. Cohen has had innumerable clients like Miranda, addicts who strip or steal cars or break into garages to fund their addictions. Cohen would like to see more spending on drug treatment and job training, less on "judges, cops, prosecutors, guards, and prison cells."

Cohen once sang a different tune. In the mid-1980s he was a Cook County prosecutor assigned to the office's narcotics unit. But he says that unit focused on high-level dealers and was lenient with addicts. Prosecutors today are less interested in drawing distinctions, and get-tough laws have limited the discretion of judges as well, Cohen says. "It's the Eichmann mentality. Isn't it simple if you don't have to think?"

To Cohen, the fact that one dose of treatment failed to cure Miranda's addiction isn't cause for giving up on that remedy. Even if it has to be repeated, he says, treatment saves money in the long run compared with warehousing an addict in prison. And it's the compassionate approach: "Imagine that it's your child who becomes an addict. Are you going to put him in prison? Or are you going to try to get him some help? I believe we're the family of man. What are we going to do with that child of ours?"

Cohen thought he might be able to win one of Miranda's two cases. But the other one seemed a sure loser, and beating one case wouldn't help Miranda much since the state could also prosecute him for violating his probation. Because of his previous convictions, and because he allegedly committed one of the car thefts while on bond, he was looking at twelve years minimum.

Locallo had worked out a way to give Miranda just ten years. At a plea conference earlier this month, the judge had said he would sentence Miranda to ten years on one of the car thefts if the state would drop the other case. Locallo would also give Miranda four years for the probation violation. This would run concurrent with the ten-year term, so it wouldn't increase the total sentence, but it would give the state a second conviction. Prosecutor Alesia had grudgingly agreed to the judge's proposal. Miranda had then asked for a continuance to consider the offer—annoying Alesia. "We're bending over backwards to give this guy a deal," the prosecutor had told Locallo. "It can only last so long."

Today Cohen tells the judge his client will take the offer. Locallo leads Miranda through the admonishments, and soon it's official. With day-for-day credit, Miranda will be incarcerated for five years. That'll cost taxpayers at least $100,000.

• • •

AT THE LUNCH BREAK the gallery empties, except for Bates. He doesn't have money for lunch. He drained his pockets earlier on a Snickers bar from the Gangbanger Café, but he's decided to save that for later, when his stomach is less jumpy, when he's on his way home. He hopes.

He still finds it hard to believe how low he's sunk. "I used to buy my first wife coats and things," he says in the gallery. "We never were starving, never got set out [evicted]." That was back in the 1970s, when Bates was stocking shelves and filling orders in a pharmaceutical warehouse in Oak Brook. The job paid well enough that Bates could keep his wife, himself, and his Monte Carlo looking good. "During the time when the Pierre Cardins was out? I had me a couple pair of them boots. Big ol' leather coats, suede, cashmere. Guys at my job would ask me to lend *them* money sometimes. Had a bank account."

He didn't drink or use drugs until his mid-twenties, he says. His father, a truck driver, worked steadily but stayed with the family off and on. A heavy drinker, he died of liver cancer. Bates, the oldest of twelve, wanted to set a better example for his siblings. His mother was a teetotaler and an ardent Pentecostal, and Bates followed in her footsteps. At first.

He graduated high school in 1973. Two years later he married a fellow church parishioner named Vanessa. They had daughters in 1976 and 1977. Soon after the second child, Latisa, was born, Vanessa took her back to the hospital with nosebleeds on several occasions. Bates recalls a doctor insinuating that he or Vanessa was causing the nosebleeds by sticking something up the child's nose. "Do you really want this baby?" Bates remembers the doctor asking. Bates didn't know what to make of it. In retrospect, he thinks he was afraid to admit to himself that something was wrong with Vanessa. She'd been acting oddly since Latisa was born. She seemed jealous when he gave the baby any attention, she talked vaguely of voices she was hearing, and she called Larry so often at work it was irritating his bosses.

Then one morning Vanessa called him at work again, distraught. Someone had broken into the house and taken Latisa, she shrieked. Bates rushed to their west-side flat. Detectives were searching the house and the alley when he arrived. They said they saw no sign of a break-in, and it was clear they doubted Vanessa's story. The next morning Vanessa called the detectives and told them where they could find the baby—submerged in a covered diaper pail. Latisa was twenty-two days old; the cause of death was drowning.

At Vanessa's murder trial at 26th Street, psychiatrists testified she was paranoid schizophrenic. Before Larry left for work on the morning of the killing, Vanessa and Larry had argued—an argument that a psychiatrist said "was probably responsible for finally precipitating a psychotic breakdown of an already stressed and vulnerable Vanessa Bates." She was found not guilty by reason of insanity and committed to a mental hospital.

Larry Bates says he started drinking regularly not long after Latisa was killed and Vanessa jailed. After he was laid off in 1980, his drinking jumped, from two six-packs a day to as much as a case. "I guess it's like they say, you drink to drown your problems, but the next day you wake up, they're still right there." He was smoking marijuana regularly too then. In 1983, his twenty-two-year-old brother was stabbed to death on a street corner. Bates married twice in the 1980s, but both marriages quickly failed.

One afternoon in 1986 or 1987 he walked in on some friends just as they were passing a pipe. "They said, 'Man, you ever smoke cocaine? C'mon, Larry, check this stuff out.' So I checked it out. *Boom.* You know how you feel when you making love? It felt like that, just all over your body. I thought, man, where'd they come up with *this*? The rat race begun then."

He moved to Milwaukee in the early 1990s "to try and turn my life around." He spent three years there working in factories and warehouses. He was still smoking cocaine but less often; it was easier to avoid it when he wasn't surrounded by friends who smoked. But in 1995 he returned to Chicago, to be closer, he says, to his four children.

Then came his first felony, in 1996, for buying one rock on a street corner for five dollars. When his PD told him he could get probation if he pled guilty, he quickly did so. The PD never asked him about his drug use or whether he was interested in treatment—not that Bates would have jumped at the idea. "I was in a whole lotta denial then. I might have did me a rock, and then right afterward if somebody asked me about it, I'd say I didn't do nothin'."

Bates kept smoking crack while on that first probation. At one point he was smoking $70 to $100 of rocks a day. There were two ways to pay for that—thieving or dealing. He still cared enough about his reputation not to steal. "It's too much publicity, you know what I'm saying? People start talking about how you not only using drugs, now you stealing, too. Nobody in my family can ever say I stole this or that from them, even when I stayed with them. I was a working addict." Working on a corner, that is. "I'd be on the spot hollering, 'Rocks and blows.'"

Then he got busted again, in 1997, for drug delivery. "I was the watch-out man," he says. Right before this arrest, he thought he recognized an undercover car coming down the block. "I said, 'Five-oh, man, five-oh!'" Too late.

Since he was on probation, there was no I-bond this time. He spent seventy-eight days in jail while the case was pending. It was his first time in the Cook County Jail, and he went in scared to death, certain he'd get beaten or raped. But early on he met a prisoner he'd gone to high school with, a man who'd since risen to high rank in the Vice Lords and who put out word that no one was to mess with Bates. The seventy-eight days were still an ordeal. Bates has often felt anxious in confined spaces. There was also the constant buzz of friction around him—guards going off on inmates, inmates going off on one another. And there was the ever-present worry that Locallo would send him to prison. At night, when his cellmates were asleep, he often cried quietly into his pillow.

He got himself transferred to the jail's drug treatment division. While in that program, he became convinced that his addiction was ruining his life. But he'd only been in the unit a few weeks when Locallo offered him probation again, in March 1997. Once again no one mentioned treatment. Bates stayed clean for a few months after he got out of jail. But now here he is again.

THE JURY RETURNS in midafternoon with a guilty verdict in the carjacking case. After Locallo meets with the jurors to thank them for their service, he mops up his calendar for the day. Probation liaison Schullo tells the judge she has one more case, and a few minutes after three, Bates is finally called to the bench. Schullo informs Locallo that Bates has indeed completed his community service, but that he's in court because he's been arrested again.

"What's the charge?" Locallo asks.

"Delivery."

"Miss Sheriff, take Mr. Bates into custody," the judge tells Deputy Laura Rhodes. Bates is scheduled to appear before a branch court judge three weeks from now for a preliminary hearing in his new case. Locallo's decision means he'll be in the jail at least until then.

Bates shuffles off toward the lockup with Rhodes behind him. Should've gone ahead and left, he says to himself.

Deputy Guerrero pats down Bates at the sheriff's station. Guerrero has little sympathy for drug offenders, even penny-ante ones. He subscribes to the domino theory regarding drug users. "You start with point-one gram, point-two grams, point-three grams—pretty soon you're robbing people and raping old ladies." Guerrero is also cranky today, the product of a late night barhopping with friends. He tosses Bates's three remaining cigarettes and one stick of gum into a wastebasket. Then he finds the Snickers bar. "Can't I just have the candy bar?" Bates pleads. But he knows what the answer will be and chastises himself for not eating it earlier. Guerrero mutters, "Not my problem," and flips the Snickers into the wastebasket, where it lands with a clunk.

IN THE DRUG WAR of the 1950s and in the present one, the courthouse has played its standard enabling role. In both instances, court officials developed strategies to process the flood of drug defendants at an amphetamine pace, allowing the wars to march onward without pause or thought.

On April 2, 1951, Courtroom 506 at 26th Street became the first court in the nation devoted solely to drug cases. Officials said the special court would help combat drug trafficking. The fifty defendants in court the first morning weren't traffickers, however—they were addicts arrested for possession. The judge locked them up for three months, six months, a year.

The court disposed of more than a hundred cases on some mornings, according to descriptions of it written by Indiana University sociologist Alfred Lindesmith, who visited it in the 1950s. It was easy to quickly convict the defendants because hardly any of them were represented by lawyers. Lawyers weren't provided in those days for indigent misdemeanor defendants, and this was labeled a misdemeanor court—although the legislature gave it the special power to sentence defendants to as much as five years in prison. (The maximum term for a misdemeanor usually is a year.) Ninety percent of the defendants were black. Lindesmith visited some of the drug court clones that other cities opened in the 1950s, and as he reported in *The Nation* in 1957, he likewise found a "long, shabby, pitiful parade of indigent drug users and petty offenders, mostly Negroes."

In the late 1980s, with 26th Street's trial judges swamped in drug cases, Presiding Judge Thomas Fitzgerald established a drug night court program, shifting most of the building's drug cases to five courtrooms that commenced business at four P.M., after daytime staff had left. The program was aimed at easing the workload of the trial judges so they could concentrate on more serious cases. Fitzgerald also reasoned that judges and lawyers who specialized in drug cases would learn routines for disposing of them more efficiently. He picked judges for the courtrooms not for their expertise in drug abuse but for their proficiency in hustling cases along; the judges came from hectic traffic and misdemeanor courtrooms and thus were adept at expediting a busy call. Fitzgerald hoped for a total of five thousand dispos from the five courts in their first full year, 1990. He got 9,700. So he added three more courtrooms to the program.

In 1992 Justice Department researchers, aware of the many other jurisdictions buried in drug cases, studied the Cook County operation. Prosecutors and PDs assigned to the drug courts told the study's researchers they had little time to prepare cases or confer with witnesses or clients.

Some PDs said they felt pressured to advise their clients to decide in five minutes whether to plead guilty or not. Lawyers interviewed labeled the drug courts a "production line," a "numbers game," a "quick way to get rid of cases," a "mill," and "cattle-call justice." Plea bargaining, of course, was rampant in the drug courts, jury trials almost nonexistent. Defendants benefited in the short run from the fire-sale offers they got from prosecutors or judges. But their plea deals often came back to haunt them. First-time offenders usually walked out of the courtroom with probation, but only four percent also got treatment. Many were soon rearrested and sent to prison. "They give them just enough rope to hang themselves," a public defender told the researchers.

But "cattle-call justice" saved time and money. And so the Justice Department researchers deemed the drug night courts an "efficient and cost-effective approach available right now for replication in other jurisdictions."

The way the Chicago newspapers raved about the night court program, one would have thought Judge Fitzgerald had developed a cure for drug abuse rather than for drug case overdose. Establishing the drug courts was "one of the smartest recent moves" in the Cook County courts, the *Chicago Tribune* crowed in 1992. The *Tribune* allowed, however, that the drug courts had become the "equivalent of a pet bear cub that kept on eating." Drug cases were coming into the courthouse more quickly than ever; the faster the bear cub ate, it seemed, the more food it had available to consume.

The drug courts are a prime example of how crime magically swells to fill the criminal courts' capacity to handle it. Before the night courts opened, police officers who found only a user amount of drugs on a person often let him go with a gruff warning, knowing that the preliminary hearing judges at 26th Street were tossing out petty cases because the trial court dockets were overwhelmed. The drug courts made this triage unnecessary: since there now were special courtrooms in which to process drug cases, the preliminary hearing judges didn't have to reject the petty cases. Police officers, in turn, knowing the petty cases wouldn't automatically be rejected, began arresting more of the addicts they caught with a single rock or packet of heroin. Special teams of cops also swept increasingly through slums and housing projects in their wittily named drug "operations"— Hammer Down, Iron Wedge, Clean Sweep, Risky Business—dropping swarms of addicts and two-bit dealers into the night court jaws.

Soon the drug courts themselves were so distended that some of the new cases had to be assigned to the day court judges. Gradually more and more were so assigned. As of March 1998, more than a third of the 383 defendants on Locallo's docket were charged with drug offenses.

The creation of the drug courts was "like opening the gates to a dam wider during a flood," the county's chief public defender, Rita Fry, told a state task force in 1992. The jail population rose from 6,500 when the night courts opened to 8,600 three years later, Fry observed—a result of the decision to prosecute the "virtually inexhaustible supply" of drug users. Fry wondered whether the drug war here would be "fought with the same vigor if it were the sons of Wilmette, Winnetka, and Wheeling"—three white suburbs—being arrested and prosecuted.

In 1996, with Judge Fitzgerald's support, the law-and-order-leaning Chicago Crime Commission proposed that lawmakers downgrade the possession of a gram or less of heroin or cocaine to a misdemeanor. The focus on small drug cases as felonies "deludes the public into thinking that we are making progress in fighting crime," the commission said. The following year a bill based on the proposal was introduced in the Illinois General Assembly. It died in committee.

"DONNA? *DONNA?*"

Public defender Kathryn Lisco is standing in the gallery aisle on an April morning, trying to rouse one of her clients, Donna Gilliam.* (Lisco recently replaced public defender Diana Bidawid in the courtroom, Bidawid having gone on maternity leave.) A skinny thirty-year-old African American in a sweatshirt, jeans, and sneakers, Gilliam is dozing on one of the benches, her head drooping above the open potato chip bag in her lap. She came alone to court, but the young man next to her, another defendant, now elbows her gently. Gilliam comes to, clutches the chip bag, and follows Lisco out into the hallway.

In January police say they saw Gilliam selling drugs on a ghetto street under the El tracks two miles northwest of the courthouse. They say she dropped five tinfoil packets to the ground as they approached, packets containing a total of 0.2 grams of heroin. She's been free on an I-bond since.

Her drowsiness today is mainly due to the heroin she snorted before she left for court this morning, she'll say later.

Now, in the hallway, public defender Lisco asks Gilliam if she'd like to opt for probation with treatment. "I know you got a drug problem," Lisco says. Gilliam dips into the chip bag and nods.

Gilliam is back in the gallery, snoring softly, when Locallo starts going through the call a few minutes after ten. Clerk Duane Sundberg calls her

---

*At her request, this is a pseudonym.

case at eleven-thirty. No response. Locallo's eyes sweep the gallery. Sundberg repeats the name, more insistently. The young man next to Gilliam elbows her again. She blinks awake. "They calling you," the young man says. Gilliam stands, the chip bag sliding to the floor. She grins sheepishly and steps through the glass doors and up to the bench.

Lisco tells the judge that Gilliam wants to be evaluated for treatment. Locallo consents to the evaluation, which will determine whether she's a suitable candidate for treatment. The judge sets June 1 as the next court date.

Gilliam returns to the gallery beaming. She's not particularly interested in treatment, she says later, but it sounds better to her than prison. After Lisco is finished with her morning cases, she escorts Gilliam to the first-floor office where Gilliam needs to make the appointment for her evaluation. Lisco wasn't confident Gilliam would get there on her own.

DRUG TREATMENT is no panacea, especially for addicts from impoverished backgrounds, who often have a host of other troubles to overcome. Even if they can get probation and treatment instead of prison, and even if they successfully complete the program, they usually return to the same neighborhood and circumstances that led to the addiction in the first place.

Gilliam grew up in a west-side slum with two sisters and a brother. Her mother liked to drink, and Gilliam preferred it when she did because it made her less ornery, less inclined to whup Gilliam and her siblings. Their father had left when Gilliam was two, but she and her siblings sometimes stayed with him on weekends. He too was abusive. One day a gym teacher at school noticed bruises on Gilliam's thighs and called the police. Gilliam wound up in foster care.

Gilliam quit school after eighth grade—because she was moving so often, she says, from foster home to group home to foster home. She got pregnant at fifteen. She says she started smoking cocaine when she was twenty-one after seeing her sister doing it. Smoking crack took away her feeling that she was worthless and unlikable. But that feeling quickly returned, and crack also made her jittery and paranoid. "It's a useless thing," she says. She craved it anyway. Like many crack addicts, she started snorting heroin to temper the jumpiness. She's supported her addictions mainly by stealing and peddling drugs, she says. Her rap sheet also shows numerous arrests for prostitution. She's worked a few legitimate jobs, but only briefly. Her lack of education has limited her to minimum-wage positions. And her frequent pregnancies have interfered with those jobs; at age thirty, she has seven children, who mainly stay with relatives.

· · ·

GILLIAM DOESN'T EVEN MAKE IT to her treatment evaluation in May. "I'm not gonna say I forgot—I want to keep it real," she says later. "I knew that day that I had to go. But I said to myself, 'I got to get this rock one more time. And toot this blow.'"

She also misses her June 1 court date. This one she really did forget about, she says later. "Drugs overruled my brain."

On the morning of June 6 she gets busted again, for allegedly peddling drugs under the same El tracks she was allegedly peddling under in January. The police catch her with another five tinfoil packets, containing a total of 0.5 grams of heroin, they say. She has a few days of vomiting and diarrhea in the jail as the heroin in her system wears off.

The police picked her out of a crowd of people under the El tracks and said the heroin they found in a bush was hers—but it wasn't this time, she maintains, and she didn't happen to be dealing that morning. "But it's always gonna be their word over mine because I'm an addict."

So in July, on Lisco's recommendation, she decides to cut her losses by pleading guilty to both charges. With two drug deliveries, probation is no longer an option. And since the second offense occurred while she was on bond for the first, her two sentences will have to run consecutively. Locallo gives her the minimum possible sentence—a total of eight years. She'll have to serve four. It'll cost taxpayers about $80,000 to keep her slum safe from her for that time—or more than $11,000 per 0.1 gram of heroin she was charged with in the two cases combined.

ON SEPTEMBER 15, 1927, after Cook County Board president Anton Cermak spread the mortar for the cornerstone, he told reporters this new courthouse wouldn't have been needed but for Prohibition and all the murders, robberies, burglaries, and arsons stemming from it.

Temperance advocates had maintained that outlawing alcohol would greatly reduce crime. Many of those who have studied the Prohibition era believe it had the opposite effect. After "intoxicating liquors" were banned in 1919, a black market blossomed to quench the public's thirst. Organized gangsters shot and bombed competitors. Mobsters bribed cops, judges, and ward bosses to let their bootleg operations flourish. Alcohol continued to be used widely by the affluent as well as the poor, and so Prohibition soon lost its political support. It was repealed in 1933.

Law enforcement corruption seems an inevitable side effect of drug prohibitions. A host of Chicago cops have gone to federal prison for extorting drug dealers in the last two decades. Bates, who lives in the

Austin police district, says no one in his neighborhood was surprised when seven Austin officers were indicted in 1996 for extorting dealers—shakedowns are routine in his neighborhood, he says.

Reductions in civil liberties are another by-product of drug wars. In 1955 Cook County state's attorney John Gutknecht acknowledged to a Senate subcommittee on narcotics that Chicago police were routinely arresting addicts without legal cause. The drug problem was so grave, Gutknecht said, "that even if we must admit some of their civil rights are being violated, you have to go along with a certain amount of that fringe violation, if you see what I mean." Everyone on the subcommittee apparently saw what he meant, as no one objected. With addicts, Gutknecht said, it was necessary "to take little extra measures."

The little extra measures today involve frequent police searches of minorities guilty of standing on street corners. If a search turns up drugs, the officers can avoid a messy Fourth Amendment problem by claiming the arrestee dropped the drugs as the officers approached. "Subject looked in arresting officer's direction and dropped small plastic bag containing white rocky substance to the ground," the arrest report typically reads. Locallo's father, August Locallo, says police officers often lied in this manner when he was on the force, and Dan Locallo says he has no doubt that officers do so today.

Bates says he's been stopped by the police and searched on several occasions when he's merely been walking down the street. Even when they find nothing on him but an empty pipe they threaten to arrest him—and then they pry him for information. "Who's dealing? Where they keeping the package?" When he tells them he doesn't know anything, they give him a whack in the chest or head, toss the pipe over a fence or into a gutter, and shove him down the street, he says.

"This drug thing is so much bullshit," veteran defense attorney Sam Adam says. "It's nothing but a numbers game. It's a colossal waste of energy, money, time. It's electing politicians, but it's stopping nothing. Narcotics court is a joke. I see people meeting each other there and making deals—right there in the gallery! A guy from Forty-seventh Street would have *never* met a guy from O'Hare Airport—now he makes a deal! Women cannot walk down the street without being attacked in a lot of neighborhoods. Poor people cannot go to currency exchanges and cash their Social Security checks without some gangbanger grabbing them and taking the money away. Over and over violent crime is taking place—and more than half of the police department is running around trying to arrest somebody on a drug case.

"I have a lot of clients who take the position that their body is their own," Adam says. "They create an analogy with abortion that is very hard to refute. They say, 'Well, I haven't hurt anybody. I got a little toot and I went home, and I relaxed and I enjoyed it, and I watched TV and I went to sleep. I don't understand why anybody would want to break into my house, or send me to the penitentiary, to stop me from doing this.'

"The first question that has to be asked—which is never asked—is 'Why are all these people using drugs?'" Adam says. "Before we can even come close to solving the problem, we've got to know why the problem is occurring."

Locallo thinks he knows why the problem is occurring. "Unfortunately, there are individuals in our society who can't get a high out of life itself, so they seek alternatives," the judge says. "That's foreign to me. I'll have a drink every once in a while. But if somebody told me, 'For the rest of your life you'll never have another beer'—so what? Now, if they said I couldn't have an Italian beef with sweet peppers . . ."

The judge says he has no idea what might improve things, just that he's sure legalization wouldn't: that would just lead to more drug use and, in turn, more birth defects. "The ones that want to take cocaine and heroin and stuff like that, and LSD and PCP—I'm saying, 'Fine. You want to have that lifestyle? I don't want to pay for your babies.' If they want to legally take drugs, sterilize 'em."

SEVEN

A Real Lawyer

AMY CAMPANELLI LOVES criminal defense work, but she's burned out by the caseload of a courtroom public defender. So early in 1998 the ten-year veteran decides to quit.

Fifty cases would be manageable, she says in her office on a February afternoon, as she packs boxes on her final day at work, but she had more than a hundred. "Nobody can adequately represent that many people. If you're in court all day doing case after case, you don't have time to prepare for trials." So she had to repeatedly ask for continuances. Most of her clients were in the jail, and they wondered why their cases were taking so long. "I'd tell them, 'Because I've got too many cases.' I *hate* saying that."

Campanelli says jail inmates represented by PDs have good reason to complain, as they often do, about how seldom their lawyers visit them to discuss their cases. Taped to a wall next to her desk are yellow sheets listing her incarcerated clients and how often she saw them. A few she never visited, and many she visited just once. She often had to rely on a brief talk with her client in the lockup the day the case was in court. She thinks lawyers advocate better for clients with whom they've developed a rapport. But PDs rarely have a chance to develop that rapport, she says.

Some PDs keep their head above water by routinely advising their clients to plead guilty, Campanelli says. They skim the police reports and decide, without any investigation, that the case is a loser. "Why would any-one want to be a public defender and work like that?"

Campanelli's replacement in 302, John Conniff, has been a lawyer for twenty-five years, a PD for eight. He believes a lawyer shouldn't get personally invested in his cases. "You should be able to pick up a file and try a case for either side. What's important is how skillful you are at representing a client in the courtroom."

Conniff says he's never felt engulfed by his caseload. He credits this to his knack for quick assessments. If his first review of the police reports and the defendant's rap sheet convinces him his client's chances are dim—the usual situation—he'll advise the client to plead, instead of "hemming and hawing" for several court dates. Clients are often disappointed when he suggests they seek a deal. The TV lawyers the clients are familiar with almost always go to trial.

Conniff acknowledges that his early appraisal of a case isn't always correct. A case that looks airtight on paper can spring leaks once the state's witnesses hit the stand and begin contradicting themselves and one another. "When the witnesses start testifying, they often open doors that weren't apparent from the police reports," he says. "Anytime you don't have a trial, the chances of that happening are foreclosed."

Before the public defender's office was created here in 1930, indigent defendants had their cases assigned to one of the novice lawyers who hung around the presiding judge's courtroom looking for work. These lawyers were willing to take such cases for the experience and in the hope that they could eventually wring some money out of the defendant. The judge usually granted the lawyer repeated continuances for that purpose, while the defendant languished in jail. Officials troubled by this injustice—and by the crowding in the jail—decided to follow the lead of Los Angeles, which had established the nation's first public defender's office in 1913.

In a 1934 law review article, Cook County chief criminal court judge Philip Finnegan raved about how cases had been flowing through the courthouse since the public defender's office had opened. The PDs rarely asked for continuances, Finnegan said, and they frequently accommodated the state by stipulating to facts when witnesses for the state weren't able to appear. Instead of trying to impress their clients by "using every legal or quasi-legal resource . . . in order to win a favorable verdict," Finnegan said, the PDs spent most of their time trying to persuade clients to plead guilty.

Public defenders made "a virtue of giving up to the prosecutor without a struggle and pleasing the judge," charged William Scott Stewart, a prominent Chicago defense lawyer, in a 1936 law review article.

PDs have since earned greater esteem among legal professionals. They can no longer be accused of routinely giving up to prosecutors without a struggle. But defendants at 26th Street, who are represented by public defenders in 80 percent of the cases, are often cynical about their free lawyers. PD stands for "Penitentiary Dispenser," some defendants say. You get what you pay for. They'd have won their cases if they could have afforded "a real lawyer."

ONE APRIL AFTERNOON Locallo hears testimony in the bench trial of Terrence Pouncy, charged with residential burglary.

Conniff, who's representing Pouncy, studied the police reports and advised his twenty-five-year-old client to seek a plea deal. But Pouncy insisted on a trial.

Conniff then counseled Pouncy to request a bench trial and not a jury—a recommendation that had been a no-brainer for Conniff. Tying up a judge's courtroom with a jury trial in a mere burglary case is ordinarily a flagrant violation of protocol at 26th Street. A private attorney might be able to get away with such an affront, if his client was acquitted by the jury and didn't have to face sentencing by the judge, and if the lawyer didn't have another case before the judge in the near future. Not so a public defender anchored to the courtroom, who had to work with the judge every day. The PD might find the judge offering his other clients less favorable plea deals for a time, or issuing stiffer sentences after guilty verdicts, as a punishment for his impropriety. Thus the decision to recommend a bench instead of a jury trial is a pragmatic one, not always in the interests of a particular defendant. But in Locallo's courtroom, a PD can advocate a bench with no pangs of conscience—for, as Conniff observes in his first weeks in 302, a defendant's chances in a bench trial here are good. Too many judges in the building try to read between the lines in a case—to the state's advantage—rather than making their judgment on the evidence that's presented, according to Conniff. Locallo seems to show a "greater willingness to follow the law of reasonable doubt" than many of his colleagues, Conniff believes.

Pouncy distrusts judges and at first intended to demand a jury trial. But on trips to 302 for pretrial matters, he heard from other defendants in the courtroom bullpen that Locallo is a "law judge," a judge who follows the law and isn't biased against defendants. Pouncy, an African American who's had other cases at 26th Street, had rarely heard positive appraisals from prisoners about any of the judges, and so he agreed to the bench.

All felony trials used to be conducted in front of a jury, in accordance with that Sixth Amendment right. But jury trials are an awful nuisance to those responsible for keeping things moving in a courthouse. Not only does picking the jury sap the court's time, but the trial itself moves slowly. The judge has to repeatedly instruct the jury on the rules, and the lawyers often must tread a circuitous path in order to avoid exposing the jury to what's been deemed inadmissible. (A judge exposed to inadmissible evidence during a bench trial supposedly will simply disregard it.)

In the late nineteenth century the Illinois Supreme Court, like other state high courts, fended off numerous attempts by trial courts to institute bench trials in felony cases. The jury trial was too fundamental a protection to be cast aside when a person's liberty was at stake, the Illinois high court ruled.

But with felony courts throughout the nation overwhelmed with cases in the 1920s, reviewing courts and lawmakers decided that the jury trial could be cast aside after all. Bench trials were approved by the Illinois Supreme Court in 1930. "Rules of law must struggle for existence in the strong air of practical life," the court observed (quoting from Sir William Holdsworth's classic *A History of English Law*). A bench trial could be held only when the defendant waived his right to a jury, the justices said. And judges should ensure that defendants did so "with caution," the court added, because "the value of trial by jury has been established by long experience and the institution should be safeguarded."

Once a vehicle as streamlined as the bench trial was green-lighted, however, there was no way that judges were going to keep bumping along in the Model T. And with deft use of the jury trial tax, they made sure they rarely had to. Bench trials in Cook County outnumbered jury trials by five to one in 1961, eight to one in 1985, and eleven to one in 2003.

The Pouncy trial opens to an empty gallery. The state's first witness, seventy-three-year-old Washington Demus, is the victim of the burglary Pouncy is charged with. Demus works as a security guard, and he's come to court in uniform: navy pants, black tie, sweater-vest, and powder-blue shirt with his firm's patch on a sleeve.

Prosecutor Andrew Dalkin handles the direct examination. Demus tells Locallo he lives with his wife in a house on the 6700 block of South Peoria. On the afternoon of May 5, 1997, he returned home, parked his car in the garage, headed for the back door of his house, and then saw someone on his back steps. The person looked in Demus's direction and then ran into the house. Demus at first thought it was one of his grandsons and wondered why the grandson would be running from him. Demus then headed into the house. Inside he heard someone say, "He's here, he's here," and then saw someone race out the front door. Then a second person emerged from his wife's bedroom. Dalkin asks Demus if he sees that second person in the courtroom, and Demus points at Pouncy at the defense table.

The intruder was carrying clothes and fur coats belonging to his wife and daughter, Demus says. Atop the pile Demus saw the rifle he keeps in the bedroom. When the man saw Demus, he backed toward the front door.

Demus tells Locallo it looked to him as if the man were about to drop the clothes and try to shoot him with the rifle. He's authorized to carry a gun, and he had his .38 on him, so he pulled it and fired a warning shot into the ceiling, he says, hoping the intruder would drop everything and run. But the man just edged out the door, onto the front porch.

"Then what did you do?" Dalkin asks.

"Look like he was grabbing my rifle, so I shot for his heart," Demus says.

But the shot hit the butt of the rifle instead, shattering it, he says. "Everything fell out of his arm, then he ran."

The intruder fled down the front steps and to the right, with Demus firing a third shot at him again from his porch, Demus continues. He believed he'd hit the man with this shot, because he went down on his front lawn, but the man quickly regained his feet and raced off, leaving his cap and one shoe behind. It looked to Demus as if he'd wounded him in the arm.

Demus stayed on the porch "sending the bullets out there"—four more shots at the fleeing man, then one at another man he spotted in the gangway next to his building, whom Demus assumed had been the other intruder.

Then Demus called the police. While he waited for them to arrive, he surveyed his house. His wife's bedroom "was tore up like a tornado had been in it." A back window was broken, as was the lock on the back door.

At the defense table, Conniff is studying a detectives' supplemental report about the burglary. He's found several discrepancies between the account the detectives say Demus gave them and the one Demus just gave on the stand. According to the report, Demus told detectives the intruder had moved to the front door and had turned toward Demus as he exited. Conniff figured Demus was now saying the man had backed toward the door because that would have given Demus a better chance to identify him. There also was nothing in the report about Demus firing a warning shot inside. And according to the report, Demus shot the intruder as the intruder exited the door, not after he reached the lawn. When Conniff highlights the discrepancies on cross, Demus insists he told the detectives the account he just testified to. But another contradiction develops on cross: Demus now says he actually missed Pouncy with his third shot and winged him with his fourth.

Demus reiterates his testimony regarding the direction the man took as he fled from the house, saying again that the man ran to the right. Locallo hands Demus a photo of his house and asks him to draw the path the offender took.

As Conniff presses Demus, Demus gets defensive, volunteering information about heart pills he had to take, about the "state of shock" he was in, about how "it wasn't no cool and calm at my age."

"If you can, Mr. Demus, just concentrate on the question," Locallo says impatiently, "and we can maybe finish this bench trial sometime today."

The next witness, Chicago police officer Jesse Jeffries, says he was at St. Bernard's Hospital on another matter during the afternoon in question when he heard a radio message asking police to be on the lookout for a young black man in a white T-shirt and black pants who'd just been shot in the arm. Then someone fitting that description walked into the hospital cradling his arm and wearing only one shoe—Pouncy.

Detective James Cavanaugh, who follows Jeffries to the stand, says that while Pouncy was administered to in the emergency room, he and his partner examined Pouncy's bloody shirt and pants, which ER personnel had put in a plastic bag. They found two rings and a watch in a pants pocket, Detective Cavanaugh says, along with a photo of Pouncy. Other officers brought Demus to the hospital, and he picked Pouncy's photo out of an array that Cavanaugh showed him. Demus also identified the rings and the watch found in Pouncy's pants as his wife's. An evidence technician later brought to the hospital the black sneaker with red laces that had been left near Demus's house. It matched the one Pouncy had worn to the hospital, Cavanaugh says.

After the state rests, Conniff calls Catherine Crittenden to the stand. Crittenden, who tells Locallo she recently retired from thirty years' work for the phone company, says Pouncy was working on her car on the afternoon in question. Her daughter, an acquaintance of Pouncy's, had recommended him to her. The car was parked on the 6700 block of South Peoria. She was sitting in her car, with the hood up, when she heard what sounded like firecrackers. She got out of the car to see what was happening, and then she saw an old man with a gun chasing a young man south down Peoria. Pouncy was still at the front of her car, she says. Soon the old man returned, and then he approached Pouncy and began threatening him. "He started swearing, and he was asking Mr. Pouncy, 'Is that your friend?'" Crittenden says. She told Pouncy he'd better go call the police. But as Pouncy tried to edge away down a gangway, the old man followed him, Crittenden says, and then she heard gunshots. Pouncy didn't return.

Two other witnesses corroborate Crittenden's account—a young woman who says she knows Pouncy from the neighborhood and happened to be in the vicinity, and Pouncy's younger sister, who says she was sitting on the curb next to Crittenden's car at the time of the incident.

Then Pouncy himself takes the stand. He's short and slight with cherubic features. He's been on home monitoring while his case has been pending, and so he's dressed in civilian clothes—white dress shirt and dark slacks. He never went into Demus's home, never took any of his property, he says. He was just fixing a car next door, in front of a girlfriend's house, when Demus approached him "saying things like, 'Are those your friends?'" When Pouncy told him no, Demus "said something about, 'You going to jail,' 'I'll shoot you,' 'I'll kill you,' other words, you know, threatening words." Then Pouncy made for the gangway, hoping to get into his girlfriend's house through a rear door, but the door was locked. In the gangway he stumbled over a low gate, and his shoe stuck in the gate. Demus fired at him three times in the gangway, the last shot wounding him in the arm.

The rings and the watch found in his pants pocket at the hospital belong to a girlfriend of his, Pouncy says. "Me and my girlfriend got into an argument the day before that and she threw them at me."

Conniff rests after Pouncy is through. Dalkin calls Officer James Yu in rebuttal. Yu says he participated in the investigation of the burglary, and he saw the sneaker on the lawn in front of Demus's house.

Sitting at the defense table along with Conniff and Pouncy is Mia McPherson, a third-year law student clerking for the PD's office. While she is perusing the photos taken outside Demus's house by a police evidence technician, something catches her eye. The photo of the black sneaker with the red laces that Pouncy left at the scene is a close-up shot, so it's not clear where exactly the shoe was, but directly behind the shoe there appears to be the bottom of a downspout. In a second photo, showing the front of Demus's house from a distance, McPherson spies a downspout in the gangway north of the house—the gangway through which Pouncy says he fled from Demus. The angle and distance from which the second photo was taken make it unclear whether the sneaker was indeed at the bottom of that downspout. But McPherson thinks the two photos together suggest that the shoe probably was in the gangway, and not out front, when the police took the picture. That would match Pouncy's account of what happened and not Demus's. In excited whispers, McPherson shares her discovery with Conniff.

On cross, Conniff shows Officer Yu the photo of Demus's house and asks if it shows a downspout in the gangway. Yu allows that it does. Then Conniff shows the officer the close-up of the sneaker.

"That is the shoe, is it not?" Conniff asks.

"Yes, sir," Yu says.

"And that is a downspout, correct?"

"Yes, sir."

In his closing argument, Conniff stresses the differences between Demus's account on the stand and the one he gave detectives, concerning where Pouncy had been when Demus shot him. "*Falsus en partes, et falsus en omnia,* Judge," Conniff says. (False in part, false in all.)

"Common spelling, Miss Reporter," Locallo says. The court reporter flashes a grin at the judge as she taps away.

Conniff leans heavily on the credibility of Catherine Crittenden, stressing her three decades of work for one company. "Why is she going to come in here and lie for Mr. Pouncy?" the PD says. When Demus returned from chasing one young man down the block, as Crittenden and the other defense witnesses say he did, he likely was frustrated over not having caught the man, Conniff says. Then he saw Pouncy on the street near his house and assumed he'd been involved in the burglary. Demus "clearly indicated from the witness stand he's not afraid to take shots at people," Conniff says. "And I think that under this circumstance, he just didn't hit the right guy, Judge." Conniff adds that the state offered no evidence, just Demus's word, that the rings and watch found in Pouncy's pockets belonged to Demus's wife. And he says Pouncy would have been a "very foolish man indeed" to burglarize the home next door to one he frequents.

Conniff believes there's enough doubt to acquit Pouncy. But he senses that Locallo thinks otherwise. Something in the judge's demeanor during the trial—Conniff can't put his finger on it—has told the PD that Locallo doesn't buy Pouncy's story, or the testimony of his witnesses. Conniff would bet on his client going down.

Except for that sneaker. For how can the state, the judge, or anyone else explain how the shoe ended up in the gangway that Pouncy says he got chased through, instead of being out front, where Demus says Pouncy left it? So Conniff spends much of his argument focusing on the black sneaker with the red laces, and where the photo seems to show it to be.

Apparently with effect, because before Dalkin even begins his argument, Locallo asks him to explain how the shoe ended up in the gangway. Dalkin says it's not clear from the photo that the shoe was in the gangway.

"If the shoe *is* in the gangway," Locallo says, "then that certainly contradicts Mr. Demus's testimony that he saw the defendant run down the stairs and make a right-hand turn."

Locallo, whose own father is seventy-two years old and moonlighted as a security guard, tells the lawyers he found Demus to be a "sympathetic" witness and that he's "not real crazy" about the defense witnesses. "However, seeing that shoe in the gangway—"

"But there's no evidence that the shoe is in the gangway," Dalkin reiterates.

Locallo asks Dalkin for the photo showing the sneaker, and he studies it again. He tells Dalkin that there does indeed seem to be a downspout behind the shoe.

"That's like reasonable doubt at this point, Judge," Conniff says.

"Not necessarily, Mr. Conniff," Locallo says. The judge says there's only one way to resolve the uncertainty. "We'll take a road trip."

Dalkin offers to have an investigator snap some more photos of the area instead.

Conniff doesn't think much of that proposal. "I think a road trip would be more appropriate than their investigator taking some more pictures. Or maybe *our* investigator should go and take some pictures."

"We're going to take a road trip tomorrow," Locallo says. "Lunchtime."

Dalkin says he already has plans to attend a party at lunchtime tomorrow for a prosecutor who's being elevated to judge.

"We'll go after the party," Locallo tells Dalkin. "We'll go in two cars. You take your car, I'll take my car."

"Do I have to ride with Mr. Dalkin?" Conniff asks.

PEOPLE HAVE BEEN accusing Pouncy of taking things for much of his adult life.

In 1990, just two months after his seventeenth birthday, Pouncy and several others were seen hauling away the proceeds of a neighborhood burglary, according to police—a Nintendo system, a color TV, some coins and jewelry. The complaining witness didn't show in court, and the case was dropped.

Two months later police caught Pouncy and another young man cruising in a 1981 Impala with a broken side window, no plates or sticker, a peeled steering column, and no keys in the ignition. According to police, Pouncy said he'd just bought the car from a man for $50, but a computer check showed it had been stolen earlier that day. Another dropped case.

Two days after that arrest Pouncy was arrested again, when two people who said they knew him told police they'd seen him leaving a house from which a VCR had been taken. Police say Pouncy claimed he'd only acted as a lookout for the real burglars. The burglary charge was eventually dismissed.

In 1992 a woman accused Pouncy of breaking into her back porch and pointing a gun at her through a kitchen window. Pouncy was charged with home invasion and attempted armed robbery. This case made it all the way to trial. Pouncy maintained he'd been watching videos at a girlfriend's house at the time of the offenses. His girlfriend's father testified on his behalf, recalling that Pouncy had been with the family watching *Home*

Alone. Pouncy was acquitted. He says his accuser was a former girlfriend who was mad at him.

While he was in jail awaiting trial on that case, police happened to run fingerprints they'd lifted from a can of spinach and a can opener from a burglarized south-side apartment—and the prints matched Pouncy's. Three VCRs, a stereo, and two handguns had been swiped in that burglary. But a judge later threw out the case for reasons that are unclear from the court file.

Pouncy's winning streak in court ended in 1994 when he pled guilty to two burglaries. He told the judge he was addicted to drugs and sought probation with treatment. The judge instead sentenced him to a state boot camp, in which he served five months. Pouncy says that the judge probably suspected he didn't really have a drug problem and that the judge was right. Except for an occasional marijuana joint, he's never used drugs, he says; he just claimed he did to try to get probation.

AT TWO-THIRTY the following afternoon, a cool, overcast day, a white sheriff's bus pulls up behind the courthouse, and the Locallo entourage boards.

The judge wasn't serious about driving to the scene in private cars. This morning he asked the sheriff's office for the bus and a driver, annoying the chief of security in the courthouse, Ed Hassel, who would have preferred a little more notice. But it's par for the course for Locallo, according to Hassel, who says Locallo makes more special requests of the sheriff's office than any judge at 26th Street, and often with little regard for the difficulties the requests might impose.

Locallo has made a half-dozen field trips in his twelve years as a judge thus far—more than any of his colleagues, he thinks. His first came during a 1989 preliminary hearing. The defendant was charged with drug and weapon offenses. Police had entered his apartment with no search warrant and seized cocaine and shotguns. The issue was whether the officers had probable cause to believe the contraband was in the apartment. An officer testified he'd been able to see the guns and drugs from the entryway to the flat, but a defense photo suggested otherwise. After visiting the scene, Locallo suppressed the seized evidence and the state dropped the case.

During a bench trial in 1995 Locallo went to a nursing home to get the testimony of eighteen-year-old Jerome Triplett, who'd been rendered a quadriplegic after a shooting and beating by rival gang members. Triplett testified through a lip-reader since he couldn't speak above a whisper. He sat in an adjustable hospital chair, his ventilator on one side of him and the lip-reader on the other. When Triplett's whispers couldn't be understood by the lip-reader, Triplett pointed at letters on an alphabet board with a stick in his mouth. Triplett also used the stick to identify photos of the four defendants as his attackers. (The defendants had waived their right to be present for the hearing.) Locallo later found the defendants guilty and sentenced them to long terms.

When a key witness can't make it to the courtroom, or when a trip to the crime scene may clarify an ambiguous exhibit, a field trip makes sense, Locallo says. He's not sure why judges don't make such trips more often. "To me, what's the harm? It's no big deal—you get on the bus and you go. It makes it interesting."

The crew boarding the bus this afternoon consists of Conniff, Pouncy, prosecutors Dalkin and Mark Ostrowski, Deputies Guerrero and Rhodes, a court reporter, Locallo, and myself. It's a midsize bus with a dozen two-person seats. The prosecutors take a seat at the front while Pouncy, the only black on board, heads straight for the rear. Conniff parks himself in the seat in front of his client, and Locallo settles in across the aisle from Conniff.

The bus crawls southward through midafternoon congestion on California. "You got a siren on this thing?" Locallo calls to the deputy who's driving.

"Yes. *Why?*" The driver's tone suggests he's not using the siren, whether Locallo wants him to or not, and Locallo doesn't push the subject.

Dalkin says something to Ostrowski about a recent vacation. Guerrero, overhearing, asks Dalkin whether he smoked dope on the trip. Guerrero's antennae are always feeling for hypocrisy. He figures a lot of prosecutors must have gotten high in college, and he'd bet that some still do. He finds it funny how they always deny it.

"That what *you* like to do, Gil?" Locallo calls out to Guerrero.

"If I did, I'd probably be in front of you now, asking for a contact visit," Guerrero says, and everyone laughs.

Everyone except Pouncy, that is, whose gaze is fixed out the emergency exit window next to him. He's not sure how to act during this odd exercise, so he's just trying to be as inconspicuous as possible. He still can't believe this is happening. Last night he told some friends about the coming trip to the scene, but they just rolled their eyes. Even his girlfriend said, "Yeah, *right.*"

"Where we at—Sixty-first Street?" Locallo is saying. "Beautiful. Officer Battaglia, you're making good time," he shouts to the driver.

"I'm Silva," the driver shouts back.

Earlier today, Locallo made his ruling in the bench trial of a defendant named Hector Padilla, who'd been accused of shooting a young man to death in a south-side Mexican neighborhood. Padilla's mother, father, and sister had testified that Hector had been with them on the evening in question, watching a video. But that hadn't been enough to overcome the confession Padilla had given and the two eyewitnesses who'd fingered him. Locallo found him guilty, declaring, with unusual vehemence for him, that he believed the Padilla family had simply lied for him.

Now Ostrowski, who prosecuted the case, tells Locallo he thinks Padilla was expecting to be acquitted.

"Hector must have misread," Locallo says.

"I was surprised you used the word *lie* on the record," Ostrowski says. "You usually say something like *not credible.*"

"Wonder what video Hector was watching that night," Locallo says. "Probably *The Usual Suspects.*" He looks across the aisle at Conniff. "You ever seen that movie?"

Conniff shakes his head.

"One of the absolute great movies," the judge says.

Pouncy turns away from the window for the first time, looks at Locallo, and says excitedly, "*I* seen that!"

"Good movie, Terrence?" Locallo asks.

"*Yeah.* That Keyser—"

"Keyser Soze," Locallo says. "There's just so many twists to it." He pauses, eyeing Pouncy in the backseat. " 'Terrence Pouncy, usual suspect,' " the judge says. He and Pouncy trade grins, and then Pouncy quickly and bashfully turns back to his window.

"A road trip would be beautiful for the Caruso trial," Locallo muses to no one in particular. "Can you imagine that? Going into Bridgeport? Jurors would get a good look at the scene. . . ." His voice trails off wistfully.

The bus rumbles along on gritty south-side streets, past body shops, fast-food joints, taverns with Old Style signs. Pouncy feels confident, mostly, that this trip will clear him, but he also worries, as he passes familiar street corners, that this could be his last glimpse of these places for years. If the judge finds him guilty, it'll be his third burglary conviction—which means a sentence between six and thirty years.

After twenty minutes, Officer Silva swings the bus onto the 6700 block of South Peoria. A hodgepodge of homes, brick and frame, are squeezed together behind tiny lawns. The bus groans to a stop in front of the Demus home, a weary frame two-story. An elderly man and woman standing on the sidewalk a few doors down look up at the bus and then at each other as the passengers spill out. Pouncy is glad to see no one he knows—he's been concerned about the embarrassment.

Locallo and the lawyers survey the gangway on the north side of the house, the one Pouncy claims Demus chased him through. There they do indeed find the crucial downspout, attached to the building next door. It appears to be a match with the downspout in the photo of the sneaker. It's good news for Pouncy.

After just five minutes, the entourage reboards. The court reporter sets up her steno on a tripod in the aisle of the bus. For the record, Locallo says the principals have made a trip to the scene, and that the sneaker appears to have been in the gangway north of Demus's house.

"All right. John, any questions?" Locallo asks Conniff. It's not clear who Conniff would address them to, but the PD says he has none.

"Andy, any questions?" the judge asks Dalkin. Dalkin likewise has none.

"Gil, any questions?" Deputy Rhodes asks her partner softly.

Guerrero rubs his stomach. "Yeah. When can I get something to eat?"

On the return trip, Locallo begins telling Conniff about the annual touch football game the state's attorneys and the PDs played when he was a prosecutor. His very first year he returned a kickoff for a touchdown, Locallo says, ending a two-year scoring drought for the prosecutors.

A judge spends his workday listening to the stories of others, and perhaps he yearns for times when the situation is reversed. Locallo can see he has an attentive audience in Conniff, whose eyes never wander from him, and Conniff soon pays the price, as Locallo relates in excruciating detail the key plays of several years of the football battles. "The next year the game was six to nothing in the snow. . . . The next year the PDs go ahead with two minutes left in the game. . . . Then we had time for one more play. . . ." The saga ends thrillingly, with wide receiver Locallo serving as a decoy, the PDs triple-teaming him, and another prosecutor grabbing a deflected pass for a last-second touchdown and a come-from-behind victory for the state. Locallo gazes blissfully out his window after finishing the chronicle. Conniff steals a look at his watch.

Conniff mentions that he's hoping to get to his daughter's high school softball game later this afternoon. Locallo grabs the ball and heads downfield, launching into several minutes of his daughter's exploits in cross-country races and his son's feats on basketball courts.

When Dalkin says something to Ostrowski about a case on the courtroom's call involving the northwest-side Edens Motel, it prompts Locallo to tell another story, relating to that motel.

He was sleeping over at a friend's house one night when he was ten. In the middle of the night "we got the bright idea to go out for some Cokes"— and the two boys sneaked out of the house and over to the motel, knowing it had a pop machine. As luck would have it, police were monitoring the area because of some car break-ins in the motel lot earlier that evening. Locallo and his friend neared the motel just as a string of squad cars and a paddy wagon rolled by. The boys darted across a busy street and into a forest preserve. "Then we heard 'Halt!' And then *boom*!" Locallo says; one officer had fired a warning shot. "We hit the dirt. They walked us back to the squad cars at gunpoint."

Locallo informed the officers his father was Sergeant August Locallo. "They said, 'Well, you'd better call him.' It was three o'clock in the morning. I said, 'I think he's asleep.' They said, 'Call him.'" Fortunately for Locallo, his father's wrath was exhausted mostly on the officer who fired the shot, and at the drawing of weapons to round up two youngsters. But "needless to say it was a while before I went on any more sleepovers," Locallo tells his audience.

Soon after the group returns to 302, Locallo calls Pouncy to the bench. The judge says for the record that the police photo of the sneaker, along with the visit to the crime scene, suggests a version of events "diametrically opposed to the testimony of Mr. Demus, and under the circumstances creates doubt in this court's mind regarding the whole set of facts. . . . Therefore, the court having said that, the defendant is not guilty."

"Thank you, Mr. Locallo," Pouncy says meekly. He confers briefly with Conniff, then takes a seat in the empty gallery. He'll have to wait while Conniff prepares a court order for Locallo to sign explaining to the home-monitoring officials why Pouncy wasn't home today. Pouncy's acquittal ought to make that point moot, but Pouncy can imagine some sheriff mistakenly hauling him back down to 26th Street for violating his bond.

Once Pouncy is in the gallery, Dalkin approaches the bench, shaking his head. He asks Locallo if the microphone is off, and the judge leans forward and cuts the sound to the gallery.

"It just strikes me as odd," Dalkin says, "that when a person gets found not guilty of a residential burglary, that he shows no emotion."

Conniff, who's writing the court order for Pouncy at the defense table, springs to his feet. "You know why that is, don't you?" Conniff asks Dalkin.

"Yeah, I know why, because he's guilty," Dalkin says.

Conniff glares at the prosecutor. "Your office has that rare myopia, that even when the evidence doesn't support the charge, you still believe the guy's guilty."

Ostrowski comes to Dalkin's aid, reminding Conniff of the difference between not guilty and innocent. "We just didn't have the evidence," Ostrowski says.

"I think you had a witness who took the stand and lied," Conniff replies. "I'd worry more about that part than about, 'Well, he [Pouncy] must have been guilty of *some*thing.'"

"We can continue this philosophical discussion another time, John," Locallo says. "You're gonna be late for your game."

"I feel very strongly about this," Conniff says.

Locallo, passing through the gallery on his way out of the courtroom, admonishes Pouncy to "stay out of trouble. You go down on another burglary, you're looking at six to thirty. Get a degree. Get a job. Be productive." Pouncy nods.

"You wouldn't think a judge would come to your neighborhood like that," Pouncy says after Locallo leaves. "I appreciate that. Like they say, he's a law judge. That's why he found me not guilty, because he went by the law. I have did some bad things, and at some point you got to be punished. But not for a crime you ain't did." He says he does indeed plan to return to school and to find work, but that he first needs surgery on his arm. He's had little feeling in the first three fingers of his right hand and trouble moving the arm since he was shot by Demus, he says.

Conniff is still steaming about Dalkin's reaction when the PD gives Pouncy his court order in the gallery a few minutes later. "These people on the other side—they read everything as evidence of guilt," he tells his client. He cautions Pouncy to watch his step back in his neighborhood, warning him that the police will be "looking to put a case on you. Whenever you win one, you better stay out of sight for a long time."

Pouncy thanks Conniff, then pays him the highest compliment a PD can get. "Hey, you good," he says. "Why ain't you become a real lawyer?"

Considering Conniff's philosophy about a lawyer remaining detached, he got surprisingly worked up about this case. He also showed a concern for Pouncy—but not one that would last. "I subscribe to the bathtub theory of litigation," Conniff says a few weeks later when he's asked something about the Pouncy trial. "You have to bathe in the waters of the case. But after it's over, you pull the plug and let out the water. Mr. Pouncy is now down the drain."

ON A MONDAY MORNING in late April, Locallo and his staff take a different kind of road trip from 302.

Jury selection is set to begin this day for Frank Caruso and Victor Jasas in the Bridgeport case. (The third defendant, Michael Kwidzinski, has asked for a bench trial.) To accommodate the anticipated throng of media and spectators, Locallo has been granted use of one of the building's older, spacious courtrooms, number 600. He takes the bench at 9:40 and runs through a few miscellaneous matters on his call. The oak pews in the gallery are beginning to fill with reporters and spectators even though the main attraction isn't scheduled to begin until 10:30. The judge is sporting a fresh haircut. So is Deputy Guerrero. So is clerk Duane Sundberg.

But when the lawyers assemble at the appointed hour and Sundberg calls the case, prosecutor Adrienne Mebane asks for a three-week continuance, citing new "security concerns" regarding a witness.

Locallo is clearly taken aback. "We'll address the issue in chambers," he says testily.

While Locallo and the lawyers meet in chambers, Conniff and his partner, Kathryn Lisco, huddle near the defense table, wondering whether jury selection will begin today or not. They look forward to their respite from the courtroom grind once the trial begins and the private lawyers do battle for a week or so. It will allow them to catch up on jail visits and case investigations. "I think he'll make 'em go," Lisco says to Conniff. "I mean, he got a haircut."

Locallo can't make them go, however. When the principals return to the courtroom fifteen minutes later, the judge says for the record that he can't force prosecutors to trial before they're ready. But since Caruso's and Jasas's lawyers are ready today and demanding trial, the delay will count against the 160 days the state has to try the defendants. The delay will be much longer than the three weeks the state asked for, since Caruso's lawyer has a federal trial scheduled for May and Jasas's lawyer has a trial set for June. Locallo sets July 6 as the new date for this case.

The witness about whom prosecutor Mebane has "security concerns" is nineteen-year-old Richard DeSantis. He's a key witness for the prosecutors, having signed a statement implicating all three defendants in the attack on Lenard Clark and Clevan Nicholson. The "security" problem is that DeSantis is missing. Sometime after the three defendants were arrested, the DeSantis family moved from Bridgeport to Scottsdale, Arizona. The prosecutors knew about the move, but when authorities went to Scottsdale recently to subpoena DeSantis for the trial, his mother and sister told them they hadn't seen him in weeks.

DeSantis's father reputedly has been a member of the same wing of the Chicago mob that Frank Caruso's father allegedly belonged to, the 26th Street Crew, which operated near 26th and Princeton. So prosecutors aren't worried about the younger DeSantis's safety. They feel certain that he's ducking.

The latest delay frustrates Locallo. He'd hoped to dispose of the case well before his retention election this coming November, to allow time for any animosity the case might generate toward him to dissipate. He's further annoyed the following morning by the jowly sketch of him in an article in the *Chicago Sun-Times.* Any publicity is good publicity, he believes, but if they're going to use his likeness, they may as well get it right. He soon delivers a personal photo to the *Sun-Times*'s courthouse reporter, asking her if in the future the paper would use the photo instead of a sketch, and adding that he's considering charging the illustrator with impersonating an artist. Guerrero is fonder of the sketch. He trims it from the newspaper and tapes it to a wall in the sheriff's station with the caption: "Ehh! All right, Gil—give him a contact visit."

EIGHT

Charlie Chan

THREE FRIENDS of Frank Caruso have signed statements implicating him in the Bridgeport beatings. Unless Richard DeSantis is located, only two of them can be witnesses against Caruso at his trial. One of the two is Mike Cutler.

Cutler told police—and the grand jury—he was in Caruso's Jeep Cherokee on the night of the beating, riding through Bridgeport, and that when they drove past two young black boys and a Hispanic youth, Caruso said he was going to "beat the fuck out of those niggers" because they "shouldn't be in this neighborhood." Caruso then parked the Jeep and confronted the youths. Cutler said he saw Caruso knock the taller black boy off his bike and chase him down the block. He said he didn't witness the stomping of the black youth around the corner, but that he heard Caruso brag later about how he and others "beat the fuck out of the nigger."

Cutler had been a year ahead of Caruso at De La Salle Institute, a Catholic high school. He graduated two months after the beating, then attended Union College in Kentucky on a football scholarship. Early in May 1998 he returned to Bridgeport for the summer.

Cutler was a shade under six feet tall, muscular, and brown complected. His mother was white, and his biological father, whom Cutler never knew, was Puerto Rican.

On the evening of May 14 Cutler went on a date with a new girlfriend, a young African American woman from a southern suburb who attended college downstate. Cutler and the young woman, Linda,* had gotten to

---

*"Linda" requested that I not use her real name, nor those of her friends.

know each other in an Internet chat room while at college. They'd talked on the phone, but this was the first time they'd met in person. They planned to go to a movie, but Linda and her best friend, Donna, got to Cutler's mother's apartment, on Halsted Street, later than expected—it was around ten P.M. The three young people then drove to the west side, to the home of a former high school classmate of the two women. The former classmate, Edward, lived in a small middle-class enclave of Austin, a solidly black, generally impoverished neighborhood.

Linda parked the car in front of Edward's house, and Donna got out to visit with him. After a half hour or so Cutler told Linda he was getting tired. Linda said she'd get a drink of water in the house and then drive him home.

Linda was still inside the house, and Cutler in the car, when two young African American men in hooded sweatshirts or jackets walked up. The hooded men approached Donna and Edward on the porch, and the taller one pointed a handgun at them and announced a robbery. Edward tossed his wallet to the men and pulled Donna into the house.

A moment later Edward, Donna, and Linda heard a gunshot out front. They called 911, and then Edward and Donna went outside to check on Cutler—they wouldn't let Linda come out. They found Cutler facedown next to the car, bleeding and barely moving. He'd been shot once in the chest. The nineteen-year-old was pronounced dead an hour later at Mount Sinai Hospital.

Detectives told reporters that they had no suspects but doubted there was any connection to the Bridgeport case. The shooting of Cutler likely stemmed simply from the robbery, they said.

But there's speculation nonetheless, in the newspapers and at the courthouse.

"Was it a hit?" Locallo asks prosecutor Joe Alesia from the bench the Monday morning after the news breaks. Alesia has assisted the two prosecutors assigned to the Bridgeport case with the pretrial hearings in 302.

"The way I heard it, it was," Alesia says.

LOCALLO IS OVERBOOKED on this particular May Monday. A jury is waiting in the jury room for the beginning of the second day of the retrial of Kevin Betts. Locallo also has two bench trials and thirty other defendants on the day's docket. If a judge always schedules only the cases he definitely will have time to hear in a day, he'll often be left with little to do, given the inevitable cancellations. Even the simplest "status hearing," in which the lawyers update the judge on progress toward trial or a plea, requires the presence of the defendant, his lawyer, the prosecutor, the judge, and a court reporter. A trial or a hearing on a motion usually requires the presence of witnesses as well. Lawyers frequently get delayed in other courtrooms, witnesses get sick or arrested, and mix-ups in the jail sometimes result in a defendant not being sent over for his court date.

The prosecutors and PDs assigned to 302 don't blame Locallo for over-booking, but they think he should be quicker to make adjustments on mornings such as these, when no one cancels and there's clearly more work than can be handled. Public defender Kathryn Lisco, who's involved in both of the bench trials set for today, thinks the judge should continue the two benches now since he knows he'll be tied up with the Betts trial. Locallo, however, still hopes to nibble away at the two benches during breaks in the jury trial. Judges frequently hear bench trials in bits and pieces over several days or even weeks. Locallo asks Deputy Rhodes to bring in the Betts jury and tells Lisco he'll start the bench trials as soon as he gets a chance. Lisco stares at him speechlessly. She'd hoped to get back to her office in the administration building to catch up on some of her out-of-court work; but now she'll be tethered to the courtroom most of the day. (When I ask Locallo later about the complaints of some of his lawyers about being tied to his courtroom and thus unable to get other work done, he says, "Here's my suggestion to them. Get to work earlier.") A prosecu-tor tells the two police officers in the jury box who are waiting to testify in one of the bench trials to come back this afternoon. "This is ridiculous," one of the officers says as she gets up to leave.

The defendants in the gallery are restless as well; it's becoming clear to them that their cases won't be called until lunchtime at the earliest. As Lisco takes a seat in the front bench of the gallery, a middle-aged black man grumbles to her about the delay. Lisco tells him, "I'm in the same boat as you are. I can't do my work because I have to wait around."

The Kevin Betts retrial began the previous Friday, with prosecutor Ale-sia telling the jury the case was about "a violent act committed by a violent person"—a verbatim repeat of his opening statement synopsis in the Feb-ruary trial, delivered with the same glare at Betts. Alesia and partner Mark Ostrowski feel no need to alter their strategy, since only one bullheaded juror spoiled things last time, in their view. Public defender Tony Eben, on the other hand, aware of the eleven votes against Betts in February, adjusted his tenor. (With Amy Campanelli having left the office, Eben is being assisted this time by Homicide Task Force colleague Ann Collins.) Eben's opening statement in the first trial had been restrained—he'd ques-tioned the "appropriateness" of the investigation and had said merely that "the evidence will show" that another inmate did the shanking. This time he came out swinging, saying the state and the defense were "in absolute and complete dispute" about the evidence and baldly asserting that Betts "was not the offender in this case."

Betts didn't like the makeup of the first jury, and to him this panel seems only marginally better. He's glad this jury is a little younger, and that there are six women instead of five, and three blacks instead of one. But half of the jurors in the first trial were from the city, and this time only two are.

On Friday the jurors heard from the victim's grandmother, Ora Lee Carter, and from Officer James Jackson, the guard in the jail barbershop. This morning Officer Johnnie Debergh tells about the call he got from Officer Jackson after the shanking and how he stopped Betts in the hallway.

Locallo recesses the trial for lunch at one P.M. He asks the court reporter, Kenneth Madoch, if he needs a break. Madoch flexes his fingers but shakes his head. The judge arraigns one defendant, scoops into custody a probationer who hasn't done his community service, and then tells Lisco and the prosecutors in one of the bench trials that he won't be able to get to that case today. Then he calls the other bench, a sexual assault case.

No reporters from the city's dailies or TV stations are covering this dime-a-dozen, not-even-a-murder, black-on-black rape case, this muddled picture of what happened, or didn't, in an abandoned building in a south-side slum more than a year ago. Twenty-sixth Street mostly offers tangled messes such as this, as opposed to nice clean TV lessons. Some courthouse veterans like to affect a knack for seeing through every snarl and detecting every lie. More prudent veterans here humbly admit there's often much about a case they'll never know.

The defendant's accuser is on the stand when the Betts jurors, having finished their lunch in the administration building, suddenly march into the gallery, led by Deputy Rhodes, through the glass doors, and into the well of the courtroom. Lisco is cross-examining the woman about her testimony that the defendant "was on top of you and having sex with you." Locallo looks up from the ledger in which he's taking notes, sees what's happening a moment too late, and signals to Lisco to pause. The woman on the stand lowers her head and covers her eyes as the deputy, twelve jurors, and two alternates parade past her to the jury room.

Ten minutes later Lisco is still questioning the woman, and the judge is frowning at the PD impatiently. He's got the jury waiting in the jury room, the lockup crammed, and defendants in the gallery. He hoped to at least complete the woman's testimony today.

"How much more?" he asks Lisco.

"I still have some, Judge—"

"Well, as soon as the lawyers [for the Betts trial] get here, we're gonna have to break."

This irks Lisco. It wasn't her idea to squeeze this testimony in over lunch, and she doesn't appreciate the judge rushing her. Locallo soon gives up on the prospect of getting all of the woman's testimony in and suspends the rape trial for the day. Lisco and the prosecutor gather up their files; the lawyers from Betts settle in; Deputy Guerrero takes the rape defendant to the lockup and trades him in for Betts. Meanwhile, Locallo issues four continuances.

Over the next two hours the Betts jury hears from three of the convicted murderers who were in the barbershop when Bernard Carter was attacked. As in February, they say the late Angelo Roberts was the culprit and not Betts. At 4:25 Locallo gives the jury a washroom break. The judge needs the break as much as the jury: he's got to deal with that lockup full of defendants and the ones waiting in the gallery. "Uh, Kathy, tell the sheriff to take five at a time," he says to Lisco, as he heads to his chambers for a moment.

"Five at a time? Any *particular* five, Judge?" Lisco says sarcastically when the judge is out of earshot. Guerrero starts lining up the prisoners in the deputies' hallway.

Locallo, back on the bench, begins calling cases and dispensing with them rapid-fire. There's not enough time even for status reports; he simply continues most of the cases to dates in the near future. When he continues one case to Wednesday, two days hence, his clerk, Duane Sundberg, warns him that "Wednesday's becoming a nightmare." "All days are nightmares at this point," Locallo says. A file is missing (continued), a lawyer is missing (continued), a defendant is missing (warrant). A defendant wants his bond reconsidered: denied. A defendant wants to plead guilty, but there's not even time for that. Bring him back tomorrow, the judge says.

At 4:50 he calls for the Betts jury again, and testimony resumes before an empty gallery.

PUBLIC DEFENDER EBEN'S closing argument for Betts the following day is laden with baseball metaphors—fitting, perhaps, after the murderers' row of witnesses who went to bat for his client.

Prosecutors get to speak first and last in closing argument, although they're allotted about the same amount of total time as the defense. During the state's first summation, by Mark Ostrowski, Eben noticed the rapt attention paid by the middle-aged black juror in the first row, Rufus McGee. Every time Ostrowski made a point, McGee had smiled and nodded. So now Eben tries hard to catch McGee's eye, but McGee looks everywhere else.

Prosecutor Alesia jabs his finger at Betts and glowers at him during the state's rebuttal argument but fails to goad Betts into an outburst like the one he made in the first trial.

The jury gets the case at 2:50 P.M. The prosecutors and PDs return to their offices in the administration building. Locallo heads downstairs for a hot dog from the Gangbanger Café. The court reporter stays in the courtroom, tapping away at a transcript on her laptop.

At 3:10 angry voices rise from the jury room. The court reporter cocks her head, fingers suspended above her keyboard. Then she swivels out of her chair and tiptoes into the hallway outside the jury room, where she nearly collides with Deputy Rhodes, who has tiptoed there faster. They trade silent grins. A man is doing most of the yelling: "They put it on a dead man! It don't take no Charlie Chan to figure this one out!"

The door at the rear of the courtroom suddenly swings open, and Locallo strides into the gallery. "Uh-oh, judge is back," the court reporter alerts Rhodes in a whisper. The two women don't want Locallo to catch them eavesdropping on the jury, and so they duck into the sheriff's station. Locallo, jamming home the last of his hot dog, heads to his chambers.

Eben returns to 302 a few minutes later, and Rhodes and the court reporter fill him in on the Charlie Chan remark. Eben guesses the source was Rufus McGee.

"Maybe they'll make him foreman," Rhodes suggests with a smile.

There's a relaxed air in the courtroom now, typical after a jury trial, like the relief at home once company has left. The company in 302 hasn't quite departed, but it's safely lodged in the jury room; no need now for solemn airs. Locallo takes the bench to mop up his call, then notices a fly buzzing over the well of the courtroom. He descends from the bench, armed with a folded *Sun-Times* and a purposeful look, a black-robed little-game hunter. In the middle of the courtroom he eyes his prey near the ceiling, swats vainly once with the tabloid, shrugs, and returns to the bench.

The deputies line up the prisoners in the deputies' hallway, and Locallo commences holding brief status hearings and doling out continuances. Public defender John Conniff represents the defendants, and prosecutor Mark Ertler has the honors for the state. Ertler has just this week been rotated into 302; he's replacing Alesia, who's moving on to another courtroom. One of the defendants, Todd Hayden, a tall, bearded African American charged with attempted murder and armed violence, breaks the routine. Hayden doesn't want a PD or a private lawyer; he wants to represent himself.

On the rare occasions when defendants at 26th Street tell the judge they'd like to go *pro se* (speak on their own behalf), the judges try to talk them out of it. Few defendants have the legal knowledge and experience necessary to mount an adequate defense, and case law directs judges to inform defendants of the disadvantages of self-representation. Moreover, pro se defendants usually insist on jury trials, which they make unbearably long with their ignorance of trial procedures. Pro se defendants are always a nuisance to the court, but they're not always foolish. In 1994 a pro se defendant named Gregory Hudson won acquittal from a jury in a double-murder trial. Defense lawyers dubbed his victory the "Miracle at 26th Street," and the losing prosecutors were the butt of jokes from colleagues for weeks. (But the miracle had an expiration date. A year later Hudson was back at the courthouse, charged with armed violence; he represented himself again, was convicted, and got an extended sentence of fifty years.)

"I'm gonna remind you of a saying," Locallo tells Hayden. " 'A lawyer who represents himself has a fool for a client.' The law allows you to represent yourself, but I don't recommend it. But that will be your choice."

Hayden tells Locallo he's taken criminal justice classes at a city college. "I've studied law all my life—civil, criminal, domestic," he says.

When Locallo asks Ertler for Hayden's background, the prosecutor lists convictions going back more than twenty years, for car theft, burglary, robbery.

"Let the record reflect that I'm demanding trial," Hayden says.

"We may be picking the jury tomorrow," Locallo bluffs.

But Hayden isn't deterred. "I'm demanding trial. If you say it's tomorrow, it's tomorrow."

"Well, I'm not saying it'll be tomorrow," Locallo retreats, "but get your witnesses ready, and we'll see what the situation is."

The judge continues the case for only one day. He hopes Hayden will come to his senses overnight and agree to accept a PD. In the meantime just one day will be lost toward the speedy-trial deadline.

After Deputy Guerrero ushers Hayden back to the lockup, normalcy returns; one by-agreement continuance after another. At 3:36 there are shouts from the jury room again.

And five minutes after this latest hubbub, the jury buzzes. It's had the case less than an hour. Rhodes returns from the jury room a moment later and informs Locallo that there is indeed a verdict.

"All right, call the other attorneys, please," the judge says.

Fifteen minutes later the principals are at their respective tables in the courtroom. There are no loved ones in the gallery rooting for Betts, nor any survivors of Bernard Carter's praying for a conviction. (Carter's grandmother, Ora Lee Carter, left after testifying on Friday, saying she didn't see the need to sit through the trial again.) A PD from another courtroom on the floor is here out of curiosity. He's predicting a not guilty; fast verdicts are usually acquittals, he says. Next to him Kenneth Madoch, the court reporter for most of the trial but not today, forecasts a guilty verdict but acknowledges that this may be wishful thinking. "I always predict guilty. You ever hear of anyone appealing his case after he gets acquitted?" Appeals mean transcript orders for the court reporter at a dollar-eighty a page.

The jurors file into the jury box. Locallo asks the foreperson to rise and hand the verdict to Rhodes. At the defense table, Eben's head drops subtly; the foreperson *is* Rufus McGee. Betts, too, is disappointed. McGee's body language throughout the trial convinced Betts that McGee "wanted to find me guilty *bad*," Betts says later. Rhodes walks the verdict over to Locallo. The judge reads it to himself and then hands it to clerk Sundberg to read to the court.

Not guilty. Betts beams and claps twice, then hugs his lawyers while Alesia and Ostrowski silently gather their files at the state's table.

"I DIDN'T EVEN WANT to be on this jury," foreperson Rufus McGee says later. "I would've rather worked."

McGee, forty-four, a resident of a south suburb and a mail carrier for nineteen years, says he was stunned to learn, when deliberations began, that not everyone was convinced of Betts's guilt. In fact, the first vote had been nine to three for acquittal, with McGee and two white men comprising the minority, and all six women voting not guilty. "I thought it was gonna be the blacks against the whites," McGee says. "But most of the whites were saying not guilty! I was the only black guy who said 'Fuck him.' I wanted to hang his ass. I don't care nothin' for no gangbangers."

He says he didn't fight harder for his view, even though his instincts said Betts was guilty, because he found the evidence lacking. There were conflicts in the testimony of the officer in the barbershop and the officer down the hall, he says. But McGee allows that practical considerations also persuaded him to give in quickly. "They got us cramped up in this little room, and I was ready to get the hell outta there, man. But I still held out—for about twenty minutes. Then I thought, let's get this over with. I was tired of being in that room with them ladies. Them broads let him off. I don't even think they should let any ladies on the jury, period. They're too sentimental. And they use the washroom too much. How many times you gotta piss in an hour?"

McGee had followed the Bridgeport case in the newspapers and knew it was assigned to Locallo. The killing of Mike Cutler had occurred on the first day of the Betts trial, and McGee had read the stories about it with interest. "Those white guys are gonna walk now, man," he says of the

Bridgeport defendants. "They probably paid some stupid black guys to do it. Of course it was a hit. It don't take Charlie Chan to figure that out."

"MAN I'M TELLING YOU, ain't no feeling like that," Betts says later about what it was like for him to hear the clerk read "Not guilty." "Only way you could feel like that is if you hit the Lotto for about a hundred million dollars."

Betts says that he and the victim, Bernard Carter, were affiliated with different factions of the Vice Lords, factions that were in conflict at the time of the shanking. While Carter was giving Betts the haircut, he whispered something to Betts concerning the gang dispute. Betts wouldn't say what he whispered, just that it angered him. "So then I stood up and punched him," Betts says. "But I didn't stab him. When I punched him, he fell back, and a bunch of guys grabbed him, and he fell down. And I ran out of the barbershop." He says he's not sure who actually shanked Carter, but that Carter "got what he had coming."

Betts's witnesses had said nothing about Betts punching Carter; they'd testified that Betts had simply walked out of the shop after his haircut. So if Betts is telling the truth, then all of his witnesses lied.

Betts soon is returned to a prison in Joliet to continue serving the sixty-five-year term he got in 1993 for a different murder. He hopes this victory in Locallo's courtroom can be used to get his time reduced in the other case. The judge who gave him sixty-five years had taken into account the shanking of Carter that Betts then stood accused of. Judges can consider other pending criminal charges, not just convictions, in determining a sentence. But now that he's been acquitted of the shanking, Betts plans to petition for resentencing in that case. His ultimate hope is to win a new trial and an acquittal of that murder as well. It might seem a pipe dream, but not to someone who's beaten a case he'd once pled guilty to. What's to say he can't win the Lotto again?

THE FOLLOWING DAY, with Betts finally out of the way, there's some real movement on Locallo's docket. The judge had twenty-eight defendants on his calendar, but now he's got time to hold plea conferences and rack up dispos. He tempts one defendant after another—conditional discharge, probation, boot camp or, at most, a brief prison stay—and one after another pleads. An accused pickpocket grabs an offer of three and a half years, total, for guilty pleas in his three cases. That's three dispos. The pro se defendant, Todd Hayden, also brightens Locallo's day. He tells the judge he might still want to represent himself, but he agrees to allow Lisco to represent him for now. Locallo continues the case for a month "by agreement" between Lisco and the state.

Locallo chalks up an exceptional fourteen dispos on the day. All of these are by plea except for one case, and the judge disposes of that one expeditiously, too—with a stipulated bench trial.

"Stip benches," as they're called at 26th Street, are Cliff's Notes versions of real trials. They're usually conducted when the state won't reduce a charge that the judge thinks should be reduced. The two sides go through the motions of a trial as rapidly as possible, substituting for actual testimony the capsule stipulations of what they believe witnesses would say. Also known as "slow pleas" and "try-downs," stip benches are popular in courthouses throughout the country because of the time they save. The judge informs the defendant of the result ahead of time. "Verdict and sentence first—trial afterward," the Queen of Hearts might say.

The defendant in today's stip bench is charged with possession of 1,277 grams of cannabis with intent to deliver. Locallo asks the state to reduce the charge to simple possession so he can give the defendant probation, but the prosecutors won't. The "trial" takes three minutes. Locallo finds the defendant guilty of the lesser charge, as he promised he would. The defendant gets his probation, the state gets its conviction, the public defender momentarily has one fewer client, and Locallo has another dispo.

NINE

Perseveration

LOCALLO USUALLY BRIGHTENS when he talks about his days as a prosecutor. But not when you bring up his most significant case—the prosecution of George Jones.

Locallo was the lead state's attorney when the nineteen-year-old was tried for murder, rape, attempted murder, home invasion, and burglary in 1982. Before Locallo finished putting on the state's evidence, Jones was cleared of all charges.

The case led to two federal lawsuits. One forced changes in the procedures of detectives and prosecutors. The other resulted in an $801,000 award to Jones—damages assessed against the city and seven Chicago police employees for false arrest, false imprisonment, malicious prosecution, and intentional infliction of emotional distress.

"A frightening abuse of power by members of the Chicago police force" was at work in the Jones criminal case, a federal appeals court panel said in 1988. Detectives "were determined to put away George Jones regardless of the evidence."

IN THE EARLY MORNING hours of May 4, 1981, on Chicago's far south side, twelve-year-old Sheila Pointer and her ten-year-old brother Purvy were bludgeoned in their beds.

Their parents, Doris and Purvy Pointer Sr., had left Sheila and Purvy and their four-year-old sister, Tiaa, sleeping at home and driven to a hospital in the middle of the night because Doris was having stomach pains, they told police. They said they left for the hospital at about three-thirty A.M. and returned home at six-thirty A.M., after Doris was treated in an emergency room. That's when they found Sheila and Purvy blood-spattered and motionless in the bedroom they shared. Tiaa, who'd been sleeping in her parents' bedroom, was unharmed. Purvy, unconscious, was rushed to a hospital with multiple skull fractures. Sheila was dead. She was on her back across the width of her bed, her legs dangling off the edge, a woman's wool coat rolled up under her hips. She was naked from the waist down, and her red terry-cloth top was pulled up above her breasts. The autopsy revealed no vaginal injury, but a lab test found semen in her vagina.

The parents told police that a window at the rear of the house, in the kitchen, had been slightly ajar when they left for the hospital but wide open on their return, and the screen was gone. A friend of the Pointers found the screen down the alley and directed police to it. Near the screen the police also found a small TV taken from the parents' bedroom, and a bloodstained steel pipe—the weapon with which the children were bludgeoned. The pipe belonged to Purvy Pointer Sr.; he used it to work on cars and kept it in the house.

Pointer was the detectives' initial suspect. His whereabouts between four and six A.M. couldn't be confirmed. Both he and his wife said he'd driven her to the hospital, nine miles away, but he hadn't gone inside; he dropped Doris off at the emergency room entrance, they said, and waited in his car until she returned. Something an evidence technician noticed about the open window in the Pointers' kitchen also provoked suspicions. The technician found an undisturbed line of dirt running the length of the windowsill, suggesting that no one had really come in through the window.

Detectives questioned Pointer at their station much of that first day. They brought him downtown early in the afternoon for a lie detector test. Pointer engaged in "purposeful noncooperation" during the test, the polygraph examiner wrote in his report. The examiner recommended he be retested at a later date. Detectives released him that evening.

The only lead that first day came from a woman who lived around the corner from the Pointers. She told police she'd seen a male youth in the alley behind the Pointer home at 6:10 A.M. She described the youth as about seventeen, slender, clean-shaven, and "clean-looking."

Purvy Junior remained in a coma for four days and lapsed in and out of consciousness for most of the rest of the first week after the attack. Detectives questioned him for the first time seven days after the attack—almost immediately after a breathing tube was removed from the youngster's throat. Area 2 detectives James Houtsma and Victor Tosello asked Purvy if the offender had been a family member. Purvy said no. The detectives asked if he knew who'd attacked him. Purvy whispered something that sounded like "George." Because nurses told the detectives it was probably painful for Purvy to talk, Detective Houtsma held the youngster's hand and instructed him to squeeze it, once for yes and twice for no, in response to other questions. According to the memo Detective Tosello wrote after the brief interview, Purvy communicated that "George" was a teenage gang-banger, lighter complected than Purvy was, and that he lived near the Pointer house.

Police soon learned of an eighteen-year-old named George Jones who lived around the corner from the Pointers. Jones was in school when detectives came by his house. They got a photo of him from his father, who himself was a Chicago police officer. The photo was a color shot of Jones dressed in a suit—the picture taken in anticipation of Jones's graduation from Fenger High School, where he was a senior. The photo showed Jones to be darker complected than Purvy. Jones also wasn't a gangbanger, as detectives later learned. He was the editor of his high school newspaper, a hurdler on the track team, an above-average student known to his classmates as "Bookworm," and a junior deacon at his church. He'd never been in trouble with the law.

That evening two other detectives showed Jones's photo to Purvy at the hospital. Purvy indicated he recognized the person in the photo but "gave no response when asked if he were the offender," according to the detectives' memo about the visit. Purvy also "kept trying to say a last name" for the offender—a last name that "sounded like Anderson–Henderson–Harrison," according to the memo.

The next day, May 12, Detectives Houtsma and Tosello took Jones's photo to the hospital and showed it again to Purvy. As soon as Purvy saw it, he "began to cry and stated that was the man who had come in his house and hit him and his sister on the head," Houtsma and Tosello would write in their official report about the investigation.

Houtsma and three other detectives went to Fenger High School, arrested Jones, and took him to Area 2. Jones told detectives he'd gone to bed around nine P.M. on May 3 and awakened around seven-fifteen the following morning. His parents, likewise, said he was at home in bed during those hours.

Two detectives brought a photo array to the home of the neighbor who'd said she'd seen a "clean-looking" youth in the alley behind the Pointer house the morning of the crime. The photo array consisted of Jones's color graduation picture and black-and-white mug shots of six other young men. The neighbor identified Jones as the man she saw.

That afternoon assistant state's attorney Bryan Schultz decided that Jones would be taken from Area 2 to Purvy's hospital room for a "show-up," a one-on-one identification procedure. Schultz worked for felony review, the unit that decides whether felony suspects should be charged and with what offenses. Schultz told Jones's lawyer, Peter Schmiedel, that he could be present for the show-up—a concession Schmiedel believed was made because Jones's father was a police officer. Show-ups are generally considered more suggestive and less reliable than lineups, since the viewer is presented with only one subject. Besides Schmiedel and Schultz, two nurses were in Purvy's hospital room when Detective Houtsma brought Jones in.

Jones was ushered to Purvy's bedside, and Schultz asked Purvy if this was the man who'd hit him. Everyone in the room would later agree that Purvy first said no. But there'd be little agreement beyond that regarding what happened during the show-up.

According to Houtsma and Tosello's official report, Purvy at first "said no, but at this time the overhead lights were off and the offender was wearing dark horn-rimmed glasses. The offender was then asked to remove his glasses and the overhead lights were turned on. At this point, without conversation from anyone else, [Purvy] stated, 'That's him,' and pointed at the offender. Purvy Jr. was shaking at this time."

According to later testimony from Schmiedel, Purvy first "said, 'No, that is not the man, no, no, no, that is not the man.'" After Jones's glasses were removed and Purvy was asked again, "Purvy responded, 'Yes, no, yes, no, yes, no.'"

Liwayway Hilario, one of the two nurses, would testify that when Purvy was asked if Jones was the offender, he first said, "No," then said, "Yes." Then Detective Houtsma "asked him, 'What is it, Purvy? Is it no, or is it yes?' and Purvy said 'Yes, yes, yes,'" emphatically. Hilario didn't recall any lights being turned on between the two identification attempts. The room was already brightly lit, she'd say—it was afternoon and the curtains were open.

The other nurse, Dorothy Harvey, would remember Purvy first saying, "No, no, yes," and then, after Jones took his glasses off, saying, "Yes, yes, yes, no, no." Purvy "was confused" and "appeared to not know what was going on," Harvey would testify.

Assistant state's attorney Schultz was the only person in the room who would later contend that Purvy's identification of Jones was unambiguous. Even Purvy's initial negative response was really an identification, Schultz would testify. "Purvy reacted in fear, exclaiming, 'No, no, no,'" Schultz would say. In Schultz's mind, this was Purvy's "first confrontation with the man that he had seen beat his sister and beat him and . . . his reaction was terror."

Schultz's account not only didn't jibe with the detectives' report—it also conflicted with the account Purvy himself would offer of what happened in the show-up. At Jones's trial, Purvy would testify that he first said, "No, no, no," because "I didn't know who he [Jones] was." But then "they cut on the lights and he took off his glasses, and I started crying and I said, 'Yes, yes, yes, yes.'"

A federal appeals court would ultimately conclude that the show-up identification of Jones—"equivocal, made in suggestive circumstances by a child with a severe head injury"—had been "worthless."

But it wasn't worthless to the person with the power to charge. After the show-up in the hospital room, "I said, 'There's my murderer,'" Schultz would testify.

The neighbor-witness was brought to Area 2, where she viewed a lineup and identified the person whose photo she'd identified—Jones—as the youth she saw in the alley. Schultz approved murder and aggravated battery charges against Jones. Rape and other charges were added later.

The following morning, May 13, Jones was taken from the Area 2 lockup to 26th Street for his bond hearing. A prosecutor cited the evidence against Jones, relying on Detectives Houtsma and Tosello's report—a report "full of falsehoods" and omissions, the federal appeals panel would later say. Judge Joseph Urso set bond at $250,000. Jones's parents didn't have the $25,000 needed to keep their son out of jail.

"STUDENT WHO 'HAD IT ALL' charged in rape slaying," read the headline of the front-page story in the *Chicago Tribune* on May 18, 1981, five days after Jones was jailed.

The morning the article ran, Purvy's mother called police to report she'd found two pairs of panty hose behind a radiator in the bedroom in which the attack had occurred. The hose weren't hers and hadn't been her daughter's, she said, and the legs were knotted in a way that suggested they'd been used as masks.

Detectives Houtsma and Tosello were unavailable, and so Detectives Frank Laverty and Thomas Bennett were assigned to pick up the stockings and reinterview Purvy at the hospital.

This time Purvy told the detectives there'd been not one but two offenders, both of whom had worn stocking masks, and one of whom had had a gun. The man without the gun was the "George" who'd beaten him and his sister. George had taken off his mask during the attack, Purvy told the detectives, had punched him in the eye, and had asked him where the jewelry was. But Purvy kept calling this attacker "George Anderson." George Anderson wore a cap with a P on it, Purvy said, and was the leader of a gang that lurked near West Pullman Elementary School. Other children had warned him to watch out for George Anderson, he told the detectives. Whenever Purvy said "George Anderson," an aunt who was present for the interview would correct him. "You mean George Jones," she'd tell Purvy, showing him the photo of Jones in the morning's *Tribune*. Purvy would agree with the aunt but soon would be talking about George Anderson again.

The interview left Detective Laverty with "serious doubts" about Purvy's trustworthiness as a witness, he'd later testify. Aside from the details Purvy had given during the interview that didn't match Jones, there was the basic problem that Purvy was now saying there were two attackers. Laverty didn't think a murder case should hinge on a witness who "can't count the difference between one offender and two offenders," he'd later say.

Laverty told his boss at Area 2, Commander Milton Deas, about the interview and about his doubts regarding the charges against Jones. Deas would later testify that although he found it "very significant" that Purvy was now saying there were two offenders, and that the youngster was now describing an offender who didn't sound like Jones, he didn't find it significant enough to direct the lead detectives on the case, Houtsma and Tosello, to reopen their investigation. Nor did he inform the state's attorney's office about the development. According to the commander's own later testimony, he told Laverty that "our hands were tied" because Jones had already been charged. Deas put the responsibility for any further investigation in Laverty's lap. "I told Laverty that if he thought George Jones was not the proper party to have been charged with the homicide, and he thought someone else was, and he had information who it was, or he had leads, I told him to follow it up."

Meanwhile, Jones remained in jail. On June 11 Schmiedel persuaded Judge William Cousins, to whom the case had been assigned, to lower Jones's bond to $60,000. Jones's parents took out a second mortgage on their house and posted the necessary $6,000. Their son came home on June 18, after thirty-six days in jail.

ONE DAY THAT JULY, two months after the Pointer attack, Laverty heard that a man named Lester Pigue was in custody at Area 2, having just confessed to murdering a twenty-one-year-old woman three blocks from the Pointer home. The woman, Sharon Hudson, had been sexually assaulted and bludgeoned with a brick. In his initial statements to police, Pigue blamed Hudson's murder on two men he called "Big Black" and "King George," but in his confession he said "that was just some bullshit I made up." Laverty speculated that "King George" might be the "George"

Purvy had said was an offender, and that he might have committed the Pointer crime with Lester Pigue. Laverty decided to question Pigue. According to the memo Laverty later wrote about the interview, when he asked Pigue whether he'd been involved in the Pointer crime, Pigue said he didn't know because he sometimes did things in fits of rage and then forgot what it was he'd done. According to Laverty, Pigue also correctly "guessed" that the weapon used to bludgeon Sheila and Purvy had been a pipe and indicated with his hands a pipe the approximate length and diameter of the one that had been used. And Pigue also said "he remembered something about a little boy and girl . . . and a screen being out of a window, but could not or would not elaborate," according to Laverty's memo. Laverty didn't ascertain from Pigue whether "King George" really existed.

Laverty brought Pigue downtown for a polygraph. Pigue told the polygraph examiner he had nothing to do with the Pointer crime. The examiner found "questionable motion disturbances" on some of Pigue's answers, which, though "not dramatic . . . precluded the examiner from eliminating him as a suspect" in the Pointer attack, according to the examiner's report.

The detective sent scalp hair samples from Pigue to the crime lab for comparison with scalp hairs that had been in the panty hose Purvy's mother had found behind the radiator.

CHICAGO DETECTIVES USED TO RELY on a double-filing system. A detective's "official" report was sent to police headquarters downtown. When an assistant state's attorney requested the police report in a case he was prosecuting, this was the report he received and the report he tendered to defense lawyers. But the detective retained his memos and handwritten notes—his "street file." When the lead detective in an investigation wrote an official report, he was expected to incorporate into it any relevant information from his memos and handwritten notes, and from the memos and notes of any other detectives who participated in the investigation. Most commanders let their detectives decide what was "relevant."

Locallo's father, August, says that when he was commander of robbery detectives at the north-side Area 6 station in the 1970s, he insisted that his detectives include in their official reports "everything that was said and done" by witnesses, even statements not consistent with the defendant's guilt. But the homicide detectives at his area, and the detectives in many other units throughout the city, followed a different practice, he says. Witness statements that strengthened the case against the defendant went into the official report; statements that might hurt the case—"negative evidence," as some prosecutors and detectives called it—went no further than the street file. Many detectives "had the philosophy, 'I'm not gonna put anything in the [official] report that's gonna help the defendant,'" August Locallo says.

The double-filing system was a handy way of skirting the requirement that prosecutors disclose any evidence suggesting the defendant's innocence—a requirement since the 1963 U.S. Supreme Court case *Brady v. Maryland.* According to August Locallo, prosecutors at 26th Street turned a blind eye to the double-filing system. When a defense lawyer asked a prosecutor if the reports he'd been tendered were all the records that existed, the prosecutor would simply say they were, rather than ask a detective to turn over his street file. Prosecutors knew that anything in the street file that hadn't been incorporated into the official reports wasn't likely to help their cases. Likewise, if a detective was asked on the stand if he'd written any reports, memos, or notes besides the ones that had been produced, he'd say he hadn't. (Police reports generally are not directly admissible as evidence, but they can be used to guide or challenge a witness's testimony.)

The elder Locallo says he complained about the whole practice to superiors, and to judges and prosecutors at 26th Street. "I would question them [judges and prosecutors]—'Do you think it's right?' They'd say, 'Well, yeah, it's an accepted thing—you don't want to put a lotta shit in [an official] report, the less you put in the better.' Well, the 'lotta shit' can be something that shows the guy is innocent. But I was all alone in my thinking."

After Jones was arraigned in June 1981, his lawyers, Peter Schmiedel and Jeffrey Haas, made the standard discovery motion for all police records, including "any material or information which tends to negate the guilt of the accused as to the offense charged . . . and any other material or information favorable to the accused."

Among the few records they got in response was the official report of Detectives Houtsma and Tosello, written the evening Jones was charged. That report made Jones's guilt seem obvious, mostly because of what was omitted from it.

Houtsma and Tosello neglected to mention that Purvy Pointer Sr. had been interrogated at Area 2 for most of a day and that a polygraph examiner had found him noncooperative. They neglected to mention that in their first interview with Purvy Junior, the youngster had said the attacker was a gangbanger with lighter skin than his, and that the first time Jones's photo was shown to Purvy, he'd given no response when he was asked if Jones was the offender, and that he'd offered a last name for the attacker that had sounded like Anderson, Henderson, or Harrison.

In a second report supplied to Jones's lawyers, Houtsma and Tosello acknowledged the discovery of the panty hose a week after Jones was charged, and Purvy's revised account that there'd been two attackers. But this second report omitted mention of Purvy's statement to Detectives Laverty and Bennett that the attacker had been a gangbanger who hung around the West Pullman school, and it didn't say anything about Purvy's repeated references, again, to "George Anderson," or about his aunt reminding him that he really meant George Jones.

The omitted information was all on paper, in memos and reports—inside a street file folder at Area 2.

That October, at the request of Commander Deas, Laverty wrote a memo detailing the information he had about the Pointer case, including the results of his interview with Lester Pigue. The report wasn't turned over to Jones's prosecutors or defense lawyers.

Jones's lawyers did get a report that month from police crime lab micro-analyst Mary Ann Furlong. A comparison of Jones's scalp hair with the hair found in the panty hose was inconclusive, the report said. Furlong had also compared Lester Pigue's head hairs with the panty hose hairs, pursuant to Detective Laverty's request—but she didn't mention that in this report. The Pigue comparison had also been inconclusive. But had Furlong mentioned it in this report, it would have tipped Jones's lawyers that there'd been another suspect. Furlong would later testify she put the results of the Pigue hair comparison in a separate report, which she placed in the Sharon Hudson file—Hudson being the young woman Pigue had confessed to killing—even though she'd done the hair comparison for the Pointer case.

In her October report, Furlong disclosed some other lab results. She'd determined from samples of Jones's blood and saliva that he had type A blood and that he was a "secretor"—meaning his blood antigens would be secreted into his bodily fluids, including his semen. Furlong also wrote that she'd found semen on a vaginal swab taken from Sheila Pointer. But in her report, Furlong neglected to mention that antigens found on the vaginal swab had been those of a type B secretor, not a type A secretor like Jones.

After a phone call from Jones's lawyers, Furlong issued a second report the following month, acknowledging the type B results. She'd later testify she'd "inadvertently" left this out of her previous report.

Jones's lawyers would contend, during his civil suit, that the type B finding positively excluded Jones as Sheila Pointer's rapist. But that wasn't necessarily so, Furlong would testify during that suit. Sheila Pointer herself was a type B secretor, and her blood antigens could have masked the antigens of the offender, according to Furlong.

Mary Pierson, a California forensic scientist who has testified frequently about blood and semen evidence, told me that masking was indeed a possibility in such circumstances. But Furlong herself would acknowledge in her testimony during the civil suit that the type B finding was "very important information" that should have been included in her original report.

LOCALLO GOT the Jones case when he became the lead prosecutor in Judge Cousins's courtroom in the fall of 1981.

The most important part of preparing a case for trial, Locallo learned as a novice prosecutor, was preparing the state's witnesses for their testimony. From a veteran colleague named Ray Garza, Locallo learned to make a special effort to develop a rapport with his witnesses. Garza would never have someone else in the office call a witness for a "prepping" session Garza was going to conduct; he always made the call himself, introducing himself not as "State's Attorney Garza" but as "State's Attorney Ray." Locallo's witnesses, likewise, were apt to get a call from "State's Attorney Dan" when he wanted to go over their testimony before trial. That fall, Locallo met repeatedly with Purvy to prepare him for his testimony against Jones.

Preparing witnesses is a "necessary and acceptable part of the prosecutor's function," Bennett Gershman, law professor at New York's Pace Law School and a former prosecutor, wrote in a 2002 article in the *Cardozo Law Review*. But it can be tempting, Gershman wrote, to suggest answers to witnesses that "eliminate ambiguities or contradictions." Because of the prosecutor's status, a witness "may try to conform his recollection of the event to what the witness believes the prosecutor wants to hear," Gershman wrote. He added that children are especially vulnerable to suggestive questioning. Like prosecutors, defense lawyers can cross the line when preparing a witness, Gershman noted; but the power of prosecutors and their special duty to serve justice make it even more important for them to stay within bounds, he said.

Locallo allows that prosecutors who pose leading questions to their witnesses in prepping sessions can end up eliciting erroneous testimony at trial. He avoided that risk by sticking to open-ended questions in his sessions, he says.

The Jones case represented a particular challenge for Locallo. Since no physical evidence linked Jones to the crime, and since Jones had made no admission, it was clear from the outset that the case would turn on Purvy's testimony.

Locallo prepared for the case with his usual zeal. In his meetings with Purvy he found the youngster to be "very slow." The attack had apparently left him with some brain damage. He was only ten years old, "and because of the injuries, he was like maybe six or seven," Locallo says. Even before the attack, Purvy had scored in the lowest two percent in intellectual functioning in standardized tests. Locallo says he met with Purvy five to ten times before the trial. Purvy was "tentative" at first, "but the more he saw of me—we were able to communicate pretty well." "State's Attorney Dan" brought Purvy into Cousins's empty courtroom one afternoon and had him sit on the witness stand. He showed the youngster where the judge would sit, where the jury would be, and where he and the other prosecutor would be. But no, he didn't show Purvy where Jones would be sitting, Locallo says. That wouldn't have been proper, given that he planned to ask Purvy to point out Jones in the courtroom during his testimony.

In his meetings with Purvy, Locallo was trying not only to build a rapport with the youngster but also to "jar his memory," he says at first—but then quickly adds that he doesn't think the youngster had any difficulty remembering the assault. During one of Locallo's early meetings with Purvy, however, the youngster's account of the attack changed again. Purvy said Jones hadn't himself pulled off the mask he'd been wearing; Sheila had ripped it off him, after which she'd cried, "Why are you doing this to us, George?" This both weakened and strengthened Locallo's case. It made Purvy a more dubious witness to have his account of the attack shift yet again. But it made more sense for Sheila to have pulled the mask off than for Jones to have gone to the trouble of wearing a mask, only to take it off in the middle of the attack. And the statement Purvy was now saying Sheila had made would explain how Purvy had known that the attacker was named George.

ON THE EVE of the trial, Locallo and his second chair, James Varga, informed Judge Cousins they'd be seeking the death penalty if Jones were convicted. It was a superior's decision, Locallo says, but a decision he agreed with because of the viciousness of the crime.

The trial, before a jury, opened on April 6, 1982, with testimony from both of Purvy's parents. Purvy himself took the stand on the trial's second day.

On Locallo's direct examination, Purvy gave a lucid account of the attack, from the time it began to the time he was knocked unconscious.

He was awakened by noises in the house that night, he told the jury. He peeked out his bedroom door and saw two men in the living room. He shook Sheila awake and told her about the men. He heard them go into his parents' bedroom. He put his ear to the wall and heard them "taking apart the TV." He heard dressers slam. Then the two men came into his and his sister's room and turned on the lights. Both of the men were wearing masks; one had a gun and the other had his father's metal pipe. The man with the pipe climbed on top of Sheila, began pulling off her clothes, and "started raping her." Then "he pulled off—she pulled off his mask," Purvy told the jury; and then Sheila "said, 'Why are you doing this to us, George?'"

Locallo asked Purvy if he saw this "George" in the courtroom. Purvy pointed at Jones at the defense table.

After Sheila asked "George" why he was doing this, George hit her on her head with the pipe, Purvy said, and she stopped moving. Purvy told the jury he jumped onto the man's back, but the man knocked him off. He ran to the kitchen and hid under a table, but George dragged him back to the bedroom. Then George hit him on the head—and the next thing Purvy knew, he was waking up in the hospital.

There hardly was anything Purvy couldn't recall on direct examination; he had an answer for almost every one of Locallo's 278 questions. His memory quickly clouded, though, when Locallo sat down and defense attorney Jeffrey Haas began his cross. What happened before Sheila got hit? Purvy had known on direct, but now he didn't. Did the attacker have the pipe when Sheila said, "Why are you doing this to us, George?" Now Purvy didn't know. Did Sheila get hit with the pipe right after she said that? He didn't remember. When he jumped onto the attacker's back, was the man still wearing a mask? He was, Purvy said at first; then corrected himself. What happened after he ran out to the kitchen? He didn't recall at first. Then he said both men dragged him out from under the kitchen table. Then he said only the man with the pipe dragged him out.

Purvy's explanation for the changes in his account of the attack before the trial—regarding how many attackers there were, and whether they were wearing masks, and who pulled George's off—was that he'd made no such changes. He insisted he'd said from the very first time detectives questioned him that there were two attackers, both wearing masks and one carrying a gun, and that Sheila had pulled the mask off one of them.

Purvy allowed on cross that although he recalled seeing Jones twice in the neighborhood before the attack, he hadn't known his name until Sheila said it during the attack. The youngster also allowed that he thought his parents were in the bedroom, right next to his room, when he saw the men in the living room, but that he never tried to go to them for help.

Sheila had been found across the width of the bed, legs dangling off the edge, a coat rolled up under her hips; but according to Purvy's testimony on cross, she was lying in her bed in a normal position when she was hit and when she stopped moving.

To Haas, this was further indication that Purvy's recollection of the attack was contrived. His testimony on direct was mostly "a lie that he rehearsed," Haas asserts today. "It was suggested to him."

Haas says he doesn't know who did the suggesting or whether it was intentional. "Sometimes police and prosecutors deliberately put information in a witness's head, knowing it's probably not true. Sometimes they guess at things with a compliant witness, and the witness repeats what's said to him." Because of Purvy's age, his intellectual deficits, and the injury he suffered, Haas says, "in this case, you were almost starting with a blank slate."

During Jones's civil suit five years later, a nationally renowned neurologist would review Purvy's medical records at Jones's lawyers' request. The neurologist, Harold Klawans of Chicago's Rush-Presbyterian-St. Luke's Medical Center, had treated hundreds of victims of brain injury, edited two clinical neurology handbooks, and written popular books and dozens of articles on neurology. Klawans told U.S. District Court judge Harry Leinenweber that Purvy had sustained an "extremely serious" injury involving both frontal lobes of his brain. The medical records indicated that when Purvy emerged from his coma several days after the attack, he'd been disoriented for nearly a month—he'd had trouble answering even simple questions put to him by medical personnel. The records also indicated that Purvy tended to "perseverate," Klawans said. The doctor explained that "perseveration" involves making a response that appears to be appropriate, then continuing to repeat that answer "when the answer may no longer have any relevance whatsoever."

Moreover, Klawans told Judge Leinenweber, Purvy likely had no memory of the attack. Almost everyone who loses consciousness after a head injury suffers some amnesia, he said. In less serious cases, it may be limited to the blow that caused the injury, and it may be temporary. But victims of head injuries as serious as Purvy's almost inevitably suffer some "retrograde amnesia"—a loss of memory of the period from the moment of the injury, backward. The longer the coma, the longer the period of retrograde amnesia. Given the length of Purvy's coma, Klawans said, it was likely that Purvy had permanently lost any memory of what had happened for "at least a half hour and up to hours, perhaps even longer," before he was struck.

Klawans also said it was "extremely common" for victims of head trauma to "confabulate"—to fill their memory gaps with details they themselves make up, or that they hear from others. As they become less disoriented, their tendency to confabulate diminishes, he said. "But often what they remember is what they confabulated."

"I don't necessarily agree with that opinion," Locallo says today of Klawans's views. "All I know is what Purvy told me."

DESPITE PURVY'S STRUGGLES on cross-examination, Jones's lawyers hardly felt confident after the youngster finished testifying. "These are the cases where you get wrongful convictions," Haas says. "There's a horrific crime. The prosecutor shows the jury the victim and points at the defendant."

And the jury got a vivid reminder of the horror of the crime near the end of Purvy's direct examination. Haas feared that what happened then might overshadow the flaws in Purvy's subsequent testimony on cross.

Locallo pulled out People's Exhibit Number 27—Sheila's bloodstained terry-cloth shirt—and asked Purvy if he could identify it.

Purvy screamed. "That's my sister's shirt!" he wailed, bursting into tears. Judge Cousins quickly called a recess and had the jury ushered out. Purvy was helped down from the stand and led from the courtroom "still hysterical," the *Tribune* would report the following day.

Haas and Schmiedel were livid. They demanded that Cousins declare a mistrial. Haas accused Locallo of inciting Purvy's reaction to elicit more sympathy for the youth from the jury. Locallo responded that he'd told the defense lawyers he was going to show the shirt to Purvy, and that they hadn't objected as he'd laboriously removed it from a plastic bag before displaying it. Cousins said there'd be no mistrial. When the jurors returned to the courtroom, he admonished them "not to allow any sympathy . . . for the victim or for the victim's family" to influence their decision.

Locallo still recalls Purvy's "bloodcurdling" scream, but he says he was as surprised as anyone by it. He'd shown Purvy the shirt while he was prepping him that morning, and Purvy had displayed no emotion, he says.

Why show the shirt to Purvy at all while he was on the stand, except to elicit sympathy from the jury? "It was an exhibit—it's part of the evidence," Locallo says, though he could have introduced it through a witness with less emotional attachment, such as one of the police officers who'd surveyed the scene of the crime.

Locallo allows that while he didn't anticipate Purvy's reaction, he was elated by it. He felt it certainly wasn't going to hurt his case.

But as it turned out, it may have torpedoed it.

"Witness, 11, hysterical at murder trial," read the headline in the next morning's *Tribune*. Detective Frank Laverty saw the story.

Laverty was stunned that the case had actually gone to trial, he'd say later, having been assured by colleagues at Area 2 that the charges against Jones were being dropped because Purvy was an unsuitable witness. After reading the story, he called Cousins's courtroom and asked to speak to anyone connected with the Jones trial. The trial was in recess for lunch, but Haas and Schmiedel were still in the courtroom, and Haas got on the phone. Laverty identified himself and said he had information bearing on the case. Then the detective drove to 26th Street.

That afternoon, with the jury out of the courtroom, Laverty took the stand and told Judge Cousins about his interview with Purvy at the hospital, and about his interview of Lester Pigue. He also told the judge he'd written memos about these interviews.

Haas and Schmiedel asked Cousins to dismiss the case because the state had failed to turn over exculpatory evidence to the defense. Prosecutors Locallo and Varga told Cousins they knew nothing about the memos. But the state is accountable for the withholding of such evidence regardless. Cousins recessed the trial and scheduled a hearing on the defense motion to throw out the charges. At that hearing, pursuant to a subpoena from Jones's lawyers, Area 2 commander Milton Deas produced the case's street file. In it were Laverty's memos.

Commander Deas acknowledged to Cousins that it was standard procedure for detectives to withhold written information they deemed irrelevant. The danger of this practice was apparent from the Jones street file; the detectives had deemed irrelevant anything that might hurt the chances of convicting Jones.

Besides the Laverty memos, the street file contained a memo written shortly after the first interview with Purvy, in which Purvy had communicated that the offender was a gangbanger who was lighter-complected than he himself was. There were memos written while Purvy was still in a coma noting the warnings of doctors that even if Purvy did recover, he might not remember anything about the attack.

And there was a memo recounting a suggestion from Purvy's father to detectives that the next-door neighbor might have been involved in the crime. Purvy Pointer Sr. had related this suspicion to detectives several days after the crime, while Purvy Junior was still lapsing in and out of consciousness. (Purvy Junior was "responding to parents" but "still not available for interview," according to the memo.) The neighbor that Pointer said he suspected, a middle-aged man, was named George. It was just a few days later, when Purvy was able to be interviewed by police, that he whispered the name "George" when asked who the attacker was.

After hearing testimony from Commander Deas and Detectives Houtsma and Tosello regarding the reports that had been withheld, Judge Cousins declared a mistrial "with prejudice"—meaning Jones couldn't be retried. The judge found no wrongdoing on the part of prosecutors Locallo and Varga. But he said the actions of the detectives had bordered on "deliberate misconduct," and that it was his "firm belief" that the wrong man had been prosecuted.

JONES'S LAWYERS then filed a class action suit in federal court seeking an end to the police department's double-filing system. The suit charged that the system was aided by the willingness of Cook County prosecutors to look the other way. It prompted the state's attorney's office to direct its prosecutors not only to call police headquarters when seeking police reports but to also call the relevant detective area and to ask the lead detectives on the case if they had additional records. The suit also compelled the police department to instruct its detectives to turn over to prosecutors not only reports pointing to the guilt of the accused but also "any information . . . that may tend to show his possible innocence or aid in his defense."

August Locallo says he'd bet that detectives "still cheat" by not turning in notes of exculpatory statements by witnesses, or by simply not writing such statements down.

Dan Locallo was among the defendants when a second suit was filed—the one in which Jones sought compensation for false arrest and imprisonment and malicious prosecution. Prosecutors are generally immune from such suits, however, and a judge dismissed Locallo, Varga, and the state's attorney's office from the case. Locallo and Varga were subsequently designated "unsued co-conspirators." Locallo says he wasn't surprised by the filing of the civil suit. "That's how they make their money," he says of Jones's lawyers.

The $801,000 awarded Jones in that suit included damages assessed against Area 2 commander Deas ($25,000), detectives Houtsma ($15,000) and Tosello ($5,000), and the crime lab's Mary Ann Furlong ($10,000). After rendering their verdict, the jurors fumed in the monthly *Chicago Lawyer* about the actions of the authorities who arrested and brought charges against Jones. "I was amazed at how lackadaisical the police and state's attorneys were about everything," said one juror. "They couldn't admit they made a mistake." Said another, "We wanted [the award] to be a warning to the police: Don't do this again." Jurors said they were particularly angered that the lawyers who defended the city in the lawsuit didn't just argue that police had probable cause to arrest Jones; the city's lawyers instead continued to maintain that Jones had indeed committed the attack on the Pointers. (The two lawyers for the city, like Locallo and Varga, are now Cook County judges.)

The appeals court panel that affirmed the jury's decision in 1988 observed that Detectives Houtsma and Tosello had had a hunch that Jones was guilty "and were not going to let a mere absence of evidence stand in their way." There was little question that the detectives' superiors "had known every false step taken by the subordinate officers, had approved every false step, and had done their part to make the scheme work," the panel said. "We cannot say that the jury acted unreasonably in finding that all of the individual defendants were voluntary participants in a common venture to railroad George Jones."

DURING JONES'S CIVIL SUIT, the city's lawyers implied that Laverty had his own agenda in the Pointer case—that he was bent on clearing Jones because Jones's father was a police officer. They raised doubts about the veracity of his memos. Thomas Bennett, the detective who accompanied Laverty for the interview of Purvy after the panty hose discovery, testified that the information about "George" that they got from that interview—that George was a gangbanger who hung around the West Pullman school—was suggested to Purvy by Laverty with leading questions. Bennett also said Laverty reminded him once that Jones was "a policeman's son" and that prosecutors were "going to try to give him the chair." Detective David Edison, who was with Laverty for the interview of Lester Pigue, testified that Pigue never really described the weapon used in the Pointer crime—Laverty had suggested to Pigue the pipe's length with his hands and had gotten an acquiescent assent from Pigue.

Jones's lawyers contended that Detectives Bennett and Edison were merely closing ranks to aid colleagues who were being sued, and to repudiate the colleague who had broken the code of silence.

Laverty maintained he'd talked with Pigue because of the similarities between the rape and murder of Sheila Pointer and the sexual assault and murder of Sharon Hudson, to which Pigue had confessed. But as the city's lawyers pointed out during the Jones suit, there were significant dissimilarities as well. Hudson had been killed on the street, not in her home, and Pigue had been an acquaintance of hers. The sexual assault of Hudson had consisted not of intercourse and ejaculation; Pigue had stuck a tree branch into her vagina, probably after she was dead. Hudson was twenty-one, Sheila Pointer twelve. Pigue was convicted of the Hudson murder and sexual assault in 1982 and sentenced to eighty years. In the 1970s he also had convictions for voluntary manslaughter and robbery and arrests for battery and contributing to the sexual delinquency of a child.

The panel of judges for the Seventh Circuit Court of Appeals that dealt with the class action suit observed that Laverty had "upheld the highest ethical standards of the United States justice system" when he came forward during Jones's murder trial. The panel suggested that Chicago police administrators award him a commendation "for his adherence to the principles of honesty, decency, and justice."

Laverty got a disciplinary investigation instead. He was, in fact, the only detective investigated by the department for his conduct in the Jones case. He was accused of testifying for the defense without first notifying his bosses. Laverty, who maintained he'd called Commander Deas before he testified, was ultimately cleared of that charge. But his testimony in the Jones case finished him as a detective. Assigned to a one-man car and given clerical duties at Area 2, he soon requested a transfer. Until he retired from the department in 1986, he was relegated to an administrative job at police headquarters. His responsibilities included standing in a washroom and observing police department applicants and officers as they gave urine samples.

The Pointer crime remains unsolved. Police never reopened the case. The consensus at Area 2 was that there was no need to reinvestigate, since Jones had been the real offender. But even earlier, after Purvy said there were two offenders, detectives had made little attempt to find the second one, as they acknowledged in testimony during Jones's civil suit. "Sometimes detectives just get something in their heads and they don't want to hear anything else," Laverty says today.

Purvy's father had been discounted as a suspect as soon as Purvy said the attacker wasn't a family member. Likewise, the middle-aged "George" next door was ruled out after Purvy said the attacker was a teen.

While Purvy was still in his coma, detectives had interviewed a man named David Thomas, the family friend who'd found the kitchen screen in the alley. An Area 2 lieutenant had wondered later that day how Thomas had happened to be on the scene, and he'd asked detectives to talk to Thomas. Thomas said he'd been dating Purvy and Sheila's aunt, and when the aunt heard about the crime that morning, she asked him to drive her to the Pointer home. There, when he heard that the TV and the kitchen screen were missing, he strolled down the alley and found the screen.

After Purvy whispered "George," detectives quickly forgot about Thomas. Court records show that in 1981 Thomas already had a conviction for pandering (soliciting a woman to work for him as a prostitute). Since the Pointer crime, he's gone to prison four times—twice for drug dealing, once for violating his parole, and once for aggravated criminal sexual assault. The victim of the sexual assault was a girlfriend's daughter, an eleven-year-old.

TESTIMONY DURING the class action suit supported what August Locallo had said about street files—that many prosecutors knew about them before the Jones case but pretended they didn't. The elder Locallo also said he'd complained widely about the double-filing practice, and that among the people he'd talked to about it was his son. But Dan Locallo says his father never told him about street files until after the Jones trial. The first he ever heard of such files was when Laverty came forward, he says.

It wasn't only Detectives Houtsma and Tosello who kept Locallo in the dark during the Jones case; his supervisors apparently did as well.

Laverty hadn't informed only his commander about the information he'd gotten that cast doubt on Jones's guilt; he'd also informed the state's attorney's supervisor of felony review, Larry Hyman, of his belief that Jones was innocent.

During testimony in the class action lawsuit, Hyman acknowledged that Laverty had visited him at his office at 26th Street in October 1981 and had told him that he thought someone else was guilty of the Pointer crimes. Hyman testified that he relayed this information to Michael Angarola, chief of the Felony Trial Division, and William Kunkle, chief deputy state's attorney, while Laverty waited in his office. But according to Hyman, he then merely told Laverty to come back to him with evidence to support his "theory," as Hyman called it. (Hyman contended that Laverty didn't give him any particulars during the visit; Laverty testified that he did.) Laverty at this point had been a police officer for thirteen years, a detective for nine of them, and he had an unblemished record. But Hyman said he made no inquiries to Area 2 about the Pointer case after the visit from Laverty. He also said he didn't inform the trial prosecutors, Locallo and Varga, of what Laverty had said.

Locallo says none of his bosses told him that a detective who'd participated in the Pointer investigation had doubts about the case. He says he doesn't know why they didn't and that he wishes they had. "If they had information that we possibly had the wrong guy, yeah, I would have liked to have checked it out."

THE JONES CASE was "an eye-opener, a good lesson learned," Locallo says. "I learned that when you talk to police, just as when you talk to any other witness, you have to check out what they say. You can't just accept what they tell you automatically."

But unlike Judge Cousins, the federal jurors, and the federal judges, Locallo wasn't outraged by the actions of police, or by the felony review attorney who approved charges against Jones. He was "devastated" when Laverty came forward, he says—not because he learned he'd been an unwitting pawn in a wrongful death penalty prosecution but because it meant his case had suddenly and irreparably collapsed. "I was more shocked about what happened to the case, because I felt strongly about it," he says.

Detectives Houtsma and Tosello were wrong to suppress evidence, he says, but he wasn't angry at them. "The culture of the police department at that time was to take notes but not necessarily turn over everything," Locallo says. And it's unfair to contend that anyone was trying to "railroad" Jones since, he believes, the detectives sincerely thought Jones was guilty: "It's hard for me to conceive that detectives would go out of their way to zero in on X, if X is not the person, because then they're letting the real killer go free."

He felt bad for Purvy and his parents after the case caved in because they "didn't get any closure." He never felt bad for Jones. Judge Cousins and the federal jurors and judges were "entitled to their opinion," he says, but he still thinks Jones was guilty "based on my conversations with Purvy."

"If George Jones was not the guy, then whatever he received [in the lawsuit] is fine," he says. "But I don't necessarily buy that he wasn't."

During testimony in the civil suit, a psychiatrist said Jones had suffered anxiety attacks, nightmares, and chronic depression after his imprisonment—classic symptoms of post-traumatic stress disorder. He'd had to fend off a rape attempt in jail. Jones was no longer the "sensitive, hopeful" person he'd been, according to another psychiatrist; he'd been "deeply wounded" by the wrongful prosecution.

"Bullshit," Locallo says.

TEN

Freely and Voluntarily

JUST BEFORE A HEARING BEGINS in 302 on the last Friday in May, the two guards behind the defense table remove the chains from the ankles of the bald, broad-shouldered, middle-aged African American in the green penitentiary uniform. The prisoner, forty-six-year-old Leroy Orange, has been on death row for thirteen years.

A jury convicted Orange of a quadruple murder in 1985. On the advice of his private lawyer, Earl Washington, Orange opted to have Judge Arthur Cieslik, rather than the jury, decide whether to invoke the death penalty. A death penalty hearing, like any sentencing hearing, is a balancing of "aggravation" and "mitigation," as the state pushes for severity and the defense for mercy. But Washington, the subject of three disciplinary complaints at the time, called no mitigation witnesses for Orange. No relatives or friends told Judge Cieslik that Orange was worth saving or that his death would be a loss to them. Cieslik quickly sentenced Orange to death.

Orange now is represented by Thomas Geraghty, director of the Northwestern University Legal Clinic. Geraghty has convinced the Illinois Supreme Court to send the case back to 26th Street for consideration of whether Orange was denied effective assistance of counsel at that 1985 death penalty hearing.

On five dates last year, Locallo heard testimony from relatives and friends of Orange about the kindness he'd shown throughout his adult life despite the violent home in which he'd been raised. All of the witnesses said they'd have testified for Orange at his sentencing hearing had they been asked. Geraghty had to persuade Locallo there was a "reasonable likelihood" that the testimony of these witnesses would have changed the judge's sentencing decision in 1985. If Geraghty succeeded, Orange's death sentence would be thrown out and he'd get a new sentencing hearing—fresh consideration of whether he ought to be executed or sentenced to natural life (the minimum sentence for a multiple murder). Geraghty and prosecutor David O'Connor would make their closing arguments today, and Locallo was expected to rule this summer.

The murders had occurred on January 12, 1984. While fighting a blaze that morning in an apartment building on Chicago's far south side, firefighters discovered the bodies of a man, two women, and a ten-year-old boy in a third-floor apartment. The victims were bound and gagged, and they'd been stabbed repeatedly. A neighbor told police that Orange had been at the apartment the preceding evening. Area 2 detectives took Orange to their station, on East 111th Street, and twelve hours later he gave a confession in front of a court reporter. According to that confession, he'd committed the murders after freebasing cocaine and then arguing with Ricardo Pedro, the adult male victim. Orange's half brother, Leonard Kidd, confessed to being present when Orange was tying up the victims and stabbing them. Both Orange and Kidd were charged with the slayings.

Orange was tried first. He acknowledged being at the apartment that night but said he left before any violence occurred, spending the rest of the evening at a girlfriend's. (Later in the trial, the girlfriend corroborated this alibi.) Orange testified that detectives induced him into confessing to a crime he didn't commit by shocking him electrically, placing a plastic bag over his head repeatedly, and squeezing his testicles. Detectives who participated in the investigation denied coercing Orange in any way. A doctor who examined Orange after his arrival at the Cook County Jail testified that he found no evidence of torture.

Leonard Kidd took the stand, against his own lawyer's advice, and said that he alone had bound and stabbed the victims and torched the apartment, in a crazed, drunken, drug-induced state, after Orange left the flat. Prosecutor Timothy Quinn told the jury that Kidd was trying to do "a nice thing for his brother" by taking the rap, but that one person couldn't have tied up and stabbed four people—certainly not Kidd, who at five foot six and 120 pounds was much smaller than Orange. "Leonard Kidd isn't big enough to handle three adults and one child," Quinn said. "Leonard Kidd needed help." The jury convicted Orange. Prosecutors used Kidd's admissions in the Orange trial against Kidd in his trial, and he too was convicted and sentenced to death. Kidd later got a second death sentence for another multiple murder involving arson: he was convicted of setting a fire that killed ten children in a south-side apartment building in 1980. Like

Orange, he's now been on death row for thirteen years while various appeals have been litigated.

On this May morning, Geraghty begins his argument by summarizing the testimony he'd presented from Orange's supporters. Relatives had depicted Orange's upbringing by an abusive, alcoholic mother and an abusive, alcoholic stepfather (Leonard Kidd's biological father) who fought constantly, pulling knives on each other and sometimes firing guns in the family's home on the south side. In spite of this horrific childhood, Orange had become a generous and dependable adult, Geraghty's witnesses had said. Orange's sister had related how Orange helped her raise her first child after she got pregnant at thirteen. His niece had recounted how Orange rescued her and her mother from her mother's abusive boyfriend. His daughter had told how her father helped her with her schoolwork and took her to shows. Locallo had arranged a field trip to hear testimony from Orange's hospitalized stepson, a sickle-cell patient. The stepson had described how Orange would tell jokes and stories to distract him from his illness. Orange's former landlord and boss had characterized Orange as gentle and quiet, a good tenant, and a trustworthy worker. The witnesses had described a "caring, respectful, loving, responsible, hardworking, and protective person," Geraghty now tells Locallo. These qualities "are precisely the kinds of attributes that are most important for a sentencer to hear"—but the sentencing judge didn't hear them, Geraghty says, because of the neglect of Orange's lawyer.

Orange's disciplinary record during his fourteen years in prison was exemplary. At a new sentencing hearing, Geraghty could raise that as a mitigating factor, but he couldn't do so in this hearing because it was limited to matters that could have been made known to Judge Cieslik before he sentenced Orange in 1985.

Before prosecutor David O'Connor begins his argument, he places montages of the four bloody corpses, as they were photographed at the crime scene, on two easels he's aimed at Locallo. He asks the judge to remember the "gallery of death" left by Orange and Kidd. "The blood, the brutality, the viciousness, the ties, the bindings, the gags, the incisions, the slices, the stab wounds . . . this sounds almost like an outline for a Stephen King book," O'Connor says. "But unfortunately, Judge, it isn't fiction. . . . It's an outline of the abilities of that guy over there. . . . In short, it's an outline of evil." O'Connor adds, "No mitigation on this planet" could outweigh the crimes Orange committed.

O'Connor had found nothing compelling in the testimony of Orange's relatives. "Adolf Hitler and John Wayne Gacy probably had families, too," he says. "So *what*?" As for Geraghty's portrayal of Orange as a loving family man, O'Connor says, "He's closer to a meat cleaver than a Ward Cleaver."

O'Connor says the aggravation evidence against Orange includes the "wild allegations" he's made about being tortured by detectives—allegations that show his "utter contempt for the legal system."

And now it's up to Locallo to deny Orange the "break" he's seeking, O'Connor says. The prosecutor concludes: "Someone once said that all it takes for evil to thrive is for good men and women to do nothing. And I think that is directly applicable here."

Before Geraghty begins his rebuttal, he flips over the montages so they're no longer staring at Locallo. "It's difficult to look at these photographs and not react emotionally to them," Geraghty says. The hideousness of the crime is not the point, he says; the point is Orange's right to a genuine sentencing hearing. He adds that evil thrives when defendants are deprived of their constitutional protections.

Locallo tells the lawyers he'll rule on the sentencing issue in July.

Geraghty's concern about the effect of the photos on Locallo was understandable, given their gruesomeness. But the judge had remained impassive when the montages were facing him. The sphinxlike expression he wears on the bench befits his role, of course, but it also betrays a genuine numbness that's developed over the years. "There are pictures I've seen, both as a prosecutor and as a judge—heads chopped off, gunshot wounds to the head where you see the brain matter," he says. "When you hear about man's inhumanity to man, twenty and thirty and forty times— it's not like you become completely indifferent to what you hear, but you build up a mechanism to deal with it."

Other staff in his courtroom likewise seem unaffected by the gory photos they see and the tragic tales they hear. "A normal person would hear some of these stories, and they'd go, 'Holy *shit*,' deputy Guerrero says. "I'm like, 'Yeah? So what?' You hear this stuff every day, and you're like, 'Let's go, let's go, let's get this over with and go to the next thing.' What actually am I supposed to do? Should my heart go out to every person we hear about getting hurt? My heart would be going out every single day—I wouldn't have a heart left."

THE JUDGE HAS another matter to consider in the Orange case this morning. Yesterday Geraghty filed a petition asking Locallo to conduct a hearing that could lead to a new trial for Orange. The petition cited "compelling new evidence" that detectives were torturing suspects at Area 2 in the 1980s, evidence Geraghty says corroborates what Orange said happened to him.

Claims of police coercion are hardly unusual in cases involving defendants who've given confessions. But a host of defendants who'd given confessions at Area 2 in the 1980s have alleged more than coercion. Like Orange, many of them have described being "bagged" (suffocated with plastic bags or typewriter covers) or electroshocked. In 1990 the chief administrator of the police department's Office of Professional Standards, David Fogel—an appointee of the city's first African American mayor, Harold Washington—directed one of his investigators to conduct an inquiry into the Area 2 torture allegations. That investigator, Michael Goldston, identified fifty criminal suspects who claimed they'd been tortured at Area 2 between 1973 and 1986, the vast majority of them during the 1980s. Thirteen of these alleged they'd been bagged, and nine said they'd been electrically shocked. Goldston concluded from his review that "systematic" abuse of suspects had indeed occurred at Area 2—abuse that hadn't been limited to "the usual beating" but that had included "planned torture." Commanders at Area 2 failed to end this practice, according to Goldston, and some had participated in it themselves.

Lieutenant Jon Burge, commanding officer of the Area 2 violent crimes unit for most of the 1980s, was fired in 1993, and two of his detectives were suspended for fifteen months.

Burge had served as a military policeman in Vietnam in 1968 and 1969, where he earned a Bronze Star for meritorious service, the Vietnamese Cross of Gallantry, and a Purple Heart for a minor shrapnel wound. He joined the Chicago police in 1970, at the age of twenty-two, and soon was winning commendations and promotions. He was named commander of violent crimes at Area 2 in 1982. In his off-hours, he relaxed on Lake Michigan aboard his cabin cruiser, the *Vigilante*.

The charge that led to Burge's dismissal from the force was made by a man named Andrew Wilson, who was interrogated at Area 2 in 1982 during an investigation of the murder of two police officers. Wilson and his brother Jackie confessed to those murders and were convicted of them. In 1986 Andrew Wilson sued Burge, three other Area 2 detectives, and the City of Chicago, alleging they'd violated his civil rights by torturing him. In testimony during that lawsuit, Wilson said that at one point during his interrogation, Burge had brought a black box into the interview room. The box had a crank and two wires with clips on the ends. Burge said, "Fun time," attached the clips to Wilson's ears, and began cranking, according to Wilson. The pain from the electric current, Wilson testified, "stays in your head . . . and your teeth constantly grinds and grinds and grinds and grinds and grinds. All my bottom teeth was loose behind that." Photos taken of Wilson when he arrived at the Cook County Jail after leaving Area 2 showed a pattern of U-shaped scabs on his ears.

Wilson said that Burge later moved the clips from his ears to his fingers, "and then he kept cranking it and kept cranking it, and I was hollering and screaming." Wilson said his wrists were handcuffed to two separate rings on a wall of the room, so that he was stretched out in front of a radiator he sometimes brushed against, from which he sustained burn marks on his chest and thigh, burns that were also documented in the jail photos. But Wilson said he didn't notice the radiator burning him while he was being shocked. "That box . . . took over. That's what was happening. The heat radiator didn't even exist then. The box existed."

Wilson said Burge also shocked him with a round black device with a wire sticking out of it that he plugged into the wall. "He took it and he ran it up between my legs, my groin area, just ran it up there very gently. . . . Then he jabbed me with the thing and it slammed me . . . into the grill of the window."

During Wilson's lawsuit, his lawyers received several anonymous letters from someone who professed inside knowledge of the workings of Area 2 in the early 1980s—"Deep Badge," as Wilson's lawyers would come to refer to him. One letter advised the lawyers to interview a man named Melvin Jones, who was in the Cook County Jail on a murder charge. The lawyers located Jones and learned that he'd been interrogated at Area 2 nine days before the Wilson brothers were. Jones told the lawyers that Burge had shocked him with an electrical device on his penis, foot, and thigh. He said he'd testified about the electroshock at a motion to suppress his confession in 1982. The lawyers obtained the transcript. Jones had testified that after Burge shocked him, he told the lieutenant, "You ain't supposed to be doing this to me," but that Burge had responded, "No court and no state are going to take your word against a lieutenant's word." Jones also testified that Burge told him he'd given the same treatment to two men nicknamed "Satan" and "Cochise." According to Jones's testimony, Burge said the two men thought they were tough but that he'd had them crawling over the floor.

Wilson's lawyers found Satan—Andrew Holmes—in the Stateville Correctional Center in Joliet. Holmes said Burge had used the black box on him in 1973. Wilson's lawyers also found an inmate in a Danville prison who said Burge had shocked him with a cattle prod in the genitals and stomach, and an inmate in a prison in Pontiac who said Burge had shocked him in the arms, armpits, and testicles.

Police brass at first suspected that Deep Badge was Frank Laverty, the detective who'd come forward during the George Jones trial. But the content of one of the informant's letters indicated that the person was still working at Area 2 after Laverty had been transferred from that station. The informant also mentioned in one letter his need to remain anonymous so he wouldn't end up "shunned like Officer Laverty" had been.

After two trials, Andrew Wilson's lawsuit was still unresolved in 1994. But by that time the Goldston report had been released to the public, along with a report by a second investigator for the police department's Office of Professional Standards that concluded that Burge had tortured Wilson. And Burge had already been fired. In filings in the Wilson suit in 1995, the city's lawyers—who previously had denied Wilson's allegations—conceded that Burge had tortured Wilson and Melvin Jones at Area 2 and that the torture had included electroshock. Burge had "plainly inflicted punishment far out of proportion to the necessities of the city's interest in solving a crime," the city's lawyers said. The commander's conduct had been so out-rageous, in fact, that the city couldn't be held responsible, its lawyers con-tended—Burge and his colleagues had clearly acted "outside the scope of their employment" in torturing suspects at Area 2.

U.S. District judge Robert Gettleman didn't buy the lawyers' argument that the officers were liable but the city wasn't. In 1996 Gettleman assessed the city a million dollars in damages. (None of the money went to Wilson. The judge directed that $900,000 go to his lawyers, who'd been litigating the suit for most of a decade without pay. The other $100,000 went to the family of one of the slain officers who'd won a wrongful death suit against Wilson years earlier.)

The city's admission that suspects were tortured at Area 2 in the early 1980s "strongly supports the allegations that Mr. Orange has made from the beginning," Geraghty contended in the petition he filed yesterday.

And now, in the courtroom, Geraghty tells Locallo that Orange's claims can hardly be dismissed as "wild allegations"—prosecutor O'Connor's term for them earlier this morning—considering that "the city has admit-ted that that's what went on."

O'Connor responds that the city made no admission about Orange's particular case.

Locallo, likewise, tells Geraghty that even if some suspects were abused at Area 2, it doesn't mean Orange was. "The court is well aware of what Mr. Orange had claimed," the judge says. "The court is also well aware of what witnesses were called [at Orange's trial] to rebut that. And there's no evidence at this stage in the record which established torture."

Locallo tells the lawyers he'll consider this new matter at a later date.

· · ·

LOCALLO ALREADY HAS the Bridgeport case to contend with. Now he has a second issue with special resonance for African Americans. All of the suspects who alleged torture at Area 2 were black. All of the detectives who allegedly did the torturing were white.

That race may sometimes be a factor in police abuse of suspects in the United States isn't something new. In 1931 the National Commission on Law Observance and Law Enforcement—commonly called the Wickersham Commission, after its chairman, former U.S. attorney general George Wickersham—reported that use of the "third degree" by police was widespread in the nation, that "poor and uninfluential" suspects were the usual victims, and that Negroes were the victims "in some of the worst cases."

Criminal suspects were sometimes punched, slapped, kicked, whipped with rubber hoses, poked with blackjacks, and deprived of sleep and food in attempts by police to extract confessions from them, the Wickersham Commission found. And sometimes they were subjected to electric shock: informants told the commission of a storage battery device called the "electric monkey" used by Dallas police until about 1925. "It had two terminals, one of which was put against the victim's spine," the commission's special field investigator, Ernest Hopkins, wrote in his 1931 book, *Our Lawless Police*. "The police called this 'giving him a needle in the back.' It was chiefly used upon Negroes, at night, and in outlying woods to which they were taken with an implied threat that there might be a lynching. It got confessions."

The third degree was "thoroughly at home" in Chicago, the Wickersham Commission reported. The favored methods here included a rubber hose to the back or to the pit of the stomach, a club to the shins, or a telephone book to the head. "The Chicago telephone book is a heavy one and a swinging blow with it may stun a man without leaving a mark," the commission said. Likewise, the marks left by a rubber hose usually disappeared in a few hours. A room at police headquarters was known as the "goldfish room," and suspects were taken there "to see the goldfish"—to be beaten with rubber hoses. The Wickersham report noted that when someone suggested to Chicago police officials that the department try using the recently invented lie detector, the response wasn't enthusiastic. "Here's the best lie detector," one police official said, extending a clenched fist.

The Wickersham report also cited examples of suspects who succumbed to their interrogators' pressure and confessed, only to have their innocence established later. It noted that in the late seventeenth century King William III had "tried the thumbscrews on his own thumbs, and said another turn would make him confess anything."

Psychological ploys have since displaced physical abuse as the dominant method for extracting confessions, many criminologists say today. For detectives bent on inducing confessions, psychological coercion has an advantage over physical abuse: since it doesn't leave marks, it's even harder to prove. But a ruse such as falsely threatening a suspect that a death sentence is inevitable if he doesn't confess or suggesting that freedom is likely if he does can wring a confession from the innocent as well as the guilty, so confessions deemed to have been involuntarily given are legally inadmissible, whether they're obtained through tricks or brutality.

Police perjury was another evil inherent in the reliance on coerced confessions, the Wickersham Commission observed. A detective who relied on the "best lie detector" during an interrogation was hardly going to admit to it on the stand.

If a defendant happened to have sustained observable injuries, police explained them away in court with one of their stock excuses: he fell down stairs while being arrested; his cellmates beat him up; he rolled off the bench in the lockup; he banged his head on the cell door as he was being taken out.

No matter how transparent the explanation, police could almost always count on a wink from the judge—could expect, that is, that the judge would find that no abuse had occurred, that the confession had been voluntarily given, and that the state was therefore free to use it against the defendant. A statement from the suspect that he was confessing "freely and voluntarily" was routinely included in confessions, and judges would point to it as evidence that no coercion had occurred. Hopkins, the Wickersham field investigator, criticized the "general judicial tolerance of the fantastic fiction that a third, or a half, or three-quarters of our felony suspects are so gentle-natured that they voluntarily sob forth their guilt on the nearest detective's shoulder."

When Cook County Criminal Court judge Joseph Fitch stunned police and prosecutors by deciding, during a 1921 robbery trial, that the confession of nineteen-year-old Harvey Rogers was inadmissible because police had beaten it out of him, the local press was stirred to action—not by the police abuse in question but by the audacity of Judge Fitch. COPS PROTEST COURT BAN ON CONFESSIONS read the headline of the story rebuking Fitch in the next day's *Chicago Herald-Examiner.* A police official warned in the article that 95 percent of the police department's work would be nullified if other judges followed Judge Fitch's example. "We are permitted to do less every day," another police official complained. "Pretty soon there won't be a police department."

Defendant Rogers was convicted even without his confession. In affirming the conviction in 1922, the Illinois Supreme Court took time to praise

Judge Fitch for banning the coerced confession "at the expense of severe and unjust criticism" and to blast Chicago police for its "criminal practice" of beating confessions out of suspects. The high court directed trial judges to suppress confessions unless they were certain the statements hadn't been coerced.

Through the years, Cook County judges have largely ignored that direction, suppressing confessions only when the evidence of coercion is overwhelming—and often not even then.

Lawyers for Andrew Wilson, the man who the city ultimately admitted was tortured by Commander Burge at Area 2, had been unable to convince a judge at 26th Street that his confession had been beaten out of him. At his suppression hearing in 1983, doctors testified that Wilson had sustained at least fourteen fresh injuries the day of his interrogation—cuts that needed stitching on his head, bruises on his chin and torso, and burns on his chest and leg consistent with his account that he'd been forced against a radiator and electically shocked. The interrogating detectives and the felony review attorney who took the confession insisted that Wilson hadn't been mistreated in any way at Area 2, and the judge deemed the confession voluntary. Wilson was convicted and sentenced to death, but the state supreme court ruled that the confession should have been suppressed. Wilson was convicted on retrial without the confession and sentenced to natural life.

In October 1983—four months before Leroy Orange was interrogated at Area 2—twenty-one-year-old Gregory Banks confessed there to a murder and armed robbery. At his suppression hearing, Banks said that during his thirty-one hours at the station he was beaten with a flashlight and kicked in his side, stomach, and ankles. Accourding to Banks, one detective put a gun into his mouth and threatened to blow his head off; when he continued to assert his innocence, another detective told him, "We have something for niggers," and put a plastic bag over his head.

Banks arrived at the Cook County jail with numerous lumps and bruises. But eight police officers and the felony review attorney took the stand and denied that there'd been any abuse at the station. Several detectives maintained that Banks had tried to escape and had been tackled on a stairwell. But a jail doctor said Banks's injuries were not consistent with a fall down stairs—he'd more likely been struck repeatedly with a blunt object. The judge decided that Banks had confessed voluntarily. In 1985 he was convicted and sentenced to fifty years.

The appellate court reversed the conviction in 1989. Justice Dom Rizzi observed in the ruling that trial judges who "do not courageously and forthrightly exercise their responsibility to suppress confessions ... pervert our criminal justice system" as much as the detectives who do the coercing. The state declined to retry Banks without his confession. In 1993 the city paid him $92,500 to settle the suit he filed.

Leroy Orange didn't even have a suppression hearing before his trial. His lawyer then, Earl Washington, filed a motion to suppress the confession, but when the judge deemed it legally insufficient, he failed to file another one. It therefore was the jury and not the judge who rejected Orange's claim that he was tortured and who accepted the word of the authorities that he hadn't been abused or coerced in any way.

CHICAGO POLICE LIE "pervasively" in court and "throughout the investigative process"—and their perjury is "nurtured by prosecutors and tolerated by judges," Myron Orfield asserted in the *University of Colorado Law Review* in 1992.

Orfield's conclusions were based on the assessments of forty-one Cook County judges, prosecutors, and public defenders he interviewed and surveyed. For a 1987 study Orfield had interviewed Chicago narcotics officers, the majority of whom also said police lie in court. Orfield conducted these studies as a research associate at the University of Chicago Law School. He later served as a special assistant attorney general in Minnesota and a Minnesota state representative.

In the court study, 92 percent of the respondents said police lie "at least some of the time" in motions to suppress evidence; 22 percent said police lie more than half the time. Prosecutors acknowledged telling their police witnesses what they needed to say on the stand if a case was to be won.

Orfield found a "sliding scale of procedural justice" in Cook County. The bigger the case, most respondents said, the more likely police were to lie. "If you got a person for a murder or who sells narcotics to grade school kids, the police are more tempted to alter or fudge their testimony," a prosecutor said. But most respondents also said judges were less likely to challenge a police officer's veracity, and suppress evidence, in such "heater" cases, even when a judge suspected an officer was lying. "In the criminal courts in Chicago, the general rule is, the hotter the heater, the less likely the judge will protect the defendant's constitutional rights," Orfield said. Seventy-two percent of the respondents, including 58 percent of the judges, said the judges were less likely than they should be to find police testimony incredible in heater cases. Many respondents commented that police testimony "that would not pass muster in a small case suddenly becomes believable in a big case," Orfield noted. He said judges don't suppress evidence in heater cases both because of their personal revulsion to violent crimes and because of their fear of adverse publicity. "Judges can afford to have principles in a small case," a public defender in Orfield's study said.

ORANGE'S REQUEST to have his torture allegations reconsidered will be granted only if Locallo is willing to entertain the possibility that the detectives, and possibly the felony review lawyer who took Orange's confession, lied about the circumstances of his interrogation.

Locallo is a former prosecutor and the son of a police officer—and in that regard, Orange's chances seem dim.

But there also is reason for Orange to be hopeful. For in Locallo he has a judge who's learned in a variety of ways that a police officer's word isn't gospel—and who's dared to say so from the bench.

Locallo's father warned him when he became a judge not to always trust a police officer's version of events. And Locallo learned this himself as a prosecutor, most notably in the George Jones case but in other matters as well. He learned, for instance, that the "reliable informant" on whose information a police officer bases his request for a search warrant often isn't as reliable as the officer claims—if the informant exists at all.

In 1979 Locallo prosecuted a teacher and part-time musician who'd been charged with drug possession. Executing a search warrant, police had found cocaine and marijuana in the teacher's south-side motel room. In a preliminary hearing the teacher's lawyer asserted that the affidavit submitted to a judge by a police officer to secure the warrant had been a "total fabrication." In the affidavit the officer had maintained that a "reliable informant" had told him he'd bought $50 of marijuana from the defendant in his motel room at three-thirty A.M. on January 17, 1978, and that he'd seen more marijuana in the room. But at the time in question, the defendant had been playing saxophone in a band that was performing at a south-side lounge, according to affidavits from the bandleader, the owner of the lounge, and a waitress at the lounge.

The officer had also sworn in his affidavit that his informant had given him information leading to arrests in seven other drug cases in the previous year. When Judge Kenneth Wendt asked the officer to identify the seven cases, the officer was unable to do so. Wendt granted the motion to quash the search warrant and the evidence resulting from it. "He tried to con me," Judge Wendt told Locallo, referring to the officer.

As a result of that experience and others like it, Locallo says he now quizzes police officers carefully when they come to his courtroom seeking

his signature on a search warrant. The search of a person's home is a serious matter, the judge says, and he wants to feel confident he's not author-
izing it based on a perjured affidavit. (If he turns an officer down, however,
the officer can shop around for another judge willing to sign.)

Locallo's father advised him that police would falsify their testimony in
drug cases when they'd found the drugs after an illegal search. August
Locallo recalls: "I told him, 'Danny, when these police testify that they
saw a suspect walking down the street and he dropped the package, it's
usually bullshit. You can catch a guy seven days a week by just saying he
dropped it.'"

His son hasn't limited his distrust of police testimony to penny-ante
drug cases. In November 1997 Locallo considered a motion to suppress
evidence of two women charged with trafficking five kilos of cocaine—
$475,000 worth. The women faced 30 to 120 years if convicted. They'd
been arrested at Midway Airport after a DEA agent found bricks of
cocaine taped to their abdomens. The women, who were black, were being
watched because they'd flown to Chicago from Los Angeles on one-way
tickets bought with cash by two male Hispanics shortly before the flight.
The case turned on whether the women had consented to the search, as the
DEA agent and her partner contended, or whether they'd been forced to
submit to it, as the defendants maintained. Locallo said he doubted that
someone with bundles of cocaine under her clothes would freely agree to
a search. He suppressed the evidence, and the charges against the two
women were dropped.

In written opinions in cases in which Locallo has suppressed evidence
because he's disbelieved a police officer, he's sometimes quoted liberally
from a landmark 1886 U.S. Supreme Court case, *Boyd v. United States*.
"Illegitimate and unconstitutional practices get their first footing . . . by
silent approaches and slight deviations from legal modes of procedure,"
Locallo has quoted from *Boyd*. "It is the duty of the courts to be watchful
for the constitutional rights of the citizen, and against any stealthy
encroachments thereon."

Locallo says he realizes that many people think judges are handcuffing
cops by scrutinizing their every action and claim. "But the Constitution
was set up to guard against the abuses of law enforcement," he says.

When it comes to the interrogation room, though, Locallo's concerns
about the abuses of law enforcement seem in line with the "sliding scale"
that Myron Orfield noted in the Cook County courts. He's shown a much
greater willingness to suppress evidence in drug cases than in cases involving violent crimes. Despite his exposure to police duplicity, he's been as

reluctant as his colleagues at 26th Street to suppress confessions. By his own estimate, he's been asked at least a hundred times to suppress a confession by a defendant who's alleged coercion. After listening to the denials of detectives, and usually also of the felony review attorney who took the confession, Locallo has ruled in every single instance that the defendant confessed voluntarily.

ELEVEN

Father and Son

WHAT MORE COULD a father do to help his son, once the son got charged with a serious crime, than Frank "Toots" Caruso has done to help Frank Caruso Jr.?

He's hired the best defense lawyers money can buy. Edward Genson and Sam Adam have represented a congressman, state legislators, aldermen, judges, attorneys, doctors, real estate developers, commodities brokers, and a host of other wealthy businessmen. Now they'll be going to bat for an eighteen-year-old from Bridgeport. At 26th Street most lawyers would be happy to get $5,000 for an attempted murder case that went to trial. A source close to Genson says Caruso's defense will easily run into six figures.

The elder Caruso has also fought to counter the news stories portraying his son as a despicable racist. He's promoted "racial healing" prayer services in Bridgeport and in an adjacent black community, services that have attracted overflowing multiracial crowds. B. Herbert Martin, the prominent black minister who leads the services, stresses the advantages of forgiveness over vengeance, although he's also assured reporters it is "highly unlikely" that Caruso beat Lenard Clark.

Father and son are in 302 on a morning in late spring, along with defense lawyer Genson. Genson is going to make a special request to Locallo today regarding Caruso's curfew. A condition of Caruso's bond requires him to be home between seven P.M. and seven A.M., except when he's working in his father's cigar shop. Caruso's first cousin is getting married on Saturday at Holy Name Cathedral downtown, and Caruso would like the curfew extended so he can attend not only the wedding that afternoon but also the reception at the Hilton that evening.

Locallo isn't in the courtroom when the Carusos and Genson arrive shortly after ten. The judge started court at nine-thirty sharp, but at ten he left to attend a graduation ceremony at the Cook County boot camp. (The boot camp, two blocks southeast of the courthouse, is a prison alternative for nonviolent offenders, and Locallo has been a big supporter of it.) Deputy Guerrero informs Genson that the judge should be back shortly. Genson communicates this to the Carusos, then takes a seat at the defense table, while the Carusos slide into a bench in the gallery.

The younger Caruso is short, slight, and clean-shaven, with trimmed dark hair, brown eyes, and an olive complexion. He's wearing a white dress shirt and brown dress slacks. He looks anything but relaxed. This morning, as he has the other times he's been in court for his case, he mainly studies the ceiling tiles or stares vacantly at the walls while he waits. His brow is constantly furrowed, and he nibbles regularly on his lips, repairing the damage now and then with lip balm.

His fifty-three-year-old father is short and pudgy, with graying curly hair. He's more casually dressed than Frank Junior—sport shirt, blue jeans, sneakers. He accompanies his son for every pretrial date and uses any waiting time to lobby people in the gallery and in the hallways. "Say a prayer for us, will you?" he'll implore strangers; or he'll caution them, "Don't believe all the things you hear about this case."

This morning he tells me again that this is a political prosecution. The powers-that-be in Chicago want Frank Junior's head, whether he's innocent or guilty, he says, because they fear the racial fallout if he's acquitted. He says the authorities have made their attitude clear ever since Frank Junior was arrested fourteen months ago. County officials have badgered the family with phone calls, ostensibly to make certain Frank Junior isn't breaking his curfew. State's attorney's investigators follow Frank Junior's mother, Sherry Caruso, when she goes shopping, he says. Sherry had also come to court for every pretrial date until recently, when she started experiencing chest pains—which Caruso Senior attributes to the harassment.

"There's a saying the Romans had," he says. "I know it better in Italian, but it's like, 'When the people who are supposed to protect us become the aggressors, the world is in turmoil.'"

The allegations in the papers about the family's mob ties are entirely unfair to Frank Junior, he says. Not only are they mere innuendo, but they concern Frank Junior's relatives and ancestors as opposed to Frank Junior himself—yet they're used to tarnish Frank Junior.

There's no way Frank Junior will get an open-minded jury, his father goes on, given how reporters have convicted him in their stories. The reporters have focused on the racial prejudice involved in the Bridgeport attack, while fostering another kind of bigotry, he says—the idea "that if you're Italian, you must be guilty of something."

THE CHARGE THAT the Carusos are mob connected has usually been made by law enforcement sources, who maintain that Frank Junior's father has been an active member of the "outfit," as the mob is usually called in Chicago, and that his grandfather was an outfit gambling boss. But the family's mob connections are older than that.

Frank Junior's great-grandfather, Bruno Roti, came to Chicago from Italy in 1909, at the age of twenty-eight. He was a beer distributor and a leader of the Democratic Club in the city's First Ward—a ward not known for its integrity. He was questioned about numerous murders and bombings, including a bombing in front of a judge's house in 1932, and each time he was cleared.

In the 1940s a growing number of blacks were moving into the neighborhood near the Rotis' home, on 23rd Street near Princeton—nine blocks due north of where Lenard Clark would be beaten and stomped a half century later. A series of arson fires in 1946 drove many blacks from the neighborhood. The city's black-owned newspaper, the *Chicago Defender,* suggested that the wave of fires had at least the tacit approval of local politicians and noted that the community was dominated by the "sometimes paternal, sometimes ominous influence of Bruno Roti." The *Defender* acknowledged that Roti and his sons, most of whom were on the city payroll, had come to the aid of burned-out victims, arranging relief and offering them jobs. But the paper was suspicious of the Rotis' professed ignorance of the origin of the fires, noting that the Rotis would "give the go signal or the halt signal" for whatever happened in the neighborhood.

When Bruno Roti died in 1957, at age seventy-seven, he was sent off in style, with a marching band, fourteen flower cars, a dozen limousines, and scores of Cadillacs. "Hoodlums, politicians, and police characters from all over the Midwest" attended his funeral, according to the *Chicago Daily News.*

Several of his six sons were murder suspects—one was picked up regarding the slaying of a black man, another for allegedly killing a Chinese man, another for allegedly killing a Mexican—but all were cleared. His son Fred had a little less luck with the law, going to federal prison in 1993, at the age of seventy-three, for fixing a civil court case and a city zoning change. Before his conviction, Fred Roti had been a state senator for six years and a Chicago alderman for twenty-two.

Upon Bruno Roti's death, control of gambling in the area near the Roti home was inherited by a son-in-law, Frank "Skid" Caruso—Frank Junior's grandfather. As the outfit's boss of the 26th Street Crew, Skid Caruso was arrested repeatedly for gambling but spent little time in jail. In 1970 a state investigative commission listed him in the "upper stratum" of Chicago juice racketeers. (*Juice racketeering* consists of making loans with exorbitant interest rates and relying on threats and violence when necessary to collect payments.)

Skid's son Frank, also known as "Toots"—the present Caruso Senior—worked in the 26th Street Crew when he was younger, moving up to a supervisory role when Skid died in 1983, according to federal authorities. Caruso Senior has also held office in several Chicago unions representing low-skilled laborers. He quit one post in 1995 the day after investigators probing that union notified him that they wanted to question him about his alleged mob ties. But now, in 1998, he's still an associate director of a $775 million union pension fund.

At a hearing in 1997 on mob influence in the Chicago affiliate of the Laborers International, Charles Bills, an outfit turncoat, described growing up with Toots Caruso. Bills said that Toots's father had assigned him to look after Toots, making it clear to Bills his intention to "kill everybody if anything happens to Toots or if he gets in any kind of trouble." Bills said he sometimes got in fights on Toots's behalf, fights that started when "somebody looked at his girl funny." Toots Caruso never had to pay a dime in any of the neighborhood restaurants in which he ate, and he could get served in any bar before he was of drinking age, according to Bills. "He was like a little prince in the neighborhood," Bills said.

Toots Caruso has never been convicted of any crime. In 1982 he and three Bridgeport friends were charged by federal authorities with extortion, but all four men were acquitted.

"NOBODY GIVES A SHIT whether he's guilty or innocent," Ed Genson says at the defense table, about his client Frank Junior. It's ten forty-five, but Locallo hasn't returned from the boot camp graduation yet. Like the elder Caruso, Genson seizes every opportunity to lobby for Frank Junior in the court of public opinion. "People say, 'It will deter other racists if he's convicted,'" Genson says. "This is what you get from the government all the time—'We need to send a message'—as opposed to considering the individual case. I find it obscene when people want to fuck a guy up for principle."

The anti-Caruso sentiment is such that even friends and family urged Genson not to take the case, he says. "My wife, my kids, people I work

with—they all said, 'It won't be good for your reputation.' I was having dinner at a country club in Atlanta, and two people at the table wouldn't talk to
me when they found out I was involved in this case. If ever a lawyer is supposed to take a case, it's when it's unpopular. I was brought up to believe that
if you don't take a case because it's unpopular, you're not being a lawyer."

The suggestion in the newspapers that Mike Cutler was killed because
he was a witness against Caruso is another example of the prejudice his
client must contend with, Genson says. There's no reason to believe the
killing was related to anything but a robbery attempt, he says: "Don't you
think if it was a hit, police would have said so? Do you know how much
the police wanted it to be a hit? Do you know how much the prosecutors
wanted it to be a hit?"

He's made repeated change-of-venue motions. In one such motion he
wrote that due to the media reports about the Bridgeport attack, "any
prospective juror would perceive that a vote of not guilty would constitute
a vote against the Mayor of the City of Chicago, a vote against the head of
Operation PUSH [Jesse Jackson], a vote against racial relations, a vote in
favor of race riots, indeed, a vote against the President of the United
States." Locallo has rejected all the change-of-venue motions. He has
pointed out that under the law jurors needn't be unfamiliar with a case; as
long as they promise to put aside what they've heard, and to base their verdict on what's presented in court, they can serve. Locallo has told Genson
he expects to be able to find enough jurors who meet that standard here in
Cook County. The judge also distrusts Genson's requests to move the trial,
he'll say later. He figures Genson simply wants the case moved to a whiter
county from which he can pick a whiter jury. In one pretrial hearing,
Locallo facetiously offered to move the case to Cairo, a majority-black city
in southern Illinois.

Genson tells me this morning that he's pessimistic about Caruso's
chances. He says he's told Caruso and his parents the best they should
expect is a hung jury, which would force a retrial. The second-best outcome, he's told them, would be an acquittal on the attempted murder
charge—which carries a term of six to thirty years—but conviction on the
lesser charges of aggravated battery (two to five years) and hate crime
(one to three years). That would result in a shorter sentence, but it'd still
mean prison. Genson says his pessimism isn't based on the evidence
against Caruso. He sees enough holes in the case that Caruso could win a
complete acquittal, he says, if not for the drumbeat for his scalp. "There
are certain kinds of cases where emotions override the facts," he says.

A fair resolution of the case would be a five-year sentence for Caruso
"with a lot of restitution so the kid [Lenard Clark] gets some money," he

says. If the prosecutors offered a deal like that, he says he'd probably take it—except that Caruso's parents "truly believe their son is innocent" and might not agree to such an offer. The issue is moot, however, he says, because the prosecutors aren't about to plea-bargain, what with all the attention on the case. The state is hoping to send Caruso away for twenty years, he says.

Genson recalls representing a black man in a civil suit stemming from a racial beating. The man's car broke down in a white neighborhood, and when he went into a tavern to call a mechanic, "he got the shit beat out of him." The men who beat the black man were convicted in criminal court, but they "only got a year, year and a half," Genson says. "If this [the Bridgeport case] was a case without heat, it wouldn't be worth anything."

GENSON HAS SPARSE, curly red hair and a thin beard. He suffers from dystonia, a genetic disorder most prevalent in Ashkenazi Jews and their descendants (his father was a Russian Jew) that makes his head bob incessantly. It bobs more vigorously when a judge, a prosecutor, or a witness annoys him, a frequent occurrence. The disorder also causes him to limp. Prosecutors have noticed his limp growing more conspicuous during jury trials. Genson says jury trials wear him out, and the limp worsens as he tires, and he'd never exaggerate it to win sympathy from jurors.

His father was a bail bondsman who dearly wanted his son to become a lawyer. Genson was not yet ten when his father began bringing him to 26th Street. He got sweet rolls for deputies and ran messages between courtrooms for clerks. His father parked him on a gallery bench for many a heater case. Genson was struck by the way lawyers could trap and humiliate a witness on cross. "*That's* what I want to do," he told himself.

His father brought home books discarded by lawyers for his son to read. Genson devoured them, even those laden with the dry and obscure prose of the criminal code. The writings of and about Clarence Darrow moved him. He pictured himself winning justice for the downtrodden. When he started practicing at 26th Street in the mid-1960s, many of his clients were poor. But in 1973 he won a federal fraud case for Jimmy "the Bomber" Catuara, rackets boss for the outfit on the far southwest side and in the southwest suburbs. Soon reputed mobsters were displacing the downtrodden as his clients. Then came politicians charged with corruption, businessmen accused of fraud, and indicted judges and lawyers—clients who could afford him.

Genson prepares for cases prodigiously. He's a fierce cross-examiner, and he pulls out all the stops for his clients. He once begged a jury to send his client home to his wife and kids, gesturing to a young woman and her three children in the gallery. The client was actually childless, the woman the client's girlfriend. Genson says one of his goals when trying a case "is to make sure that no one on the other side wants to ever try a case against me again."

He's already helped Frank Junior avoid jail once since he was charged with the Bridgeport beating. In August 1997, after a Bridgeport restaurant owner said Frank Junior had threatened to burn her place down, prosecutors asked Locallo to revoke his bond and jail him. In a hearing before Locallo, the restaurant owner, an elderly woman, testified that a young man had parked his car in her lot and seemed about to leave. She hollered to him that the lot was for customers only and that the car would be towed if he left it there. She said the young man yelled back, "Fuck you, motherfucker, I'll burn you," before returning to his car and screeching away. She saw the license plate: ITALIA. That plate was registered to a car belonging to the Carusos. But Genson argued that many cars bore decorative ITALIA plates, and that the woman might have seen a car with one of those. And Locallo ruled that since the restaurant owner wasn't asked right after the incident to pick the offender out of a lineup, the evidence was insufficient to revoke Caruso's bond. But the judge added that although he'd granted previous requests to extend Caruso's curfew to allow him to attend novenas and to visit his grandparents, he'd no longer do so.

It was Genson who defended Caruso Senior when he was charged with extortion in 1982. During that trial jurors heard undercover recordings in which one of Caruso's codefendants threatened to stick an ice pick into the head of a man who was tardy on a juice loan, or to cut his heart out. In his closing argument Genson mocked the government's case: "It's a lot of nonsense and it's a lot of Hollywood and it's a lot of showtime. . . . What you got is guys that hang around the street corner in the old neighborhood. You don't got no juice gang." He asked the jury "to stop this right now and send Frank Caruso home to his family." And the jury did.

LOCALLO RETURNS from the boot camp graduation at 11:10 and, after quickly disposing of a couple of other matters, calls the Caruso case.

Genson tells the judge about the wedding and about Caruso's desire to have his curfew extended that day until midnight, so he can also attend the reception. He adds that Caruso would be under his parents' supervision the entire time. Prosecutor Ellen Mandeltort says the state would object to the curfew being extended.

Locallo says Caruso can go to the wedding but not the reception. The judge reminds Genson of the hearing to revoke Caruso's bond last year and of his avowal then not to relax the conditions of Caruso's bond for any reason. "I'm not taking any chances with your client," he tells Genson. Then he adds forcefully, "This court will not allow him to *party* with his family. . . . The motion is respectfully denied."

AFTER THE CARUSOS and Genson have left, Locallo and the lawyers in another case go to his chambers for a conference. During the break Deputy Guerrero and probation liaison Rhonda Schullo, standing near the jury box, appraise the judge's decision regarding Caruso's request. Schullo, who's Italian American, thinks Locallo ought to have let Caruso attend the reception as well as the wedding. "Italian weddings are big things," she tells Guerrero. Guerrero shakes his head. "When I was in the army, I missed a lot of holidays," he says. "Sometimes there are things you gotta miss."

Guerrero soon is waxing prophetic on the broader matter of Chicago's ethnic conflicts. They're deeper and more complicated than commonly understood, he says. "You see, your north-side Italians don't like your south-side Italians," he tells Schullo. And Mexican Americans such as himself, from the southwest side, often don't see eye to eye with Mexican Americans from the southeast side or Mexican Americans from the north side.

Any Chicagoan who wants to stay safe needs to be aware of the variations in ethnicity and attitude from neighborhood to neighborhood, he says. He learned his lesson as a kid, when he and some Mexican American friends biked into Bridgeport and were chased out by threats, curses, and thrown bottles. Lenard Clark should have known better than to bike through Bridgeport, Guerrero tells Schullo: "I'm not saying he deserved to get beat like that. But you gotta know where you can go and where you can't go. I mean, you can say you should be able to go wherever you want, but c'mon—this is Chicago."

TWELVE

Defective Products

THE FIRST WEEK OF JUNE, Locallo puts in especially long days. When he's not on the bench, he's tapping away on the computer in his chambers, finishing up the ruling he's promised this month in a case involving more than a ton of marijuana, and updating the speech he gives each June on traffic-related law at Bradley University in Peoria. One day he gets to the courthouse at five-thirty in the morning and doesn't leave until eleven at night.

The hours seem to be wearing on the judge. He's unusually testy when Larry Bates is ushered before him the morning of June 4. Bates is in a jail uniform; he's been locked up since March 25, when Locallo ordered him into custody after he was arrested for a new drug offense while on the judge's probation. In April another judge found probable cause for the latest charge, and in May Locallo continued the case to this date at the request of Bates's lawyer, public defender Kathryn Lisco. That gave Lisco time to have Bates evaluated by the county's drug treatment agency, Treatment Alternatives for Safe Communities (TASC), to determine whether he was an acceptable candidate for treatment.

Now Lisco tells the judge that although the report hasn't arrived in the courtroom yet this morning, TASC has informed her that Bates has been deemed suitable for treatment. Lisco wants the judge to give Bates probation with treatment in exchange for his guilty plea. Locallo responds that he thinks the county's boot camp would be better for Bates—he believes its military regimen is more likely to turn a life around than a drug treatment program. (He also has a gentlemen's bet with another judge regarding who will send more defendants to the boot camp this year.) But Lisco points out that Bates, at forty-four, is too old for the boot camp—the maximum age is thirty-five.

Locallo frowns. He reminds Lisco he's given Bates probation twice for drug cases, and both times Bates has been rearrested.

"You gotta give him a chance," Lisco says.

"He's had a chance. He's had two chances," Locallo says.

Locallo passes the Bates case pending the arrival of the TASC report. A group of students from Northeastern Illinois University have been watching the morning's activities from the jury box. The judge now recesses court and invites the students to his chambers.

Lisco's partner, John Conniff, arrives, and Lisco tells him about her colloquy with Locallo regarding Bates. If another judge were reluctant to grant a third probation to a defendant, no one would bat an eye. But Locallo usually leaps at the chance to quickly shed a minor case from his call. "You think he's mad at us?" Conniff asks Lisco. "We haven't been getting enough dispositions?"

In the gallery, Bates's mother, sixty-five-year-old Ann Bates, waits patiently with one of his sisters for the judge to retake the bench. Larry Bates has what many defendants here lack: loved ones who show up for his court dates. His mother was also present for his brief appearance before Locallo last month, along with his daughter and girlfriend, and she's visited her son in the jail every week. Larry was sick last week, she says—he was having trouble stomaching jail food: "I told him, 'The food ain't *supposed* to be any good—that's part of your punishment.'"

"Sometimes he gets very depressed," she says. "He says, 'I don't like being in a place all closed up like this for this long. It's tearing me down, Mom.' I tell him, 'Don't let it do you like it does all those other people that's stuck in jail.' So many people, they just give up in there and then they come out worse than when they went in. I say, 'Don't you fall into that. You hold up.'"

The visits drain her emotionally, although she tries to hide it from her son. "He's on one side of a window, you're on the other, and you can't touch him," she says. At the end of their visits, they each press a hand against the glass.

She says Larry was an obedient boy who loved to work, even as a youngster, and who sometimes made the honor roll. She thinks his troubles started when he married the woman who ultimately drowned their baby daughter in 1977 and was subsequently diagnosed as paranoid schizophrenic, adjudged insane, and institutionalized. The sudden loss of his wife and daughter "tore him up all to pieces. He never was right after that," she says. He started "picking up different habits" like excessive drinking and drug use. "I don't blame it all on that," she says. "I told him, 'We all lose people sometime, but you got to get over that and move on.' But— some people are stronger than others."

She says her son is foolish to be messing with drugs, but she thinks the war on drugs is foolish, too. "They can lock up Larry and thirty or forty thousand like him, it ain't gonna do no good. All it does is make them more bitter and more resentful. They should get these people real jobs. But they just want to keep putting these Negro boys in jail."

Locallo returns to the bench, and Lisco resumes her pitch on behalf of Bates. She tells the judge that Bates is the father of three and a widower whose wife died in 1995 after battling "depression" for years. In Lisco's brief interview with Bates in the lockup, the drowning of his daughter by his wife hadn't come up. Bates is a high school graduate with a city college certificate in auto mechanics, Lisco continues, and he's worked as a dry-waller, a roofer, and a machine operator. Neither of his previous probations included drug treatment even though he's been using for at least a decade. He's been working on his addiction in the jail's drug treatment unit while this case has been pending, Lisco says.

Locallo asks her what guarantee there is that Bates will make it through a treatment program.

"Judge, there are no guarantees in life," Lisco says. "I'm telling you that I think Mr. Bates is a good risk."

Locallo says he doesn't see what makes Bates a good risk considering how he keeps getting arrested.

Lisco asks Bates if he wants to tell the judge anything. Bates mumbles something the court reporter asks him to repeat. Raising his voice slightly, Bates says he's never really tried to do anything about his addiction, but that now he sees the need. "I think everyone deserves a second chance," he adds.

"You've had two already," Locallo says.

Lisco pipes in: "Why rush to judgment on Mr. Bates on this?"

"Because he may be taking up a bed of someone who's serious about addressing his problem," Locallo says.

Lisco insists Bates is serious.

"Yeah, at the moment of judgment everybody's serious," the judge shoots back.

"Mr. Bates sounds sincere, and I believe he is sincere," Lisco says. "And if he doesn't do what he's supposed to, you'll be right and you can sentence him accordingly."

With a sigh, Locallo surrenders. He tells Bates that for his guilty plea, he'll get probation and inpatient treatment. Bates will have to remain in the jail until a bed opens up for him in a treatment center. That could take weeks or months. Locallo gives Bates the guilty plea admonishments.

Bates whispers something to Lisco, and Lisco asks the judge if he'd consider freeing Bates next weekend so he can attend his son's high school graduation.

"No sir," Locallo snaps. "No sir."

But then the judge's thoughts shift to his own children. A year from now his daughter Lauren will be graduating from high school, his son Kevin from elementary school. He can't imagine missing those events. And so he suddenly reverses himself. He tells Bates he'll give him a recognizance bond next Thursday, the day before the graduation, allowing Bates to leave the jail for the weekend. When Bates returns to court the following Monday morning, he'll be formally sentenced. Lisco thanks the judge on behalf of Bates. Inwardly, though, she's disappointed about Locallo's change of heart, as she says later. Now she'll have to worry about Bates getting carried away during his weekend of freedom and failing to return to court, or getting brought back in handcuffs. Then this deal would be voided, and off to prison Bates would go. Plus, she'd never hear the end of it from Locallo, she tells herself.

In the gallery, Ann Bates is delighted. She understands the judge's doubts about her son's willingness to change; in fact, she shares them. "But with some people," she says, "it takes three or four hits on the head before they learn them some sense."

Larry Bates's head is swimming as he's ushered back to the lockup. One moment prison had seemed unavoidable; the next, the judge gave him not only the sentence he wanted but a weekend I-bond as well. Bates credits this to Lisco's staunch lobbying in his behalf, he says later. He's never had a PD fight so hard for him. The brief ten minutes Lisco spent quizzing him about his background through the lockup bars this morning was probably twice as long a conversation as a PD had ever had with him, he says. When I tell Locallo later about the drowning of Bates's daughter by his paranoid schizophrenic wife, the judge is immediately sympathetic. It makes Bates's struggles with drugs easier to understand, Locallo says. He adds that had he known about it, he'd have granted the request for probation and treatment a lot quicker.

LOCALLO AND HIS ONLY SISTER and one of his two brothers did well in school, mostly avoiding the kind of youthful indiscretions that would have embarrassed their police officer father. But the oldest son in the family, Victor, was a long-haired pot smoker in his teens who often clashed with his father. Shouting matches between the two were common in the house, and one of them culminated in Victor pulling a knife on August. This was when Victor was in his early twenties. The police were called, but the officers were hesitant about intervening; August ended the standoff himself by swatting the knife out of Victor's hand with his billy club. Victor was taken to a hospital, diagnosed as paranoid schizophrenic, and institutionalized for two years.

In February 1975 Victor was home on a brief furlough to celebrate his mother's birthday with his family. On the afternoon that Victor was to return to the hospital, the family gathered for birthday cake at the home of Locallo's other brother. August and Victor left the party first—August was going to drop Victor back at the hospital on his way to work after a stop at home. Locallo drove his mother home a short time later. There was an ambulance in front of the house. When they rushed inside, they found blood sprayed throughout the dining room and the paramedics working on Victor, who was unconscious with a bullet wound near his temple. August almost always locked his gun up when he was home, but this time he'd left it on a dresser while taking a shower, and Victor shot himself with it. He died soon after his arrival at the hospital. He was twenty-four.

Given the friction between Victor and August, Locallo was relieved that Victor "didn't take my dad out with him, which could have easily occurred."

Locallo believed that his brother killed himself because he had "lost hope" and because he didn't want to go back to the hospital. There was no question his death was a suicide, the judge says. But according to records from the Cook County medical examiner's office, a coroner's jury ruled the death an accident. Locallo says he presumes the jury did so "as a favor to my father" because of the stigma of suicide.

In the years before Victor killed himself, Locallo says there were times when he and his other siblings had rued the burden he'd become, particularly to their parents. "In the back of your mind you're feeling, 'Jesus, I wish this problem would just go away.' But when your thoughts become a reality, it's a lot different situation. You wish you had the last moment to say, 'I'm sorry about what's happened to you.' Because we didn't understand."

Locallo says he learned from Victor's life and death "to be more compassionate and more tolerant of people who are different. My other brother and I, and my sister, we had the same parents as Vic. But unfortunately for Vic, he had a number of things that weren't in his favor. The rest of us were able to be achievers, be successful in many aspects. Vic had a lot of good qualities, but God didn't give him the same opportunities that we had."

. . .

"INTELLIGENT PEOPLE now know that every human being is the product of the endless heredity back of him and the infinite environment
around him," Clarence Darrow told a judge in a Cook County criminal
courtroom in 1924. Darrow was asking the judge to spare the lives of
Nathan Leopold and Richard Loeb after they'd pled guilty to the kidnapping and murder of fourteen-year-old Bobbie Franks. "When I think of the
light way nature has of picking out parents and populating the earth," the
renowned defense lawyer said, "I cannot hold human beings to the same
degree of responsibility that young lawyers hold them when they are
enthusiastic in a prosecution."

Darrow argued that crime would not be reduced until the focus of
courts shifted from meting out punishment to addressing motives and
causes. "If a doctor were called on to treat typhoid fever, he would probably try to find out what kind of milk or water the patient drank, and perhaps clean out the well so that no one else could get typhoid fever from the
same source," he said. But a lawyer called on to treat a typhoid patient
"would give him thirty days in jail, and then he would think that nobody
else would dare to catch it."

The prosecutor opposing Darrow scorned his "weird" and "dangerous"
ideas. The responsibility for the Franks murder belonged to no one but the
defendants, whom he called "snakes," "cowardly perverts," and "mad dogs."

Darrow saved Leopold and Loeb from the gallows, but determinist
views such as his rarely fared well in criminal courtrooms in the 1920s.
Nor are they given much credence today at 26th Street, where the bedrock
doctrine is free will and individual responsibility.

Locallo is a strong free-choice disciple, notwithstanding what he says
he learned from his brother Victor's life. "There's nothing I'm aware of
that programs somebody to rob people or kill people," he says. "Nobody's
putting a gun to anyone's head and forcing him to do that."

As a prosecutor in 1982, Locallo won conviction of a defendant named
Mark Clements for setting a fire that killed four people. Clements was a
sixteen-year-old eighth-grader when he was charged with the murders.
He'd become a ward of the state at age three after his parents abandoned
him. He had an IQ of 58. At his sentencing hearing before Judge Cousins,
public defender Brian Dosch said the state bore some responsibility for
how Clements had turned out, given that he'd been its ward most of his life
and it had done little to set him on a proper path. Locallo responded that
the state didn't set the fire, Clements did. Clements delivered a rambling
plea for mercy, sketching his troubled childhood and talking about racism
in society. He spoke for an hour and fifty-five minutes. (Clements's other

lawyer, Bob Cooney, says it was the longest speech by a defendant before sentencing he'd ever heard "by about an hour and fifty-four minutes.") Clements was wasting his breath; a life sentence was mandatory with the multiple-murder conviction. Locallo was unmoved by the speech. "I felt, 'So what?'" As Clements talked on and on, Locallo says he was mainly thinking about his next case.

EVERY FEW WEEKS this spring and summer Dan Young Jr. is steered by guards from his bunk in the jail's mental health unit, through the tunnels, and up on the elevator to the lockup behind Courtroom 302. The other prisoners in the lockup are called one by one before the judge; by lunchtime, Young frequently has the lockup to himself. After lunch one of the deputies walks him out to the defense table in the courtroom, where he takes a seat next to Mr. Mayfield, his PD. Then Mr. Mayfield and the lady prosecutor and Judge Locallo and the witnesses say Dan Young this and Dan Young that for most of the afternoon. Then he goes back to his bunk in the jail.

Young is a short, slight, thirty-seven-year-old African American with wide, wondering eyes and a jutting jaw. His IQ is in the fifties. "He knows the judge is going to make a ruling," public defender Mike Mayfield says. "He doesn't really know what it's about. He just knows that he wants to go home."

That won't be happening anytime soon—not without help from Locallo. Young is doing life for a murder and sexual assault. An appellate public defender recently won him a hearing to determine whether the medicine he was being given in the jail at the time of his trial, in 1994, impaired his fitness for trial—that is, whether the drugs made him too groggy or disoriented to understand the nature of the proceedings and to help his lawyer defend him. If Locallo rules that the drugs did indeed impair Young's fitness, Young will get a new trial.

In May two county psychiatrists testified about the typical effects of the medicine Young was given in the jail at the time of his trial, lithium, a mood stabilizer used to treat manic depression, and Stelazine, an antipsychotic. But the psychiatrists told Locallo their exams of Young showed no signs of these disorders, and they weren't sure why he was given the drugs. They were powerful medicines with sedating qualities, the psychiatrists said, but they doubted they made Young particularly sleepy at his trial—he'd been on them for months by then and likely would have developed a tolerance.

Judge Thomas Durkin, who presided over the trial, also testified in May. He allowed that Young had seemed to doze at times during the trial and that he'd also made some outbursts. According to the trial transcript, Young had called out during the testimony of one witness, "You don't even know me"; another time he'd suddenly announced from the defense table, "I didn't kill Kathy Morgan. I didn't kill anybody." But Durkin testified that nothing Young did during the trial made him question the defendant's fitness.

That assessment by Judge Durkin hurt Young's chances of a favorable ruling from Locallo, especially given Locallo's relationship with Durkin. Locallo considered Durkin a friend, and before Durkin left 26th Street in 1994 for a civil courtroom, Locallo considered him a mentor as well. "He was a great source of knowledge, has good common sense, a great sense of humor—he's just a wonderful man," Locallo says.

If a potential juror knew a witness in a case and had such a high opinion of him or her, the potential juror would almost certainly be dismissed. But when the appellate or supreme court sends cases back to 26th Street for hearings, judges are frequently called upon to appraise decisions made by colleagues. The judges almost never recuse themselves in such situations; it's presumed they won't let their personal relationships affect their rulings.

On the afternoon of June 9 public defender Mayfield calls Cheryl Bormann, a fellow PD, to testify about Young's behavior during his trial. Bormann represented a codefendant of Young's at the trial, so she sat at the defense table near Young. He was a constant distraction, she tells Locallo. She remembers him frequently rolling his fingers across the table and tapping his feet, as if he were playing a piano. Once when she was at a lectern questioning a witness, she noticed that the jurors' attention was on the defense table. She glanced over and saw Young looking "like something out of *The Exorcist*"—he had one arm in the air "like it was reaching for something that was above him" and his face turned backward. Bormann also observed Young in the courtroom lockup during breaks in the trial while she was talking with her client. He was often "incredibly agitated, walking in circles, babbling to himself," so the other inmates kept their distance, she says.

The second witness this particular afternoon is Steve Greenberg, the lawyer who defended Young at his trial. Greenberg recalls Young contorting his body at the defense table and dozing through some of the testimony. Greenberg says he realized when he first met Young that he was "not a normal functioning adult." But whereas before the trial Young had been "somewhat helpful in terms of describing how he was arrested and what had occurred," during the trial he was "basically no help at all, totally worthless in terms of an assistance," Greenberg says. "I mean, I felt like I was all alone."

On the state's cross-examination, Greenberg allows that during the trial he never described for the record his client's odd body movements; nor did he tell Judge Durkin about the difficulty he was having with Young. This was only his second or third murder trial, and he didn't know it might prove important to put such matters on the record, Greenberg says.

After Greenberg is excused, Locallo continues the hearing until July.

In the hallway outside the courtroom, Greenberg tells me he usually charges $5,000 to $10,000 for a murder trial; but he'd continued representing Young even when it became clear Young's mother couldn't pay him any more than the $1,000 she gave him originally. He simply felt sorry for Young, Greenberg says. "He was the most disadvantaged of the disadvantaged—the poor retarded guy nobody cared about."

Greenberg asked for a psychiatric evaluation of Young before the trial. He didn't see how Young could meaningfully help him put on a defense, given the extent of his retardation. But two psychiatrists had deemed Young fit for trial. Then he was convicted, largely on the basis of a confession he'd signed.

"The case makes me sick to my stomach," Greenberg says. "I don't think Dan Young said any of that stuff that's in his confession. I have no doubt that the detectives concocted his statement. There's only a couple of defendants whose cases I've lost who I thought were innocent, and he's one of them."

YOUNG WAS SLOW to walk and talk. As a child in Yazoo City, Mississippi, he would sometimes "foam at his mouth like a mad dog," his mother, Lillie Young, testified at his trial in 1994. Other children in the neighborhood "didn't never want to play with him when he was coming up," she said. "All the other kids used to call him, you know, crazy, and they just didn't—they didn't like the way he looked."

In 1969 Lillie Young and her five children moved to Chicago. (Later she had a sixth child, who's also retarded.) The family settled on the south side, and Lillie enrolled Dan, then age nine, in school for the first time. He was placed in classes for the trainable mentally handicapped, the lowest level of classes for retarded children. When he was about twenty, an acquaintance introduced him to booze, according to his mother, and soon he'd do most anything for a drink. He'd walk into a tavern, announce the arrival of the Cigar Man, put five cigars in his mouth, and light them. Sometimes he'd light cigarettes in his ears as well. A glass of wine was a sufficient reward. The police picked him up on occasion for being drunk and disorderly. They'd keep him in their lockup overnight and let him go in the morning.

On a March evening in 1992 detectives brought Young in for questioning about a sexual assault and murder.

That crime had occurred in October 1990. While putting out a blaze in an abandoned building in Englewood, a south-side slum, firefighters had found the body of thirty-nine-year-old Kathy Morgan. She was nearly naked, and her face was bruised and swollen. Wooden dowels had been shoved deep inside her rectum and into her vagina. The medical examiner attributed her death to the blunt trauma to her head and the internal injuries caused by the dowels. The extensive internal bleeding made it impossible to say whether semen was present.

The Morgan case soon was just another of Englewood's many unsolved rapes and murders. But the night before the detectives picked up Young, they'd stumbled onto a lead while working on another case. Detectives were questioning eighteen-year-old Harold Hill about a robbery when, according to the detectives, Hill said he knew something about the Morgan murder. Hill subsequently confessed that he and two other men had forced Morgan into an abandoned building and raped and killed her before torching the building. He identified the other two offenders as Dan Young and Peter Williams.

Young, who'd been living in Englewood seven blocks from Morgan's apartment, at first denied any involvement in the crime. But several hours later he admitted joining in the attack with "Harry" and "Pete," according to detectives. An assistant state's attorney wrote up his confession. Young can't read and can write just a few words, but he could sign his name to a confession.

When the detectives picked up nineteen-year-old Peter Williams, he too at first denied any involvement in the crime. But before long he gave a detailed, court-reported confession, in which he acknowledged committing the crime with Hill and Young.

After Williams signed his confession, however, he asked a detective not involved in his interrogation when exactly this crime had occurred. The detective gave him the date—October 14, 1990. Williams said he was pretty sure he was in jail that day. Jail records confirmed that he was locked up on a drug charge from September 26 to October 25, 1990, so he wasn't charged in the Morgan case. But Young and Hill still were, even though they'd confessed to doing the crime with a man who was locked up.

Williams testified for Young and Hill at their trial. He told the jury that during his interrogation, a detective had slapped him in the face and hit him in the chest and legs with a blackjack and had told him he'd never go home again if he didn't cooperate. Williams said the detective showed him photos of the crime scene and drilled him on the details of the rape and murder, and he'd then spat the story out in front of the court reporter. The lawyers representing Young and Hill argued that their clients, likewise, had been coerced into false confessions. Young's lawyer, Greenberg, told the jury that Young, the "neighborhood idiot," would have signed the confession in exchange for an M&M. Young testified that he didn't rape or kill Morgan and that he signed the confession after the detectives threatened him, kicked him, hit him in his stomach, and "tore my fifty-dollar coat up."

But several detectives testified that they didn't coerce Young, Hill, or Williams in any way. Separate juries convicted both Young and Hill, and Judge Durkin sentenced them to life.

At Young's sentencing hearing, the prosecutor declared him "not fixable." Judge Durkin, who had referred to Young during hearings in the case as a "mental defect" and a "defective product," conceded that "life hasn't been fair to Mr. Young," that "he was dealt something less than a full hand." But the judge quickly added that Young "chose, and the operative word here is *chose*," to involve himself in Morgan's rape and murder. When Durkin asked Young if he wanted to say anything before sentencing, Young responded, "I'm going to the penitentiary for something I didn't do."

THE SPECIAL SUSCEPTIBILITY of the mentally retarded to the giving of false confessions has long been recognized by experts in retardation. "The retarded are particularly vulnerable to an atmosphere of threats and coercion, as well as to one of friendliness designed to induce confidence and cooperation," John F. Kennedy's President's Panel on Mental Retardation observed in 1963. "If a confession will please, it may be gladly given."

Since it was first published in 1962, the book *Criminal Interrogation and Confessions,* by Fred Inbau and John Reid, has been considered the leading authority on interrogation by many police departments, including Chicago's. The latest edition, published in 2001, includes a new chapter on "Distinguishing Between True and False Confessions," which concedes that according to "anecdotal accounts," a high proportion of false confessions are obtained from "mentally handicapped" suspects. A suspect with mental disabilities "generally lacks assertiveness and experiences diminished self-confidence," the book says. "In many cases he will have a heightened respect for authority and experience inappropriate self-doubt," and therefore may be "more susceptible to offering a false admission when exposed to active persuasion." The new chapter advises investigators to use persuasive tactics cautiously with such suspects, to rely instead primarily on "simple logic to convince the suspect to tell the truth," and to "take great care in obtaining corroborative information to verify the trustworthiness of the statement."

But in this latest edition, as in earlier ones, investigators also are advised that they "may have to resort to dramatic tones and gestures" with unintelligent subjects, and that it "may even become necessary at times to invoke some feigned displays of impatience." The book counsels that "throughout the interrogation of an unintelligent, uneducated offender with a low cultural background, the investigator must maintain a positive attitude, without ever relenting in the display of a position of certainty regarding the suspect's guilt (unless there are clear behavioral indications reflecting truthfulness). It is only a matter of how, when, where, or why the offender did the act in question."

Before Young's trial, Greenberg asked Judge Durkin to suppress his confession on the grounds that Young's retardation had rendered him incapable of understanding his Miranda rights and the implications of waiving them. The landmark *Miranda v. Arizona* ruling of 1966 not only requires that authorities inform anyone taken into custody of his right to a lawyer and to remain silent; it also imposes a "heavy burden" on the state to show that anyone who waives those rights and talks to police does so "knowingly and intelligently."

But abiding by this requirement—like abiding by the requirement that a confession be given "voluntarily"—would result in the freeing of a not-inconsiderable number of defendants who'd confessed to dreadful crimes. So judges instead have frequently found the decision to decline a lawyer and speak to police to be knowing and intelligent even when it's made by a person in his early teens or with an IQ in the fifties.

The two psychiatrists who deemed Young fit for trial had also told Judge Durkin that Young was too retarded to knowingly and intelligently waive his Miranda rights. So had the third mental health expert who evaluated Young, Dr. Edward Blumstein, director of the psychology department for the Cook County courts. Blumstein told Durkin that Young had the mental age of a six- or seven-year-old. "This man is not simply slow," Blumstein testified. "This man is not merely mildly retarded. This man has very serious and severe intellectual deficits."

But Mike Rogers, the assistant state's attorney who wrote up Young's confession, testified he'd worked with retarded children in a recreation program his senior year of high school and therefore felt he knew how to explain something so a retarded person could grasp it. Rogers maintained he gave the Miranda rights slowly and plainly to Young, asking him questions to make sure he understood them.

Judge Durkin decided that the "extensive experience" of prosecutor

Rogers with the retarded kids in the recreation program trumped the experience of the three doctors on the Miranda issue. Young may have been a "mental defect" and a "defective product," as Durkin had called him, but he had "exercised sufficient intellectual competence" in deciding to talk with police.

Locallo likewise thinks a retarded person can intelligently waive Miranda if the rights are carefully explained to him.

The authors of a study published in the *University of Chicago Law Review* in 2002 tested that idea. The authors read the Miranda warnings to forty-nine mentally retarded persons who had an average IQ of 55.5. The subjects were given simplified synonyms for the key words in the warnings, then were tested on their understanding of the warnings. A control group of nondisabled subjects displayed an overall comprehension of the Miranda warnings, but the retarded subjects didn't understand the key words of the warnings, or the simplified synonyms, or the basic purposes of the warnings, or the implications of waiving Miranda rights. The study's authors concluded that waivers of Miranda rights by retarded persons "are 'voluntary, knowing, and intelligent' only if we are willing to manipulate and distort the very meaning of these terms."

One of the detectives who helped get the confessions to the Morgan murder, Kenneth Boudreau, has had a checkered career. In 1995, Boudreau got a murder confession from a man who was later exonerated by DNA evidence. That defendant, Derrick Flewellen, maintained he signed his confession after Boudreau slapped him, choked him, and slammed him against a wall. Flewellen, who was locked up for four and a half years before he was cleared, sued the city and won a settlement of $250,000.

Boudreau has also gotten murder confessions from at least three other retarded suspects who were acquitted at trial, and from a thirteen-year-old with an IQ of 73 whose confession was suppressed by a judge who ruled that the youth couldn't have intelligently waived his Miranda rights.

Boudreau, who has received numerous commendations during his career, once served as a detective under Jon Burge, the commander who ultimately was fired for torturing suspects at Area 2. Like many police officers, Boudreau helped pay for Burge's defense when he was facing those charges by selling raffle tickets and contributing money.

BECAUSE OF THE MEDICINE Young was being given the year of his trial (1994), he was brought to the jail hospital monthly that year for brief evaluations. Judge Durkin had ruled that Young was fit for trial, that he could assist his lawyer in his defense, and that he understood the nature and purpose of the proceedings against him. Young's understanding of the proceedings against him apparently included the idea that his release was imminent: every month, according to jail hospital records, he told the doctor or the aide who saw him that he was going home soon. He was also seen in the hospital after he was convicted but before he was sentenced. "I should be going home pretty soon," Young said again.

Now, four years later, during the hearings in Locallo's courtroom, he still seems blissfully unaware of his life sentence. Deputy Laura Rhodes says, "Once he told me, 'My mama's going to Mississippi next month, I hope I can go, too.' I said, 'Yeah, I hope you can go, too.'"

When Young was born in 1960, the nation's mentally impaired were far more likely to end up in a mental hospital than they are today. The rate of hospitalization for the mentally ill declined from 400 per 100,000 in 1960 to less than 50 per 100,000 by 1990. The deinstitutionalization movement that began in the 1970s was supposed to provide a higher quality of life for the mentally retarded and mentally ill, in community settings, at less cost for government. But the money promised for community services for the deinstitutionalized wasn't provided, and many of the mentally disabled have wound up homeless, or in a different kind of institution—a jail or prison. The Department of Justice estimated in 1999 that 16 percent of the inmates in U.S. jails and prisons were mentally ill. That would equal 333,000 of the current inmate population—which doesn't include the number of mentally retarded inmates. Retardation often isn't formally identified in jails and prisons, so estimates of its incidence are less certain. The number of patients in state and county mental hospitals has dropped from 370,000 in 1969 to 55,000 in the year 2000.

Despite the prevalence of mental disabilities among defendants, and notwithstanding a widespread public belief that insanity acquittals are common, insanity defenses are rarely even attempted. An eight-state study funded by the National Institute of Mental Health, published in 1991, showed that the insanity defense was raised in less than one percent of all felony cases and was successful only 26 percent of the time it was raised. In Cook County thirty-one felony defendants were found not guilty by reason of insanity in 2003—out of thirty thousand felony cases. Nor is an insanity verdict a get-out-of-jail-free card. Insanity acquittees are almost always committed to secure mental hospitals and usually can't be released without a judge's approval. Insanity acquittees often spend more time in custody than defendants convicted of similar charges and sent to prison.

Defendants who have mental disorders or defects but are deemed able to "appreciate the criminality" of their conduct can be found guilty but mentally ill instead of insane in thirteen states, including Illinois. Such convicts go to prison and, in Illinois and most states, often receive no more mental health treatment than other prisoners.

Locallo has never had an insanity acquittal in his courtroom. An insanity defense "might work on the East Coast and the West Coast, but it doesn't go over too well in the Midwest," he says, because of the "good common sense" of midwesterners. If a person can appreciate the criminality of his conduct, "then no matter what his mental disease or defect is, he should suffer the consequences," the judge says.

The consequences suffered by mentally disabled convicts often are especially harsh. They kill themselves and try to do so far more frequently than other prisoners, and they have many more run-ins with guards and other inmates. Mentally retarded prisoners in particular often have trouble comprehending what's expected of them, which leads to frequent punishment, including solitary confinement, and sometimes to longer sentences. Retarded inmates are also more likely to be exploited and injured than other prisoners.

Deputy Guerrero doesn't believe in giving a prisoner a hard time if the prisoner hasn't caused him any problems, and Dan Young never has—he's been docile in the lockup. But after one hearing in Young's case, an idea struck Guerrero that the deputy couldn't resist.

Guerrero and Rhodes were sitting in the sheriff's station, Guerrero gazing idly at the lockup monitor, when the inspiration hit. Young was alone in the lockup, sitting on a bench. "Watch this," Guerrero said to Rhodes with an evil grin. He leaned over to the lockup mike. *"Daan Youung,"* the deputy said in a ghostly tone. *"This is God."* Guerrero and Rhodes watched on the monitor as Young's head jerked from side to side and up and down in search of the disembodied voice. Rhodes frowned and shook her head while Guerrero roared.

Locallo will ultimately decide not to grant Young a new trial. In a May 1999 ruling the judge will conclude that Young's mental functioning wasn't impaired by the psychotropic medicine he was being given at the time of his trial. He will note that nothing about Young's behavior had caused Judge Durkin to order a psychiatric examination of Young. "This court has the highest respect for the manner in which Judge Durkin has conducted himself as a member of the judiciary," Locallo will say of his friend and former mentor. "He is well aware of the due process that is owed to defendants."

LARRY BATES and his mother are the first arrivals in 302 on Monday morning, June 15, the day Bates is required to turn himself back in from his weekend I-bond.

He enjoyed his son's graduation ceremony at Orr High School, on Chicago's west side. One of the school's deans, Thomas Hill, addressed the graduates, and Bates felt almost as if Hill were speaking directly to him. The dean advised the graduates to be "ready to battle being tired and disgusted because things aren't going right." And he urged them to take charge of their lives. "If you don't have any passion, get some," he said. "If you don't have any will, get some."

After the ceremony Bates and his family had ribs and cake at a relative's house. Bates declined the beers and cocktails he was repeatedly offered, opting for pop instead. A relative tried to give him a bottle of Crown Royal whisky with which to celebrate his brief freedom; he turned that down, too. Booze had led to cocaine in the past, and he was being careful about such triggers. Bates was surprised at how much temptation went with a weekend I-bond. Before he'd departed the jail, some of his fellow inmates counseled him to grab his chance and never come back, to consider moving out of state. "No, I'm trying to change my life around," Bates told them.

The graduation ceremony and the party afterward were tainted by one matter, however. Five days before the graduation, Larry's son himself had been arrested for selling drugs. Police say they saw him dealing in a westside alley and that they found 0.2 grams of crack nearby. Since it was his first arrest, he was released the next day on his own recognizance. Father and son thus both attended the graduation on I-bonds from drug cases.

In the gallery this morning, Bates blames his son's dealing on the influence of his son's cousins, who Bates says have been raking in cash on drug spots and convinced Bates's son that he could, too. "It don't take much to turn an individual to that, especially when his pockets are empty," Bates says. Over the weekend Bates told his son to think long and hard about what he was doing and warned him that jail "ain't no party." Bates says he feels guilty about being in jail when his son could use his guidance. "I hope he'll do something decent, not end up in here like his dad. All I can do is try and turn my life around, try to be a better provider and a better role model for my kids."

Locallo begins the court day by reading aloud the ruling he's written in the one-ton marijuana case. The defendants, four Hispanics in dress shirts and slacks and shiny black shoes, are clustered around an interpreter in the jury box. Their private lawyers are at the defense table. The defendants have been free on bond since shortly after their arrests, having posted $30,000 each.

Police say they caught the four men unloading bundles of marijuana from a van in a south-side garage. The officers had no search warrant, however. In a hearing on the defendants' motion to suppress the evidence, one officer testified that the garage door was open, allowing him to watch the unloading from his position behind a stockade fence, and that he could see and smell the marijuana because some of the bundles were open.

Locallo recounts the testimony for twenty-five minutes, the interpreter in the jury box struggling to keep pace. Finally, on page thirty of his thirty-one-page ruling, the judge reaches the bottom line. "This court does not believe the police version of the events surrounding the unloading of the van," Locallo says. "The first time the bundles of marijuana were observed was when the police made a warrantless entry into the garage. . . . The first time the smell of marijuana was detected was when the officer entered the garage." He suppresses the evidence. When the defendants learn this from the interpreter, they tactfully suppress their glee. The charges against them will soon be dropped.

Locallo has another drug case on his docket this morning, involving two white defendants, Larry Ramacci and Richard Wilson. Both have private lawyers and both are free on bond. They were arrested in 1995. The case has been continued thirty-two times, and today it's continued for another three weeks. Ramacci and Wilson are charged with possessing with intent to deliver 1,163 grams of cocaine. The defendants in the marijuana case were charged with possessing with intent to deliver 2,182 pounds of marijuana (989,733 grams). Bates is waiting nervously in the gallery while Locallo dispenses with these other defendants. His case involved 0.4 grams of cocaine. Soon after the marijuana defendants get their good news, and Ramacci and Wilson leave with their continuance, Locallo calls Bates to the bench. Bates meekly asks the judge if he'd consider assigning him to outpatient instead of inpatient treatment so he won't have to wait in the jail for a treatment bed to open. Locallo says no, and Guerrero escorts Bates to the lockup.

THIRTEEN

Fixes

"HAVE ANY OF YOU seen a cold-blooded killer before? Let's take a look over here," prosecutor James McKay is telling a jury in 302 one July morning. McKay steps behind the defense table and brushes Dino Titone's shoulder lightly with one hand. "This man, sitting over here with the suit and the glasses on, is a cold-blooded killer. What the evidence is going to show you, ladies and gentlemen, is that Dino Titone is an executioner."

Titone, who's sharply dressed in a gray suit that his mother had tailored for him for this trial, is repelled by McKay's touch. But he knows the prosecutor would love to have him fume in front of the jury, so he remains stone-faced, doesn't flinch.

It used to be easier to provoke him, Titone says later. As a youth, "I was always one to fight. But I'm more laid-back now. Over the course of time you learn that fighting's not the way you solve things, and that you can do more with kindness than with anger."

Titone is solidly built, just under six feet tall but over two hundred pounds. He has a broad face, a small mouth, and a full head of wavy black hair that's graying at the temples. There was no gray when he was arrested in 1982 for the double murder for which he's now on trial for a second time. But he was twenty-two then; now he's thirty-eight, and much has happened in the interim. The judge at his first trial is in prison for taking bribes, and the lawyer who represented him is on parole for giving them.

ON THE MORNING of December 12, 1982, a forest preserve ranger was patrolling a secluded tract of land near the Des Plaines River for illegal duck hunting. This was in unincorporated Lemont Township, fifteen miles southwest of Chicago and barely within Cook County. Around nine-fifteen A.M. the ranger came upon a powder-blue Oldsmobile on the river's south bank. He parked his patrol car and walked toward the Olds, planning to look through its windows for hunting gear. As he approached, he heard banging from inside the trunk and a voice: *I'm running out of air! Get me out of here!*

The ranger radioed for help. A Lemont police car arrived, then an ambulance. The ranger and a police officer used a tool from the ambulance to pop open the trunk. Inside were two blood-spattered men, one writhing and moaning, the other pale and still. Their hands were tied behind their backs. A .38 revolver lay in the trunk. Police later found another gun, a small semiautomatic, on the ground not far from the car.

The motionless man, thirty-nine-year-old Aldo Fratto, had been shot in the head, chest, back, abdomen, and shoulder. He was dead. The other man, Fratto's nephew, twenty-six-year-old Tullio Infelise, had four bullet wounds in his chest and abdomen. The two men had been shot about six hours earlier. As paramedics worked on Infelise in the ambulance, the police officer asked him who had done this to him. Infelise's gasping response sounded to the officer like "Robert Gotch." In the emergency room at the hospital, Infelise said another offender was "Dino."

Police determined that Fratto and Infelise had lived on the south side, in Bridgeport. Soon their prime suspect was twenty-eight-year-old Robert Gacho, who lived with his wife and two young children in Bridgeport. Police brought Gacho in for questioning that afternoon, and by evening he confessed. He implicated two other men: twenty-year-old Joseph Sorrentino and twenty-two-year-old Dino Titone.

Gacho said the two victims had come to his house on the evening of December 11 with three-quarters of a kilo of cocaine they'd arranged to sell him. But Gacho, Sorrentino, and Titone had decided to take the cocaine instead of buying it. They pulled guns on Fratto and Infelise and bound their hands. In the early morning hours of December 12, they drove them from Bridgeport to the secluded spot near the Des Plaines River. Sorrentino and Titone shot them while Gacho and his mistress waited in a second car. Back at Gacho's house, the three men split up the cocaine and the $1,500 that Sorrentino and Titone had taken from the two victims.

Police also arrested Sorrentino on December 12, and he gave a similar confession. According to Sorrentino, at the Des Plaines River, Titone ordered Fratto and Infelise to climb into the trunk of the Olds, which was Fratto's car. Titone told Sorrentino that if he didn't shoot anybody, "he would shoot me, and he started firing about three times on Aldo," Sorrentino said. He said he himself then shot Infelise. Then he threw his gun aside, and Titone dropped his into the trunk.

Police located Gacho's mistress, Katherine De Wulf, and brought her to the station. According to police, her account of the crime matched Gacho's and Sorrentino's. She wasn't charged.

That same evening, December 12, officers went to the home of Titone's parents, in west suburban St. Charles, but his father told them Dino wasn't there. The next morning Titone, accompanied by his father, turned himself in at a police station. He declined to answer questions. After De Wulf picked him out of a lineup, he was charged with murder and attempted murder. Gacho and Sorrentino had already been charged. With Infelise's death two weeks later, the three defendants were facing a minimum of natural life if convicted and a possible death sentence.

In separate trials two years later in the courtroom of Judge Thomas Maloney, all three defendants were convicted—Gacho and Sorrentino by juries, Titone by Maloney. Sorrentino's jury sentenced him to natural life. Gacho's jury sentenced him to death, and Maloney condemned Titone as well. Gacho's and Sorrentino's convictions were upheld on appeal. Gacho's death sentence was then vacated because of a procedural error by Maloney, and he was resentenced to natural life.

Titone's conviction and sentence were upheld on appeal. But on a January morning in 1990 a new lawyer for Titone stood before Judge Maloney asserting that his client deserved a new trial. He had novel grounds for his claim. The lawyer contended that Titone's father had given Titone's trial lawyer $10,000 to fix the case—money the lawyer was supposed to pass on to Maloney—and that Titone had been convicted and sentenced to death because the fix had gone bad.

The new lawyer, Ian Ayres, was just thirty and a novice attorney when he made these charges. Titone, in fact, happened to be Ayres's first client. After graduating from Yale Law School in 1987, Ayres had come to Chicago to teach law at Northwestern. He'd volunteered his services to the Illinois Coalition Against the Death Penalty, which had asked him to represent Titone. Maloney on this January morning was sixty-four and a thirteen-year veteran of the bench. Prosecutors and defense lawyers alike considered him rude, contemptuous, and state-minded. He once scolded a jury from the bench for acquitting a defendant. He was a former boxer. Ayres was aware of Maloney's reputation and didn't expect him to retreat timidly to his corner when confronted with these allegations. Ayres had brought his own lawyer to court in the event Maloney tried to jail him for contempt.

And indeed, Maloney "went ballistic," recalls Ayres, now a law professor at Yale. The judge asked him where he was born, how old he was, and how long he'd been practicing law. When Maloney learned that Ayres was barely out of law school, he berated him for his naïveté. Ayres remembers the judge saying that when Ayres got some experience, he'd realize that such charges by a defendant "were 'just a bunch of crap,' or words to that effect." Maloney soon summoned Ayres and the prosecutor to his chambers, where the judge resumed his tirade against the defense lawyer, now lacing it with profanity.

Ayres supported his charges with affidavits from Titone and from his father, Salvatore. Salvatore Titone said in his affidavit that his son's trial lawyer, Bruce Roth, had told him after Dino was indicted "that Dino could walk if I paid him some extra money"—money that would be passed to Maloney. According to Salvatore Titone, Roth originally said the fix would cost $60,000, but after the elder Titone said he couldn't come up with that, Roth said Maloney would take care of the case for just $10,000. This was in addition to the $20,000 Salvatore Titone had agreed to pay Roth for his legal services. The elder Titone said he gave the $10,000 to Roth in March 1983.

Dino Titone said in his affidavit that Roth had told him after he was indicted that he "would find a judge that he could work with" to preside over the case. The case originally was assigned to a different judge, but it was transferred on Roth's motion.

In August 1983, before the case came to trial, an ongoing federal probe of corruption in the Cook County courts—Operation Greylord—became public. Dino Titone theorized in his affidavit that Greylord had scared Maloney out of following through on the deal, and that the judge had convicted him and sentenced him to death to prove his integrity. Titone said it was also possible that Roth had made a deal with Maloney but had pocketed the $10,000. In either case, Titone said, he believed he hadn't been convicted because of the evidence against him but because either Roth or Judge Maloney had reneged.

On the January morning Ayres confronted Maloney with these allegations, he also asked him to transfer the case to a judge who could consider the petition for a new trial without bias. The chief judge at 26th Street later reassigned the case to Judge Earl Strayhorn, a twenty-year veteran of the bench known for his honesty.

Ordinarily the Titone allegations would have been written off as the desperate fictions of a defendant and his father. But certain developments during the 1980s lent credence to the claims. When the case reached Judge Strayhorn, Titone's trial lawyer, Roth, was already serving a ten-year federal term for bribing judges and extorting defendants in other Cook County cases, having been convicted in 1987. And federal agents were completing an investigation into other fixes involving Maloney, a probe that would result in the judge's indictment in 1991.

In 1990 Judge Strayhorn vacated Titone's death sentence and ordered a new sentencing hearing based on Roth's woeful work for Titone at sentencing. Ayres had learned that Judge Maloney had warned Roth that if he left the sentencing decision up to him, he'd condemn Titone. Roth had nonetheless advised Titone to put his fate in Maloney's hands. Roth had then offered no mitigating evidence in Titone's behalf, and Maloney made good on that promise. But Judge Strayhorn denied the request for a new trial that was based on the fix allegations.

In 1992 the Illinois Supreme Court affirmed Strayhorn's rejection of a new trial for Titone, observing that his fix allegations hadn't been proven. The federal charges pending against Maloney were "not germane" to Titone's case, the court said.

In 1993 Maloney, by then retired, was convicted in federal court of taking bribes to fix four cases, three of them murders. He was sentenced to fifteen years and nine months. One of the cases involved a failed fix remarkably similar to the one alleged by the Titones. According to testimony at Maloney's trial, a leader of the El Rukn street gang had paid the judge $10,000 to acquit one of two gang members charged with a double murder. But on the last day of the trial Maloney returned the bribe, perhaps because of the presence of numerous FBI agents in his courtroom, the FBI having been tipped to a possible fix. Maloney then convicted the defendants and sentenced them to death.

In 1996 another 26th Street judge granted the El Rukn defendants a new trial because of Maloney's proven corruption in that case. By this time Ayres—the lawyer who'd raised the corruption issue in Titone's case—had left Chicago for a job at Stanford University. Titone's new lawyer was Thomas Geraghty, director of the Northwestern University Legal Clinic (the lawyer who now represents Leroy Orange). After the El Rukns were awarded their new trial, Geraghty went before Judge Strayhorn and said Titone deserved as much.

Strayhorn repeatedly delayed his final ruling on the matter. His hesitancy was understandable. If the allegations about the fix attempt were true, Titone himself had hardly played a virtuous role—he'd at the least acquiesced in his father's attempt to buy his acquittal. And now he wanted a new trial because the fix attempt had backfired.

In July 1997 Strayhorn finally rendered his decision. "I cannot truly articulate the pain that I have borne in listening to the horrible things that went on in this case in what is supposed to be a court of law and justice," he said. He'd decided that "this entire corrupt process be wiped off the books," and that Titone "be given an opportunity to have his case heard in a courtroom not tainted and besmirched with a corrupt judge and a corrupt defense attorney."

AND SO HERE SITS the impassive Titone at the defense table in Locallo's courtroom, with a second chance at freedom.

In his opening statement, prosecutor McKay tells the jurors they'll learn that when Titone described the shootings to Robert Gacho, and to Gacho's mistress, Katherine De Wulf, he laughed about how Infelise and Fratto begged for their lives.

Relatives of Infelise and Fratto are in the gallery today. McKay knows from talking with them that they still want what they wanted fourteen years ago: Titone's execution. And McKay would like to do his part. It hasn't been lost on him that Titone is getting this second trial because an attempt to rig the first one backfired. "The more I think about it," he's said, "the more upset I get."

The forty-year-old McKay has a stern mien, with a hawkish nose and unflinching eyes. His voice is strong and clear. He's been a prosecutor for thirteen years. Defense attorneys say he's a formidable opponent. He'd be the top prosecutor in the building, some say, but for his occasional overzealousness—the reason defense lawyers occasionally call him "Mad Dog." McKay doesn't mind the nickname. "I think it means I'm tenacious and determined in the courtroom. You have to be tough if you're a prosecutor because this system is designed to protect the defendant's rights, not the victim's. And the burden of proof is on the prosecutor's shoulders. The defense lawyer doesn't have to do *shit*." He says another prosecutor actually gave him the nickname, back when he was a relative novice and "just fire and brimstone." Like Titone, he claims to have softened. "If you're always shouting and pointing and yelling, the jury is going to turn off to you. I guess with age and experience you tend to mellow somewhat. But I'm still a mad dog once in a while."

McKay says that if money were his prime concern, he would have left the state's attorney's office years ago. But he gets "unmitigated personal satisfaction" from his job. "Representing victims of crime is the most noble thing a lawyer can do," he says. "I can't think of an assistant state's attorney who does not love his or her job. I would suspect there are tons of lawyers in private practice who hate their jobs. Maybe they like driving around in their Mercedes, but they hate their jobs."

Locallo has barred prosecutors from referring to Titone's previous conviction in this case. The lawyers aren't even to mention that there was an earlier trial. When they refer to a witness's testimony at the first trial, they're to refer to the trial as a "proceeding." McKay knows that the jurors will wonder about the many years between the crime and this trial, and he expects some will guess that Titone was convicted before but won a new trial with an appeal. Such a presumption probably won't benefit Titone, and so McKay will remind the jurors repeatedly of the time lag. "Here we are, fifteen and a half years later, and a lot has changed in that time," McKay now tells the jury. "But the truth hasn't changed about what happened in a desolate area by the Des Plaines River in unincorporated Lemont."

Titone's lawyer for this trial, Frederick Cohn, tells the jury that Titone will testify that he was playing cards miles from Bridgeport and from Lemont on the night of the shootings—an alibi that two of the other card-players will corroborate, Cohn promises. He says Titone's fingerprints weren't found on Fratto's Oldsmobile or on either of the two guns recovered at the scene. He says the state's main witness, De Wulf, feared she might also be charged with the shootings, and so made up "this cock-and-bull story that accuses my client."

Cohn, sixty, has been trying cases at 26th Street for more than three decades. He's tall and obese, with a large round face. He grew up in New York, and although he moved here more than forty years ago, he hasn't completely shaken his Brooklyn accent. In 1955, when he was still living in New York, he joined protests in Harlem after Emmett Till was murdered in Mississippi: "There were four hundred thousand blacks and me." In 1964, when three civil rights workers were killed in Mississippi, he took two weeks off from his job with the Cook County public defender's office, rode a Greyhound to Mississippi, and worked as a volunteer civil rights lawyer. As a public defender, he once got a letter from a client addressed to "Mr. Fred Cohn, Public Dissenter," a description he still considers apt: "If I see something going on that I think is wrong, it's my nature to say something about it."

He shares McKay's passion for his work. Being a lawyer is a "vocation, not just a profession," he says. He often tells people that the first criminal lawyer was Abraham, who tried to convince God to spare the people in Sodom and Gomorrah. "I tell people that I was there, whispering in Abraham's ear. That's basically what a defense lawyer does—he argues on behalf of bad people to try to save them." Cohn wraps up his opening statement by telling the jurors they will hear "absolutely no credible evidence" to support the charges against Titone.

There's plenty of evidence incriminating Titone that the jury won't hear. There are Gacho's and Sorrentino's confessions, both naming Titone as the third offender. The Sixth Amendment right to confront one's accusers precludes the use of such statements at trial (because a statement can't be cross-examined). And the Fifth Amendment protection against self-incrimination means Gacho and Sorrentino can't be forced to testify. (They still have appeals pending in their cases.) There's also Tullio Infelise's alleged emergency room statement that one of the offenders was named Dino. Since Infelise can't be cross-examined either, that also can't be used. The police officers who say they heard the statement can't testify that they did; that would be hearsay. (Infelise's "Robert Gotch" statement at the scene had been deemed admissible as a "spontaneous declaration," an exception to the hearsay rule. But Infelise's naming of Dino wasn't spontaneous; it was in response to prolonged questioning by police in the emergency room.) There's also the fact that Titone didn't originally tell police he was playing cards at the time of the shootings, that he instead refused to answer questions about the crime. Prosecutors can't suggest that a defendant's decision to remain silent is a sign of guilt; they can't even inform the jury the defendant wouldn't talk. To do so would penalize a defendant for having exercised a constitutional right. Cohn and McKay agree that these protections are elemental to the U. S. justice system, but they speak of them in different tones—Cohn as though he's talking about chocolate cake, McKay, lima beans. "Those are the rules, and I'm not gonna argue that the rules are bad," McKay says. "But all too often a jury gets very little of the story."

BRUCE ROTH, Titone's original lawyer, worked as a Cook County prosecutor for seven years before he went into private practice in 1976. As a defense lawyer, Roth not only fixed cases, he forged court documents, suborned perjury, and used cocaine with his clients, federal prosecutors said at his sentencing in 1987. He was the "public's worst nightmare of what the criminal justice system is all about," the prosecutors said.

Roth's résumé of corruption, as chronicled at his trial, shows how some attorneys and judges have worked in Cook County.

In 1980 Roth represented a defendant named Rocco Filipponio who'd been caught with a machine gun and cocaine in his car. Roth managed to get the case assigned to a Judge Alan Lane, and Lane acquitted Filipponio— after Roth passed the judge $15,000 from Filipponio.

In 1981 Roth brokered a deal between Judge Lane and another defense lawyer who was representing an accused armed robber. That defendant had confessed to the crime. Though Cook County judges rarely find a reason to suppress a confession in Cook County, Lane found a reason to suppress this one. The reason was $4,000. The state had to drop the case.

In 1982 Roth appeared before Judge Adam Stillo on behalf of one of three defendants charged with dealing cocaine. Roth's client advised his two codefendants that Roth could fix the case for all three of them, but the two codefendants opted for other lawyers. In a bench trial Judge Stillo acquitted Roth's client and convicted the other two defendants. Before sentencing, the two convicted defendants, having seen Roth's success with the judge, visited the lawyer at his office. Roth told them he could keep them out of prison, despite their convictions, for $25,000 apiece. One of the two paid up. Judge Stillo changed that defendant's conviction to a lesser charge and granted him probation. The nonpaying defendant got six years.

Also in 1982 Roth tried to extort a bribe from Cook County Jail inmate Michael Davis, who was awaiting sentencing by Judge Lane on a rape conviction. In Roth's unsolicited visit, the lawyer told Davis that Lane would toss out the conviction for $10,000; otherwise Lane would give him ten years. Davis said he didn't have that kind of money. Roth suggested that relatives or friends raise it for him. Davis gave Roth some phone numbers, and soon Davis's girlfriend and several relatives got calls from Roth's office squeezing them for the money. Instead of paying Roth, the relatives called the state's attorney's office.

Lane was voted off the bench by fellow judges in 1983 amid questions about his integrity. (He was an associate judge, and associates face a retention vote of the circuit judges every four years.) Federal agents stopped investigating Lane in 1984 after he was diagnosed with terminal cancer. He died the following year, at forty-two. In 1994 Judge Stillo, then seventy-seven, was sentenced to four years for fixing a half dozen cases.

"Bruce Roth didn't create what we have now learned to be a very bad state court system," Roth's lawyer, Patrick Tuite, said at Roth's sentencing in 1987. Tuite, who himself had practiced for many years at 26th Street, added that defense lawyers are occasionally confronted by clients who want to be assured they'll win—and that the lawyers sometimes fear losing clients if they don't give such assurances.

Although Titone swore in an affidavit, when he was lobbying for a new trial, that he'd understood from early on that Roth was trying to fix the first trial, now that he *has* a new trial he's retreated from that position. He says he was mostly in the dark about the fix. His father told him the first trial "was being taken care of," and he didn't ask his father what that meant, he says. "He told me not to worry about it, I tried not to worry about it."

Titone's present lawyer, Cohn, says the convictions in the 1980s and 1990s—of eighteen judges and fifty-two lawyers, along with nineteen deputies, police officers, and clerks who mainly served as bagmen—were a help to honest lawyers here. "It's hard to compete against guys who are getting business because they're guaranteeing cases."

Cohn doesn't drive a Mercedes; he drives a Dodge minivan "with no automatic windows or any of that junk." Like most solo criminal practitioners, he's had lean times. His willingness to work long hours has helped him survive those periods—that, and his frugality. "With too many lawyers, when the big money is coming in they assume it's always going to continue, and so they spend it. Then they have no money to pay their taxes and they get in trouble. It pressures them to charge more, to steal from clients— just a lot of things."

From time to time during his career, a potential client has asked Cohn if he could fix his case. Cohn says he's thrown such people out of his office. "You don't fix a case, because it's *wrong* to do it," he says. "It's got nothing to do with whether you need the money. Yes, you have obligations to support yourself and your family, and to pay your rent and your secretary. But it's *not* just a business. For a lot of lawyers, though, it *is* just a business."

BEFORE THE TRIAL Locallo informed Cohn and Titone that he and McKay lived in the same neighborhood, and that his daughter had babysat for McKay's daughter. The judge said he'd recuse himself if Titone wanted him to.

Titone chose to stick with Locallo. From his first appearance before the judge, Titone's impression had been that Locallo would bend over backward to be fair. He also appreciated Locallo's respectful manner toward him in the courtroom. In Titone's experience, most judges, lawyers, and courtroom staff made little attempt to hide their disdain for defendants.

No one ever accused the judge at Titone's first trial, Thomas Maloney, of being overly respectful. In a 1990 survey of prosecutors and defense lawyers conducted by the Chicago Crime Commission, Maloney got the worst score of the county's forty-five criminal court judges in "treats defendants with consideration." The lawyers also ranked Maloney last in how he treated witnesses and in how he treated lawyers.

"He was arrogant, the Lord High Justice," Cohn recalls. "He basically believed that defendants should be convicted and should go to the penitentiary—unless, of course, he got paid."

At Maloney's trial, prosecutors presented financial records indicating that in his first six years on the bench—1978 to 1984—his expenditures exceeded his known legitimate income by $400,000. As one federal appeals court judge later noted, this raised the "distinct possibility" that the four fixes he was convicted of were "merely the tip of the iceberg."

Fixes most likely were not uncommon in earlier years, at 26th Street and in other urban felony courts. When veteran defense lawyer Sam Adam started trying cases here in 1961, "there was all kinds of fixing going on," he recalls. A defendant with mob ties would rely on a bondsman to broker a fix with the judge, he says, while a defendant with political connections would have a ward committeeman call the judge. Judges often owed their seat on the bench to the ward committeeman. "The judge knew he couldn't cross the committeeman," Adam says. "He'd say, 'I'll see what I can do'— but invariably he'd do what the committeeman wanted him to do."

In those years the investigation of corruption in state courts was left to local prosecutors. But local prosecutors weren't about to expose the corruption of judges with whom they usually teamed for convictions. Federal laws passed in the 1970s made investigations such as Greylord feasible.

In 1980 a judge at 26th Street became the first judge in the nation to have his chambers wiretapped by federal agents. On a November night that year Greylord agents hid a microphone in the desk of Judge Wayne Olson, who presided over a first-floor courtroom in which preliminary hearings were conducted in drug cases. Greylord investigators had heard he was taking bribes. On the first day court was in session after the bug was planted, it picked up a conversation between Olson and a defense lawyer—Bruce Roth.

"I love people that take dough, 'cause you know exactly where you stand," Judge Olson told Roth.

"Sure, that's the way to do business," Roth replied.

Olson pled guilty in 1985 to racketeering, extortion, and mail fraud and was sentenced to twelve years. Locallo's present clerk, Duane Sundberg, worked for Olson for three years when the judge was assigned to divorce court. Sundberg thinks too much has been made of Olson's transgressions. "When every fish in the brook is swimming downstream, it's hard to swim upstream," the clerk says. Besides, he adds in Olson's defense, "He never fixed a murder case."

As a prosecutor, Locallo learned from colleagues about a ruse that defense attorneys employed to squeeze money out of clients—a ploy known as "selling the judge" or "selling the prosecutor." A defense lawyer who knew that the judge would sentence the defendant to probation, given the facts of the case, would warn his client he was in for a prison term—a term that could only be averted if the client gave the lawyer a bribe to pass to the prosecutor or the judge. When the client got his probation, he'd figure he'd bought it, not knowing that the bribe had gotten no farther than the defense lawyer's wallet.

Before Greylord, Cook County judges often were mere patronage products, chosen for their political clout more than their legal ability. Politics still matter today but less so; Locallo says Greylord convinced political bosses to sponsor more capable candidates.

He feels sympathy for most of the judges who got convicted. Several of his friends have gone to jail. One was Maloney, whom Locallo got to know when he was a prosecutor. Federal judges and prosecutors have called Maloney a "mafia factotum," a "racketeer sending men to the death chamber in the name of the state," "one of the most ruthless judges," and "depraved." Locallo says he has doubts about Maloney's guilt and still considers him a friend.

THE STATE'S KEY WITNESS against Titone, Robert Gacho's former mistress Katherine De Wulf, takes the stand after lunch on the trial's first day.

De Wulf, now forty-four, tells the jury that Gacho called her on the night in question and summoned her to his house in Bridgeport saying he needed a "backup car." She parked in the alley behind his house, as he'd directed over the phone. Joseph Sorrentino pulled up behind her in a light-blue Olds—Fratto's car. Then Fratto and Infelise, their hands tied behind their backs, were marched out of the house by Titone, who ushered them into the backseat of the Olds. Titone got into the front passenger seat, next to Sorrentino, and Gacho got into her car. She says Gacho told her they were going to "take Aldo and Tullio somewhere, and they were going to have to waste 'em."

They followed the Olds through Bridgeport to the Stevenson Expressway—Interstate 55—and then southwest, De Wulf tells the jury. After a short drive off of I-55, they reached the area near the Des Plaines River in Lemont. She says Sorrentino drove down into a gully, while Gacho, who was driving her car, parked nearby. Gacho told her he was waiting to hear shots. After fifteen or twenty minutes, they did. Then Titone and Sorrentino got in the backseat of their car. Gacho "asked if it was over," De Wulf says. And Titone "said, 'Yes, they're gone. They're dead.'"

McKay asks De Wulf if she noticed anything about how Titone reported that they were dead.

"He was laughing, like he was bragging about, that he had shot them," De Wulf says. "He seemed like he was proud about it. . . . He said that they were begging for their lives, that they were pleading for him not to shoot them."

Through his questions on direct, McKay lets the jury know that De Wulf left the state twice in 1984 to try to avoid testifying at a previous "proceeding." McKay knows that Cohn will be going into this on cross, to cast doubt on De Wulf's trustworthiness. De Wulf explains that she still loved Gacho back then, and that he'd told her that if she didn't testify, the case against him would be dropped. Authorities found her both times she fled and brought her back to Chicago, and she testified against all three defendants.

On Cohn's cross, De Wulf acknowledges that when police questioned her about the shootings, she worried about getting charged herself. Cohn is suggesting to the jury that she may not have told police what really happened. And, yes, she knew it was a crime for her to flee the state, she says, but she did it anyway.

BRIBING THE JUDGE is usually a last resort for fixing a case. It's easier and cheaper to get to the witnesses.

While Gacho was in jail awaiting trial in 1983 and 1984, he wrote long, adoring letters to De Wulf, invariably signing them "Your Future Husband." Next to his signature he'd draw a heart and write inside it, "Bob and Kathy 4-Ever." In the letters he told De Wulf he planned to marry her just as soon as he beat the case and got out of jail—which he could do only if she stayed off the witness stand. He asked De Wulf to leave Illinois and hide from authorities, and De Wulf complied, fleeing to Gacho's sister's home in Arkansas. "The state made just about their whole case around you," he wrote De Wulf after she fled. "Now they are going to have to change their plans, and they don't have all that much time with all their other cases." But authorities found the time, and De Wulf.

Most witnesses comply with their subpoenas. But it's not rare for a witness to get cold feet or amnesia, or even to disappear, as a trial nears. One witness did so in another Titone case, in fact.

In 1980—two years before Titone was arrested for the shootings of Fratto and Infelise—he was charged with the armed robbery of a northwest-side trucking dock. Titone and his brother-in-law, Robert Caparelli, were accused of tying up a dock employee at gunpoint and taking 116 cartons of clothing worth an estimated $60,000. The two men were taken in for questioning the day after the offense and picked out of a lineup by the victim.

Before the case came to trial at 26th Street, Titone and Caparelli replaced their original lawyer with Bruce Roth.

On the morning of the trial, the employee who'd been tied up informed prosecutors that he could no longer identify the defendants as the culprits. "It caught us totally by surprise," recalls Jeffrey Pattee, one of the prosecutors. Pattee, now in private practice, says Titone was smirking throughout the bench trial that day. "Usually a defendant on trial for a serious offense is a little worried," Pattee says. "He wasn't the least bit concerned." Without the witness's identification, Judge Robert Collins acquitted Titone and Caparelli.

Titone told me he did in fact commit this robbery. He said he didn't know exactly how his acquittal was won—just that his father had told him not to worry about the case, that he'd take care of things.

THE DOUBLE-MURDER CASE against Titone turns out to be an exception to the axiom that cases get harder to prosecute as they age. Fourteen years after the first trial, not only is the state's chief witness, Katherine De Wulf, still available to testify against Titone, but now she's joined by Robert Gacho's former wife.

Judy Gacho testified at her husband's trial in 1984 that although she was home on the evening in question, she mainly stayed in her bedroom and didn't hear if anyone stopped by.

But she and Gacho are now divorced. On the second day of Titone's retrial, she tells the jury that Titone and Sorrentino did indeed stop by the Gacho home on the evening in question. She heard them talking with Gacho about how Fratto and Infelise were going to bring over a large quantity of cocaine. She recalls Titone saying that although he didn't have money, "he wanted the drugs anyway." Fratto and Infelise arrived later. She was in her bedroom but could smell cocaine being smoked. Later, when she got up to use the bathroom, all five men were gone.

Cohn badgers her on cross about the differences between her testimony in 1984 and her testimony today. She acknowledges that she knew she was committing perjury back then. On redirect, McKay asks her who instructed her to lie in 1984. "My husband Bob and his lawyer," she says.

Her testimony not only corroborates De Wulf's, it torpedoes Titone's alibi that he was playing cards that night and never went to Gacho's house.

Although the Illinois Supreme Court affirmed Titone's 1984 conviction (before evidence surfaced that Maloney and Roth were crooked), one justice, Seymour Simon, vehemently dissented. Simon had observed that the case rested entirely on De Wulf—an untrustworthy witness, he said, given her own involvement in the crime. "I do not understand how, based on the testimony of such a witness, the defendant could properly be convicted of murder," the justice wrote. This dissent underlined an irony that Titone had thought of many times since the first trial: had there been no fix attempt, and had the 1984 trial been before a jury or an uncompromised judge, he could well have been acquitted. Now, with the testimony of Judy Gacho, the chances of that have greatly dimmed.

. . .

"CORRUPTION ISN'T GONE from 26th Street—it just went underground," Titone says. "That's the way they do business, not just in Chicago but everywhere."

Locallo disagrees. "In Dino's world, at the time his case first came in, corruption very well may have been happening. But today I just can't see it." The salaries of circuit judges in Cook County have risen markedly since Greylord (from $65,500 in 1984 to $150,000 in 2004). Locallo thinks this makes judges less vulnerable to bribery and less willing to put their seat at risk. He also thinks Greylord taught ward bosses "that they're not supposed to be calling [judges] seeking favors" and taught judges not to accept such calls. "If any of my colleagues are accepting phone calls from committeemen with respect to cases—I mean, it's the highest of stupidity. The bottom line is, 'I can't help you. Don't call me.'" Locallo says the only person who ever sought a favor from him was an acquaintance who asked him to intercede on his behalf with the judge who was presiding over his divorce case. Locallo politely but firmly told the person he couldn't. "For the most part, I think it's a pretty straight ship," Locallo says. "But if the authorities get lax, corruption can always resurrect itself."

Greylord showed that a key to corruption was the ability to get a case assigned to a corruptible judge, which defense lawyers accomplished by bribing clerks in the presiding judge's office. The clerks would ignore the results of the Randomizer—the computer program that determines which trial judge gets a particular case—and assign the case to the judge chosen by the bribing lawyer.

After the Greylord revelations, a commission was formed to recommend anticorruption measures for the court system. One of the recommendations was that the random assignment system "be routinely audited to ensure that the cases assigned through the computer are, indeed, assigned on a random basis." But no audit has ever been instituted. And Marcus Ferguson, the clerk who's been running the Randomizer at 26th Street since 1996, says a dishonest clerk could still "easily" subvert the system. No one looks over the clerk's shoulder to make sure the judge's name that appears on his monitor after he runs the Randomizer is the name he calls out to the prosecutor assisting him with the process. Ferguson says it would be even easier for a prosecutor to direct a case to a preferred judge (as defense lawyers here have long suspected prosecutors sometimes do). On occasion the assistant state's attorney working with Ferguson instructs him to send a case to a certain judge. There are valid reasons to bypass the Randomizer; if the defendant is already on probation, for instance, his new case is supposed to be sent to the judge who gave him probation. But there's no one checking to ensure that the reason given by the assistant state's attorney is bona-fide. "They can make it sound official and I would never know," Ferguson says. Although defense lawyers can watch the randomizing process that's conducted every weekday, he says they never do.

COHN PUTS ON his defense witnesses after lunch on the trial's second day. The audio feed to the gallery isn't working, so Locallo asks Deputy Rhodes to open the gallery doors so the spectators can hear.

The first witness is Titone's brother-in-law, Robert Caparelli. He's the man who was acquitted with Titone of the 1980 armed robbery of the trucking dock.

Caparelli, who testified for Titone at his first trial, says he and Titone and two other friends were playing cards on the evening of December 11, 1982, at a home on Chicago's northwest side. The game began at about eight-thirty P.M. and went on until four the next morning, he says, and Titone was there the whole time.

On cross, Caparelli acknowledges that he never told police that Titone had been with him on the evening of the murders. He says Titone's lawyer, Roth, instructed him not to tell anyone about the card game until he testified.

The next witness, Thomas Caccavele, also testified for Titone at his first trial and also recalls playing cards with Titone that night. (The man who testified at the first trial that he'd hosted the game, Michael Wesley, died two months before this retrial.)

Titone takes the stand after Caccavele. He tells the jury he didn't shoot Fratto or Infelise. He was playing cards at Mike Wesley's that night.

He acknowledges that he knew Gacho before all this. They worked for the same trucking company. Titone says he stopped working for that company five years before the murders. Then, about two weeks before the crime, he says Gacho called him and asked him to meet him at a motel on Chicago's southwest side. Titone says he drove from his parents' home in St. Charles to the motel. When he arrived, Gacho was already there, and De Wulf was with him. He says they asked him to help them rip off a large amount of cocaine from some men but that he declined. Gacho called him a week later, asking him to reconsider, he says, but again he said no.

"So you had nothing to do with this homicide, did you?" Cohn asks.

"No, sir," Titone says.

McKay's cross is an entertaining squabble, but it offers the jury little substance about the crime or Titone's alibi. Titone's answers aren't always directly responsive; McKay reminds the jury of this with jabs such as "Was that hard to answer that question?" and "How's your hearing?" "My hearing is good," Titone thrusts back after the latter remark. "I don't want you to manipulate the conversation."

Titone allows that when Gacho invited him to the motel meeting, he made the forty-five-minute drive there from St. Charles even though he hadn't talked with Gacho in five years and Gacho wouldn't tell him on the phone what the meeting was about. When he's asked to describe this meeting of almost sixteen years ago, Titone's memory is remarkably vivid: "Bob threw his jacket on the bed, sat down. I was still standing up. I believe she [De Wulf] even offered me something to drink and I turned her down." Then Gacho and De Wulf proposed the rip-off, Titone says, and he told them he wouldn't participate. McKay wonders why he turned them down. "Because I won't—I'm not into that," Titone says in an offended tone.

TITONE AND HIS PARENTS and siblings moved to the western suburbs when he was ten. Before that he lived on Chicago's northwest side, in a home at 2125 North Melvina. A noted Chicago crime syndicate figure, Anthony Spilotro, also lived at that address for many years. Spilotro went on to become the Chicago outfit's top lieutenant in Las Vegas, a position he held until he and a brother were beaten to death in 1986 in an apparent mob hit. Their bodies were found buried in an Indiana cornfield. Titone allows that he and members of Spilotro's family grew up together in the same building. In the fall of 1983, while Titone was in jail awaiting trial in this case, Anthony Spilotro went to trial at 26th Street, also for a double-murder case. The victims in Spilotro's case, like the victims in Titone's, had been found in a car trunk. And Spilotro had somehow also ended up before Maloney. Members of Titone's family sat with members of Spilotro's in Maloney's courtroom while Spilotro was tried.

Spilotro chose a bench trial. Given Maloney's inclination toward the state, that was usually an unwise choice—but it wasn't unwise for Spilotro, whom Maloney acquitted. Titone has since wondered whether suspicions raised by that acquittal caused Maloney to convict him when he was tried the following year. "There was a lot of heat on his courtroom," Titone says.

Maloney had been tied to the mob from his days as a defense lawyer, federal prosecutors maintained. They also contended that Maloney's harshness on the bench toward most defendants was calculated. "Showing defendants little mercy had the effect of diverting any conceivable suspicion from Maloney while at the same time giving defendants a strong motivation to cough up big bribery dollars," a prosecutor said at Maloney's sentencing.

Mob leaders here had long advised their allies on the bench to favor the state in most cases, mob expert William Roemer has written. Roemer was an FBI specialist on the Chicago outfit for many years. He wrote that Murray Humphreys, the mobster in charge of corrupting public officials in Chicago from the 1930s through the 1960s, encouraged mob-tied judges to cultivate reputations as hanging judges. Then, according to Roemer, such a judge "could do a favor for the mob, and if someone criticized him, he could just say, 'Look at my record; look at my statistics. You can't just pick out this one case.'"

If Maloney did indeed balance his books on the backs of nonpaying defendants, then there are a host of convicts who are at least as deserving of new trials as Titone—defendants who paid the price for not paying Maloney.

Federal judges have wrestled with that issue since 1993. Four months after Maloney's conviction that year, two men sought relief in federal court from the murder convictions and death sentences they received as co-defendants in Maloney's courtroom in 1981. William Bracy and Roger Collins asserted that Maloney had made sure they were convicted and condemned because they hadn't tried to bribe him. Bracy and Collins won a partial victory in 1999 when a federal district judge here vacated their death sentences but affirmed their convictions, a ruling upheld in 2002 by the Seventh Circuit Court of Appeals.

The federal judges who considered the case agreed that it was "plausible" that Maloney was biased against nonpaying defendants, and that he may at times have ruled against such defendants as part of his bribery scheme. But they split regarding what a defendant would have to show to get relief. The majority said a defendant would have to demonstrate not only that Maloney was biased in a particular case, but that the bias stemmed from corruption and wasn't simply his usual orientation toward the state. The majority judges have voiced concern about the implications of granting Bracy and Collins a new trial, noting that to do so might nullify all of the convictions in Maloney's thirteen years as a criminal court judge—along with, possibly, the convictions in the courtrooms of other judges who were found corrupt.

Judges in the minority have contended that Maloney's proven crookedness could indeed invalidate most every guilty finding he made in his courtroom and that reviewing judges shouldn't be factoring in the implications. One of these dissenters, Seventh Circuit appellate judge Ilana Rovner, has noted the irony of granting retrials to defendants such as Titone, whose fix attempts soured, while denying them to defendants who never tried to bribe Maloney. "It is a sad day indeed when defendants who attempted to purchase their way out of a conviction receive a greater measure of justice than those who did not," Rovner wrote in 2001. In an earlier opinion, she criticized the idea of deciding the issue on pragmatic grounds. If retrials had to be ordered for all defendants convicted before Maloney, "there are doubtless many guilty individuals, murderers even, who would go free" because of the age of their cases, she allowed in 1996. But this "appalling" prospect, she said, didn't change the fact that every defendant deserved a trial before a judge who wasn't crooked. "The Constitution was not written for easy cases and likeable defendants," Rovner wrote.

THE AUDIO IS WORKING again in Courtroom 302 on the morning of the trial's third and final day, but now the air-conditioning isn't. So the trial moves down the hall, to Courtroom 306.

In his closing argument, Cohn observes that the state failed to produce "one iota of physical evidence" tying Titone to the crime. He reminds the jurors that Titone testified even though he didn't have to. He says that when Titone learned from his father that the police wanted to question him, "he didn't run away. He didn't hide under the bed. He didn't check into a motel. He did nothing to demonstrate knowledge or acts of guilt. He came to the police station with his father. He didn't even go and get a lawyer to come to the police station."

McKay immediately objects, and Locallo calls a sidebar.

The lawyers and the judge huddle on the far side of the courtroom from the jury, where Locallo tells Cohn: "Now, you know from the facts that were brought out in the opinion that he showed up at the station with Mr. Roth." Locallo is referring to the Illinois Supreme Court opinion that affirmed Titone's conviction.

"I didn't know that," Cohn says.

"Yes, you did," McKay says.

"Your honor, I'm confused," Cohn says. "I will tell the court I made a mistake."

"All right," Locallo says.

But it's Locallo who's erred. The supreme court opinion didn't say that Titone had come to the station with Roth, and in fact, he hadn't. A police report indicates Titone arrived at the station with his father, was advised of his rights, refused to talk about the crime, and then phoned Roth, who showed up later. Cohn's mistake is in failing to catch Locallo's. As a result, Cohn's attempt to show the jury that Titone acted as if he had nothing to hide turns into an apology that suggests the opposite. "Ladies and gentlemen of the jury, I apologize," he says after the sidebar. "He came with a lawyer. I didn't realize that. I'm the first one to admit it if I make a mistake. As I've said various other times, I'm not only broad in the belly, I'm broad in the shoulders."

He switches to an attack on the credibility of Judy Gacho and Katherine De Wulf. Since Judy Gacho admitted that she lied under oath in 1984, how could her testimony be trusted now? As for De Wulf, by her own admission she was involved in the crime herself. She accused others of the crime "instead of taking it on her own shoulders," Cohn says. "She's not like me. She's not broad in the shoulders."

When it's McKay's turn, he wins instant grins from the jurors. "You know, ladies and gentlemen, Mr. Cohn, he has broad shoulders with a broad belly, but he can't have his cake and eat it, too. He can't stand here and say Judy Gacho's lying and Kathy De Wulf is lying, too. . . . Judy and Kathy, as far apart as you can possibly be, a wife and a mistress, and never the two shall meet to put their testimonies together."

Of Cohn's assertion that no physical evidence links Titone to the crimes, McKay says, "You know where Dino's fingerprints are? They're right on his fingertips, which are attached to his fingers, which are attached to his hands, which are attached to his arms, which are attached to his shoulders, which are attached to his collarbone, which is attached to his neck, which is attached to his head. And on his head, ladies and gentlemen, is the biggest print of all—his face print . . . permanently embedded in the memory of Judy Gacho, permanently embedded in the memory of Kathy De Wulf. We don't need fingerprints. It was cold that night. You can't lift fingerprints in conditions like that. Oh, by the way, Aldo Fratto's fingerprints weren't on the car either. It was his car. He was in the trunk. Tullio Infelise's prints weren't at the scene. Is Mr. Cohn saying they weren't there?"

In 1997 McKay and a partner won a conviction and a death sentence against an accused killer of a police officer. But the conviction would later be overturned by the Illinois Supreme Court, and the defendant awarded a new trial, because of the prosecutors' "overbearing conduct in pursuit of defendants' convictions." The high court chastised McKay for his closing argument, in which he exhorted the jury to make its verdict a message of support for police. Now, in his closing argument against Titone, McKay has the jurors in his palm. They're leaning forward, smiling, nodding. But then he takes a gratuitous shot at Titone, the kind an appellate panel might frown upon. Referring to De Wulf's testimony against Titone, he says, "What does Kathy De Wulf get out of this? How would you like to be her life insurance agent right now?"

Locallo sustains Cohn's objection. "Sometimes you can snatch defeat from the jaws of victory," Locallo says later about McKay's remark. He says prosecutors on occasion can't restrain themselves from taking a jab at a defendant, even when it puts their case at risk.

Titone's alibi is "nothing more than a card trick on you," McKay says. "You know that if a family member or a friend were with you on the night somebody says they're committing a crime, you would come forward right away. You would tell the police. You would tell the state's attorneys, somebody who has the power to dismiss the case, what you saw, what you know."

McKay concludes: "So what's in the cards for Dino Titone today? There was no poker game that night. The only card playing going on that night was three of a kind beating a pair. The three of a kind was Bob Gacho, Joe Sorrentino, and Dino Titone. Tell Dino his bluff didn't work."

THE JURORS HAVE BEEN deliberating for less than an hour when they scribble out some questions for Locallo: "Where are Bob and Joe now? Where has Dino been since 1982? Why is this case just now coming to trial?" Locallo confers with the lawyers, then writes out the same answer to all of the questions: "You have heard the evidence. Please continue to deliberate."

The buzz from the jury room comes four hours later.

The longer the jury was out, the more confident Titone had felt. But the first juror to enter the courtroom stares at the floor as she takes her spot in the box. Titone's heart sinks. It's guilty, he tells himself.

He's right.

"THAT TRIAL WAS SQUEAKY CLEAN," McKay says afterward. "But unfortunately for Dino the evidence was overwhelming, and the jury did the right thing."

Titone still may benefit from this second chance. He knows that Locallo has never sentenced a defendant to death, and so he's opted for Locallo and not the jury to decide whether he should be sentenced to death or natural life. Locallo has scheduled that sentencing for October.

FOURTEEN

A Sensitive Area

IN JULY, Locallo rules on Leroy Orange's bid for a new sentencing hearing.

The written ruling, which the judge reads to the parties in the courtroom one morning early in the month, is long even by Locallo standards—fifty-eight pages. Locallo recounts the testimony of the witnesses for Orange in profuse detail and cites eleven cases in his discussion of the legal issues. The aggravation evidence against Orange was "quite substantial," the judge says, given that four people were "savagely murdered." He agrees with the assessment that prosecutor David O'Connor made in May that Orange was not deserving of a "break." But Orange does deserve an authentic sentencing hearing, the judge says. The failure of his trial lawyer, Earl Washington, to investigate and present mitigation had effectively deprived Orange of that. So now he'll get one, Locallo says.

He doesn't set a date for the sentencing hearing. First he wants to resolve the other petition filed by Orange's present lawyer, Thomas Geraghty, the petition asking the judge for a hearing revisiting Orange's torture claims. Through that hearing Geraghty hopes ultimately to win Orange a new trial. Locallo says he'll listen to arguments on the petition in August. But he again voices skepticism regarding Orange's claims. Referring to Orange's allegation that a detective squeezed his testicles—and the fact that no evidence of injury to the testicles was found when Orange was examined after his arrival at the jail—the judge tells Geraghty, "You're a man, I'm a man. When there's injuries to the testicles, they don't just disappear. It's a very sensitive area.

"You're gonna have a long road to get over the hill" regarding the torture claims, Locallo tells Geraghty.

. . .

IN EARLY AUGUST Geraghty continues his push to get over that hill with a bulky filing. A cover memo addresses Locallo's earlier insinuation that Orange was merely trying to exploit the revelations about Area 2. Orange was not just "jumping on some bandwagon," Geraghty says in the memo. "Years before the evidence about the pattern and practice of torture by Area 2 police officers emerged, Orange was telling everyone he could about the horrors he had been through."

The balance of the filing consists of affidavits and other documents backing up that contention.

There's an affidavit from Jeffrey Howard, the public defender who represented Orange and his half brother, Leonard Kidd, at their bond hearing at 26th Street on January 14, 1984, a few hours after Orange and Kidd were transported to the courthouse from Area 2 after giving their confessions. Howard didn't speak with Orange or Kidd until they were brought into the courtroom that day, he says in his affidavit. But "when Leonard Kidd and Leroy Orange were brought out of the lockup, one of them complained to me that the police used a 'black box' to electroshock him," Howard says. He couldn't remember whether it was Orange or Kidd.

The "black box" allegation sounded ludicrous to Howard at the time, and so he didn't tell the judge at the bond hearing about it, the PD says in his affidavit, reasoning that such an outlandish claim could later be used by the state to impugn the credibility of the defendant who made it.

The transcript of the bond hearing is included in the filing. Like most such hearings, it was abrupt. Orange and Kidd were brought simultaneously before Judge Matthew Moran, who dealt first with Kidd. Noting the four counts of murder, Moran declined to set a bond. Howard noted for the record that Kidd had limped into the courtroom, and he asked Kidd which leg was injured. "I am hurting between my leg where they jumped on me and made me tell that I had said I done something I did not do," Kidd said, over the objection of the prosecutor. Judge Moran said Kidd's statement would "be made a matter of record."

After Moran likewise declined to set a bond for Orange, Orange said, apparently to Howard, "Talk about my injuries."

"You have injuries?" Howard responded. "Hold it, your honor. He says that he also is injured as well."

"I got pin marks on my butt," Orange said. "Only bruise I got to show. Other things happened. That is all that is visible right now."

"The record will show your statements," Judge Moran said.

Among other documents in Geraghty's filing:

• A February 9, 1984, *Chicago Tribune* article, in which attorney Earl Washington, then representing both Orange and Kidd, charged that both of his clients had been electrically shocked at Area 2 with "a mysterious 'black box,'" as the article put it.

• Records of visits by Orange to the Cook County Jail hospital in 1984, in which he repeatedly complained of rectal bleeding and weakness of his rectal muscles. A notation from a February 16, 1984, hospital visit said Orange attributed the bleeding "to electric prong being placed in rectum which he alleges police did upon his arrest 1/12/84."

• Affidavits from several people who said Orange had recounted the torture to them while he was in the jail in 1984. Alfred Girtley, who was in the cell next to Orange's from January through November of that year, said Orange began talking to him about his arrest a week or so after Orange was jailed. Orange told him the police "used a cattle-prod to shock him to get him to sign the confession," according to Girtley. Orange's ex-wife, Mildred Dixon, said Orange told her "the police had a black box and that they shocked him with it." Patricia Moore, a former girlfriend, said Orange told her "that the police put an electrical device inside of him that gave him an electric shock." Wanda Walton, a friend, said Orange told her the police had put "some sort of cattle prod up his anus," and that they'd also put a plastic bag over his head. Marie Jamison, another friend, recalled Orange talking about a black box that "had something electrical in it which gave him a shock."

In the filing, Geraghty also addresses Locallo's assertion that injuries to the testicles "don't just disappear."

Orange had alleged that a detective had squeezed his testicles shortly before he agreed to confess. His confession was taken beginning at 3:56 A.M. on January 13, 1984. He was examined by Dr. Sharish Parikh at the jail on the afternoon of January 14, not long after his bond hearing. Parikh testified at Orange's trial that he examined Orange's scrotum and testicles after Orange told him his testicles had been squeezed by police. Parikh said he didn't find any bruises, marks, or swelling, and that when he palpated the testicles, Orange reported no pain.

But Dr. Anthony Schaeffer, chairman of the department of urology at Northwestern Medical School, maintains in one of Geraghty's affidavits that it was "entirely possible for a patient to sustain a very painful squeeze" of the testicles and "have no signs of trauma, including palpable tenderness, 36 hours later."

And there's an affidavit from Dr. Robert Kirschner. As a Cook County medical examiner for seventeen years, Kirschner had testified in court here more than five hundred times, the vast majority of them as a state's witness testifying about a murder victim's cause of death. But he'd also investigated torture internationally. He'd served as a forensic consultant to the United Nations Truth Commission in El Salvador, to the International Criminal Tribunal for the former Yugoslavia and Rwanda, and to the Office of the Archbishop of Guatemala. He'd investigated many allegations of police abuse in Chicago, finding in "numerous instances" no evidence supporting the claims, his affidavit says.

Kirschner had interviewed Orange in the courthouse in early August. He'd reviewed Orange's trial testimony, his confession, the police records pertaining to his arrest and interrogation, and the relevant medical records. The methods of torture described by Orange—the bagging, the electroshock, the squeezing of the testicles—were "used on persons in custody in many countries" because the methods "usually leave no marks," Kirschner observes in his affidavit. The rectal bleeding Orange complained about in the jail could have been caused by the insertion of a foreign object into the rectum, the medical examiner says.

Orange's description of his near-suffocation with a plastic bag was "consistent with that of someone who has actually experienced this event," Kirschner says, as was Orange's account of his physical reaction to being electroshocked. Orange had extended his hand and fingers when describing the shock administered to the back of his forearm, and he'd flexed his hand and fingers when describing the shock to the front of the forearm. This was exactly the kind of "involuntary neuromuscular response" such shocks caused, according to Kirschner. Orange had also said he clenched his teeth so hard while being shocked that his upper front teeth had cracked. Kirschner had examined Orange's teeth and found them to indeed be cracked. In Orange's previous accounts of the injuries he suffered from his treatment at Area 2, he'd said nothing about cracked teeth. But it was common for torture victims "to be uncertain of some details of their torture, or to recall other injuries at a later date," Kirschner says.

In sum, Kirschner says in his affidavit, Orange's description of his physical reaction to being shocked made it "virtually certain that Mr. Orange was subjected to electric shock torture."

ON A MORNING in late August, Locallo hears arguments on Orange's petition for a hearing regarding his torture claims.

Geraghty contends that the affidavits and other documents he's submitted show that Orange made his allegations promptly and repeatedly. Kirschner's affidavit attests to the validity of the allegations, Geraghty adds.

Locallo soon starts finding fault with Geraghty's position. Regarding Orange's complaint of rectal bleeding, the judge points out that Geraghty has neglected to mention Orange's history of hemorrhoids. (Orange had been treated for hemorrhoids in 1978.)

"Well, he did have a history of hemorrhoids," Geraghty says. "But he didn't complain about hemorrhoids. He complained about something being shoved up his butt."

Locallo asks Geraghty what physical evidence he has corroborating Orange's claims. Geraghty says the corroboration isn't physical—it's in the multitude of evidence of similar torture at Area 2 in the early 1980s. Evidence of injuries to Orange might have been found if he'd been more carefully examined after his bond hearing, Geraghty says. But the complaint Orange voiced to his public defender, about being shocked with a black box, had seemed too outlandish to be believed. "We just did not know what was going on at Area 2 back then," Geraghty says.

Geraghty, who's well aware that Locallo has recently presided over Dino Titone's retrial, now draws a parallel between Orange's quest for a hearing and the appeal that won Titone the retrial. It was hard to believe Titone's account of the attempted fix of Judge Maloney, Geraghty says—until evidence surfaced of other fixes involving Maloney. Just as Titone made his allegation before Maloney's corruption was widely known, Orange made his torture claims before Area 2 became notorious. But Orange's case is even stronger than Titone's was, Geraghty says, because Orange voiced his complaint almost immediately, whereas Titone had waited years.

Prosecutor David O'Connor responds that Orange's allegations have grown "more grandiose, more ludicrous" over time, as witness his latest claim that the electroshock caused his teeth to crack. O'Connor says that torture allegations have been made against Area 2 detectives for years now, and people in the "criminal element" talk to each other, and thus defendants "know that these are the type of allegations that should be made" to try to get new trials.

Geraghty shoots back that Orange was hardly a member of a "criminal element"—he had only one conviction before this case, for criminal damage to property, sixteen years before he was arrested for the murders, and he'd been steadily employed for years.

Locallo interjects, "Your client did also admit to taking cocaine. So there's a worker, Leroy Orange—there's also a Leroy Orange who takes cocaine. . . . So Mr. O'Connor's argument is not beyond the realm of possibility."

The judge says he'll rule in late September on the request for a hearing.

FIFTEEN

What Really Happened

"DO *NOT* BE FOOLED by her appearance today," prosecutor Michael Nolan is warning the jury in 302 as he points at defendant Leslie McGee.

McGee watches Nolan studiously as he continues with his opening statement. There's a pen in her hand, a legal pad on the table in front of her. Her pigtails frame a bright-eyed, cherubic face. Winnie the Pooh, hunched above one breast pocket of her jumper, is gazing at the clutch of balloons above the other breast pocket. McGee also has on a white blouse, crew socks stretched halfway up her calves, and green tennis shoes. She's an average-sized eighteen-year-old. She was sixteen when she shot the cabbie in the head with the .357.

Nolan reads the jury the climactic passage of McGee's confession: "I said, 'God bless you,' and a couple other words that I don't remember. Then I gave him a peck on the cheek and I shot him." "Where did you shoot him?" "Somewhere in his head." "And how did you know that you shot him?" "Because he gasped and his eyes opened wide."

With those "chilling" words, Nolan says, McGee told police how she murdered thirty-six-year-old Jean François, a Haitian immigrant with three children, on the first day of March 1997.

Nolan has been looking forward to this trial. He's had his fill of gang-banger cases "where so-and-so shoots so-and-so because he had his hat cocked the wrong way." He'll take a "weird little murder" like this one any day, he's said. When he read the case file, what stood out to him was the blessing and kiss McGee gave François, according to her confession, before he killed him. Nolan didn't know what to make of it, but he found it intriguing.

The courthouse reporters are elsewhere this fall morning, this "weird little murder" not weird enough. It's another black-on-black case. The gallery benches are draped with the usual smattering of yawning, heavy-lidded minorities, anxious for a break in the trial so they can get their continuances and leave. The sole spectator with a personal interest in the trial has only a peripheral connection—she's the sister-in-law of the common-law wife of the deceased cabbie. McGee's father can't watch the trial because he's listed as a potential defense witness, but McGee's mother, who lives in Chicago, isn't here either. McGee hasn't heard from her since she was arrested for this murder a year and a half ago.

Pacing in front of the jury, Nolan now relates the circumstances preceding the shooting. François was in his cab when he spotted McGee near an El station on the south side. He offered her a ride even though she told him she had no money. McGee got into the front seat. François couldn't have known about the .357 she had in the back of her pants, under her coat. She'd stolen the gun from her father's house, intending to shoot her boyfriend, who'd recently broken up with her. When François reached 51st and Aberdeen—two blocks from where McGee said she wanted to be driven—he "did something that was wrong, but that should not have cost him his life," Nolan says. He pulled the cab over, suggesting that McGee pay him for the ride in another way. "He was suggesting that he would like to have some kind of sexual relations with the defendant." When McGee said she wasn't interested in paying that way, François "at that point touched her left breast over her shirt." When McGee again rebuffed him, François "slapped her and said, 'Get out of the cab, bitch.'" That's when McGee instead delivered her fatal mixed message to François.

Nolan paints such a vivid picture, it's as if he'd been in the cab's backseat. But there were only two people in the cab, as far as anyone knows, and one of them is dead. So Nolan's source for these details is the confession of the young woman he's already cautioned the jury to distrust. Nolan isn't at all sure the shooting unfolded this way—in fact, he doubts it did. "To be perfectly honest, I didn't know what was true in her statement and what wasn't," he says later. He could have told the jury what he really thought: that McGee definitely shot François but exactly how, or why, he wasn't sure. There's no percentage in betraying such doubts to a jury, however. "Why should twelve people who don't know you be willing to convict someone and send her to prison if you seem unsure of what she did? You're selling your case. I mean, that's just being a lawyer."

After shooting François, McGee jumped out of the car and fled, Nolan continues—and then spent the next few hours drinking and playing pool at a lounge. "That's how she mourned the death of Jean François."

Nolan has also been looking forward to this trial because he gets to do battle with Marijane Placek of the public defenders' Homicide Task Force. A trial is never boring with Placek in the mix. A PD more than twenty years, she's a formidable opponent and, at least in her attire, the most flamboyant lawyer at 26th Street. McGee isn't the only one at the defense table dressed for effect today. Placek has on an admiral's shirt, navy with gold stripes and buttons. A gold horse pendant hangs from her neck. She's platinum blond this morning. She changes the color of her hair, and the tint of her contact lenses, to suit her mood (or, she claims, the needs of a case). Now Placek, who's fiftyish and has knees that always ache, pushes herself to her feet and hobbles to the lectern. In the well of a courtroom she's in her favorite place, the center of attention. "We're all actors," she says of lawyers, "but we're too egotistical to say someone else's lines."

Nolan, thirty-four, has been a prosecutor for eight years. The main thing he's learned is that "everybody lies." Defendants, witnesses, defense lawyers, prosecutors, judges, cops—"we all have our own agenda. It's part of the game, I guess." It bothers him at times.

It never bothers Placek. One judge dubbed her the "Queen of Obfuscation," to her delight. She freely acknowledges being "sharp and manipulative." The only trouble with being manipulative, she says, is that sometimes it doesn't work. "Certain people you just don't lie to, you don't even practice on," she says. "Everyone else is fair game." Are the courts fair game? "Of course," she says. "That's where you play the most important game in the world."

Placek hates to lose—"it's ashes in my mouth." Winning causes no ambivalence. After she won a rape case for a client, she got a letter in the mail signed by "A Rape Victim." "I hope that what happened to me happens to you," the letter read. "And when it does, I hope you come up against a public defender just like you." Placek proudly pinned the note above her desk. Despite her wish to win them all, she prefers cases such as this one, with the odds stacked against her. "It's like Henry V said at Agincourt—'So much greater the victory.'"

In her opening statement, she doesn't deny that McGee shot François. Instead she glares at Nolan and tells the jurors that the prosecutor "forgot to tell you" that McGee was suffering from post-traumatic stress disorder when she encountered François. She developed the disorder after she was abducted at gunpoint a year earlier—an abduction that culminated in police finding her "running naked from her captors who had had her for several days." Placek says she isn't looking for sympathy for McGee because of this ordeal—although the girl clearly hasn't been the same since, she adds. She says the point is that McGee's behavior in the cab was understandable given what she'd been through a year before. François's actions revived her terrifying memories of her earlier abduction, and that was why she shot him. PTSD can also induce bouts of amnesia, Placek says, which explains why McGee went partying after the shooting: "She had at that time blotted the killing from her mind."

THE FRANÇOIS CASE was misleading from the start. On that March evening, shortly after nine, neighbors flagged down a squad car and directed it to the scene of a car accident at 51st and Aberdeen. The officers found François inside a crumpled Chevy on the sidewalk. He was unconscious, covered with blood, and sprawled across the front seat. A mangled Ford sat nearby, sideways in the street. Neighbors said they'd heard the collision but hadn't seen it, and that the Ford had been parked before the accident. The officers, and the paramedics who took François away, assumed the crash caused his injuries. He was pronounced dead at Cook County Hospital shortly after his arrival. The officers were back at their station, completing the paperwork about the accident, when they got a call from a worker at the morgue who'd discovered a bullet hole in François's cheek. The autopsy later attributed his death to the bullet found in his brain.

François's Chevy looked like it might have served as a taxi—its hood and trunk were painted red, the rest of the car white. A business card in his pocket led detectives to his employer, a livery service at 79th and Colfax. A driver there, a friend of François's, told detectives he'd seen François on the evening he was killed, parked near the livery office, with a woman in the front seat. François had borrowed $10 from the friend, saying he planned to take the woman to a nearby motel, the Skyview, and that he was a few dollars short of what he needed for a room. The friend said he hadn't seen the woman's face.

At the Skyview, detectives learned that François had indeed checked in on the evening of his death, at 6:20, renting a room for four hours for $26. He registered alone, but a clerk saw a female in his Chevy in the parking lot when he checked out at eight.

Detectives still didn't have a suspect when, in the predawn hours two days after François was killed, police got a call reporting a girl with a gun to her head on East 75th Street. This was McGee. She was pacing the sidewalk, holding a blue steel .357 revolver in her mouth and against her temple. She was distraught. "I'm scared and I just want to die," she told the officers who arrived, according to their reports. "I killed my boyfriend—I shot him in the face at 51st and Aberdeen." One of the officers, Sergeant Linda Szefc, asked her why she shot her boyfriend, and McGee said because he'd been beating her. Szefc changed the subject, gradually calmed McGee down, and, after two hours, finally convinced McGee to toss the gun away. She was taken to Jackson Park Hospital for psychiatric evaluation.

At the hospital, Sergeant Szefc asked McGee again about who she'd shot. This time McGee said it was a cabdriver who had asked her for sex as payment for a ride, and who grabbed her breast. After he also struck her in the head, McGee pulled out the gun and shot him, according to Szefc's report. McGee told Szefc she stole the gun from her father, intending to shoot her boyfriend because he'd been beating her.

Police realized the cabbie McGee was talking about was François. Detectives headed to the hospital and found McGee in restraints on a gurney in the emergency room, her mother at her side. She'd been at the hospital only about half an hour. When hospital personnel refused to release her to police, a detective pulled out a knife and cut the restraints. Then McGee and her mother were driven to the detectives' headquarters. Four hours later authorities had her court-reported confession.

According to that confession, McGee had taken the gun from her father's home, intending to shoot her ex-boyfriend "Melvin"—not because he'd been beating her, but because they'd broken up and McGee had seen him with another girl. François was just an unknown cabbie who offered her a free ride but who then molested her when she refused his advances. She shot him, but not until after he ordered her out of the car. Still in drive, the car lurched forward after the shooting, and McGee jumped out and ran.

The detectives, and the assistant state's attorney who took her confession, had little reason to doubt that McGee shot François. But they had good cause for disbelieving her assertion that she didn't know him, considering that she first told police that she'd killed her boyfriend, and given her admission that she'd taken the gun intending to shoot her ex-boyfriend. Detectives also knew that François had had a female in his car at a motel just over an hour before McGee shot him. And they knew that McGee and François had been neighbors: McGee's home was at 80th and Colfax; the livery service François worked for was at 79th and Colfax; and up until two months before the shooting, François had been staying with another woman at 81st and Colfax.

McGee's account in the confession of her actions after the shooting also had a fishy odor. She said she left the gun next to a garbage can in an alley, then ran to Halsted, a busy street three blocks away. Another stranger honked at her, offering her a ride, which she accepted. She told this stranger—"Mike"—about the shooting. They drove to the Why Not lounge at 109th and Michigan, where she drank, shot pool, and danced. She began worrying about her fingerprints on the gun and told Mike she needed to retrieve it. They drove the eight miles back to near the shooting scene, she picked up the gun, and they drove back to the lounge. She took the gun into the lounge in a bag. She drank, shot pool, and danced some more. Mike left, and McGee's ex-boyfriend—who at this point in the confession she called not "Melvin" but "Man"—happened into the lounge. "Man" wanted to reconcile with her. So they left and spent the night together.

The confession, with its soap-opera flavor, cried out for scrutiny, especially considering the age of its author. Instead, Kari Mason, the assistant state's attorney who put the questions to McGee during the confession, stepped lightly over the story's soft spots. Mason didn't ask McGee why she first told police the man she shot was her boyfriend; or why she told François "God bless you" and kissed him on the cheek before shooting him; or why she didn't just get out of the car when François ordered her to. She didn't ask McGee for the complete name of "Melvin"/"Man," so detectives could talk with him (or determine if he even existed); nor did she send detectives to the Why Not lounge to see if McGee had been there.

But then, from a prosecutor's point of view, it was a solid confession. McGee had admitted shooting François. Her statement that François ordered her out of the car would make it hard for her to claim later that her only option was shooting him. Her tale about partying afterward wouldn't win her points with a jury. If it remained a mystery why she shot François, well, that was hardly important. The law doesn't require police and prosecutors to get to the bottom of a matter; halfway in is close enough. After McGee signed the confession, Mason's supervisor approved a first-degree murder charge.

FRANÇOIS'S COMMON-LAW WIFE, Elizabeth August, leads off for the state. She tells the jury she and François had lived together off and on since 1988, and that their children are aged nine, eight, and seven. She saw François three days before he was killed, and the next time she saw him was at the morgue. Her brief testimony is unemotional.

While she's on the stand, her sister-in-law, Lisa Hampton, complains in the gallery that McGee's confession unfairly maligns François. "They're full of shit, that lawyer and that girl," Hampton says, gesturing at the defense table. François liked to play around, she says, but he wouldn't have tried to force sex on anyone the way McGee claims he did. She says that after François was killed, the word in the small south-side Haitian American community was that McGee and François had been involved for months. She guesses François was breaking off the relationship and that McGee shot him because she couldn't accept it.

August joins us on the bench when her testimony is over. She tells me she knew François fooled around, but that she appreciated that he "didn't do it in my face." About once a month he'd precipitate an argument with her, then stalk out of their apartment and stay out all night. This happened the last time she saw François. He got angry because his dinner wasn't ready when he arrived home, and he stormed out.

August says other Haitians did indeed inform her after his death that he'd been seeing a young woman, who she presumes was McGee. She says she told Nolan about this, "but he said he could convict her on what he had."

Nolan says later he didn't feel obliged to check out what August told him, or to inform McGee's lawyer, Placek, of it, because it was "just rumor and innuendo" and because it wouldn't make McGee less culpable if she and François were in fact involved. He says he wouldn't doubt that they had a relationship, though, "because it doesn't make sense that after a ten-minute cab ride, she kisses him on the cheek and then shoots him."

Evidence of a prior relationship could have strengthened his case in one way, he says—along with McGee's admission that she'd taken the gun to shoot her boyfriend, it would have indicated that the killing was premeditated. But it also would have muddled things for the jury, he says, because it would have contradicted McGee's confession. "You usually don't want to put in evidence that doesn't coincide with what's in the defendant's statement, because then it makes the statement seem unreliable."

Had Nolan investigated what August told him, another issue might have surfaced: this could have become a battered-woman case. In recent years jurors have occasionally acquitted women, or found them guilty of lesser charges, after they've killed their batterers. Placek could have maintained that McGee's first statement to police was the truth: she'd shot the boyfriend who'd been beating her—François—when he attacked her once again. Then, panicking about the potential repercussions, she concocted a story she thought made her less culpable, the story about the unknown cabbie.

Though only McGee knows for sure, this defense might have had the added benefit of actually being true. According to August, François was indeed a batterer. He was a good father to their children, August says, but short-tempered with her, sometimes slapping her around in the middle of arguments. "I picked up the phone and called police I don't remember how many times," she says, although when police arrived she invariably chose not to press charges.

Based on the police reports about the shooting, Placek says she suspected that McGee and François *had* known each other. But Placek had her own reasons for not pursuing this angle. While the battered-woman defense succeeds occasionally, Placek knows it usually doesn't, and she wanted to steer clear of anything that suggested a premeditated killing.

This image of the shooting that Placek and Nolan are presenting to the jury may well be mostly a mirage, Placek will allow later. But that's not unusual in a criminal trial, she'll say, and it doesn't trouble her at all. The truth is a nebulous thing, hard to determine under the best of circumstances: "How do I feel about the fact that the truth never comes out in court? The truth never comes out in *life*."

KARI MASON, the assistant state's attorney who took McGee's confession, reads it to the jury, employing a normal tone for the questions she put to McGee and a singsong voice for McGee's answers.

On Placek's cross, Mason acknowledges that when she arrived at the station to question McGee, the detectives informed her they'd brought McGee to the station from a hospital. "Did you inquire what she was in the hospital for?" Placek asks. Placek is backing Mason into a corner. If Mason says she knew McGee was at the hospital because she'd threatened to kill herself, Placek's next question certainly will be about the appropriateness of questioning a sixteen-year-old in such a fragile state. Perhaps Mason can see this coming. "You know, I don't think I did ask," she says. Placek screws up her forehead and glances at the jury. She presses Mason further, and Mason allows that she "might have" asked detectives where the gun that was used in the shooting had been recovered from. (It was recovered from the sidewalk where McGee dropped it to end her suicide threat.)

Mason also acknowledges on cross that she never asked McGee specifically why she shot François. Placek says later she thinks she knows why Mason didn't pose that question during McGee's court-reported confession: because had McGee responded that she shot François because she feared he was going to rape her or continue attacking her, it would have impaired the murder case. (Mason didn't return my phone calls.)

"Didn't you consider it relevant why a sixteen-year-old girl would shoot a cabdriver?" Placek presses Mason. "Or wasn't that good for the state's case?" Nolan objects, and Locallo directs Placek to rephrase the question.

"Did you ever say, 'Well, Leslie, he was letting you out of the car. Why did you shoot him?'"

"No, I didn't ask her that."

MCGEE WASN'T LEGALLY an adult at the time of the shooting, but it was always certain she'd be tried as one. Under Illinois law, a person is a juvenile until she or he turns seventeen, and McGee was three months shy of that when she shot François. But in Illinois, fifteen- and sixteen-year-olds accused of murder, rape, armed robbery, and certain other felonies are tried as adults. Thirteen- and fourteen-year-olds are also tried as adults for these crimes when prosecutors request it and a juvenile court judge approves. Most other states have similar provisions.

The Juvenile Court of Cook County, the world's first such court, opened in Chicago in 1899. Similar courts were soon born across the nation. The movement was founded on the idea that young offenders lacked the maturity to be fully responsible for their acts and that the punitive approaches of adult court were therefore inappropriate. The focus in juvenile court was on the child, not on the alleged offense. As Julian Mack, one of the first judges of Cook County's juvenile court, wrote in 1909: "The problem for determination by the judge is not, 'Has this boy or girl committed a specific wrong?' but, 'What is he, how has he become what he is, and what had best be done in his interest and in the interest of the state to save him from a downward career?'"

But even in the earliest years of the juvenile court here, juveniles in their early and mid-teens, charged with murder, rape, and armed robbery, were often tried as adults. Critics of this practice protested that it was inconsistent with the juvenile justice philosophy; if juveniles were too immature to be responsible for lesser crimes, why were they responsible for more serious ones? Pragmatism was behind the inconsistency. Supporters of the fledgling juvenile justice movement, already fending off complaints that juvenile courts were just havens for young hoodlums, were unwilling to fight to retain jurisdiction of notorious young offenders.

In more recent years, Judge Mack's philosophy of trying to determine how to save a youth from a downward career has been displaced by another tenet: "If they can do the crime, they can do the time." Across the nation in the last two decades, legislators have raced one another to introduce bills calling for more and more youths to be tried and sentenced as adults. Lawmakers have done so even though the in-vogue mantra apparently has a corollary: when they do adult time, they do more crime. Studies indicate that transferring youths to adult court increases the recidivism of those youths. Perhaps this is in part because those who are convicted as adults and sent to adult prisons before they're twenty-one suffer many more violent and sexual attacks while incarcerated than do similar youths kept in juvenile facilities.

BEFORE THE TRIAL, Placek asked Locallo to bar the state from introducing any testimony or evidence regarding a certain tattoo on McGee's calf. Placek knew the state had a photo of the tattoo, taken when McGee was jailed. "To put it bluntly, Judge, it's a hand holding a penis," she'd told Locallo. She argued that it was irrelevant to the case and that the state wanted to use it simply "to besmirch Miss McGee's character." Nolan countered that McGee's character might be relevant, depending on how Placek conducted her defense. Locallo at first responded as if it were a tattoo of Snow White he was considering. The tattoo "doesn't besmirch her character," he said; what McGee chose to put on her body was simply a "matter of free expression." But he ultimately sided with Placek regarding its admissibility. "I'm the gatekeeper," he told the lawyers. "We'll not talk about a tattoo of a handheld penis until it becomes relevant."

Now, on the afternoon of the trial's second day, before McGee takes the stand, Nolan asks Locallo to reconsider this ruling. Nolan wants to ask McGee about the tattoo on cross-examination, he tells the judge. Of course he'd like to show the jury the photo of the tattoo as well. "I think it's relevant based on the way she's been appearing before the jury with Winnie the Pooh clothing on . . . obviously, to make a different impression in front of the jury than is normal," the prosecutor says. But Locallo decides the tattoo is still irrelevant.

Nolan is worried that the jurors might not be too disturbed about François's death. "Under our theory, he's a scumbag cabdriver trying to cop a feel," as Nolan says later. He's concerned the jurors might sympathize with McGee instead, because she's young and female. He wanted to use the tattoo to undermine her sweet-little-lamb appearance.

Before the trial, McGee said in the jail that the tattoo was just something she got to retaliate against a boyfriend after he got himself a tattoo of a half-naked woman. She hadn't thought about how it would look to others, she said. "I wasn't nothing but fifteen."

Placek believes the tattoo represents more than that. She guesses that McGee had been compelled to get it by a "sadistic pimp" who pushed her into prostitution. "It's not a saucy, sexy, cute thing," Placek says. "It's like an advertisement, a branding, showing that she was some man's property." But Placek had no delusions about jurors sympathizing with McGee if they were allowed to see a photo of the tattoo. "Jurors want to feel superior," she says. "When they get into court, they're with a bunch of strangers, and they want to show that they're different from the defendant, that they're nice, normal, middle-class people. If they saw the tattoo, the reaction would be, 'My *God,* what kind of an arrogant little whore *is* she?'"

IT'S NOT RARE, Deputy Rhodes says, for a prisoner in the women's lockup to "flash" the males in the lockup across the way—to raise her shirt or lower her pants for a cigarette or a piece of candy that the men will toss to her. Rhodes says she's seen McGee flash the males for no obvious reward. Except for the flashing (which doesn't particularly disturb Rhodes but annoys Guerrero), McGee has been a docile prisoner, Rhodes says. Sometimes she curls up on the lockup's tile floor, sucking her thumb. This offended one of Rhodes's bosses, a sergeant, when she saw it one day this summer. The sergeant had come to the lockup to escort the female prisoners back to the jail. "Get that thumb out of your mouth," the sergeant snapped at McGee. "How old are you? If you don't stop sucking your thumb, I'll leave you here, I don't care."

McGee has frequently been a soothing influence on her cellmates in the lockup, Rhodes says. One morning a female defendant who was in court for a mental fitness hearing was ranting and raving in the lockup, alarming the other females—all except McGee, who calmed the woman by launching into a Supremes medley. "The other female defendants were cowering in the corner, and Leslie's there singing 'Baby Love,'" recalls Placek, who witnessed the episode. Deputy Rhodes has never seen McGee particularly upset and believes she's resigned to going to prison. But Rhodes has seen McGee comfort weeping cellmates after Locallo has sentenced them to prison. One image stands out in Rhodes's memory: that of McGee sucking her thumb while cradling the head of a sobbing woman in her lap and stroking the woman's hair with her free hand.

"I always have loved to take care of others," McGee said in the jail before the trial. "I don't worry about me first."

She started running away from home when she was twelve, she said, to get away from her parents' constant fights. She started drinking at that age, too. She liked "the feeling of absence from this world" that drinking gave her.

McGee said she was close to her father even though he was a harsh disciplinarian. She didn't fault him for the frequent whippings she says he gave with belts and extension cords. ("That's what he felt was right to do.") He was also fiercely protective of her. The police charged him with battery one time for beating a classmate of hers with a fiberglass fishing rod at her school. McGee had complained to her parents that the boy was picking on her. McGee was then nine, as was the boy. Her father "grabbed that boy by the ankles, he hit him in the head and everything. He beat him like he was his own child," McGee recalled. According to the police report, the elder McGee also attacked several other children, aged six to ten, at the school that day. The battery charge was thrown out when the complaining witnesses didn't appear in court. James McGee says he only hit one of the children. ("A little boy jumped right in front of me, so I spanked his ass.")

James McGee allows that he was a "pretty strict" parent. He only whupped Leslie "when she did something she wasn't supposed to do," but that became fairly often as she advanced into her early teens and "started listening to the wrong people and wouldn't listen to me," he says. When she began running away, he whupped her for that. Leslie was "strong-willed," he says. "She didn't want nobody to tell her what to do. She got that from me."

Leslie McGee is her father's second child to have killed someone as a teen. When she was six, her seventeen-year-old half brother plunged a butcher knife into the face of his mother's boyfriend during a fight. He said he'd caught the boyfriend slapping his mother. He got six years for voluntary manslaughter.

McGee described her mother as "paranoid, schizoid." She remembered her frantically stuffing suitcases one morning, telling Leslie, then seven, and her brother that they had to flee their home because their father was plotting to burn them up so he could collect the insurance money. "We believed her—she's Mama, and she'd never whipped us," McGee said. They spent nearly a year living with her maternal relatives in a decrepit flat before Leslie's mother was willing to return home with the children.

Court records indicate McGee's mother has been arrested once, for selling incense on a city bus.

McGee's parents divorced when she was ten, reunited, and split for good when she was fourteen. She kept her things at her mother's after that and stayed there or "with friends," she said. To her drinking she said she added an occasional snort of cocaine. She stopped attending school her freshman year and found work as a cocktail waitress at a south-side lounge whose owner didn't ask her age.

After she was charged with the murder of Jean François, she was held at first in the county's juvenile detention center. The county commemorated her seventeenth birthday, in June 1997, by shipping her to the adult jail at 26th Street. She was scared at first about being locked up with adults. But she learned that "it's a lot of talented, intelligent people locked up. It's a lot of people who do things out of necessity. Some people have unique situations."

She's been diagnosed in the jail as having bipolar disorder, a mood disorder characterized by swings between extreme highs and lows. McGee said she'd had days "where I do flips over the furniture" in the division day room, "I turn the TV [channel] rapidly, I run across the room, I do everything all in one breath, and I don't care who's watching me." But she'd also had "horrible crying spells, where nobody could calm me down." After vomiting one evening six months before the trial, she told the jail doctors she'd taken a two-week supply of her antidepressant—she'd been pretending to take the pills daily but was saving them up, she said. She told counselors she'd tried to kill herself several times before—at age eleven with rat poison, at age fourteen with muscle relaxers, at age fifteen by cutting her wrists. The jail overdose was prompted by her thoughts "about something bad that happened a long time ago," she told a counselor.

McGee has also told counselors, in response to their queries, that she was physically and sexually abused by relatives while growing up. She was reluctant to talk about sexual abuse when I raised the subject, other than to say that for a period of her childhood, a relative had indeed sexually assaulted her, and to stress that the perpetrator wasn't anyone in her immediate family.

McGee said she thought she needed to be locked up for a few years regardless of how her trial turned out. "If they just let me go home I know I'm gonna have problems again. Maybe they could send me to a mental institution, somewhere I can close myself off from the world, clear my mind of all the negatives." Placek later said McGee's professed desire to stay locked up awhile was immaterial for her. "What do I look like, a social worker?" the lawyer asked. Her job was to get McGee off if she could, she said, and otherwise to keep her sentence as short as possible.

Prosecutor Nolan had been assigned to juvenile court before he came to 26th Street. There he learned of the "hideous things" that adults, and often parents, sometimes do to children. He also saw how little was done to help the children: battered kids were often returned to their families or moved to homes that were even worse: "We certainly weren't solving any problems over there. Just trying to control things, I guess."

He doesn't doubt that McGee was a victim before she became a culprit: "I think most defendants were victims at some point. They're part of a situation that perpetuates itself. That doesn't absolve them, though. You can't ignore the new crime." Not that he has any illusions about what adult court achieves. As at juvenile court, "you're just solving the problem you have today. And you're not really solving that. You're just saying, 'Here are some consequences.' All it is is a Band-Aid."

PLACEK DOUBTED she could win McGee an outright acquittal based on self-defense, given McGee's admission that François ordered her out of the cab before she shot him and the fact that McGee was carrying the gun in the first place.

So Placek was aiming mostly for a conviction of only second-degree murder. In Illinois, a person is guilty of second-degree murder if he or she believed the circumstances justified the use of deadly force, but that belief was "unreasonable." (Second-degree murder was formerly known as vol-

untary manslaughter—the charge McGee's half brother was convicted of.)
The minimum sentence for first-degree murder is twenty years. For second-
degree, the minimum is four years, but a judge can give probation. And
since McGee was a juvenile at the time of the shooting, if she's convicted
of only second degree, Locallo could send her back to juvenile court for
sentencing. If she were locked up under juvenile law, she'd have to be
released by her twenty-first birthday at the latest—just two and a half years
from now.

Placek's plan is to convince the jury that post-traumatic stress disorder
made McGee believe—though unreasonably—that she had to shoot François.

Doctors had long noted in military veterans the symptoms of what is
now known as PTSD—flashbacks, nightmares, and a pronounced agitation
that sometimes erupts into violence. Doctors called this "shell shock" or
"combat fatigue." PTSD became a formal diagnosis after the Vietnam War.
It's currently defined by the American Psychiatric Association as a "development of characteristic symptoms following exposure to an extreme
traumatic stressor." That stressor can be not just combat but also an accident, a natural disaster, or a sexual or violent assault—anything threatening death, serious injury, or harm to one's physical integrity.

PTSD was first used as a criminal defense in the early 1980s by Vietnam veterans. These veterans would typically maintain that they had committed their crimes while reliving a combat experience—in some cases,
that they believed they were under enemy attack and responded accordingly. More recently, PTSD evidence has been used to buttress battered-
woman defenses, the women contending they were mentally reexperiencing
an assault at the time they lashed out. Juries and judges rarely acquit defendants because of PTSD evidence. Probably they'd agree with Locallo's
assessment of PTSD: "It exists, but a lot of it is bullshit." Sometimes, however, PTSD evidence helps turn a likely first-degree murder finding into a
lesser conviction.

In June, Placek had had McGee evaluated by a forensic psychologist
named Larry Heinrich. Placek and Heinrich have known each other for
years and consider each other friends. Heinrich had testified for about eight
of Placek's clients. They wrote an article in a law journal on the battered-
woman defense. Heinrich interviewed McGee in the jail for several hours,
talked with her father, and reviewed her jail records and the police reports
in the François case. Then he diagnosed McGee as having bipolar disorder,
borderline personality disorder, and "features of PTSD." The PTSD finding was especially significant. In a first-degree murder trial, judges won't
give the jury the option of a second-degree verdict unless there's evidence

supporting such a verdict. Illinois courts have deemed PTSD, but not mood disorders or personality disorders, as a possible basis for the "unreasonable belief" needed for second-degree murder.

Placek had another decision to make before trial regarding the PTSD defense: she had to decide what to attribute McGee's PTSD to.

Placek knew that PTSD was considered to be common in victims of childhood sexual abuse and that McGee fit the profile of such a victim. According to the National Center for PTSD, child sexual abuse victims often show sexual behavior or seductiveness inappropriate for their age; tend to have behavior problems, including running away; may try to injure themselves or attempt suicide; are frequently agitated or depressed; and often use alcohol and drugs to help soothe emotional pain.

But jurors dislike assertions by a defendant that an abusive upbringing played a leading role in their crime, Placek says. They're not inclined even to reduce a murder verdict to second degree unless substantial abuse can be proven, she says. And proving child abuse is often difficult. McGee might fit a profile, but that wasn't proof. There were no records, as far as Placek could determine, of abuse in McGee's home. Without supporting evidence, all there would be was what McGee herself would say on the stand. And McGee was disinclined to testify that she'd been sexually abused, which didn't surprise Placek. "Can you imagine how hard it is to talk about sexual abuse, even to one other person? And then can you imagine saying it in an open court, with sheriffs, jurors, lawyers, a judge, and a court reporter taking everything down? And saying it so you don't sound like a whiner?"

So Placek decided to attribute McGee's PTSD not to childhood sexual abuse but to an abduction she says she suffered a year before the shooting. There were definite advantages in relying on this 1996 abduction instead of on childhood sexual abuse. McGee was willing to testify about it; and there was a police report, albeit a vague one, about the incident.

As with her rejection of the battered-woman defense, Placek decided to stay away from the subject of childhood sexual abuse for strategic reasons. Lawyers don't try their cases according to their assessment of what really happened, Placek says, but on their estimation of what might work: "Both sides put on a case they think they can win."

ON THE SECOND DAY of the trial, McGee is dressed like a private school student—white dress shirt, red-and-black-checked blazer, black skirt—as she heads for the stand. Her crew socks are pulled up on her calves again, lest a juror glimpse the tattoo.

Placek has decided to let her second chair, public defender Camille Calabrese, handle the direct examination. Placek figured that McGee's testimony would seem less stage-managed if the junior lawyer on the case did the questioning. The testimony would, of course, be stage-managed, to the extent possible. Placek and Calabrese had rehearsed McGee repeatedly on her testimony, going over the questions Calabrese would ask, as well as the questions Nolan would likely put to her on cross. "We worked and worked and worked with her," Placek says later. "You can script a client as much as you possibly can, but when she hits the stand, all you can do is pray." Placek will hasten to add that by "scripting," she doesn't mean telling a client to lie, just advising them "what light to put things in."

"Calling your attention to April of 1996," Calabrese begins, "did anything unusual happen to you?"

"Yes, I was kidnapped by a man," McGee says.

McGee had been staying at a friend's in the suburb of North Chicago, she tells the jury. As she walked to a neighborhood pay phone to call her mother, she was accosted. A man forced her at gunpoint into the basement of a nearby house, where he made her strip and tied her to a couch. The man, who seemed to be Jamaican or Haitian, started smoking cocaine. He kept the gun nearby, and he had a knife in his hand as well.

"He took lighter fluid from out of the house, and he brought it into the room—and I don't want to talk about this, I don't want to talk about it, please don't make me talk about it," McGee says with a short sob.

"Leslie, if you need a moment, we can rest a moment," Calabrese says.

"I can't do it," McGee says.

"Leslie, I'm sorry, but I have to ask you these questions," Calabrese says. "And the jury needs to know what happened to you. What did the man do with the lighter fluid?"

McGee licks her lips and abruptly resumes. The man poured the lighter fluid over the couch to which she was tied. He smoked seven or eight bags of cocaine. He gagged and blindfolded her, then raped her. He kept threatening to kill her and kept saying "all types of nasty things he wanted me to do to him sexually, what he wanted to do to me." He raped her "twice. Or three times." He stroked her body with the knife, asking her where she'd like to be stabbed. McGee's face is blank and her tone flat as she relates these details—she could be describing last night's dinner. Her answers are almost inaudible; Locallo asks her repeatedly to speak up.

The man smoked more cocaine, McGee continues. He "kept trying to make me kiss him, telling me, 'Bitch, if you scream, I'm going to kill you now.'"

"And what were you doing?" Calabrese asks.

"Crying, pleading with him, pleading, 'Spare me.'"

Calabrese doesn't ask McGee how she could have said anything if she was gagged. And when McGee says the man showed her a lighter and threatened to ignite the couch, Calabrese doesn't ask her how she could have seen the lighter if she was blindfolded. At the defense table, Placek, ever aware of the jurors' watchful eyes, is affirming McGee's responses with nods but wincing inwardly.

The man left her alone after seven or eight hours, McGee says. She freed herself from her bindings and removed the gag and blindfold. Upstairs she found a sweater and pulled it on, and she wrapped a towel around her waist. Then she raced, screaming, to the house across the street. The man there let her in and called the police, who took her to their station. Placek suppresses an urge to groan. McGee's account doesn't even match the lawyer's opening statement, in which Placek had said police found McGee "running naked from her captors who had had her for several days." (Placek says later she based this on what McGee told her.)

McGee tells the jury she led the North Chicago police back to the house where she'd been held captive. But no one was there, and to her knowledge no one ever was arrested.

(The North Chicago police report about the incident says police got a 911 call from a "hysterical female." The officer who responded to the home from which McGee called found her wearing just a T-shirt and a towel wrapped around her waist. She said she had been abducted at gunpoint by a black man with a Jamaican accent, who forced her into the basement of an apartment building. He took her clothes from her and tied her up on a couch, she said, but he didn't rape her. The apartment in which McGee said she had been held was in "complete disarray." Police found masking tape on the floor, along with cords, wire, string, several socks—one of them tied into a loop—and an unopened package of condoms. In the kitchen they found a small amount of what appeared to be rock cocaine, along with a broken ink pen, presumably used to smoke the cocaine. A neighbor in the apartment complex told police he had heard a girl yelling during the night but that he couldn't tell whether she was laughing or crying.)

McGee now tells the jury she had trouble sleeping and eating after the North Chicago attack. Men unnerved her, Jamaican and Haitian men in particular.

She says she took the gun from her father's house because she had an abusive ex-boyfriend and because she feared for her life after the abduction. Calabrese doesn't ask her to elaborate on her ex-boyfriend's abuse or to explain why she didn't take the gun until eleven months after the kidnapping.

When François grabbed her breast and hit her, "It wasn't him I saw," McGee says. "I saw the man that kidnapped me."

"And when you thought you saw the man who kidnapped you, what did you do?" Calabrese asks.

"I guess I shot him."

She says she got into the front seat of François's cab when he invited her to "because I'm a trusting person. I trust any- and everybody."

On Nolan's cross, McGee says she doesn't know the last name of the friend she stayed with in North Chicago. The person was actually a friend of another friend—whose last name she doesn't know either. She allows that she didn't tell the North Chicago police that her abductor raped her.

When Nolan presses her for specifics about the shooting of François, McGee's memory dims. She doesn't recall much about the shooting, or about what she did afterward that night, or about her standoff with police two days later, or about confessing. "I don't remember things I do from the last five minutes," she tells Nolan.

When her testimony is complete, Locallo dismisses the jury for the weekend.

After Rhodes escorts McGee from the courtroom, Placek, gathering her files at the defense table, tells me she doubts that the jury believed McGee's account of the abduction. Jurors expect a great show of emotion from witnesses recounting how they've been victimized, when in fact victims of traumas often closely guard their feelings, she says. Did Placek herself believe McGee was raped in North Chicago? The lawyer hesitates, then says, "I believe she believes she was raped."

After Placek leaves, Deputy Rhodes tells me that she too doubts that the jurors bought McGee's testimony. "I think something bad really did happen to her, but it's not what she's testifying about," Rhodes says. "I keep thinking: 'Leslie, why don't you just say what happened?'"

NOLAN HAS LITTLE REGARD for most psychologists and psychiatrists who offer expert testimony in criminal trials. "A lot of them are just whores," he says. "That goes for the state's experts as well as the defense's. They can take any set of facts and arrive at whatever conclusion they want."

On the trial's third day, psychologist Heinrich tells the jury that when he interviewed McGee in the jail, she described the abduction in North Chicago. She also told him that after that "very life-threatening episode," as Heinrich calls it, she lost weight and had trouble sleeping; she was anxious and fearful; and she had unsettling flashbacks of the abduction. She was constantly on her guard around men, fearing "that she would be sexually assaulted or possibly killed." These are classic PTSD symptoms, Heinrich says.

Then Placek has Heinrich connect the PTSD to the shooting. A PTSD flashback can cause a person to "do something impulsive," Heinrich tells the jury. And François triggered such a flashback with his actions in the cab, the psychologist says. When François "was going to force her to have sex," it revived for McGee an image of the North Chicago episode, when she was tied to the couch "and the man was threatening her life."

Heinrich relates this with certainty, a certainty reminiscent of Nolan's opening statement. Heinrich and Nolan were relying on the same source for their accounts of the shooting—McGee. But whereas Nolan told the story as if he'd been in the backseat, Heinrich is providing an even more immediate perspective: the view from inside McGee's head. When McGee shot François, the abduction in North Chicago was "the primary . . . thing on her mind," Heinrich asserts.

Heinrich says that besides PTSD, McGee also has bipolar disorder and borderline personality disorder. People with borderline personality disorders are "fairly poorly adjusted individuals" who "have trouble reasoning issues through," he says. He attributes her suicide attempts, her running away from home, and her dropping out of school to this disorder.

On cross, Heinrich concedes that when McGee described the abduction to him, she didn't mention being raped.

He also acknowledges that he's being paid by the defense for his work on this case—$125 an hour, or about $2,000 so far.

Heinrich has testified in more than fifty criminal trials, he tells me later, nine times out of ten for the defense. "Despite all of our efforts to be objective, we will have some bias that we take into the evaluating process," he allows. "I try to wed my opinion to the evidence I've reviewed. But it's an adversarial process, and it becomes a matter of convincing the jury, a matter of salesmanship sometimes."

He also allows that the shooting could have been mainly a product of McGee's borderline personality—but that PTSD was "certainly more dramatic as a defense argument."

He never considered that McGee and François might have been involved before the night of the shooting. When I raise that possibility with him, he says that that would explain the blessing and kiss McGee said she gave François before killing him. Heinrich found that blessing and kiss "frankly bizarre." He asked McGee about them, but she wasn't able to explain them. If McGee and François were indeed involved, "that would have changed the whole dynamic of the offense—and maybe it would have changed my opinion, to be honest with you," Heinrich says.

Now, in the courtroom, Nolan's answer to Heinrich is psychiatrist Roni Seltzberg. Seltzberg, who's employed by the county, has a diagnosis of

McGee that is less likely to engender sympathy: McGee's main problem isn't PTSD; it's drug abuse. McGee acknowledged in her interview with Seltzberg that she'd been a heavy drinker, a habitual smoker of marijuana, and an occasional user of other drugs before her arrest. She told Seltzberg she'd started using drugs at age twelve because of "family problems" that she wouldn't specify. Seltzberg says the sleep trouble and anxiety McGee described could have been products of the drug withdrawal she likely experienced after she was locked up. She doesn't think McGee showed any particular fear of men before the shooting, pointing out that according to her confession "she apparently willingly went with at least three different men in one night."

Placek counters Seltzberg with psychiatrist Alexander Obolsky.

This is Obolsky's maiden trip to the stand for a Placek client—the beginning, Placek hopes, of a long and mutually beneficial relationship, like the one she has with Heinrich. Placek heard Obolsky speak at a recent psychiatry convention where she was "trolling for experts." She's planning to have him testify for another of her clients with even more at stake than McGee, a paranoid schizophrenic facing the death penalty for a quadruple murder. Today's testimony is in part a dry run for that case, Placek has said, a chance for her to develop a "rhythm" with Obolsky.

Now Obolsky seconds Heinrich's diagnosis of McGee. He tells Placek it's reasonable to conclude that McGee was suffering from PTSD, given her symptoms and her "validated story of kidnapping," and that the PTSD prompted the shooting of François. His conclusions regarding McGee are based on his review of the relevant records and reports; he never actually talked with her.

"YOU'VE HEARD A LOT of people tell you that Leslie McGee suffers from this or Leslie McGee suffers from that," Nolan's partner on the case, second chair Mark Ertler, tells the jury in his closing argument. "But did anybody tell you that she was not in control of her actions?"

The shooting was McGee's "way of saying, 'Somebody is going to pay for all the things that I feel have been done wrong to me,'" Ertler says. To render a verdict of only second-degree murder would be to give McGee a "license to kill because of the problems that she says she has."

Ertler advises the jury to put more stock in McGee's confession—given before she talked with defense lawyers or psychologists—than in her courtroom testimony. When a person tells conflicting stories, the first account is likely to be more accurate, he says. And McGee's confession makes clear that McGee was bent on killing someone even before she encountered François, the prosecutor observes. She left her home that morning intending to kill her boyfriend "and to the great misfortune of Jean François, he happened to get in the way."

Once again Lisa Hampton, sister-in-law of François's wife, is the only one in the gallery with a personal interest in the case. François's common-law wife, Elizabeth August, had flown back to California, her current home, the day she testified. The only spectators in the gallery besides Hampton and myself are three assistant state's attorneys. Hampton, who's rocking her infant daughter in her arms, says she hopes McGee spends twenty-five years in prison. "That'll give her time to think about what she did."

It's five in the evening when Placek begins her closing argument. She reminds the jury of Ertler's contention that a person's original account of an event is the most trustworthy. Then she further reminds the jury that before McGee gave her confession, she told a sergeant she shot the cabbie after he molested her and struck her. Thus it's clear McGee was simply trying to protect herself from being raped, Placek says.

Placek barely mentions the North Chicago abduction. She'd just as soon the jury not dwell on that, given McGee's performance on the stand.

The PD allows that she doesn't know exactly what happened in François's cab. But the prosecutors don't either, she says. She gestures at her blank-faced client at the defense table: "I don't know if *she* knows what happened." But the likeliest explanation, Placek says, is that McGee shot François either to fend off a rape or because of her PTSD: "Otherwise, what is the motive? She did what she had to do based on her background."

In his rebuttal argument, Nolan allows that "something probably did happen" to McGee in North Chicago, but something far less traumatic than what McGee described. After McGee met with her lawyers, he says, she probably realized the North Chicago episode was her only possible ticket out of the first-degree murder charge, but that she needed to embellish on the episode for it to help her.

Nolan thinks his best courtroom skill in a jury trial is his ability to focus jurors on the bottom line. "Keep it simple" is the advice he gives younger colleagues.

Now he tells the jury that François did something in the cab that offended McGee, "and she shot him and killed him—it's that simple, folks." He urges the jurors to ignore "all the other nonsense. There is no post-traumatic stress disorder. There is a murder, plain and simple."

DEPUTY RHODES IS STUDYING a pair of mail-order catalogs at the sheriff's station, while Deputy Guerrero twirls the cylinder of the .357 McGee used to shoot François. It's seven-thirty P.M., and the jury has been out a half hour. Guerrero doesn't much care what the jury decides since "I get paid either way." The deputies' lockup monitor shows McGee stretched out atop a steel bench, sound asleep. "Maybe we'll go to a hotel, get some overtime," Guerrero muses hopefully. But Rhodes shakes her head. Though she's rooting for second degree, she's expecting first, "in an hour, tops," as she tells her partner. Then she reconsiders. "Well, their dinner is back there, so maybe an hour and a half."

At nine-fifteen, the deputies hear laughter from the jury room. "They've reached a verdict. They're all relaxed now," Guerrero says.

The beep sounds a few minutes later.

Soon Placek is at the bars to the women's lockup, calling to her client. McGee blinks awake and slowly pushes herself up on the bench. "Whatever the verdict, show nothing," Placek instructs her. She always tells her clients this. She thinks it's insensitive for defendants to celebrate in the courtroom when they're acquitted, especially in murder cases. And she'd rather not give the prosecutors the satisfaction of seeing her clients break down when they're convicted.

The parties are back at their tables a few minutes later, and the somber-faced jurors return to the jury box. Lisa Hampton has the gallery almost to herself—there's just her baby, dozing in the infant seat next to her on the bench, and myself.

Locallo directs the foreperson to hand the verdict to Guerrero, and Guerrero delivers it to Locallo. Since the clerk is gone for the day, Locallo announces the verdict himself: " 'We, the jury, find the defendant, Leslie McGee, guilty of first-degree murder.' "

"Yes!" Hampton says.

Locallo polls the jurors. Some of them are wet-eyed, but they each acknowledge the verdict was theirs. The judge thanks them and dismisses them to the jury room. He sets a December sentencing date. McGee yawns as Rhodes ushers her out of the courtroom.

"First-degree murder, and she's *yawning*," Hampton says dejectedly as she lifts her baby from her infant seat. "I wanted to see the pain on her face."

MCGEE IS IN BLUE jail togs when she returns to 302 for sentencing on a mid-December morning. Placek is in a green suit jacket, and her hair is now red. "Looks nice. Matches the season," Locallo tells her.

Both sides know Locallo has made up his mind on the sentence, and so they rush through the hearing. Nolan presents no witnesses in aggravation, Placek none in mitigation. Locallo asks McGee if she wants to say anything. McGee says she doesn't. But then she adds softly, "I feel remorseful for what I did. I would like to apologize to my father for what I did."

Locallo says that because McGee is only eighteen and has no previous record, he thinks she can be rehabilitated. The murder was the result of an "unfortunate set of circumstances." He gives McGee the minimum twenty years—and a contact visit with her father, who's in the gallery today. The hearing is over in five minutes.

The contact visit consists of McGee and her broad-shouldered father clutching each other for almost ten minutes in the hallway outside the courtroom lockup, with Rhodes and Guerrero looking on uncomfortably. Finally Rhodes tells them it's time for Leslie to be returned to the jail. Her father leaves the courtroom through the gallery. In the hallway, he tells me he's worried about how prison will affect his daughter. He fears she'll only slide farther downhill. His eyes are glistening, and he's twisting a baseball cap in his hands. He wonders whether he disciplined her too harshly. He was tough on both his kids, he says, but especially on Leslie because she ran away so often.

With day-for-day credit, McGee will have to serve ten years. (The truth-in-sentencing law enacted in June 1998 requires first-degree murder convicts to serve 100 percent of their terms; but since the François murder predated that law, McGee is still eligible for the day-for-day credit.) In the jail before she's shipped downstate, McGee says she intends to make the most of her time in prison. "I want to show my family that I'm more than they think I am. I have to forget what's happened and go on with my life. I want to make myself be somebody people can look up to instead of down to."

She's shipped to the Dwight Correctional Center the day before Christmas Eve. The guards inspecting her upon admission discover a new tattoo on her thigh, a jailhouse artist's work. The words "Live By The" and "Die By The" are printed alongside a sword.

LATER, when I outline for Locallo the numerous facts suggesting a prior relationship between McGee and François, he's at first taken aback. He says that it would disturb him if the jury was indeed presented an erroneous scenario of the crime. It would bother him, too, he says, if he sentenced McGee under a false presumption of how the crime occurred. "If what you say is true, that he was in fact her boyfriend, then the post-traumatic stress disorder is bullshit," he says. "I don't know what the truth is here." But then he shrugs and turns to the bottom line. "If he was her boyfriend, then the question might be—so what? She still killed him." He chuckles and adds, "She gave him a kiss and blew him away. So was justice done anyway? Sounds to me like it was."

The jurors did not believe McGee's account of the North Chicago episode, according to foreperson Selig Pearlstein. They speculated that the place McGee was staying was a drug house since it had no phone and since

McGee couldn't recall anyone's last name. They figured that McGee was high when she walked outside to use the pay phone. They didn't believe she was raped. And they didn't believe that the abduction traumatized her about men, particularly Haitian or Jamaican men, given that, according to her confession, she got into François's car when François offered her a ride.

But the jurors felt sorry for her nonetheless, Pearlstein says. "We felt she was a street kid who'd probably been selling her body for drugs since she was twelve or thirteen. We didn't know if Jean François was a good person or a bad person, but what we knew about him we weren't impressed with. We went into the jury room planning to give her second-degree. But then we read the instructions, and we realized that according to the law, she was guilty of first-degree. No matter how the defense tried to cloud it, there was no denying she could have gotten out of the cab without doing serious harm to him and without being seriously hurt herself."

Pearlstein wishes juries had some say regarding what happens to a defendant after she or he is convicted. "If we could have sent her somewhere where she'd get five years of intensive psychiatric help, we would have done that."

He says that when Locallo came into the jury room after the trial to thank the jurors, the jurors told the judge they wished he wouldn't just punish McGee but would find help for her. Locallo offered the jurors some reassurance, according to Pearlstein: he said he'd be giving McGee the minimum, which meant she'd probably be sent to a minimum-security prison, where there likely would be programs to help her. "All of us felt good about that," Pearlstein says. In reality, McGee would be assigned to maximum security, as are all inmates with sentences of sixteen years or more. ("I wasn't aware of the rules," Locallo says.)

Pearlstein says the jurors all wondered why McGee told François "God bless you" and kissed him before she killed him. They assumed there was more to the story than they learned of in court. Pearlstein says the trial taught him that in a courtroom, "there's three sides to every story: your side, my side, and what really happened."

SIXTEEN

Prejudice

IN THE DINGY JURY ROOM of Courtroom 500, Locallo and the lawyers are interviewing potential jurors for the Frank Caruso trial. It's an afternoon in early September, and the trial is finally about to begin. As in April—the last time the trial was supposed to start—it's been assigned to a larger courtroom because of the expected crowd.

In the courtroom this morning Locallo, sporting a fresh haircut, introduced Caruso to the venire, the panel of potential jurors, and asked anyone who'd heard of the case to stand. Just about everyone did. Laughter erupted, and the judge grinned. Locallo asked a few preliminary questions of the venire, then began calling prospective jurors one at a time to the jury room, where they sit in an armchair with torn upholstery and answer more questions.

Several acknowledge a bias against Caruso from the media coverage of the case. These candidates are excused by Locallo "for cause." So are the couple of people whose bias runs in the opposite direction. ("I find that a lot of the young blacks walk around very comfortable in the white neighborhoods, whereas the young whites wouldn't do it in the black neighborhoods," a white man says.) Some other members of the venire who show no clear prejudices get booted by the lawyers.

Locallo is hoping the trial will be a picture of color-blind justice. So it's lucky that most of the jury-picking is being done in this back room, because as usual the process is anything but color-blind. Both sides have seven peremptory challenges—they can strike seven prospective jurors without citing a reason. At 26th Street, as in many urban criminal courtrooms, the unspoken reason is often race. Lawyers tend to believe that jurors are more likely to sympathize with a defendant of the same race, and they use their strikes accordingly.

In 1986 the U.S. Supreme Court acted to curtail racial use of peremptories with its ruling in *Batson v. Kentucky. Batson* requires a lawyer accused by the other side of a racial strike to give the judge a race-neutral reason for dismissing the juror. Justice Thurgood Marshall, while concurring in the *Batson* decision, predicted that lawyers would simply concoct phony justifications for their racial strikes. The way to eliminate racial jury-picking, Marshall said, was to eliminate peremptory challenges. (Great Britain did so in 1988, and jury selection there has since become a more efficient process. But American trial lawyers tend to oppose such a reduction in their power.)

Justice Marshall's forecast has proven accurate. Since *Batson,* legal scholars and reviewing court judges have chastised prosecutors in particular for the flimsy excuses they often give for striking blacks. In a 1996 ruling, Illinois appellate justice Alan Greiman lamented the "charade" that jury selection has become. Pointing to the multitude of excuses prosecutors offer for excluding black jurors—too young, too old, unemployed, overeducated, hair unkempt, demeanor bothersome—Justice Greiman wondered facetiously whether new prosecutors were given a manual entitled *Twenty Time-Tested Race-Neutral Explanations* for excusing African American jurors.

With a white defendant and black victims, the Caruso case has things upside down. Prosecutors Robert Berlin and Ellen Mandeltort don't find any of the black prospects too young or too old or to have unacceptable hair or demeanor. They use all seven of their strikes against whites.

One of the rejected whites is Ronald Pedelty, a high school physics teacher. He says he'd base his verdict on what's presented by both sides in the courtroom. He says physics has taught him to value "objective reasoning based on the evidence." When Berlin and Mandeltort move to strike him, Caruso's lawyers make a *Batson* challenge. Locallo asks the prosecutors for a race-neutral reason for excluding Pedelty. Mandeltort notes that Pedelty "indicated that he would use objective reasoning." Besides that apparently troubling fact, Pedelty's demeanor was "not satisfactory to the state," she adds vaguely. Locallo finds these to be valid reasons for the state to strike Pedelty.

Meanwhile Caruso's lawyer, Ed Genson, uses six of his seven strikes against blacks. When the prosecutors charge Genson with violating *Batson,* Genson insists the strikes aren't due specifically to race. A jury poll he commissioned advised him against selecting jurors who are mothers or who are elderly, and this explains most of his peremptories, he tells Locallo.

Genson admits to me later that he didn't just want younger jurors and non-mothers. He wanted as many white men as he could get. He believed white men were "less likely to be swayed by things they shouldn't be swayed by."

Locallo perfunctorily does his duty under *Batson,* asking one side for race-neutral reasons when the other complains of a racial strike and immediately accepting whatever justification is offered. The judge says later he realizes the reasons cited may be contrived. "But I don't think it's my prerogative to say, 'You've given a race-neutral reason; I think it's full of shit.'" Besides, jury selection is tedious enough, and these *Batson* challenges only bog it down more. On the afternoon of the second day of the process, with two more jurors and two alternates yet to pick, Locallo closes the final *Batson* discussion in nearly one breath, with the court reporter straining to keep up: "Pursuant to *Batson versus Kentucky* and its progeny the court is required to see if the reasons are race-related or race-neutral and I've considered each of the reasons given by both the state and also defense and I've found race-neutral reasons for the exclusion of those individuals. . . . It's now one-twenty-five. Do we want to break for lunch and come back?"

After two days and consideration of sixty-two jurors, the Caruso panel is finalized. Both the state and the defense have reason to feel pleased with their efforts. The prosecutors have held the number of white males to three. There are five minorities on the jury, but the defense has managed to limit the number of blacks to two; the other minority jurors are two Hispanics and one Pakistani American. Both of the black jurors are women. As so often happens here, not a single black male has won a spot.

THE GALLERY BENCHES are jammed, and standing spectators line the side and rear walls, as prosecutor Robert Berlin steps to the lectern the next morning, the tenth of September. Sketch artists and reporters are bent over their pads and notebooks. Except for one group of African Americans squeezed in two rows, which includes relatives of Lenard Clark and the other victim, Clevan Nicholson, the gallery is mainly a sea of white faces. At the defense table, Caruso is drowning in a navy sport coat. If the intent is to suggest vulnerability, it's offset by the five lawyers sitting with him.

Berlin tells the jury about two thirteen-year-old project kids who decided to take a bike ride after school on a warm early spring afternoon. They rode into Bridgeport because Lenard's bike needed air, and he could get it for free at the gas stations in that neighborhood, Berlin says, whereas the gas stations near the project charged a quarter. On their return trip, when they were meandering down a Bridgeport side street with a Hispanic teen they'd met along the way, Berlin says, Lenard and Clevan were attacked by Caruso. After Caruso knocked both of them off their bikes, Clevan managed to flee, but Lenard was chased down by Caruso and two buddies, tackled to the street, and stomped. Maybe they'd have killed him if a neighbor hadn't interrupted the beating and threatened to call the police, Berlin says. Lenard spent a week in a hospital and five weeks in a rehab institute, where he had to relearn how to brush his teeth, dress, bathe, and feed himself. He has no memory of the attack and thus won't testify.

Berlin, thirty-six, is tall and clean-cut, with a narrow face and thinning hair. He'd originally been paired on this case with one of the few veteran African Americans in his office, but that prosecutor left in May for another job, and Mandeltort, thirty-seven, had been picked to replace her. Berlin and Mandeltort, thirteen-year veterans of their office, are both products of Chicago's wealthy north-shore suburbs.

Berlin's aggrieved expression and tone suggest a simmering outrage as he tells the jury of Caruso's vow "to beat the fuck out of these motherfuckers" when he spotted Lenard and Clevan from his Jeep, and of his complaint to a friend in the Jeep that "niggers think they can just come into our neighborhood and walk around, but we can't go into theirs and walk around." He lets the jury know that one witness is missing, another dead. He steps toward the defense table and points repeatedly at Caruso, whose eyes remain fixed on the edge of the oak table in front of him.

Berlin was vacationing in Puerto Rico when Lenard was assaulted. He was thrilled to learn upon his return of his assignment to the case. "Ninety-nine percent of the cases we do are not in the news," he's said. "It's nice once in a while to be noticed for the work you do." When he saw the intensive-care photos of Lenard, with his face battered and a tube up his nose, his reaction was mixed. On a personal level, he was repulsed and angered, but as a prosecutor, he realized how helpful the photos would be.

Now he concludes his opening statement by standing directly in front of the jury box and holding up before-and-after photos of Lenard. The first photo shows a bright-eyed youngster with a wide, toothy grin, the second a hospital patient with eyes clamped shut and the tube in his nose. "Ladies and gentlemen, this was Lenard Clark before he went into Bridgeport on March 21, 1997," Berlin says. "And this is what happened to Lenard Clark because he and Clevan Nicholson made an error in judgment to save twenty-five cents. That's what happened to Lenard Clark when he went into Bridgeport and ran into this defendant and his buddies." The jurors are riveted on the second photo, so Berlin pauses. The courtroom's silence is broken by the sniffle of one juror, a white woman. Two other white women in the box swipe at their eyes.

After Berlin sits down, Ed Genson hobbles to the lectern, where he climbs onto a tall wooden chair brought here from his office. The high perch gives him a clear view of the jurors, and the jurors of him. It leaves his feet dangling childlike above the gray carpet. The beating of Lenard is indefensible, he says, but Caruso didn't do it. He's trying to prevent another horrible crime—the conviction of an innocent man. "We will not strut, we will not walk around and point," he says disdainfully. "I'm in no position to strut anymore anyway. Don't fall for that. Indignation, anger, does not show guilt. We have to decide who committed this act. If the state wants to substitute accusations for reason, fine. And if they want to substitute anger for facts, fine. We will not join in. We are not going to accuse."

His job isn't to accuse, of course; it is to deny—which he does, over and over. Frank Caruso is innocent. He didn't punch Lenard or Clevan. He didn't chase down Lenard and kick him. He never used those racial slurs. He is falsely accused. At the state's table, Mandeltort is summarizing Genson's remarks in a blue hardback ledger. When she takes notes during a case, now and then she adds a comment in a margin, an idea perhaps for closing argument. Now she writes in the margin, "He can say it ten times, he can say it a hundred times, it does not change the evidence, it does not change the facts."

Genson is above accusing—except to tell the jury that the police rigged a lineup, and ignored evidence, and let the real culprits off the hook, in order to get the quick solution demanded from them by the mayor and the police chief.

He says that everyone, the defense included, wants sympathy and justice for Lenard. But "I ask for sympathy and justice for someone who was charged with a crime he did not commit."

"How dare he compare their plights," Mandeltort writes in her ledger.

Genson reminds the jury that Caruso is presumed innocent. "It's like a one-run lead in a baseball game," he says. Maybe he's less confident than when he defended Caruso's father fifteen years ago; then he told the jury it was like a four-run lead. Mandeltort is not impressed with the analogy in any event. "The game's over," she writes.

CLEVAN NICHOLSON is dwarfed by the witness stand. He's short, even for a fourteen-year-old, slightly plump, and dark-complected, with hair trimmed to the scalp. He's wearing a bright yellow-and-black-checked shirt. Mandeltort, who's doing the questioning, usually knows what her witnesses will say, but this time she's not sure. Clevan has told her he'll identify Caruso as the person who attacked him and Lenard. But the murder of Mike Cutler and the disappearance of Richard DeSantis have left the prosecutors uneasy about their remaining witnesses. Mandeltort has worried that someone might have threatened Clevan or somehow persuaded him not to finger Caruso. Of the state's witnesses, Mandeltort has told Berlin, "This is one of those cases where you really don't know until you hear it coming out of their mouths."

Responding to Mandeltort's questions, Clevan relates how he and Lenard had decided to go bike riding, and that Lenard had realized his bike needed air.

"Why did you go to Bridgeport?" Mandeltort asks.

" 'Cause the air free over there," Clevan says.

Clevan tells about meeting a Mexican youth, William Jaramillo, on their return trip and playing football with him and his cousins on a school playground. After the game he and Lenard were pedaling slowly in the general direction of home, Jaramillo walking between them, when they were confronted by a white youth on a side street. Mandeltort asks Clevan to get down from the witness stand and point out this person if he sees him in the room.

During a long day in a courtroom, jurors often find their attention wandering. They yawn and fidget and examine their nails. But they're spellbound now, as Clevan strides confidently across the well of the hushed courtroom toward the defense table. He stops directly in front of Caruso, whose gaze is aimed at the gray carpet. Caruso seems to notice the bright green dress slacks and green felt shoes in front of him. His eyes flicker up to Clevan's face and down again. Clevan stares straight at Caruso. He points. "It's him." In the jury box, everyone's drinking it in. "A Kodak moment," Berlin says later.

Back on the stand, Clevan says Caruso hit him behind his ear. He says he heard Caruso say, "Fuck this nigger, get off your bike." Then he saw Caruso hit Lenard in the head, and Lenard's head snap backward into the wall behind him. Lenard jumped off his bike and ran east on 33rd, Clevan says, while he himself managed to escape by running in a different direction, south on Shields.

At a police station the next day, he picked Caruso out of a lineup as the attacker, he says. Yes, he did initially pick another youth—codefendant Victor Jasas—out of an earlier lineup, and say he was the original attacker; but when he viewed the second lineup, which included Caruso, "I realized that I had picked the wrong one" the first time, he says.

Genson presses him about this on cross.

"You were positive when you said Jasas was the one that attacked you, weren't you?"

"Yes."

"You identified him as the one that hit you and hit Lenard, isn't that right?"

"Yes."

"But only one man attacked you and Lenard?"

"Yes," Clevan says. "After I had viewed the second lineup, I told the officer, I said the first lineup I had viewed, it was the wrong person I had picked."

COURTROOM IDENTIFICATIONS are quite persuasive, maybe more than they deserve to be. It isn't hard for a witness to find the defendant in the courtroom; at 26th Street, he's usually the only black person at the defense table. Clevan's job was somewhat harder, and not only because the defendant is white. One of the four lawyers Genson has hired to help him with the case, twenty-seven-year-old Michael Pagano, looks an awful lot like Caruso: he has short dark hair, an olive complexion, a diminutive build, and similar features. He is dressed like Caruso on this first day of the trial—dark suit, white dress shirt, and tie. "I think they were hoping he'd catch a finger," Mandeltort tells me later. "When you're going against someone like Genson, you have to figure on those kinds of things." Before opening statements, the prosecutors asked Locallo in chambers to bar the defense from having Caruso and Pagano sit next to each other at the defense table, as they had during jury selection the previous day. "Judge, it's obvious what the purpose is, what they're doing," Mandeltort said. But Genson pled not guilty. "I am perfectly capable of doing something like that," he told the judge. "I just didn't do it." Locallo declined to tell the defense who could sit where. And Pagano was next to Caruso when Clevan made his ID.

But as Genson brought out on his cross, Clevan had seen Caruso several times on the TV news since the attack and once at a pretrial hearing. And Berlin had shown him photos of Caruso "a lot of times," as Clevan had acknowledged. How could anyone know the basis of his courtroom ID?

This was chiefly an eyewitness case in Genson's mind. It boiled down to whether the jury should trust the IDs of Clevan and of William Jaramillo, the Hispanic youth who was also present at the beginning of the attack. Genson hadn't done an eyewitness case in recent years, and so when he'd taken on Caruso, he'd boned up on the subject. What he learned, he says, was that misidentifications are commonplace.

Genson had wanted the jury to hear from Elizabeth Loftus, a psychology professor at the University of California at Irvine and the nation's most prominent expert on eyewitnesses. As Genson outlined in a pretrial filing, Loftus would have testified that eyewitnesses err frequently, particularly when identifying a person of another race. This testimony was especially relevant, Genson had told Locallo before the trial, because Clevan and Jaramillo had both waffled on their IDs at the police station, first picking Jasas as the initiator of the attack and then switching to Caruso. Loftus would have also informed the jury that suggestions from police to a witness regarding their expectations, even subtle and unintended ones, greatly increase the chance of error. Genson maintained that this was relevant because the second lineup had been so suggestive. Caruso had been in the same position Jasas had been in—on the far left—and he'd been dressed similarly to Jasas.

Loftus had written five books on eyewitnesses and testified in 225 cases. "It may fairly be said that she 'wrote the book' on the subject of eyewitness perception, memory retention and recall," the Arizona Supreme Court once observed. But like most of his colleagues at 26th Street, Locallo takes a dim view of eyewitness experts. In barring Loftus's testimony, Locallo said he trusted the jury to use its common sense in deciding how much stock to put in Clevan's and Jaramillo's identifications. "She can write all the books she wants," Locallo would say later. "I don't have much faith in these self-styled experts."

ON WHAT WAS TO HAVE BEEN the trial's second day, a Friday, the defense comes to court without its captain. In the judge's chambers, Sam Adam tells Locallo that Genson can't get out of bed because of severe back pain. He asks that the trial be postponed until Monday. Mandeltort and Berlin say they have no objection.

The judge and the lawyers then head into the crowded courtroom to put the continuance on the record. The jury is still in the jury room. But now, when Adam formally makes his request, Mandeltort says that since Caruso has four other lawyers representing him, the trial should proceed. Locallo, taken aback, eyes Mandeltort momentarily. ("I thought it was very comical," the judge says later. "All of a sudden Ellen is playing to the crowd.") Locallo tells Mandeltort he doesn't think the trial should go forward at this point without Caruso's chief lawyer. The case will resume on Monday with or without Genson, he says. He calls the jury into the courtroom, explains the postponement and apologizes for it, then dismisses the panel for the weekend.

Mandeltort this morning has on pearls and a powder-blue dress suit she bought for the trial. Now that the jury has seen the suit, however briefly, she doesn't think she can wear it a second time during the trial. "I wasted a perfectly good fucking new suit," she says before leaving the courtroom.

GENSON IS BACK on Monday. The gallery is full again. It's now William Jaramillo's turn to point the finger at Caruso.

The nineteen-year-old Jaramillo, hefty and broad-shouldered, has a wide impassive face, bushy eyebrows, a mustache, and thick black hair. He lives in a neighborhood southwest of Bridgeport. He tells the jury that on the day in question, he was playing football with two younger cousins on a Bridgeport playground when Lenard and Clevan came by on their bikes and asked to join the game. He and his cousins didn't know either youth, but they were glad to have more players. When the five boys were finished playing, Jaramillo walked his two cousins home and then accompanied Lenard and Clevan as they pedaled east down Bridgeport streets. Jaramillo was walking between them. At the corner of 33rd and Shields, a white youth "walked up to me and said, 'What are you looking at?'" he recalls.

Berlin asks Jaramillo to get down from the stand and see if this white youth is in the room. Jaramillo walks into the well of the courtroom and points at Caruso.

Back on the stand, Jaramillo says he didn't respond when Caruso asked him what he was looking at. He heard Caruso say something about "this nigger" as he hit Clevan in the back of the head, knocking him to the ground. Then Caruso punched Lenard in the head, sending Lenard reeling into the building behind him—Jaramillo says he heard a "crunch" as Lenard's head hit the wall. Lenard collapsed to the ground, his bike on top of him. Clevan fled south on Shields; Lenard got up and ran east on 33rd, pursued by Caruso and two other youths. Jaramillo says he picked up the two bikes Lenard and Clevan had left behind and carried them to his uncle's house. Then he and his uncle went to the police station to report the attack. At the station, he first picked Victor Jasas out of a lineup as the attacker at 33rd and Shields; then he picked Caruso. On Genson's cross, Jaramillo says his initial identification of Jasas was simply a mistake.

JARAMILLO HIMSELF had been arrested just two weeks before he testified, a fact Genson would have brought out on cross—had he known about it.

In the early morning hours of August 31, 1998, Jaramillo and two other young men allegedly used a baseball bat to break windows in twenty cars on the 1100 block of West 18th Place in Chicago. The three accused offenders were charged with criminal damage to property and released on recognizance bonds.

Prosecutors are required to disclose to the defense any pending charges against their witnesses because of the inherent potential for bias—a witness could shade his testimony to help the state in return for favorable treatment in his own case. To adhere to this obligation, prosecutors do criminal history checks on their witnesses before trial, and usually again when the trial begins. "Ideally, you want to do it the day of [the witness's testimony], but that doesn't always happen," Berlin will tell me after the trial. It didn't happen in Jaramillo's case, the prosecutors will say; Berlin and Mandeltort will maintain they didn't learn of Jaramillo's arrest during Caruso's trial, either from a criminal history check or from Jaramillo himself. (Jaramillo wouldn't return my calls.)

"It would have been a good hook on cross," Genson will say about Jaramillo's arrest, when I learn of it and tell him about it after the trial. Jaramillo would have had a motive to stick resolutely to his identification of Caruso at trial, according to Genson. The defense lawyer will add that he feels certain the prosecutors knew about the arrest. "They held it back, I'm sure they did. I'm sure he [Jaramillo] would have run to them after his arrest and said, 'Help me.' "

Criminal damage to property is a felony if the damage exceeds $300. In May 1999, after seven continuances, the state will drop its case against Jaramillo.

WHEN DEPUTY RHODES ESCORTS the jurors through the hallway between the courtroom and the elevators, Caruso's father is often within their view, leaning against a wall and studying a New American Bible. His hair has grayed remarkably since the last pretrial court date four days before the trial began—a product not of stress but of hair dye, contend a few cynics, including Deputy Guerrero, who has also noted how quickly the elder Caruso closes the Bible after the jury passes. Caruso Senior's wife, Sherry, lingers in the hallway as well, a rosary in one hand, a bottle of nitroglycerin pills in the other.

Most of the spectators attending the trial are relatives or friends of the Carusos. During recesses they don't hesitate to talk up Caruso's innocence in the hallway.

"I saw the whole thing, and it wasn't Frankie that did the beating," Rocco LaMantia says during one such recess. LaMantia's father, Joseph "Shorty" LaMantia, was a codefendant of Caruso Senior in their 1982 extortion case. The elder LaMantia, another reputed member of the outfit's 26th Street Crew, pled guilty to racketeering in 1996. According to Rocco LaMantia, it wasn't Frank Junior who beat Lenard, it was some other Bridgeport kids who he hopes are caught and punished one day, because, he says, no innocent young boy should be treated the way Lenard was.

But LaMantia goes on to defend most of the assaults on blacks in Bridgeport, some of which he says he's also witnessed. The beatings aren't really racial, he says; they're just attempts to keep the neighborhood safe. They're usually administered to lawbreakers—most of whom he says happen to be black. "Are we racists because we take care of our own?

"We don't rape our women," LaMantia says. "We don't kill each other.

But the black man today doesn't want to be responsible for his actions. He doesn't take care of his children. He doesn't want to work. I think they have to quit blaming everybody else for inequalities, for their misfortunes."

LaMantia, thirty-nine, has had his own misfortunes, court records show. In 1995 he was convicted of aggravated robbery and impersonation of a police officer, for which he got probation and a year of home confinement. He also has misdemeaner convictions for weapons violations and theft. Seventeen years ago he was charged with murdering his girlfriend, twenty-year-old Martha DiCaro, who was shot in the LaMantia home one night in 1979. DiCaro's mother told police her daughter went to the LaMantia home that night to break up with Rocco. And one of DiCaro's friends told police that LaMantia once said that if he caught his girlfriend with anyone else, he'd kill both of them, and that his father would pay $20,000 to get him off.

LaMantia had opted for a bench trial, and the judge acquitted him. The judge was Thomas Maloney.

"I DON'T RECALL," Thomas Simpson tells the jury the following day. Again and again and again.

Simpson is the other friend—besides the late Mike Cutler and the missing Richard DeSantis—who gave police a damning account of Caruso's words and actions on the night of the attack.

Simpson is only twenty-five, but he's already been convicted of aggravated criminal sexual abuse, two robberies, and a burglary. He's tall, fair, blue eyed, and dyed blonde. He's wearing a gray T-shirt and a gold neck chain, his appearance less formal than that of the silver-haired, deeply tanned, navy-suited lawyer who's accompanied him to court. Simpson and the lawyer were in the courtroom the preceding day, after the jury was dismissed, for a hearing regarding Simpson's desire to invoke the Fifth Amendment. Locallo found "no basis" for Simpson's professed concern that his testimony might be self-incriminating. The judge told Simpson he'd be required to testify when the trial resumed the following day. Over the protests of Simpson's lawyer and his parents, Locallo also ordered Simpson kept under guard in a hotel overnight. Given DeSantis's disappearance and Cutler's murder, the judge considered it a reasonable possibility that if he let Simpson go home for the evening, he wouldn't be back in the morning. "The stakes are high in this case," Locallo explained to Simpson's parents in his chambers. "And I'm not going to take any chances. . . . I can't afford to lose any more witnesses."

Now, with Simpson on the stand and Mandeltort questioning him, Simpson's backup plan has quickly become evident. Was he in Caruso's

Jeep on the night in question? Did they drive past three minority youths? Did Caruso say, "Let's beat these motherfuckers up?"

"I don't recall."

The prosecutors aren't concerned at all about Simpson's amnesia, in fact, they couldn't be more pleased. His forgetfulness allows them to confront him with the statement he gave police, and with the testimony he gave to a grand jury, about what Caruso said and did on the night of the beating. So the jury hears all the details, and they're emphasized all the more by Simpson's professed inability to remember them. "This happens in tons of cases," Berlin says later. "A witness flips, and we put in his prior statement. Juries are real smart—they know what's going on." As Simpson continues to not recall, it's Caruso's lawyers who are cringing. "We're dead," Genson whispers to Adam.

An investigator who works for Genson interviewed Simpson before trial. Simpson told him he was on 33rd Street at the time of the attack, and he saw people running in different directions, but he never saw anybody hit anyone—he was too busy talking with Mike Cutler, who was standing next to him. He acknowledged that he and Cutler were in Caruso's Jeep before the attack, but he maintained that Caruso didn't say anything about wanting to beat up any black kids. He said he incriminated Caruso in his statement, and in his grand jury testimony, because the police were threatening to send him back to prison if he didn't. Genson will say later he doesn't know why Simpson chose to rely in court on a failed memory.

Mandeltort asks Simpson how Caruso reacted when he and Cutler, who was also in the Jeep, told Caruso they didn't want to beat up the black kids.

"I don't recall," Simpson says.

"Well, in your handwritten statement, sir, did you say that 'Frankie acted like he was disgusted with Tom and Mike for not wanting to beat the kids'?"

"That's what it says," Simpson replies. His tone is sarcastic and a smirk is fixed on his face. He's draped an arm across the back of the witness chair as he fields Mandeltort's questions.

"Did you further state, sir, that 'Frankie has a problem with the idea of blacks coming into his neighborhood, and this is what set him off'?"

"That's what it says in the statement."

"There came a time when the Jeep stopped at about Thirty-third and Princeton, is that correct?"

"I don't recall."

"Well, looking at your statement—'Frankie stopped the Jeep at Princeton and Thirty-third and said to Tom and Mike, "You guys are pussies"'— do you remember that, sir?"

"I don't recall."

The jury learns that according to the Simpson statement to police, Caruso then got out of the Jeep and headed west on foot toward Shields, while Simpson and Cutler stayed near the Jeep. Simpson saw Victor Jasas and Michael Kwidzinski—the other codefendants—walking toward Shields from the west. Then he saw "Victor or Frankie" take a swing at a black kid at 33rd and Shields. The black kid—Lenard—ran east on 33rd, with Caruso and Jasas in pursuit. Simpson lost sight of the three when they rounded the corner onto Princeton. Then he heard an old man yelling. When Caruso and Jasas returned to 33rd shortly thereafter, they were flushed and breathing hard. A little later, Simpson was in the Jeep with Caruso, Jasas, Kwidzinski, and Cutler, heading to a party. Caruso and Jasas bragged about the attack. "We beat the fuck out of him," Jasas said. "They think they can come in the neighborhood and talk shit." And Caruso added, "Yeah, I punched the fuck out of them. They shouldn't have been walking through this neighborhood." Caruso had rap music playing in the Jeep, Simpson said in the statement, because "Frankie doesn't hate black people, Frankie just hates niggers."

Sam Adam handles the cross after lunch. Adam is renowned at 26th Street for his talent on cross, and he prizes the memories of the legion of witnesses he's irritated in thirty-seven years. "One time a woman came down from the stand and threw the [witness's] microphone at me! Right in the middle of the cross!" he once told me proudly. "There was almost a riot right there in the courtroom! I enjoyed it; it was very exciting."

But Adam's strength is flustering hostile witnesses, and Simpson isn't that. Simpson's smirk is gone now, he's sitting up straight, and his memory cells have regenerated. He recalls being picked up by police a few hours after the beating, two blocks away from where it occurred. They brought him in because he matched the description of one of the assailants given by Jaramillo, and because a computer check showed an outstanding warrant for a parole violation. Adam asks Simpson about his time in custody and his treatment by police, deftly leading him to Adam's desired theme: that Simpson succumbed to the coercion of police and incriminated Caruso to save his own neck.

"They kept pushing you to tell a story that they were going to give to you, is that correct?"

"Yes."

"And they told you that, in fact, if you didn't go along with the story that they were going to give you, that you yourself would be charged with the beating of Lenard Clark, is that correct?"

"Yes. Actually, they told me they would charge me with attempted murder, and that there was a possibility that Lenard might die. So they might wait and then charge me with first-degree murder."

"But on the other hand, they said, did they not, 'If you say what we want you to say, then we won't even charge you'?"

"They said if I agree, that if I cooperated, that I wouldn't be charged, and that I would actually go home that day."

Simpson's selective recall is eliciting dubious expressions from some of the jurors. Genson is studying the jurors and thinking, as he'll say later, that with a friend like Simpson, Caruso doesn't need enemies.

On redirect, Mandeltort asks Simpson whether he'd had "some sort of memory-enhancing" ingredient in his lunch. Simpson says he doesn't understand.

"Well, this morning, sir, you said, 'I do not recall' approximately one hundred times. Would that be correct?"

"I don't recall," Simpson replies.

DETECTIVE STANLEY TURNER takes the stand the following day to refute Simpson's accusations of coercion, many of which were aimed at him, the case's primary detective.

Turner has a strong athletic build, though at forty-nine a paunch has set in. An African American, he has a receding hairline, glasses, and a mustache. He joined the police department as a cadet straight out of high school. His childhood on the south side left him with a distaste for bullies. He has vivid memories of older kids in his neighborhood jumping younger ones for their money, and the bullying involved in the attack on Lenard bothered him more than the racism, he says later.

It's not as if Turner evaded racism as he was growing up, however. There was the grade-school basketball play-off game that was stolen from his all-black team by an all-white one, thanks to the white referee who looked the other way while Turner and his teammates were tripped and low-bridged. "The cheating was just so blatant, I never forgot it. You look at it and say, 'Well, how do I prevent this from occurring?' And you prepare yourself so you won't get beat again."

His mother sent him to a Catholic high school, a school he wouldn't have picked since it was nearly all white. He ended up liking it except for "some fools who didn't want to accept the fact that there were blacks there." They'd cut into the lunchroom line in front of him. "It was, 'Look, we come first.' Well, I'm not gonna accept that. So you end up knocking a person on his ass."

He's sensed racial prejudice as a detective—particularly a perception, both inside and outside the department, that black detectives are inferior to white ones. He told himself during the Bridgeport probe that if the attackers weren't caught and convicted, some would see the outcome as more evidence of the mediocrity of black detectives.

Turner is dressed in a gray suit today, with a dark tie and a gold tie clasp. Under Mandeltort's questioning he matter-of-factly denies all of Simpson's allegations. He didn't threaten to charge Simpson with the beating; he didn't feed him a story. He didn't ignore Simpson's repeated requests to speak with a lawyer, as Simpson claimed; Simpson never asked for one.

Mandeltort turns the subject to the two lineups the detective helped conduct. Turner tells the jury that suspects are allowed to pick their position in lineups. Jasas and Caruso just so happened to pick the same spot in their respective lineups, the one on the far left. Yes, he made Caruso take off the dress shirt he wore to the station (leaving Caruso in a plain white T-shirt, like Jasas in the first lineup). But that was because the other lineup participants were dressed casually, and he didn't want Caruso to stand out. For the same reason, he had Caruso remove his dress shoes, he says, and he gave him a pair of green sneakers to wear. Jasas's sneakers.

Mandeltort asks Turner if he noticed anything about Clevan Nicholson when Clevan entered the room to view the second lineup. The lineup members were on the other side of a one-way mirror. Turner says he recollects Clevan walking up to the glass and then instantly retreating. He "went into almost like a frightened mode when he first looked through the glass and saw Mr. Caruso," the detective says. After each of the five lineup members approached the glass individually, Turner says, Clevan pointed at Caruso and said, "That's the one. That's the one." Clevan then said his earlier identification of Jasas had been a mistake.

This is hardly the first time Genson has heard a detective recall at trial an eyewitness's startled response upon seeing the defendant. Turner hadn't said anything about this frightened reaction by Clevan when he testified about the lineup at a pretrial hearing. On Genson's cross, Turner acknowledges he never wrote anything in any of his reports about this frightened response by Clevan. Genson also asks the detective whether the other four participants in the Caruso lineup weren't already seated when Caruso was brought into the lineup room and allowed to "choose" his spot. Turner concedes that "some may have been sitting down." (Turner's partner, Glenn Mathews, later testifies that Caruso was indeed the last to be seated.)

Turner also allows that he never noted in any of his reports that Clevan and Jaramillo had said their original identification of Jasas had been a mistake. In fact, as Genson points out, in Turner's final report on the case, the detective wrote that in the lineups, Clevan and Jaramillo had "identified Jasas and Caruso as two of the men who attacked each of them."

Turner tells me later he never acknowledged in his reports that Clevan and Jaramillo had made a mistake in the first lineup because he didn't think they did. He says he's convinced that a number of Bridgeport youths participated in the attack at 33rd and Shields, and that Caruso wasn't the only one to hit Lenard and Clevan there.

But if that's true, then both Clevan and Jaramillo lied when they testified that Caruso, and only Caruso, hit anyone on that corner. Turner couldn't explain why they would have done so. Genson says he thinks Turner wasn't sure what to do with the bad ID from the first lineup and wrote his report the way he did to leave his options open.

Turner tells me that while he's sure more Bridgeport youths were involved in the attack than the ones who got charged, he's also sure Caruso was the ringleader. When he was investigating the case and talking with people about Caruso, he got the impression that Caruso believed he could bully people without repercussions. "Little Frankie had been doing things like this for years," the detective says. "This time he just got caught." He recalls seeing Caruso in an interview room after he was picked out of the lineup. His dress shirt was in a heap on the floor next to him. "He had torn up his shirt, shredded it," Turner says. "I asked him, 'What happened to your shirt?' He looks at me and he says, 'I'm a Caruso.' Well, maybe it means something in Bridgeport, but it didn't mean shit to me."

THE DAY TURNER TESTIFIES a thirty-eight-year-old computer consultant named Jeffrey Gordon also takes the stand to describe the more brutal part of the attack, the stomping of Lenard on Princeton.

Gordon had been living in an apartment on the 3200 block of South Princeton for two years. On the night in question, he was leaving his apartment for the El station on 35th. He tells the jury that after he crossed to the east side of Princeton, he saw one person, who he later learned was Lenard Clark, come racing around the corner of 33rd and Princeton with three others after him. He saw the first of the chasers catch Lenard in the street and start swinging at him. Lenard "was just standing there taking the blows," Gordon says. Then he collapsed to the pavement. Gordon was standing on the sidewalk, his view partially obstructed by parked cars, but it appeared to him that all three attackers were kicking Lenard.

Gordon says he stepped toward the men and told them to leave the victim alone. But the initial attacker persisted. "I thought he was, you know, stomping his head or something like that, and I just screamed out, I said, 'Stop it!'

Stop it!' You know, 'Leave him alone!'" Gordon says he then walked into the street, brandishing his cell phone. "I said, 'I'm calling the police,' and then I made the distinct motions of pushing the buttons on the cell phone."

The first attacker gave Lenard "one last kick," Gordon recalls, and said to Gordon, "He was breaking windows in the neighborhood." Then the three attackers fled, south on Princeton.

Lenard was facedown in the street. Gordon called for help on his cell phone.

Gordon says he told one of the police officers who arrived that the attackers had been three white men. But then someone in the crowd told him, "'You didn't see nothing,'" he says. Feeling threatened, he didn't offer police any more information, and they didn't even ask him for his name. A month later detectives tracked him down through records of his cell phone call for help.

If Gordon can identify Caruso as one of the three attackers, Caruso might as well throw in the towel. But Gordon says he can't. He tells the jury the three offenders appeared to be in their twenties. They were smaller than he—he's five foot ten and weighs 205. They had dark hair. The chief attacker's hair was parted down the middle and feathered back, he says (as is Caruso's hair in the lineup photo). But he says he couldn't make out their facial features.

He acknowledges on Genson's cross that he previously said (in a pretrial hearing) that the three attackers were light-skinned. Genson directs Caruso to stand at the defense table, and he asks Gordon if he'd characterize Caruso as light-skinned. Gordon says he wouldn't.

THE STATE CLOSES its case with the testimony of two eighteen-year-old black youths, Lionel Johnson and Larry Dixon, who say Caruso used racial epithets against them in 1995. They both were then attending a grammar school near Armour Square Park, and their basketball team used to practice in the Armour gym. The Armour gym is at 33rd and Shields, where Caruso allegedly confronted Lenard and Clevan. Johnson and Dixon tell the jury that Caruso often played there too and that he used to call them "nigger," "skunk," and "monkey" and warn them to get out of the neighborhood.

Testimony regarding other alleged crimes by a defendant can't be admitted if it's merely to show the defendant's character or his propensity to commit the crimes he's on trial for; the jury isn't supposed to be deciding whether the defendant is likely to have committed the crimes he's accused of but whether he actually did. But other-crimes testimony can be admitted when it relates to a defendant's motive, to his dislike for the victims, or to his modus operandi. The line between what's admissible and what isn't is fine indeed.

Before the trial the prosecutors presented Locallo with a host of assaults and batteries that Caruso allegedly committed in Bridgeport but wasn't charged with. The prosecutors had learned of these alleged offenses primarily through interviews conducted in the neighborhood by investigators for their office. Besides the alleged threats against Johnson and Dixon, there was a 1994 attack on a white youth in a church parking lot that left the youth unconscious. According to the prosecutors, witnesses said Caruso had been among the attackers. There were also charges by two youth center workers—a white woman and a black man—that Caruso had been among the group of whites who shouted racial slurs at the minority children they escorted to Armour Square Park in 1995 and 1996. The black youth worker said that when he confronted Caruso about the name-calling, Caruso threatened him with a baseball bat. And there was a white woman who said that in 1996 Caruso jabbed her in the face with a baseball bat during a dispute over cars double-parked on 33rd Street by Caruso and his friends. The woman maintained that as Caruso hit her, he said, "Don't you know I'm syndicate?" and "This is our street."

A judge may bar testimony about other crimes, even if he deems it relevant, if he considers it too prejudicial. And Locallo had done so with all these charges except the ones involving Johnson and Dixon. Genson had argued vehemently, but in vain, that Johnson's and Dixon's testimony was likewise so inflammatory that it was bound to poison the jury's consideration of whether Caruso had attacked Lenard.

AS USUAL, Locallo has developed a rapport with the jury. The jurors like his sense of humor and are impressed with how quickly he's learned their names. One juror, Atif Sheikh, brought a coffee cake in one morning on the birthday of a fellow juror. Sheikh made sure a piece of the cake was sent over to the judge. Locallo reciprocated two days later, bringing in a cake for the jury. "He's a judge," Sheikh says later. "Biggest authority in the courtroom. But he's a very down-to-earth person."

Locallo and the lawyers have been impressed with the jury's attentiveness. Through four long days so far, no one's drifted off. (The full gallery every day, including the reporters and sketch artists, provides extra impetus not to.) Nor has anyone shown signs thus far of partiality. Within the jury there were the usual gripes the first day or two about missed doctor's appointments and work that was piling up in the jurors' regular jobs, but then everyone had settled earnestly into the task.

· · ·

ON THE TRIAL'S FIFTH DAY Genson calls a string of police officers to highlight minor discrepancies in the state's case. Caruso himself doesn't testify.

In the hallway outside the courtroom, Caruso Senior is distributing home-baked cookies, along with complaints about the persecution of his son. He says certain city officials don't like the role he's played in unions and Frank Junior is now paying the price. He thinks people should recognize that everyone loses when a defendant is treated unjustly. "When someone takes away my rights, they're taking away your rights, too," he tells me. "We're looking at the erosion of the core of our justice system."

Frank Junior "isn't an angel," his father says. "He's got a little Bridge-port attitude. But does anyone ever think about what this is like for him if he's innocent?"

The elder Caruso is especially irked at Mandeltort—"Little Miss Ausch-witz," as he calls her, perhaps unaware she's Jewish. Earlier today Mandeltort asked Locallo to instruct the Carusos to stay away from Lenard's mother, Wanda McMurray, during the rest of the trial—this, after McMurray and Frank Junior's mother had hugged in the hallway. Mandeltort told the judge the hug had been foisted upon McMurray for the benefit of reporters; Gen-son said it was his understanding the embrace had been spontaneous and mutual. Locallo suggested there be no further contact between the families during the trial. "What's wrong with that woman?" Caruso Senior now says of Mandeltort.

Caruso Senior's older brother, Bruno, interjects that a prison term of any length for Frank Junior would be a "death sentence," because black inmates surely would make him a marked man. "And for what?" Bruno Caruso says. "He's a kid. Skinny little piece a shit. Can't even grow a whisker yet."

The fifty-five-year-old Bruno Caruso holds several offices in local labor unions. He recently left his $220,000 job as president of the Chicago District Council, an umbrella group of the Laborers International that rep-resents low-skilled laborers in twenty-one Chicago-area locals. The inter-national has been investigating the council, under federal pressure, because of the council's alleged mob ties. A hearing officer concluded in Febuary 1998 that Bruno Caruso was "at least an associate of the Chicago Outfit," observing that "the contacts between Bruno Caruso and the mob are too numerous and too repetitive to be accidental." (Bruno Caruso's lawyer, Allan Ackerman, will later deny the allegation. Ackerman will maintain that the labor investigation had yielded no evidence that his client was in the outfit, merely evidence that he'd met with reputed mobsters, which had made him a victim of "guilt by association.") A source close to Genson says Bruno Caruso is providing the bulk of the money for Frank Junior's defense.

Bruno Caruso says the Carusos are family people above all else. They have a large dinner gathering every Sunday—brothers and sisters, aunts and uncles, nephews and nieces. It's at the Bridgeport home of his eighty-seven-year-old mother, who still does some of the cooking. "I told Ed [Genson] yesterday, I said, 'Ed, you're the most important man in the world to my family right now,'" Bruno Caruso says in the hallway. "It's like if someone was seriously ill, the doctor would be the most important man in the world. I said, 'We're counting on you. That's why you're well paid, but forget the money. We're counting on you.'"

BERLIN'S CLOSING ARGUMENT the following morning is a pep talk to jurors, delivered in front of another jammed gallery. "Some people disappear and one witness is dead," he says, over Genson's objection, overruled by Locallo. "Some things don't change, ladies and gentlemen. The truth doesn't change, and the will of the people to do justice doesn't change." He implores the jurors to "have the courage . . . to deal with the hard facts that evil men like Frank Caruso confront us with." He again climaxes his speech with the before-and-after photos of Lenard, which again draw tears. His passionate appeal is marred by one tongue slip: he says that Caruso's intention in beating Lenard was "to take care of the niggerhood—excuse me, to take care of the neighborhood."

As in his opening statement, Genson gives his closing argument while perched atop the tall chair brought from his office.

He says much of the state's case was "theater, an intentional plea by the state's attorneys to ignore the facts of this case." The prosecutors' liberal repetition of the racial epithets allegedly used, their constant pointing and glaring at Caruso, the way they'd had Clevan and Jaramillo descend from the stand and finger Caruso, and the repeated display of Lenard's intensive-care photo were all designed to elicit an emotional verdict and not a reasoned one, he says. The photo of the injured Lenard "makes you cry, and it ought to," he says. "The picture makes *me* cry. But it doesn't show us who committed the crime."

Genson gestures at Caruso, who happens to be digging his fingernails into the edge of the defense table. Caruso is wearing the same oversize sport coat he's worn each day of the trial. The subject of the state's theatrics is "this eighteen-year-old boy," Genson says, "who sits here uncomfortable in a sports coat that doesn't fit and a shirt that doesn't quite fit him and the defendant's chair he's not used to sitting in."

He outlines the state's case as he sees it. Clevan Nicholson and William

Jaramillo positively identified Caruso as the initiator of the attack—but only after positively identifying Victor Jasas as the offender. Jeffrey Gordon couldn't positively identify anyone; and in fact, he said the attackers were lighter-skinned than Caruso. That leaves only Thomas Simpson—a "bum," a "criminal," a "liar with his own agenda," Genson says. Having seen the jury's disdain for Simpson, Genson has decided to disown him; after Adam labored to help Simpson deliver his tale of police coercion, Genson now says much of that testimony probably was fabricated too. "Every time that man opens his mouth he's lying," Genson says. But given that, how can anyone believe Simpson's statements incriminating Caruso? he wonders. "There is certainly reasonable doubt when you put all this together."

The attempted-murder charge is more theater, Genson goes on. Beating a person badly isn't attempted murder unless you intend to kill him, he points out—and no intent to kill has been proven. He knows it's a dangerous point to raise: it's like insisting that Caruso didn't beat Lenard, then adding that even if he did, he wasn't trying to kill him. But if he can't win the whole war, Genson at least wants to win the most important battle; hence this suggestion to the jury that a compromise is possible.

Genson tells an Old Testament story about a ritual in which the priest and the elders of Jerusalem would send a goat into the wilderness to purge the sins of the community. "It made no difference that the goat didn't do anything. It made the people feel better. That is what the state is asking you to do here. Frank shouldn't be the scapegoat for this horrible crime."

He's not defending any racism that exists in Bridgeport, he says; he's defending "the man who hit and beat Lenard Clark." Then he quickly amends: "I am not defending the man who beat and hit Lenard Clark . . . I am defending a young man wrongfully accused of a crime."

He pushes himself off his chair, stands behind the lectern, and scans the jury. He says the urge to "send a message" that racist violence won't be tolerated shouldn't enter into deliberations. The jury's job is simply to decide whether Caruso has been proven guilty beyond a reasonable doubt. "The message I ask you to send to the community is that the rules of law will be followed in this country, this state, this county, this city, and this courthouse. And that emotion, and overzealous police officers, will not circumvent these rules of law. Frank Caruso is not guilty. Send him back to his family." He gathers his notes and limps back to the defense table.

Bob Galhotra, a public defender recently assigned to Locallo's courtroom, is among the many lawyers in the gallery, here to enjoy the show and to study the performances of these veteran lawyers. As Genson takes his seat next to Caruso and Mandeltort heads to the lectern with the state's rebuttal argument, the young PD tells me softly, "When you spend so much time talking about reasonable doubt, the jurors just figure your guy is guilty."

Mandeltort calls Caruso a "violent racist street punk," a "thug," and a "bum." She ridicules the "ill-fitting clothing" he's worn throughout the trial, designed to make him look less menacing, she says. At the defense table, Caruso pokes at a balled-up tissue. "Perhaps he could slide down in that chair just a little more so he wouldn't look quite so threatening to you," Mandeltort says. "But remember, that is not the Frank Caruso that Clevan and Lenard met . . . the Frank Caruso who will ruthlessly beat a thirteen-year-old boy simply because he's black."

She blasts the "conspiracy of silence" in Bridgeport. There were other witnesses to the beating on Princeton besides Jeffrey Gordon, she maintains, but none of them would tell police what they'd seen. "Frank Caruso beat Lenard Clark in the streets of Bridgeport because he knew something about Bridgeport," she says. Genson objects, and Locallo strikes the comment.

Earlier this morning, after Berlin finished his argument and resumed his seat next to her at the state's table, Mandeltort quietly kidded him about his one mistake—saying niggerhood instead of neighborhood. ("Nice job, Bob.") But now Mandeltort makes her own slip: she says the evidence shows that Caruso "called Clevan Niggerson—Clevan Nicholson, a nigger."

It's the only blemish in her argument. "Counsel stood here in opening statement and asked you for sympathy and justice for Frank Caruso," she tells the jury. "But the judge will instruct you that you are not to consider sympathy . . . and you know that he is certainly not entitled to it. However, there will be justice for Frank Caruso today.

"He is having a trial with all the legal protections our judicial system has. He has selected a jury to listen to the evidence. He has a judge to determine the issues of law, and he is being tried in a court of law. . . . That is more than he gave Lenard Clark on March 21, 1997. Frank Caruso declared himself judge and jury for Clevan Nicholson and Lenard Clark. He tried, convicted, and sentenced Lenard Clark in the street. The sentence was a brutal and savage beating that placed him in a coma, a brutal and savage beating . . . that has forever changed who he is and how he will live his life. The crime that Lenard committed was being a black kid who came into Bridgeport to save twenty-five cents on air. . . . That, ladies and gentlemen, is Frank Caruso's idea of justice. However, true justice in this case is Frank Caruso learning that you can't beat black children who come into Bridgeport on their bicycles."

"ANYONE WITH HALF A BRAIN can see there's too much doubt in this case," Caruso's friend Rocco LaMantia is saying on a gallery bench. The jury is still deliberating. It got the case at 1:50 P.M., and now it's almost eight. "The lineups, the identifications—nothing matches, nothing fits," LaMantia says.

Waiting patiently on a bench across the aisle is a retired postal worker named Alonzo Cooper. At eighty years, Cooper, stooped and wizened, is twice LaMantia's age and half his size. He's one of the few African Americans who attended the trial. A lifelong south-sider, he comes to trials frequently as a volunteer for Citizens Alert, a police watchdog group. Usually it's in support of a defendant who Citizens Alert thinks has been mistreated by police. Most of those defendants are black. "When a black person gets caught with drugs it's a crime, but when a white person gets caught it's a sickness," Cooper says. He followed this case hoping to see "that they don't whitewash the whole scenario."

Cooper thinks Caruso has been proven guilty. He hopes he'll be convicted and sent to prison. "If he got some time away from home, maybe he'd change his way of thinking and acting."

Cooper shakes his head perplexedly. The creases on his face deepen. "I just wonder what influenced him to be that antagonistic toward black people," he says. "Did he get that from his parents or his peers? He went to a Catholic high school, didn't he? I just wonder what effect that had on him— or did it all just go in one ear and out the other? That religious training was lost on him from what I can gather. So we have to have a reformation, or a penance. Because it's not normal for a young man to be so hateful."

A BUZZ SOUNDS from the jury room at 10:28 P.M. Two of the lawyers who assisted Genson and Adam are playing chess at the defense table. One of them jumps to his feet and rushes to the corridor leading to the jury room. Yes, Deputy Rhodes tells him, the jury has a verdict.

The news spreads quickly through the sleepy courthouse, and the gallery quickly refills. The courtroom's atmosphere, relaxed while the jury was out, quickly sobers. Ties are tightened, voices soften. At ten forty-five P.M. the gallery is once again packed. Lenard's and Clevan's relatives are in a bench near the front of the gallery. Detective Turner is behind them, along with a squad of prosecutors that includes the boss, white-haired Richard Devine. Most of Caruso's supporters are sitting in the rear benches or standing at the very back of the gallery. A dozen deputies survey the crowd warily from the front and rear of the courtroom and the center aisle.

Locallo admonishes the spectators to restrain themselves regardless of the decision. Then he directs everyone to stand, and Deputy Rhodes to bring in the jury.

The foreperson—a white suburban woman, a neuroscientist—hands the verdicts to Rhodes, who delivers them to Locallo. The judge reads through them silently once, then shuffles them into the order he wants them read and hands them to his clerk, Angela Villa. Villa reads: "We, the jury, find the defendant, Frank Caruso, guilty of aggravated battery of Lenard Clark on a public way."

There are sobs and gasps from the Bridgeport contingent.

"We, the jury, find the defendant, Frank Caruso, guilty of hate crime of Lenard Clark," Villa continues. "We, the jury, find the defendant, Frank Caruso, guilty of hate crime of Clevan Nicholson. We, the jury, find the defendant, Frank Caruso, not guilty of attempted first-degree murder of Lenard Clark."

Now there are claps and cheers. "Quiet!" a deputy barks.

Reporters rush from the courtroom. In their separate pews, Lenard's mother and Caruso Senior take deep breaths and exhale almost simultaneously. Rocco LaMantia leans forward from the bench behind the elder Caruso and rubs his shoulders. At the defense table, Frank Junior, arms folded, shows no emotion.

Locallo polls the jurors, several of whom are crying. Then he thanks them for their work. He rises, and his voice cracks as he says, "And for the final time in this case, we stand out of respect for you."

After the jury has retired to the jury room, he sets sentencing for the following month. He revokes Caruso's bond and orders him taken into custody. Genson gives his client's shoulders a squeeze before deputies escort him away.

WHEN THE VERDICT WAS READ, a police lieutenant was on a phone in an anteroom, waiting to relay the results to the police superintendent's office, from which they'd be radioed to police citywide. Locallo says later he had this in mind when he shuffled the verdicts so his clerk would read the guilty ones first. He figured that if the convictions were emphasized when the news went out, there'd be less chance of postverdict disturbances. And indeed, none were reported.

With the intensive-care photo of Lenard on the table in front of them, the jurors had quickly decided that Caruso was guilty of aggravated battery and of hate crime. Most of the deliberations were spent on the attempted murder charge. By the time everyone agreed there wasn't sufficient evidence that Caruso tried to kill Lenard, the panel was drained. "We weren't upset because we had to convict him on the other charges," one juror, a white male who asked to be anonymous, says. "We were upset because we couldn't get him on the big one. I knew he [Caruso] didn't care if the kid lived or died. And I knew that he thought he could get away with it. But he never said, 'Kill him.' He didn't have a bat or a club in his hand. It was so damned frustrating."

Atif Sheikh, the Pakistani American juror, was troubled by the acquittal even though he agreed to it. "Let's say Frank Caruso got beat up like that by a black kid," Sheikh says. "Would the black kid get convicted of attempted murder? I think it's a ninety-nine percent chance he would."

As he always does, Locallo stopped in the jury room after the verdict to thank the jury directly. The jury presented him with a thank-you card. The judge "got choked up and said, 'I'll cherish this card,'" one juror recalls. Most of the women were crying. Locallo told them he thought he knew why they were crying—because they weren't satisfied with their verdict. He reassured them that they'd made the right decision given the evidence. "Some people wanted to make sure that [Caruso] wasn't going to get a slap on the wrist," says the forewoman (who also asked that her name not be used). "The judge was sort of assuring us that that wouldn't happen."

The morning after the verdict Mandeltort woke up retrying the case in her head, wondering what she could have said or done differently to get Caruso convicted of attempted murder. But then she thought about the hurdles she and Berlin had had to leap, such as DeSantis's disappearance and Cutler's murder, to get any conviction at all. "And then I said to myself, 'You know what? We won a really tough case.'"

Genson likewise claims victory. The case "may not have ended up exactly as I wanted it to," he says, "but it wouldn't have ended up as good as it did if it had been another lawyer." And if not for the bias against Caruso, he'd have prevailed completely, he says. "I tried to get past the emotion and prejudice and innuendo, but I couldn't get past all of it. I couldn't get around the fact that it appeared to the jury he was a punk Italian kid from Bridgeport."

SEVENTEEN

Blame the Po-*lice*

ON SEPTEMBER 29, eleven days after the Caruso verdict and in front of a nearly empty gallery in 302, Locallo rejects Leroy Orange's bid for a hearing on his torture allegations.

Orange filed "inconsistent" affidavits regarding his alleged abuse, Locallo tells the lawyers and Orange. In a 1991 affidavit, Orange alleged that he'd been struck in the mouth, kicked, shocked with needles in his buttocks and anus, and bagged, and that his testicles had been squeezed. But in the affidavit he recently filed, Orange "no longer claims that he was kicked," the judge observes.

There's sarcasm in Locallo's voice, unusual for him on the bench, and his tone only grows more disdainful as he continues. He repeatedly calls Robert Kirschner, the former Cook County medical examiner who deemed Orange's torture claims authentic, the "receptive doctor." "Incredibly, fourteen and a half years after the murders, petitioner now reveals for the first time to the receptive doctor that the electroshocks caused his teeth to crack," the judge says. "Suddenly, the receptive doctor has petitioner being shocked to petitioner's front and back forearm, with no electric shocks noted to the buttocks or anus. Instead, the receptive doctor has noted that the rectal bleeding is consistent with the type of injury produced from the insertion of a foreign object in a rectum."

Orange had testified at his trial in 1985 that he'd been shocked on the arm, so that was nothing new, although Locallo seems to be suggesting it was. And in his affidavit Kirschner didn't comment specifically about shocks to Orange's buttocks or anus. He didn't say that a foreign object inserted into Orange's rectum couldn't have also shocked him, but Locallo seems to have interpreted it that way.

The judge also notes that in Orange's formal confession he "said his treatment was fine" at the police station.

Locallo says the firing of Area 2 commander Jon Burge, and the police department investigation that found that suspects had been systematically abused at Area 2 in the 1980s, don't prove to him that torture was a routine practice at Area 2, let alone that Orange was a victim of it. Orange's claims are simply "not corroborated."

The judge turns the discussion to Orange's sentencing hearing. He soon continues the case to late October. But no action regarding Orange's sentencing will be taken that month, or through the end of 1998, because Geraghty will be appealing today's ruling by Locallo to the Illinois Supreme Court.

GERAGHTY IS DISAPPOINTED BY Locallo's ruling, but he's not surprised—either by the decision or by Locallo's justification for it. Locallo had said he based his decision partly on inconsistencies he found in Orange's claims about the torture. But it's easy to find contradictions in a case that's fourteen years old, Geraghty says. People inevitably forget things, he says. "The bottom line for me is, does the person tell a story that would be difficult to make up? And is there some internal consistency to what the person is saying? The fact that there are some inconsistencies on peripheral points means little to me. But it's typical of how judges wind up ruling in favor of the state in these cases."

Geraghty thinks judges at 26th Street are reluctant to rule for defendants in cases involving allegations of police abuse because of the courthouse's "insular culture." Many judges are former prosecutors with "long-standing relationships that make it difficult for them to rule objectively" in such cases, he contends. Dennis Dernbach, the assistant state's attorney who took Orange's confession and who testified at Orange's trial that he saw no evidence of coercion at the police station, was a colleague of Locallo in the state's attorney's office, and he's still a colleague—he presides in Courtroom 301. Locallo considers Dernbach a friend. From 1983 to 1986 Dernbach was supervisor of felony review, the unit of the state's attorney's office that takes confessions. Attorneys serving under him took confessions in many of the Area 2 cases in which torture has been alleged.

Geraghty could have asked Locallo to recuse himself because of his relationship with Dernbach. But Orange's case then could easily have wound up in front of another former prosecutor. And Geraghty wanted to keep the case in front of Locallo in the event it did proceed to sentencing, since Locallo has never given the death penalty.

Locallo says later that his ruling wasn't a close call. Orange made up his torture charges to try to save himself after he confessed, the judge says. The fact that so many other defendants had made similar accusations about Area 2 didn't persuade Locallo in the least that the claims had any merit. Defense lawyers "say that because ten or fifteen people make the same claim, it must be true. Baloney. The bottom line is, that allegation is glommed onto by a lot of people. I'm telling you, I am convinced. It is a cottage industry out there: blame the *po*-lice."

Nor did it matter to the judge that Orange was one of the first to claim he was electrically shocked. "I don't care if he was the first," Locallo says. If Orange really had been tortured, he would have told Dernbach about it when Dernbach was preparing to take his confession, the judge says. "Denny Dernbach asked him, 'Well, how were you treated?' 'Fine.' 'Any problems?' 'No.' I don't think the prosecutor is gonna lie."

And if Orange didn't feel comfortable reporting the torture while he was still in police custody, he should have done so when he got to 26th Street, Locallo says. "The bottom line is, as soon as you get within reach of a judge, you yell out, 'Hey, I've been tortured.'"

When I remind Locallo that according to the transcript of Orange's bond hearing, and the affidavit of Orange's public defender at that hearing, Orange apparently had tried to do that, Locallo just shakes his head. Even if Orange *did* complain immediately, the judge says, no sign of physical abuse was found when he was examined.

Locallo isn't convinced that Commander Burge ever tortured anyone at Area 2 despite the city's admission that he did. That admission was "political," the judge says. Burge had become a "lightning rod for lawsuits," and the city "wanted to get rid of the lightning rod." In Locallo's view, Burge was a "sacrificial lamb."

But why did Orange make such a peculiar allegation? Unlike many defendants who allege coercion, he didn't say detectives slapped him around. At his bond hearing, Orange said: "I got pin marks on my butt. Only bruise I got to show. Other things happened. That is all that is visible right now." What did Locallo make of that? "I have no idea," the judge says.

EIGHTEEN

Compassion

CARUSO APPEARS IN COURT in a jail uniform for the first time on the morning of Tuesday, October 13. Like the outfit he'd worn throughout the trial, this one is too big for him. He grabs the waist of his baggy tan pants and hikes them up as he's escorted into the courtroom by two burly guards in black uniforms and shiny black boots.

The guards are members of SORT, the sheriff's Special Operations Response Team. Caruso has the special detail because he's in protective custody in the jail due to the nature of his case. That status also keeps him out of the regular courtroom lockup. "Why don't they just put him in with the niggers?" a deputy from another courtroom asked Guerrero face-tiously after the SORT guards parked Caruso in the jury room earlier this morning.

Caruso is before Locallo only briefly. The lawyers and the judge quickly hash out a procedural matter relating to his sentencing two days from now. Soon the guards usher him back to the jury room. Locallo has granted Caruso a contact visit with his father and sister before he's returned to the jail. Deputy Rhodes beckons Caruso Senior and his daughter out of the gallery for the visit.

The Carusos don't have the jury room to themselves for the visit, and not just because of Caruso's SORT guards. This also happens to be sentencing day for Dino Titone. Titone's status as a prison inmate with a potential death sentence qualifies him for special handling, too: he's hand-cuffed to a chair in the room, and his own pair of SORT guards are sitting nearby, thumbing through newspapers.

The double murder Titone was convicted of had originated in Bridgeport. The two victims were abducted on a December night in 1982 from a house at 3002 South Emerald, just nine blocks from the Carusos' home. Now, on a fall morning sixteen years later, Titone and Caruso have ended up together in a jury room at 26th Street, although not to deliberate someone else's fate.

Titone takes the opportunity to give Caruso some advice: he tells him to be grateful he'll be getting another chance in the world. Titone won't be getting such a chance, barring a successful appeal and a victory in a third trial, since the only alternatives in Illinois for a multiple murder are lethal injection or natural life—the choice Locallo will make this afternoon. Titone advises Caruso to learn what he can from his time in prison. He also promises the elder Caruso that he'll put in a word for Frank Junior regarding his safety in prison. Titone has influence with some prison gang leaders, he tells me later, having gotten to know them during his six years on death row and eight years in maximum security.

Locallo also has his usual batch of minor cases to deal with today, starring the blacks and Hispanics crammed into the lockup and those defendants on bond who are waiting in the gallery. One of the prisoners in the lockup is George McNeal, a gaunt fifty-one-year-old African American who was arrested three weeks ago after an encounter with an undercover "drunk" at an El station. A twenty, a five, and two ones were sticking out of the cop's breast pocket. McNeal allegedly snatched the money while offering to sell the officer a rabbit McNeal happened to have in a cage. Backup officers moved in and handcuffed McNeal. The officers also charged him with a weapons violation after they found a butcher knife in his backpack. The arrest report is more thorough than arrest reports are in some violent crimes, including even a description of the rabbit (two pounds, six inches, black).

McNeal has been in jail for three weeks since he was charged with swiping the $27; Caruso spent no time in jail while charged with stomping a thirteen-year-old nearly to death. Caruso's family could put up $10,000 for his bond; McNeal didn't have the $500 for his. At $51 a day in room and board, McNeal's jail stay for the $27 theft has thus far cost taxpayers more than a thousand dollars.

When McNeal is in front of the bench, his public defender, Bob Galhotra, gives his side of the story to Locallo. McNeal had just finished his second day on a demolition crew and he had yet to get paid. He was hungry. Someone gave him the rabbit. Perhaps the rabbit was going to be his dinner, Galhotra says; maybe that was what he was going to do with the butcher knife. Then McNeal happened on the fake drunk. The two men were negotiating a price for the rabbit and the cage, and McNeal plucked the $27 before the deal was finalized. "It was just a poor decision, Judge," Galhotra maintains.

"Some people might say it was a hare-raising decision," Locallo says. The judge grins, the lawyers chuckle, McNeal stares straight ahead.

Locallo dangles probation, with fifty hours of community service, for a plea to theft—an offer that would spring McNeal from jail today. "I'll take that," McNeal says eagerly.

LOCALLO GRANTS Titone his own contact visit in the jury room during lunch, with his father, sister, brother, and a friend. They came to court against Titone's wishes. He didn't want them to hear all the bad things the prosecutors were sure to say about him as they lobbied for his execution.

Titone professes a lack of concern about today's hearing. He hopes Locallo takes him off death row because it'll soothe his parents; but it's not such a big deal to him because, he says, he isn't afraid of being executed. In fact, there's nothing he can think of that he fears. "My father told me when I was young that I was blessed for I never had no fear," he says. "But as I see it now, this was a curse." Without fear, a person "enters into bad challenges," as Titone puts it.

The hearing begins with prosecutor James McKay putting a records custodian on the stand to testify about some of the thirty-eight disciplinary infractions—or in prison parlance, "tickets"—Titone has accumulated in his fifteen-plus years in prison. Titone's two SORT guards struggle to stay awake in their chairs behind him. Titone smiles from time to time as the records custodian details his tickets. When he first entered prison, he fought often with other inmates "to get my respect and space," but he rarely has to anymore. He's gotten along fine with most guards, he says, but if one is being unfair, "I'm the type of person who will stand on what I believe to be right and not back down or give in." His lawyer Fred Cohn later calls to the stand one prison guard after another—eight in all—who've had Titone under their supervision and who say he's been a model inmate.

McKay reads to Locallo "victim-impact" statements from two sisters and a sister-in-law of one of the slain men, Tullio Infelise. All three women say they want Titone put to death.

According to the statement of Tullio's sister Rosario, Tullio had described the shootings to relatives in the hospital before he died. Tullio said that Titone taunted him and the other victim, Aldo Fratto, when they were in the car trunk, telling the two men he was going to leave the trunk lid open so the light would stay on, so they could watch each other die. Titone "laughed and joked and tormented" her brother and Fratto before he and the other gunman, Joseph Sorrentino, shot them, according to Rosario.

The sister-in-law, Christine Infelise, says she and her relatives resent supporting Titone in prison with their taxes.

Titone's smile is gone and he's gazing vacantly at the carpet as McKay reads these statements. He's thought often about the Infelise and Fratto families since his imprisonment. "I know there's suffering, and hurt, and pain. These people have a right to feel hatred toward the persons they think did it."

He can especially imagine the grief of Infelise's and Fratto's parents, he says, having himself witnessed, albeit from prison, his own parents' suffering when two of his brothers died at early ages. One succumbed to cancer in 1980, at age twenty-two; another brother killed himself in 1989, asphyxiating on carbon monoxide in a garage at age twenty-five. Between these two deaths, Titone got his death sentence, in 1984, when he was twenty-three. "My parents have suffered more heartache and pain than fifty families," but they've always been loving and supportive of him, he says.

Titone fought constantly in his neighborhood as a youth and usually won. But he sees no parallels between himself at a younger age and Caruso, whom he considers a "spoiled brat living off of his father's name and reputation." Titone adds, "I would have given him a beating myself for what he did to that black kid." He senses an affinity with Locallo, however. "I know if things were different and if he grew up with me, we would have been the best of friends."

Abiding by Titone's preference, Cohn doesn't call any relatives or friends on Titone's behalf. Titone doesn't want to subject his loved ones to McKay's cross-examination, and he doubts the judge is going to be swayed by such testimony anyway.

When it's time for arguments, Cohn tells Locallo that Titone is now a more prudent person than he was in his youth. "The testosterone that sometimes causes young men to do foolish things is burned up," he says.

Cohn also asserts that it would be unfair to sentence Titone to death when his two codefendants have been sentenced to life. According to the state's evidence, Titone's responsibility for the murders was no greater than that of his codefendants, Cohn observes: Robert Gacho was the ringleader, and Titone had been an equal partner with Joseph Sorrentino—both of them had shot the victims.

And a natural life sentence is no prize, Cohn reminds Locallo. It would keep Titone locked up "until he's old and his body is falling apart," when he might be shipped to a nursing home for inmates.

But McKay parries that standard defense argument with the standard state reponse: since the only options now are death and natural life, the latter is the minimum punishment. "If you don't give him the death penalty, your honor, you're giving him what he wants. You're giving him the opportunity to watch color TV, to lift weights, to play basketball. . . . You're not sending a message to him and any other murderer out there when you give him the minimum."

McKay also points to trial testimony indicating that after Titone and Sorrentino shot the victims, Titone laughed about it. "That makes him far more evil" than his codefendants, McKay says. "That makes him inhuman. That makes him undeserving of any mercy you could show."

McKay doesn't often ponder what brings certain people to commit monstrous acts. "Maybe we're incapable of figuring some of these criminals out, because they're just so far removed from general mankind," he says later. "Maybe we don't want to figure them out." His mission is to get them locked up for as long as he can—and in some cases to get a lethal injection prescribed if possible. "They just need to be held responsible," he says.

Locallo asks Titone if he'd like to say anything before he's sentenced. Cohn quickly declines for his client. An apology wouldn't enhance Titone's appeal chances.

Locallo prefaces his ruling by saying he has no doubt that Titone took pleasure in the killings, but that he doesn't think this is indicative of Titone's character today.

He says case law generally frowns on greater punishment for one codefendant unless he's more culpable than his partners in crime. Titone, if anything, played a lesser role in the murders than did his codefendants, Locallo says. Gacho was indeed the ringleader, the judge says. And as for Sorrentino, the judge notes that according to the evidence, he used a .25-caliber gun, and both victims were shot with a .25; whereas Titone fired a .38, and only one of the victims had wounds from a .38. Thus Sorrentino likely shot both men, Locallo says, while Titone shot only one. It's a point that even Cohn hadn't made.

So Locallo says he's decided to sentence Titone to life. Titone nods slightly. In the gallery, his sister sighs loudly and claps once. The judge adds that he knows the sentence will be a disappointment to the families of the victims and to the prosecutors. "But the court has the final say on whether justice or mercy is given."

LOCALLO RECEIVED good news earlier this week, when six bar groups announced their recommendations for next month's judicial retention election. All six bar groups recommended that he be retained. This in itself was no great feat: of the seventy-two Cook County judges up for retention, only nine had been found wanting by any of the bar groups. But Locallo was one of only eleven judges to get a "highly recommended" and a "highly qualified" rating from the two bar groups with such categories.

Bar ratings are important for all judges but especially for judges with an eye on a higher seat. Locallo could never be accused of underestimating their significance. His submission to the bar groups that rate candidates "is probably the largest that they get," he says. He sends each of them every ruling he's written, every appellate court opinion issued in his cases, and all of the summaries he's written of death penalty and traffic cases. Guerrero and Rhodes share the assessment of some prosecutors that Locallo kowtows to defense lawyers with his ratings in mind because defense lawyers outnumber prosecutors in the bar groups. Upon learning of the judge's high marks this year, Rhodes said, "It's because he kisses up to all those attorneys." And Guerrero added, "It's 'cause he gives all those contact visits."

Considering his ratings and reputation, Locallo should have little reason to worry about the election. Even judges who are criticized by the bar groups rarely get voted off the bench. Illinois judges must run for retention every six years as part of a general election. They need 60 percent approval from those who actually vote on their retention. (Many voters skip the lengthy retention ballot rather than render a verdict on judges they've never heard of.) Citizens complain about the quality of their judges, but they're forgiving come election time. Since Illinois began holding retention elections in 1964, sitting judges have been retained 98 percent of the time. The retention rates are even higher in other states, a function of the fact that only 50 percent approval is needed elsewhere.

But the judges up for retention this year are concerned that because of a logistical matter, retention might not be a sure thing this time. The nonjudicial portion of the ballot is particularly lengthy, and a change in election law has eliminated one-punch, single-ticket voting—voters can no longer vote for all members of a party by punching a single number. Judges fear that as a consequence, voters will grow weary as they work their way through the ballot, and more voters than usual will skip the retention election at the end of the ballot. This will make the votes of the small but dependable antijudge constituency—the bloc of voters who turn thumbs down on all judges up for retention—more significant.

Locallo has a particular reason to be apprehensive: the fact that he is the judge in the Bridgeport case. While he enjoys the challenge of a heater and the attention and publicity it brings, he isn't naïve about the risks. A misstep in a controversial case, particularly right before an election, can jeopardize a judge's seat. With that in mind, he'd planned to dispose of the Caruso case long before the election. But several matters beyond his control, particularly the disappearance of witness Richard DeSantis, had forced him to postpone the case repeatedly, resulting in the trial of Caruso less than two months before the election.

The trial itself went well for Locallo. His name was in the papers often, his portrait was on the nightly news, and there was nothing but praise for the way he conducted the trial. The media looked with favor on the mixed verdict, the *Tribune* calling it "perfectly reasonable," the *Sun-Times* declaring that "justice has been served."

But Locallo isn't out of the woods. Caruso still has to be sentenced, and his two codefendants still have to be tried.

The newspapers are calling on Locallo to throw the book at Caruso, to "send a strong message throughout the city that hate crimes will not be tolerated in Chicago," as the *Sun-Times* has said. Mayor Daley—who, more than any other person, can make or break a Cook County judge's career— has confidently predicted that Caruso will be held "fully accountable" when he's sentenced.

The normal term for aggravated battery is two to five years. But if an aggravated battery shows "exceptionally brutal or heinous behavior indicative of wanton cruelty," the judge can give an extended sentence of as much as ten years. Caruso also faces one to three years for his hate crime convictions. Illinois law generally dictates concurrent sentences for separate convictions arising from the same offense. But the prosecutors contend that the hate crime committed against Clevan Nicholson, when he was punched at 33rd and Shields, and the stomping of Lenard Clark around the corner on Princeton, are two separate offenses—and that Locallo can therefore tack on three years for the crime against Clevan to the ten he can give for the aggravated battery against Lenard, for thirteen years in all. This argument for consecutive sentencing is a stretch, as the prosecutors themselves will later acknowledge to me, because under Illinois law offenses aren't "separate" unless there's a "substantial change in the nature of the criminal objective." But such stretching by prosecutors is standard procedure at sentencing time, particularly in a heater case. By asking for the absolute theoretical maximum, the prosecutors demonstrate to the public how seriously they consider a case. And like car dealers emphasizing a bloated sticker price, they put pressure on the judge for a result at the high end.

At the opposite extreme, Caruso, with no prior convictions, is eligible for probation or boot camp. Some staffers in 302 believe it would be hypocritical for Locallo to sentence Caruso to prison—among them Rhonda Schullo, the probation department's liaison to the courtroom. Schullo points to how liberally the judge dispenses probation and boot camp, not infrequently offering those sentences even to violent offenders, so long as it's their first conviction.

Not that Schullo or anyone else expects Locallo to keep Caruso out of prison. Given how severely Clark was beaten, the case's notoriety, and the imminent retention election, everyone understands that if Locallo sentences Caruso to probation or boot camp, he might as well look for a different job no matter how "highly qualified" the bar groups consider him. No one is betting on probation in the dollar-a-person pot on Caruso's sentence that a lawyer is running in the courtroom. The bets have all been on a prison term of from four years to ten.

While the newspapers, the mayor, and the prosecutors are pressuring Locallo to sentence Caruso severely, the judge also is getting pushed in the opposite direction.

A few days before the sentencing Sam Adam Jr., who recently became a lawyer and who is assisting his father and Genson on the case, delivers to Locallo a packet of letters written on Caruso's behalf. Locallo rarely gets any letters supporting a defendant before sentencing. For Caruso, there are 120.

The letters have been written by Caruso's friends and relatives, and by public officials, ministers, community leaders, and union officials. Letter after letter implores the judge to show Caruso compassion. Several writers assert that Caruso is more likely to be rehabilitated if he's kept out of prison. To read some of the letters, one would think Caruso had been convicted of shoplifting or joyriding. A Catholic priest observes that young people "will often disappoint us and do dumb things." A neighbor of Caruso's believes "the ordeal he has already been through in this matter has been correction and instruction enough."

Other letters depict a different Caruso than the one portrayed at his trial. Caruso's brother-in-law, Keith Vitale, tells Locallo of the time he and Caruso encountered a beggar outside a grocery store. "Frank, not having any money, removed his jacket and handed it to him, saying, 'Stay warm, it's cold outside.'"

"This boy is not what the press have insinuated and he needs a chance to prove it," writes Frank Junior's uncle and godfather, Bruno Caruso. Bruno Caruso tells Locallo that in his thirty-two years as a union leader, he's always withstood political and media pressures and made decisions in the interests of those he represents. He asks Locallo to likewise not knuckle under to pressure. Then he reminds the judge that he represents thirty-five hundred county workers as president and business manager of the County, Municipal Employees, Supervisors, and Foremen union; and that he's also vice president of the Chicago and Cook County Building and Construction Trades Council; as well as vice president of the Chicago Federation of Labor AFL/CIO; not to mention past president of the District Council of Chicago and vicinity, which represents twenty thousand laborers. Locallo also has gotten letters asking for compassion for Caruso from the president and business manager of the Water Pipe Extension, Bureau of Engineering Laborers, the secretary-treasurer of labor, AFL-CIO, the president of the Iron Workers District Council of Chicago and vicinity, the business manager of the Heat and Frost Insulators, and the president of the State of Illinois Building and Construction Trades.

The clear implication from some of the letters is that Locallo could pay politically for sentencing Caruso stiffly. Most of the letters make that point obliquely—but not the one signed by a Tina Ariola. Ariola doesn't say how she knows Caruso or where she lives. She just writes that she knows Locallo is up for retention, and that while those who want Caruso sentenced severely are vocal, those who favor a lighter sentence, as she does, predominate, "and we vote in blocs of high numbers."

Reverend Floyd Davis, president of the Southside Branch of the NAACP, is among several prominent black ministers who beseech Locallo to show Caruso mercy. Davis thinks it would be a "great travesty" if Caruso were locked up for long. There's also a petition in the packet with 795 signatures. "I am an African American," the petition reads. "I would like to see race relations improved between African Americans and whites. This is why I'm signing my name to ask for leniency for Victor Jasas, Michael Kuidzinski [sic] and Frank Caruso."

And Locallo gets this typewritten letter in the mail a few days before sentencing:

TO JUDGE LOCALLO:

"Fairly, be ye all of one mind, as having compassion one of another, live as brethren, be pitiful, be courteous, not rendering evil for evil, railing for railing, but on the contrary, blessing, knowing that ye are called to this, that you should inherit a blessing." (1 Peter 3:8–9)

YOUR HONOR:

When I first saw my son beaten, I prayed for his life and for justice. Now that both his precious life has been spared and justice has come, my soul is somewhat at ease. With all things considered, today my prayer is that justice now be tempered with compassion.

Best regards,

MS. WANDA MCMURRAY
MOTHER OF LENARD CLARK

CARUSO'S UPCOMING SENTENCING isn't Locallo's only problem. The cases of Caruso's codefendants are also looming ominously.

Victor Jasas and Michael Kwidzinski are set to go on trial on October 19, four days after Caruso's sentencing. Prosecutors have far weaker cases against those two defendants than they had against Caruso. The prosecutors know that if the cases actually go to trial, both defendants will probably be acquitted.

That would be a blow to the state's attorney's office. Never mind that it would be due to a lack of evidence and not a lack of effort by the prosecutors. In criminal cases such as this one, the public focuses on the bottom line. And the bottom line, if Jasas and Kwidzinski walk, will be that only one of the three white defendants charged with battering the black boy will have been convicted, and that one only on a lesser charge.

The prosecutors have decided to try to make the best of a bad situation—to try to extract pleas from Jasas and Kwidzinski after Caruso's sentencing. They'll have to lower the charges to make a deal enticing, of course. But if they can persuade Jasas and Kwidzinski to plead, at least their office can say it convicted all three of Lenard Clark's attackers.

Surely there will be an outcry if, in order to get guilty pleas from Jasas and Kwidzinski, the prosecutors have to give them probation, but that's better politically than going to trial and losing. State's attorney Richard Devine isn't up for reelection for another two years, so any fallout won't be lethal to him. Mayor Daley is up for reelection in February, four months from now, against a black candidate, but his victory is certain. So the only person who might be in jeopardy if Jasas and Kwidzinski get probation is the judge who would approve such deals—the judge whose retention election is just weeks away.

There's no easy solution to this dilemma for Locallo. He can't postpone the trials of Jasas and Kwidzinski until after the election, because both have formally demanded trial, and the time the state has to prosecute them is expiring. He could simply refuse to approve the plea deals. But judges almost always okay such agreements, and he'd have no obvious justification for nixing these. And if he did reject the deals, thereby forcing the cases to trial, and Jasas and Kwidzinski were indeed acquitted, he might absorb all the blame. Yet his approval of plea deals for Jasas and Kwidzinski—particularly of probation deals—would be seen widely as an endorsement of leniency toward two of the Bridgeport attackers.

Caruso's lawyer, Ed Genson, believes Locallo long ago recognized this scenario and conceived a way to offset the likely damage.

Genson had found it curious that on the day Caruso was convicted, September 18, Locallo had set sentencing for October 13—just twenty-five days after trial. Illinois law gives defendants thirty days after conviction to file their standard motion for a new trial. (The motion for a new trial is almost invariably rejected, but a defendant needs to make it to preserve issues for appeal.) Sentencing rarely occurs before the motion for a new trial is heard. Judges nearly always are willing to delay sentencing even beyond thirty days—to give lawyers more time to gather witnesses in aggravation or mitigation, for example, or to allow defense lawyers to get a full trial transcript to aid their preparation of their motion for a new trial. When Genson asked Locallo to postpone sentencing for both of these reasons, Locallo did so grudgingly, pushing the sentencing back by just two days, to October 15. The trial transcript still wouldn't be ready by then, but Locallo had said the defense lawyers would have to proceed without it.

Genson thinks he knows why Locallo is in such a hurry to sentence Caruso: he's going to use that sentence to counterbalance the harm he'll suffer if he has to approve probation deals for Jasas and Kwidzinski. If Locallo sentences Caruso severely, it'll show voters he didn't take the racial beating lightly. But sentencing Caruso stiffly won't help Locallo in the November 3 election if he waits until after the election to do it. "I've been trying cases for thirty-three years," Genson says. "I have never once had a judge order me to file post-trial motions in twenty-five days. What other reason could there be for him to do this?"

It's the timing of the sentencing that bothers Genson; he doesn't think the judge will actually give Caruso extra years for political reasons. "But the problem is, my clients believe it," he says. That's why he'd prefer sentencing be after the election.

The scenario Genson described was "completely wrong," Locallo would say later. He'd had "no idea" that Jasas's and Kwidzinski's cases were headed for probation. Yes, he wanted to sentence Caruso quickly, but not because of fears about the election. He simply wanted to sentence Caruso before the trials of Jasas and Kwidzinski began so those two defendants could see what Caruso got and then "think about what they wanted to do"—in other words, reevaluate whether they wanted to go to trial.

Genson said that even if this truly was Locallo's motive for sentencing Caruso quickly—and Genson didn't believe it was—it was an inappropriate motivation. "Should you use your sentence for Defendant A to scare Defendants B and C into pleading guilty?"

Genson would also say that Locallo was so intent on sentencing Caruso in a hurry that the judge did something that astounded him. After Genson filed a written motion asking that the sentencing be postponed, Locallo visited him in his office downtown to ask him to withdraw the motion, according to Genson. "That's the first time that happened to me in thirty-three years, too."

Judges are prohibited from initiating ex parte communications (meetings with only one of the parties) such as Genson describes. But when I ask Locallo, after the Caruso case is disposed of, about this alleged visit to Genson's office, the judge will vehemently deny it ever happened. "He's a liar," Locallo says of Genson. "He's an absolute liar. You can tell him that. I want you to call him up and say I think he is a fucking liar. . . . He is an absolute liar. That's an absolute lie. Absolute lie."

LOCALLO AND HIS STAFF move to a large sixth-floor courtroom on the morning of October 15. The early birds among the reporters and sketch artists are soon staking out territory in the jury box, while Locallo doles out continuances in other cases.

Sam Adam Jr. briefly takes a seat next to me in the jury box. He tells me he thinks the "magic number" today is five. A five-year sentence for Caruso will "appease both sides," he says, meaning those calling for Caruso's scalp and those lobbying for mercy. This seems to be wishful thinking on Adam's part. Given the credits inmates can get on their sentences, a five-year term can be completed in two years. That would hardly be viewed as the strong message against hate crimes that the newspapers have been demanding.

Adam also informs me of plans for a campaign to knock Locallo off the bench in next month's election should the judge slam Caruso today. Bruno Caruso has arranged for "Dump Locallo" buttons and flyers to hit the streets overnight, Adam says, if the sentence is too stiff—that is, more than five years.

This was a mess of Locallo's own making, Adam says, one he could have avoided simply by sentencing Caruso after the election. The Carusos' wrath is understandable, he thinks. "If you were paying your lawyer a hundred grand or two hundred grand or whatever, and he doesn't even have a chance to look at a full transcript before he has to come up with his post-trial motion, wouldn't you be pissed? Why couldn't he [Locallo] wait, so it wouldn't look like this was a political decision?" Adam, who's only four months out of law school, solemnly adds, "There must not just be the reality of justice, but the appearance of justice."

The gallery is packed when the hearing begins a short time later, with Adam Senior standing at the defense table and making the oral argument for a new trial.

When Adam began trying cases here in the 1960s, he'd kill time while a jury was deliberating by poring over the dusty transcripts of 1930s trials that were stored in the courthouse basement. Locallo looks up to Adam, respecting his experience and legal knowledge. The judge studied hard for the Caruso trial, anticipating the issues Adam would raise and researching the relevant cases. "Every time he came up with a [legal] proposition, I came up with a proposition that countered it," the judge told me proudly after the trial. He boned up again for this hearing, and now, as Adam cites one case to back a point, Locallo parries with a different one; when both men agree that a particular case is the controlling precedent, Adam says it means one thing, Locallo says it means another. The spectators are yawning and squirming. The sketch artist on my right in the jury box is sketching the crowd on the instructions of the TV reporter he's working with. "I hate doing crowd scenes even worse than juries," he says. "At least jurors sit still." He adds that the fruit of his labor will be on the air "for two and a half seconds."

Locallo may look up to Adam, but when it's time for a decision in their courtroom debates, Adam must look up at Locallo. It's like a veteran manager arguing a call with a younger ump. To no one's surprise, certainly not Adam's, Locallo ultimately concludes that all of his trial rulings were correct, and he denies the motion for a new trial.

The fidgeting in the gallery abates as the sentencing hearing begins, with the prosecutors putting on several witnesses to testify about other offenses allegedly committed by Caruso in Bridgeport. Judges are allowed to consider mere allegations in deciding a sentence.

A woman tells Locallo she saw Caruso and another youth deck a white fourteen-year-old near her Bridgeport home in 1994 and kick him while he lay on the ground. Caruso was fifteen then. Genson later calls two friends of Caruso's who say they saw the fight and that Caruso wasn't involved. Eighteen-year-old Lionel Johnson—one of the two African American youths who testified at Caruso's trial that Caruso called them niggers, skunks, and coons at Armour Square Park—tells the judge Caruso also menaced him with his car near the park one day in 1995. Johnson says he was walking down the street when a car sped up behind him. The car kept coming even after he raced to the sidewalk; it leaped the curb and swerved just past him. Caruso, who was behind the wheel, yelled out his window, "Fucking nigger, get out of my neighborhood," Johnson says. Genson later calls a private investigator to the stand who says he questioned Johnson about this incident, and Johnson told him he didn't know the name of the driver of the car.

Caruso, sitting amid his five lawyers at the defense table, is in civilian clothes—white shirt, brown tie, gray slacks. As during his trial, he betrays no emotion when these allegations are made against him, or at any other time during the hearing. He mainly studies the edge of the table, sometimes stealing glances at a witness.

Cedric Banks, a tall, twenty-six-year-old African American, describes an encounter with Caruso at Armour Square Park in 1995 or 1996. One summer afternoon Banks, then a youth worker, brought a group of kids to the park to use its pool. The children, most of whom were black, ranged in age from six to thirteen. After several children complained to him that Caruso was calling them racial names, Banks told Caruso to leave the kids alone, he says. When he and the children were ready to leave the park, a phalanx of twenty to thirty white youths, armed with sticks, bats, and chains, was waiting on the stairwell outside the pool's locker room, he tells Locallo. Caruso was at the bottom of the stairs, holding a stick or a bat. "They gave us one little pathway to walk through. . . . I had to walk through sideways," Banks says. He adds that as he passed Caruso, Caruso said, "Now, big guy, you ain't so tough out here." On Genson's cross, Banks allows that neither he nor any of the children were struck by anyone.

Mandeltort concludes the aggravation evidence by reading to the court the victim-impact statements of Clevan Nicholson's and Lenard Clark's mothers.

Jennifer Nicholson says in her statement that at first she feared that Clevan's and Lenard's attackers would get away with the crime—she'd heard of other minorities being victimized in Bridgeport and no one being punished. She hopes the case will show "that race will not make a person above the law." She says Clevan wants Caruso to get the maximum.

Mandeltort tells Locallo she understands that the judge has received a letter purportedly written by Clark's mother, Wanda McMurray. Mandeltort says she's shown that letter to McMurray—who's sitting in the gallery this morning—and that McMurray said she didn't write it or sign it. Then Mandeltort reads the official McMurray statement: "What Frank Caruso did has changed our lives forever. Frank Caruso should receive the maximum sentence that can be given by the court. Judge Locallo, please spare other children and their families the grief caused by Frank Caruso Jr."

AFTER LUNCH Genson's mitigation witnesses describe an entirely different Frank Caruso Jr. Kathie Moy, a forty-eight-year-old Bridgeport resident, relates how Caruso and his parents helped with the neighborhood's food and clothing drives, which benefited the parishioners of a poor black Baptist parish east of Bridgeport. Moy has known Caruso since he was small and considers him a "sweetheart." Moy's son, a fitness instructor at Armour Square Park since 1996, follows his mother to the stand and tells the judge he's never seen Caruso cause any trouble at the park.

Reverend Floyd Davis, president of the Southside Branch of the NAACP and pastor of a Baptist church just east of Bridgeport, tells Locallo that Caruso should be shown leniency because it's wrong to use people as "sacrificial lambs" to try to solve society's racial problems.

This comment infuriates Locallo, although he hides his anger on the bench. "It was just unbelievable that somebody would come up with that thought," he says later. "A sacrificial lamb is by definition an innocent. I was tempted to just turn to him and start cross-examining him myself." (A few days after this hearing, Davis will resign his NAACP post. His successor will stress that the support shown Caruso was Davis's personal position and not that of the NAACP.)

Genson's final witness is the Reverend B. Herbert Martin. Tall and broad-shouldered, with cropped black hair and a bushy gray mustache, Martin is dressed in his cleric's black suit and white collar. He is the minister who led the "racial healing" prayer services, promoted by Caruso Senior, in Bridgeport and in his own African American community east of Bridgeport, after the Clark beating.

Martin tells Locallo that although he himself was once the victim of a racial beating, he believes in the "power of forgiveness" and recommends mercy for Caruso. In a letter to Locallo, Martin had also said he thought some form of nonprison punishment would be "more rehabilitative, redemptive, and transformative for this young man's life and future."

Martin was nineteen when he sustained the beating he alluded to, he tells me later. He and his best friend were jumped by a half-dozen young white men on a country road outside his hometown, Mound Bayou, Mississippi, on a summer evening in 1962. He remembers being hit in the head with an ax handle, then awakening in a ditch to the moans of his friend. The friend had been kicked repeatedly in the groin and clubbed in the head. Neither Martin nor his friend reported the attack to police, because all of the officers in the county were white. Martin and his friend had been working to register blacks to vote, and he thinks this precipitated the attack. He says he didn't thirst for vengeance because he'd absorbed Martin Luther King's exhortation to turn the other cheek. "You let go of the hurt, let go of the pain, and the enemy gets destroyed by your nonviolent response."

He'd met the Carusos in the late 1980s, when they participated in those food and clothing drives for his church that Kathie Moy testified about. Martin knew that the Carusos were union heavyweights. He thought an alliance with them could yield more than canned goods and hand-me-down coats; he thought it could translate into jobs for his parishioners. And in fact, before the Bridgeport attack, Bruno Caruso had found jobs for some of the applicants Martin had sent his way, Martin would tell me. Martin had realized that the Carusos, likewise, had more on their minds than helping poor blacks—they'd seen advantages in a relationship with Martin. In the 1980s Martin probably had more political clout than any

African American minister in Chicago outside Jesse Jackson and Nation of Islam leader Louis Farrakhan. He was private pastor to Chicago's first black mayor, Harold Washington, who named him chairman of the city's public housing authority. Under the next African American mayor, Eugene Sawyer, Martin served as head of the city's Commission on Human Relations. Martin thinks the Carusos saw him as a conduit to the mayor's office. "They saw opportunities for contracts and all kinds of stuff with the city. I'm not naïve about that." Sometimes he was able to get them access to the mayor, and sometimes he wasn't, he'd tell me.

The Bridgeport attack had imperiled this alliance, what with so many African Americans, including many of Martin's parishioners, demanding that Caruso and his codefendants be severely punished. He led the "racial healing" services in part to soften that sentiment.

Now, on cross, Mandeltort says, "So I'm clear here, sir, you believe in the 'power of forgiveness,' is that correct?"

"You're right," Martin says.

"And you forgive the enemy, is that correct, sir?"

"You're right."

"And in the world of racism, the enemy would be racists, would that be fair to say, sir?"

"You're right."

Martin thinks Mandeltort is implying, with her questions and incredulous tone, "that something is wrong with forgiveness," he'd say later. This doesn't surprise him. "She's out to win a case; she's not out to transform a life. That's the difference between my profession and hers."

Genson, on redirect: "There are people that do things that are wrong . . . that are entitled to mercy and compassion, is that right?" Martin says there are indeed.

"And even though Ms. Mandeltort seems to think all black people should hate everyone—" Genson begins, but Mandeltort breaks in with an angry objection that Locallo sustains.

"There is nothing inconsistent with your religion and your ministerial and pastoral calling to come into court and ask for a judge to exercise mercy and compassion, is there?" Genson asks.

"There is nothing wrong with that, and I have done it on many occasions," Martin says.

But Martin would later tell me that while he'd written letters on behalf of other defendants, he could think of only one other defendant he'd testified similarly for—a wealthy slumlord named Louis Wolf. Wolf owned dozens of buildings in Chicago, some of which he'd allowed to become "environmental disasters and toxic waste dumps," thereby propelling "whole neighborhoods into urban decay," a lawyer for the city said at his sentencing in federal court in 1993. Wolf had failed to pay property taxes on real estate he owned. Then, after the property was sold at a tax auction, he'd bought it back through various fronts, which freed him of the tax liens, bilking the government out of hundreds of thousands of dollars in property taxes. He pled guilty to racketeering and mail fraud. At the behest of Wolf's lawyer, Martin urged the judge not to imprison Wolf but to allow him instead to redeem himself by donating his time, money, and one of his properties to Martin's church. "We feel that this would better serve to rehabilitate the man," Martin told that judge. The judge ultimately sentenced Wolf to a year in prison and fined him $400,000, directing that half the money go to Martin's church for its outreach programs, the other half to a social service agency. Martin's church got stiffed, however. Wolf later pointed out in a letter from prison that the judge had no authority to direct a defendant to pay a fine to anyone but the U.S. government, and that therefore the fine was illegal; thus, he maintained, he didn't owe a dime. An appeals court accepted only the first part of this argument, mandating that the fine be paid to the federal government. Martin would tell me later that he now realizes he was "misused" by Wolf. "I don't mind quid pro quo enterprises. However, it didn't work out that time."

IN HIS ARGUMENT, prosecutor Berlin reminds Locallo that Caruso was eighteen at the time of the attack, his victims just thirteen. Berlin is well aware that the judge himself has a thirteen-year-old son.

When no relatives or friends show their support for a defendant at sentencing, prosecutors sometimes remind the judge that the defendant won't even be missed if he goes away for a long stretch. On the odd occasion that there is an outpouring of loved ones, prosecutors instead employ the argument Berlin uses now: Caruso apparently "comes from a very supportive family," Berlin says—which only makes him more reprehensible: "Despite . . . all the love and support that he's had at home, he still committed these brutal and horrible crimes." And the letters and testimony on behalf of Caruso don't change the bottom line, Berlin says—they don't change the fact that "two innocent little boys" were "brutally and savagely beaten because of the color of their skin." He asks for the maximum extended sentence of ten years for the aggravated battery, and the maximum three years for the hate crime, and for the terms to run consecutively, for thirteen years in all.

Locallo has granted Adam's and Genson's request to divide their argument. Adam begins with the legal issues. He first contends that Caruso isn't subject to consecutive sentencing, since his convictions all stemmed from the same offense. Locallo soon tells Adam he can "move on to another area," making it clear he won't be giving Caruso consecutive terms.

This makes the maximum sentence for Caruso ten years, if he qualifies for an extended sentence. Adam, of course, says he doesn't, because the Bridgeport attack wasn't *exceptionally* brutal or heinous, as is required for an extended term. He cites several cases in which extended sentences were overturned because the crimes weren't brutal enough.

Thus Caruso can get no more than five years, Adam says. "While your honor may have a great deal of personal feelings about this case—and we all do; I don't think anybody in the community doesn't have their own personal feelings about this case—nevertheless, the law is the law."

Genson spends much of his argument reading letters to Locallo from Caruso and his parents. He starts with the one from Frank Junior.

Caruso opens his letter by saying that after the beating, he prayed that Lenard would recover from his injuries. (At the state's table, Mandeltort whispers to Berlin, "Yeah, so he wouldn't get charged with murder.") Caruso says he's also prayed that Locallo would give him the chance to work in his community and Lenard's "to try and help all people to live in peace and tolerance."

Caruso says that from an early age he was taught that all outsiders, not just blacks, were a menace to his neighborhood. "The older people would say that if strangers came into the neighborhood our relatives would lose their jobs," Genson reads. "Our families would not be safe. Drugs would come into the neighborhood. We would lose our houses." He and others "believed these lies about outsiders, and it is because of this stupidity and prejudice that Lenard and Clevan were hurt."

Caruso comes as close to admitting guilt as he can without jeopardizing an appeal. "I am sorry for the agony that I have brought to everyone," Genson reads. "I understand that being sorry does not make everything right. Everyone believes I am a monster. I never could show how I feel. If I could show it, everyone would know how scared I am."

The Bridgeport attack has been dissected by newspaper columnists, TV commentators, radio talk show hosts and callers, teachers and their students, ministers, civic leaders, and elected officials, including the president and the mayor. During the trial, thirty-one witnesses testified about the crime from myriad perspectives, and the lawyers weighed in with their addresses to the jury. It seems as if most everyone has been heard from about the crime but the person convicted of it. And even now, after Genson reads Caruso's letter to the court, it's impossible to know what part of it, if any, came from Caruso. As Adam Junior would say later, "Eddie did a nice job with the letter."

Genson next reads the letter from Caruso's mother, Sherry. She pleads with Locallo to give her son another chance, saying that despite the media portrayals, he's "shy, loving, kind, very timid," although he "does get mad like any other normal teenager." She says she "did everything for Frank. That's why it's so hard for him. He is a little boy who needs me."

Sherry Caruso is slumped forward and sobbing silently in the gallery's first row as Genson reads her letter. Genson asks Locallo to consider the agony of Caruso's parents, as well as that of Lenard's and Clevan's families, in deciding Caruso's sentence. Sherry Caruso "has suffered in this case like no other mother I have seen," he says. Caruso's father has been similarly devastated: "He now has white hair. He's lost a good deal of it. He doesn't work. He walks around crying for his child."

Locallo is listening attentively on the bench, his eyes on Genson, his chin resting on his fist. Near his elbow is a stack of stapled, four-page, double-spaced documents—copies of the speech the judge wrote a few days ago for this hearing.

Genson concludes his letter-reading with the one from Caruso's father.

The elder Caruso opens with an apology to Lenard and his mother "for whatever sorrow my son has brought." He wonders how Wanda McMurray has been able to withstand her ordeal, and he says he and his family have gained strength from her example. These are kinder thoughts than he expressed in the gallery during pretrial court dates, when he questioned McMurray's competence as a parent.

In his letter, Caruso Senior hurries past the subject of McMurray's suffering to his family's own. His account of the misery the case has brought the Carusos is far longer than the victim-impact statements of McMurray and Nicholson. He describes his wife's heart problems, exacerbated by the case, and the hate mail his family has received. He says Reverend Martin "pastored us in what we thought were our bleakest days" after Frank Junior was charged. "Little did we know how bleak the days would become." At times during the case he felt it might be easier to die "than to get up every morning with this pain."

Frank Junior was always small for his age, he continues in the letter. A slight speech impediment and hearing loss in one ear made him shy and withdrawn. Father and son liked watching scary movies together. They'd watch them in the basement with all the lights on, running upstairs at the scary parts. On Frank Junior's first day of school, Frank Senior was the only father there, and he found it hard to leave his son. As a teen the younger Caruso "got caught up with an attitude problem . . . like many young people do." The elder Caruso attributes this to the corrupting influence of older youths who wouldn't stay away from Frank Junior even when he warned them to. The source of his son's racial hatred certainly wasn't him; he spoke forcefully to his children against ethnic stereotyping.

But now he's left to agonize over what will happen to his son if he's sent to prison. One of the hate-mail letters had suggested that Frank Junior would be used as a sex object, Caruso Senior notes in his letter. "If this is true, my God, take him now," the letter concludes. As Genson reads his letter, the elder Caruso is standing just inside the door to the courtroom, where he's biting his fist, wiping his eyes, and leaning on the man next to him.

Genson tells Locallo that the attack on Lenard and Clevan was "extraordinarily stupid" and "perhaps racist" and that Frank Junior deserves punishment. But he asks Locallo to also consider "a Frank Caruso that is a loving son, that is a good member of the community," as reflected in the letters.

Caruso declines Locallo's invitation to orally address the court before he's sentenced.

Then, without explanation or introduction, Locallo launches into his prepared remarks.

It's a remarkably un-Locallo-like sentencing address, ranging far from the issue of the specific defendant before him. He recounts the unwillingness of Rosa Parks to ride in the back of the bus, President Kennedy's decision to mobilize federal troops to ensure the admission of black students to colleges in Mississippi and Alabama, Martin Luther King's dream that people be judged "not by the color of their skin but by the content of their character." Progress has been made, Locallo says, but "sadly, we have miles to go. When we as a nation or city stumble, together we must lift a hand to steady the course and keep moving in the right direction." Genson is frowning at the defense table; this doesn't appear to be moving in the right direction for his client.

Locallo lauds the courage Lenard showed in relearning to walk, talk, dress, and eat. He commends the courage of the jurors also, calling them "noble descendants" of the first jury to assemble after the signing of the Magna Carta.

"Where do we as a city go from here?" he asks. "Racist views from both sides must be rejected. Violence against others because they do not share the same race, religion, national ancestry, or sexual orientation must not be tolerated." He urges citizens to unite against the "enemies of mankind, such as poverty, hunger, disease, discrimination, intolerance, and ignorance.

"Every generation cherishes their children's future," the judge concludes. "Every generation has a common goal, and that is to make the world safe for their children, and their children's children. When one harms a child in the manner shown in this case, justice demands that an appropriate sentence be handed down."

Locallo finally turns to the matter of Caruso's sentence. He says he's decided not to consider the other allegations made against Caruso today because of the conflicting testimony.

But he says he gives great weight to the trial testimony of Jeffrey Gordon, the neighbor who interrupted the beating of Lenard on Princeton. The judge says he vividly recalls Gordon's description of how one of the three attackers gave Lenard a final kick, even after Gordon had threatened to call police. Locallo says he's convinced that attacker was Caruso. He says the crime merits an extended sentence since Caruso showed a "complete lack of concern" for Lenard, as evidenced by this last kick he gave him after he'd already been stomped unconscious. At the rear of the gallery, Caruso Senior, his arms folded in front of him, turns his back to the judge. A priest standing next to him gently turns him frontward again.

Locallo places the blame for the beating squarely on the shoulders of Caruso Junior. Attempts to portray Bridgeport residents as racists are unfair to the "hardworking and decent" people of that neighborhood, he says. The judge also fully exonerates Caruso's parents. "I have no doubt in my mind that Mr. and Mrs. Caruso did the best they could with Frank Junior. It's not their fault, but he was out of control."

For the aggravated battery against Clark, "the court finds the appropriate sentence is an extended term of eight years," he says. And three concurrent years for hate crime. Caruso nods. The gallery is silent; there are scowls but no words from Caruso's supporters. The judge offers him a contact visit with family before he's returned to the jail.

The reporters and the sketch artists hurry out of the jury box. Locallo hands the reporters copies of his speech as they pass the bench. Caruso's guards usher him to the jury room for his contact visit. His parents and sisters see him first. Then it grows into one of the strangest contact visits the courthouse has probably ever experienced. It becomes clear in the courtroom that anyone who wants to say a quick good-bye to Caruso will be allowed to. A line forms, of relatives, friends, and neighbors, and soon it stretches from the jury room to the back of the courtroom. It's a slow, somber procession, like mourners paying last respects to a VIP lying in state. As the line inches forward, Bruno Caruso and two men in green work shirts grumble to each other in the gallery. "Politics," one of the green-shirted men huffs. "When's the election?" growls the other.

• • •

THE FOLLOWING MONDAY, back in 302, Locallo calls the cases of Victor Jasas and Michael Kwidzinski. Reporters are watching in the jury box, as are Lenard's and Clevan's mothers. The two defendants step forward from the gallery to join their lawyers, who are standing with the prosecutors in front of the bench.

Jasas and Kwidzinski will be pleading guilty, prosecutor Mandeltort tells the judge. Jasas will plead guilty to aggravated battery, for which he'll get thirty months' felony probation. Kwidzinski will plead guilty to simple battery, a misdemeanor for which he'll get two years' probation. Both defendants will also have to do three hundred hours of community service "in some area of racial awareness or racial sensitivity," Mandeltort says. They're both acknowledging being "present and legally responsible and accountable for the actions of Frank Caruso" when he punched Lenard and Clevan at 33rd and Shields.

Caruso Senior is watching in the gallery. Genson is here as well, sitting at the defense table. His head is bobbing conspicuously, as it tends to when he's mad. "I hate to be fucking used," he mutters as Locallo says he'll approve the deals.

Locallo trots Jasas and Kwidzinski through their pleas. No one has promised them anything, other than their probation and community service deals, to get them to plead guilty, they both say. They're doing it of their own free will. Locallo deems the pleas knowing and voluntary. The judge asks the defendants if they have anything to say, but neither does. Locallo formally issues the sentences. Then he tells the defendants he hopes their community service "will at least give you a little bit more enlightenment as to the proper way to deal with individuals who are different than you."

In the hallway afterward Joseph Lopez, one of Jasas's two lawyers, gloats about his client's deal. "Can you believe it? He was charged with attempted murder! He gets probation! Couldn't turn *that* down." The prosecutors started with an offer of a five-year prison term, Lopez says. "Then it was three, then two. I turned boot camp down on Friday."

"It *hurt* not to try this case," Jasas's other lawyer, John DeLeon, pipes in. "I was so confident of a not guilty. When [Jasas and his parents] asked me, 'What do you think we should do?' it hurt to say, 'Take it—you'd be a fool not to.' Anytime you can walk out of this building free, it's a victory."

The bargaining had started soon after Caruso got his sentence, Lopez says. Locallo was not only aware of the negotiations, he helped them along. Lopez says the parties were stymied at first because the discussions were between himself and Mandeltort, "and she and I are like oil and water." Then Locallo "said, 'Okay, from now on Bob [Berlin] and John [DeLeon] are doing the negotiating.'"

In his chambers, Locallo is boiling. Someone has just called to inform him about the Carusos' campaign to unseat him. They've already printed thousands of "Dump Locallo" buttons, the judge learned. "It just shows the father's a big phony," he tells me angrily.

He fields a phone call, leaning back in his chair and resting his brown suede shoes on his desk. The green button pinned to the lapel of his sports coat urges "Vote Yes on Retention of Judges." "They pled," Locallo informs the caller. "Now Caruso's father is working on a campaign against my retention. All this 'racial healing' shit? Fuck him. It just shows he's a big phony. He's interested in racial healing, and then he's gonna go after somebody who does the right thing? Well, fuck *him*. My message to him is 'Fuck *you*.'"

After he hangs up, he tells me he had no involvement in the plea negotiations, notwithstanding Lopez's account.

Regarding Caruso's sentencing, he says, "There were no decisions based on the fact that I was up for retention. Politics had nothing to do with the case. As for any campaign to remove me from office, I would hope it would not be successful. But the chips will fall where they may. I'm not gonna change the way I do things."

NINETEEN

Politics

"JUSTICE WAS NOT SERVED in this case," Jesse Jackson says two days after the probation deals are consummated. Robert Shaw, an African American Chicago alderman, tells reporters the deals show once again the racism of the Cook County courts. A front-page story in the city's African American daily, the *Chicago Defender,* quotes several furious black Chicagoans: "The justice system always leans toward white people." "We all know that if the tables were turned and three black men would have jumped on a white kid, the three black men would have gone to jail." Newspapers across the country and in other nations make note of how two white men, charged with beating a black boy unconscious in Chicago, have been "let off" with probation, as the *Independent* of London puts it.

An editorial cartoon in the *Chicago Sun-Times* shows a judge telling two smirking defendants, "I'm gonna throw the book at you!" and tossing a volume labeled "Jokes" at them, and the book bouncing harmlessly off their heads.

Once again Locallo is being thumped from two sides. On the afternoon of the plea deals—October 19—Caruso's lawyers file a motion asking Locallo to reconsider Caruso's sentence. An eight-year term for Caruso is clearly unfair when his cohorts are getting probation, according to the motion.

The next day reporters are invited to a press conference at Reverend B. Herbert Martin's church. The featured speaker is none other than Lenard Clark's mother, Wanda McMurray. In tears, McMurray tells reporters she had no idea that Jasas and Kwidzinski were going to get off with proba-tion, and that she feels betrayed. In light of the probation terms, Caruso's sentence ought to be reconsidered, she says. Caruso's parents and a sister are at the press conference, having come to show their support "for continued racial healing," as Caruso Senior tells reporters.

McMurray had been in the courtroom when Locallo took the pleas from Jasas and Kwidzinski. Prosecutor Mandeltort told Locallo then that the plea agreements had been explained to McMurray, as well as to Jennifer Nicholson, Clevan's mother, who was also in the courtroom, and that both mothers had given their assent. When Locallo learns of McMurray's statements at the press conference, he assumes "that she's being used," as he says later, and that it's part of the Carusos' effort to convert the furor over the plea deals into a lighter sentence for Frank Junior.

On October 21, Locallo gets a mailgram from Reverend Martin, who informs the judge that his community is "appalled" that Caruso got such a stiff sentence while Jasas and Kwidzinski got off so easy. It's clear now that Caruso was sentenced harshly for political reasons and not in the interests of racial justice, Martin asserts. The sentencing disparities are a "blatant act of injustice against the African American community," he says.

The judge has no intention of letting this matter linger. He sets a hearing on the motion to reconsider Caruso's sentence for October 22.

THE SMALL GALLERY in 302 is jammed the following morning with Caruso friends, neighbors, and relatives, and more Caruso allies are in the hallway hoping to get in. Caruso Senior chats with a friend on one of the gallery benches. During the trial he'd dressed unassumingly—a plain dress shirt and tie and beat-up Nikes; today he's in a tailored three-piece suit and a Gucci tie. "He's gonna have something to say," Mike Jankovich told me earlier this morning outside the courthouse. Jankovich, thirty, a highly regarded junior-middleweight boxer from Bridgeport, has been chauffeuring the Carusos to court.

The front of the courtroom is packed, too, reporters and sketch artists filling the jury box, and various sheriffs and curious courthouse workers standing along the walls; it's the most crowded 302 has been this year by far. Rhodes and Guerrero are also in the front of the courtroom, but crowd control is mainly the responsibility of the half-dozen sheriffs specially assigned to 302 today.

When Locallo indicates he's ready to begin, a pair of SORT guards escort Caruso Junior from the jury room to the defense table. He's in civilian clothes, white dress shirt open at the collar and dark slacks. For the first time a bit of fuzz is evident on his chin. He takes the seat next to Genson and immediately drops his gaze to his lap.

Locallo's mood is evident as soon as Genson asks the judge if he and

Adam can split their argument in support of their motion. "Do whatever you want to do," the judge snaps.

Genson does most of the talking. He refers to Locallo's statement at sentencing that Caruso gave Lenard a final kick after Jeffrey Gordon screamed at the offenders to stop. Assuming Caruso did do that, he still didn't deserve eight years more in prison than his codefendants for one extra kick, Genson says.

Mandeltort responds that of course Caruso isn't getting eight more years for one extra kick. Jasas and Kwidzinski got probation for a simple reason, she says: their cases were far weaker, the evidence against them resting more heavily on the missing witness and the dead one.

Genson also offers Locallo an out, a way to rationalize a sentence reduction for Caruso should the judge be so inclined. He says Mandeltort and Berlin "deceived" the judge by not telling him before Caruso was sentenced that they were going to offer probation to Jasas and Kwidzinski. Had Locallo known that the other two defendants were getting probation, he surely would have given Caruso less than eight years, Genson says. It's a devious point for Genson to make if he believes, as he's told me, that Locallo foresaw the probation deals.

Mandeltort calls the charge that she and Berlin deceived the judge "outrageous, offensive, and totally, totally without merit." There was nothing mysterious about the plea deals, she says. She and Berlin met with Jasas's and Kwidzinski's lawyers and came to an agreement. The lawyers presented the agreement to Locallo, and the judge approved it. "It happens every day in every courtroom in this building," she says.

DURING THE LUNCH BREAK Caruso Senior steps through the glass doors and into the nearly empty front of the courtroom. His son is in the jury room with his guards. The elder Caruso catches the eye of the clerk, Angela Villa, who's at her desk. "Thank you for your kind smile throughout this whole ordeal," he croons to her. Villa, surprised, smiles back bashfully. "Just doing my job," she says.

Caruso Senior walks up to the lectern and taps the microphone. Then he frisks himself for the speech he hopes to read today. His brow creases. He pulls off his suit jacket and probes its inside pockets. He dips into his pants pockets and pulls out a thick bankroll but no speech. "I lost it," he mutters.

He takes a seat at the empty defense table, picks up a pen, and bends over a legal pad.

Genson soon returns to the courtroom. When he sees the elder Caruso composing at the defense table, he tells him, "You're not addressing the judge," but Caruso ignores him and keeps writing.

"Not if you want me to continue on this case," Genson says. "It reflects on me."

"Does the judge have to warn me before he holds me in contempt?" Caruso asks an onlooker. The onlooker shrugs, and Caruso resumes writing.

"It reflects badly on me," Genson repeats.

"So what? You're tough," Caruso says without looking up.

"I have a reputation," Genson says. Then he tries a different tack. "You start attacking the judiciary, and it might not help in the appellate court."

Again, Caruso seems not to hear. He frowns, crumples the page he's been working on, and starts over on a fresh sheet.

A short time later Caruso asks me if I thought one particular witness who testified against his son was a transvestite. I ask him what made him think so. "I don't know. He just looked funny on the stand," he says.

I ask him how he'd have reacted if someone had beaten his son, when he was thirteen, the way Clark was beaten.

He purses his lips and stares vacantly at the unlit cigar dangling from one of his hands. Then he tells me about something that happened to Frank Junior when he was eleven. Frank Junior had gone skateboarding one day just east of Bridgeport, he says, in the black neighborhood on the other side of the Dan Ryan Expressway. Three black men came by in a car and offered to tow him along. Frank Junior held on to the rear bumper as the car cruised up a hill. At the top of the hill the driver floored it, sending Frank Junior flying. His head slammed into the pavement, knocking him cold. A friend who happened by piled him into his car and rushed him home. The elder Caruso was horrified when he saw his son. "I didn't know a head could get that big," he says, spreading his hands in front of him. Flesh was torn from Frank Junior's face, neck, and chest. He and his wife rushed him to a hospital. "We thought we were gonna lose him," he says. Then he looks me in the eye and delivers the moral. "When the doctors said he was gonna be all right, I didn't care who did it, why they did it, or if they caught them."

I ask him again how he'd have reacted if Frank Junior had been attacked the way Clark was. "My first reaction then probably would have been violence," he says softly. "But I have more spirituality in me now."

LOCALLO BEGINS his ruling after lunch by distancing himself from the plea deals. "This court was not involved in the negotiations," he says. At the defense table Genson leans over and whispers to Adam, "I told you he'd say that." Locallo says that the prosecutors knew their case better than he did, and so it would have been inappropriate for him to reject the plea deals. It also would have been wrong to make Lenard's and Clevan's families suffer through another trial, he says, especially when the outcome likely would have disappointed them. "With the pleas of Jasas and Kwidzinski there was a guarantee of a conviction," he says. "If there was a trial, there was no guarantee of a conviction and a great possibility of acquittal."

He says Caruso deserved a harsher sentence than Jasas and Kwidzinski regardless, since he "planned the attack, led the attack, and . . . finished the attack, upon a defenseless thirteen-year-old boy. All because he was black." Therefore, he concludes, "the motion to reconsider the sentence is respectfully denied."

The Caruso supporters in the gallery have been growing louder throughout the hearing, their jeers occasionally audible through the Plexiglas. Now a woman shouts at Locallo, "You did it to further your career. *That's* why you did it!"

"Mr. Sheriff, remove that woman from the courtroom," Locallo directs a sheriff's lieutenant. But the clamor persists:

"Politics!"

"Fucking *puppet*!"

"Call the fucking mayor and ask him what he wants you to do!"

"Piece a *shit*!"

Locallo waits as a handful of sheriffs restore order.

Then Sam Adam tells Locallo that Caruso's father would like to address the court. This is highly unusual, and Locallo certainly doesn't have to allow it—the elder Caruso has no legal standing in this hearing. But Locallo says, "If he wishes."

Caruso Senior steps forward from the gallery, pulling a folded paper from a suit-coat pocket.

"Your honor," he says at the lectern, "I feel that this has a lot of political attention, feel it's got a lot of media attention, therefore I think your decision, respectfully, has been clouded. I feel that the pressure that was weighed on you from politics and the media had you boxed in a corner, and you had to do something that was forced upon you. I actually feel that the scales of justice weren't tipped—I think the robe was actually ripped off the lady."

Locallo stares at Caruso. "Is that what you wanted to say?"

"I would continue, but I don't want to burden the court," Caruso responds tartly. "You have a decision to make. You've made it, and we have to live with it."

"Well, Mr. Caruso, I take what you say and I understand where it's coming from, because it's your son. But as for your comment about the scales of justice, or what she's wearing—you're entitled to your opinion. But if there's nothing else you have to say, then I suggest that you take care of your wife and family."

"I thank you, and that's what I'm going to try to do, but with no help from you," Caruso fires back.

"All right. Mr. Sheriff, take the defendant," Locallo says.

This ignites the Caruso supporters again. Several of them pound the tinted glass, Frank Junior's girlfriend with her middle finger. Curses are shouted at Locallo and Mandeltort. The three sheriffs in the gallery are notably ineffective and unusually tolerant. They implore the Caruso allies to settle down, but they make no arrests nor threaten any. Guerrero hustles into the gallery to help. "Step *back*," he barks at one young man in the aisle. The young man doesn't budge; instead he glares at Guerrero and says, "Well, *who* are *you*?" Guerrero is about to pull him into the hallway when a sergeant steps between them. "We're not here to arrest people," the sergeant tells Guerrero. ("If that was any other family, we would have made a *bunch* of arrests," Guerrero says later.)

The sheriffs eventually manage to steer most of the spectators out to the hallway. But the spectators stay close to the courtroom door—they're going to wait for Mandeltort to emerge, they say. "You have to come out *some*time!" one of them yells. More epithets are hollered. A young man screams that Caruso got *"railroaded!"* A deputy asks him to lower his voice. "Fuck *you*," the young man replies. "*Eight* years. What are they gonna do, make it *twenty*?"

The prosecutors wait in the courtroom until they're told that the hallway has been cleared. Two retired Chicago police detectives, assigned by the state's attorney's office to guard the prosecutors throughout the case, escort them from the courtroom. A few Caruso supporters remain in the hallway. "They were still calling me names as we walked by," Mandeltort will say later.

The tepid response of the sheriffs to the uproar stunned Mandeltort. The sheriffs "were useless," she'll say. "If someone had been getting beaten, the person would have been dead before the sheriffs did anything." Had the case involved a black defendant, and had his supporters greeted the judge's ruling with screams and curses in the gallery and hallway, the sheriffs "would have locked the whole group up," Mandeltort will say.

She's never before been frightened at 26th Street. "People have always said to me, 'Aren't you afraid to prosecute murderers and rapists?' But to most defendants, who I am doesn't matter. I've put people on death row, but until this moment in my career, it had never been taken personally. The defendants and their families realize that if I wasn't trying them, somebody else would be. Yeah, I was frightened when this happened, because it really was a mob mentality. But my feeling was, the fruit doesn't fall far from the tree. You don't have to do DNA to find out where Frankie came from. These people all this time were saying, 'Poor Frankie, he's not that way,' and, 'We're calm, peaceful, loving, law-abiding citizens'—and they were like animals."

After almost everyone else has left the courtroom, Frank Junior's uncle, labor leader Bruno Caruso, is still standing in the gallery aisle, staring at the judge's empty bench. I ask him if he'll proceed with the campaign to unseat Locallo. "I'll treat him the same way I'd treat an arbitrator who makes a bad decision," he says with a wave of an unlit cigar. "An arbitrator makes a bad decision, I certainly don't want him sticking around. But it's a personal campaign. It's personal."

After Bruno Caruso finally leaves, Locallo returns from his chambers to the bench to mop up his call. He issues continuances to a string of defendants represented by public defender Bob Galhotra. Galhotra, who was present for the mayhem, was amazed that Locallo allowed Caruso Senior to make his remarks. "You have a really thick skin, Judge," the PD tells him between cases. "That went way beyond the call of duty."

"Well, I'm Sicilian, too," Locallo says with a laugh. Then he adds, "Hey, Bob, will you start my car?"

CARUSO SENIOR "wanted to see me react," Locallo says in his chambers after he's finished his call. "Sure, he was out of line, but I think I handled it right. If I go down to his level, what does that show? So he makes his statement. So he gives his shot. Does it change anything? Is his son better off because of it?"

He's reminded of a story another judge once told him, about what the judge had said to a defendant who called him an "asshole" under his breath after the judge sentenced him to prison. Locallo leans back in his chair and tells the tale gleefully:

"So this judge says to the defendant, 'You know, sir, when I get done with my court call at the end of the day, I'm gonna take off my robe, drive home, and have a glass of wine and a nice dinner with my wife. Then I'll watch a movie, or maybe read a book; and then I'll go to sleep in my own bed. In the morning I'll take a shower, have a nice breakfast, come down to work, and handle some cases. You, on the other hand—you're going to leave this building in handcuffs. You'll go back to the jail, where you'll get a cold baloney sandwich. You'll be taken back to your cell with no chance to shower. In the morning they'll stick you on a bus that'll take you to prison. So *who's* the asshole here?'"

About the Carusos, the judge adds: "All this stuff about 'racial healing'? It's all bullshit. What happened today when their motion was denied? You see? Their true nature came out. Just like Frank Junior's true nature came out on March 21, 1997."

Locallo says he isn't worried about his safety even though he has angered a reputed mob family. "It'd be different if there was an unholy alliance between me and them, and they had perceived that I was in their pocket, and I had disappointed them," he says. "But I was just doing my job. My wife will probably be more concerned." He's anxious about the campaign to unseat him, though, he says.

But even this stormy day has had a ray of sun. Locallo shows me a letter he received today from Dino Titone. Titone wrote from prison to thank the judge for the contact visit he gave Titone with his family last week on the day Locallo sentenced him to natural life. "All of the time you allowed me with my family was special, and we are all very appreciative," the letter said. "I have the utmost respect for you and your office." The judge's sentencing decision "brought peace to my father (and me), and was a sign that God has indeed been working in my life," Titone wrote. He thanked Locallo "for being humane and Christ-like."

DOMINIC DI FRISCO, president emeritus of Chicago's Joint Civic Committee of Italian Americans, was in the gallery when Locallo denied the motion to reconsider the sentence. For years, Di Frisco, a public relations executive and a friend of the Caruso family, has led the fight locally against negative stereotyping of Italian Americans, and especially against the mobster image. Locallo says Di Frisco called him before the hearing on the motion to reconsider and tried to persuade him to reduce Caruso's sentence—an accusation Di Frisco vehemently denies.

After the Caruso trial but before Caruso was sentenced, Locallo says he bumped into Di Frisco at a Columbus Day reception. He says Di Frisco praised him effusively for how he conducted the trial. Di Frisco also mentioned that he'd be helping with the telecast of the Columbus Day parade the following week, and he'd make sure to mention Locallo's name. Locallo was going to be riding on two floats in the parade—one for the retention judges, and one for the Justinian Society of Lawyers, an association of Italian American lawyers. Since he was up for retention, he'd appreciate the plug, he told Di Frisco. And Di Frisco came through: friends of Locallo's told him they heard his name repeatedly during the telecast.

It was after Genson filed his motion to reconsider the sentence that Locallo got a call from Di Frisco, according to the judge. "He starts out saying that the FBI has it in for Italians and that Italians are getting rougher treatment from the law. Then he says, 'Could you show that you're a compassionate judge by reducing Caruso's sentence? Because I fear the consequences if you don't.'"

Locallo says he was flabbergasted. He couldn't believe the "boldness of somebody attempting to muscle me like that." He didn't know what "consequences" meant, "but I took it as a threat. I told him, 'I'll make my decision based on the law and the evidence and what I think is right. This conversation's over.'"

Of Locallo's version of events, Di Frisco says: "To call that a blatant lie would be the understatement of the century. I never threatened him in any way, nor did I ask him to reduce the sentence. I said that I trusted that God would guide him toward a just and proper sentence." Moreover, Di Frisco says that when he called Locallo, he was only returning a call the judge had placed to him. "I was quite shocked to hear from him as a matter of fact. He asked me, 'Would there be any repercussions if the matter doesn't go the way the family wants it to go?' I said I thought the only repercussions would be political." Di Frisco allows that he did believe the sentence was too harsh and that Locallo gave it because he thought it would benefit him politically.

Locallo says it's an "absolute lie" that he called Di Frisco.

He also says he thinks Di Frisco used his public relations skills to burnish the Caruso image while the case was pending. "There's no doubt in my mind that he and the Carusos sat at a table and talked about what they could do to improve their image. He's got the Caruso family going to these prayer services, members of the family carrying the rosary in court, Mr. Caruso carrying the Bible, showing up with his hair all white. It was a PR scheme all the way." Genson unquestionably condoned this scheme, in Locallo's view. "Anything Ed could use to his advantage, he was going to use it."

Di Frisco says he attended the racial healing services but didn't suggest them, nor did he play a role in any effort to enhance the Caruso image. "I wish I were that talented," he says. Genson, likewise, says, "I didn't condone anything" regarding attempts to improve the Caruso image. "I don't involve myself in that sort of thing. If the family did that sort of thing, it was the family that did it."

WITHIN DAYS of Locallo's rejection of the motion to reconsider, blue-and-white placards urging voters to "Vote No!" on Locallo bedeck the front windows or yards of every home on the 200 block of West 25th

Street—Frank Caruso's block. Other anti-Locallo signs are scattered throughout Bridgeport, but they're a rare sight elsewhere in the county.

"JUDGE DAN LOCALLO LET THE TWO WHITE BOYS GO FREE," screams a large ad in the *Chicago Defender,* the African American daily, ten days before the election. "NO JUSTICE! NO PEACE! VOTE NO! NO! NO!" The ad bears the name of the Inner City Youth Foundation, a south-side not-for-profit whose executive director, Maurice Perkins, is a Caruso ally. (Perkins was among those who'd written Locallo letters on Caruso's behalf before his sentencing. His foundation had also given Caruso Senior a humanitarian award two days before Caruso Junior was sentenced.)

On Halloween, Caruso supporters pass out flyers in various Cook County locations asking voters to no longer allow Locallo "to play trick or treat with the lives of the people of this county." According to the flyers, Locallo tried to appease African American voters by giving Caruso a stiff sentence and white voters by giving probation to Jasas and Kwidzinski, thereby dividing a community "very much in the midst of racial healing." To permit Locallo to stay on the bench "is in itself a travesty of justice," the flyers say. "If you vote for only one thing, let it be to stop the injustice of Daniel Locallo."

Locallo is hardly without support, however. In fact, the campaign to oust him elevates him overnight into a cause célèbre. "By all accounts, Locallo is a fair and honorable judge who deserves to retain his seat," a *Sun-Times* editorial says. *Sun-Times* columnist Steve Neal writes that the "travesty of justice" would be "if Locallo is punished by the voters for doing the right thing." *Tribune* columnist R. Bruce Dold calls Locallo one of the best judges in Cook County. "He's fair, he explains the law to people in his courtroom, and he works like a dog. And if he loses his job in this election because he handled a tough case, every judge in Cook County will know what that means: Don't be a hero. Locallo's election shouldn't be in question. We ought to be holding a parade for him."

Leaders of bar groups and civic organizations pepper the city's dailies with letters supporting the judge. "I will never hesitate to present a case or stand before Locallo for any reason," writes William Hooks, the first African American president of the Chicago chapter of the Federal Bar Association. "His integrity is above reproach, and he is certainly not a racist."

Locallo even gets help from John Hillebrand, the foreperson in the first Kevin Betts murder trial earlier this year. Hillebrand sends letters to the jurors who served with him, alerting them to the anti–Locallo campaign. "I for one plan to tell my friends that Judge Locallo should be returned to the bench. I hope you will join me," Hillebrand's letter says.

Genson says he counseled the Carusos not to oppose Locallo's retention. The campaign against the judge "makes no sense," Genson says. "You have a guy who, as judges go, is extraordinarily competent, who works hard, who tries to do the right thing." He's confident that Locallo will be retained regardless. "But he doesn't just want to be retained," Genson says. "He wants to be on the appellate court, and he wants to be on the supreme court, and he wants to be king of the world."

THE CARUSOS' "vindictive" campaign against Locallo "provides yet another compelling reason to dump the traditional process of electing judges in favor of a nonpartisan merit-selection system," a *Sun-Times* editorial observes.

In other democracies judges are almost always appointed, as they are in the U.S. federal system. The idea is that a judge shouldn't have to worry about popular opinion when making a decision.

In the nineteenth century, fears of government power caused states entering the union to opt to elect their judges, and still today most elect some or all of their judges. In fifteen states, however, judges are now picked through some form of "merit selection," under which a commission typically nominates candidates, and the governor, the legislature, or the state supreme court makes the final choices.

Those lobbying for a switch to merit in Illinois contend that an expert nominating commission will produce more qualified candidates for the bench than do the ward bosses who choose most of the candidates now. Merit proponents also point out that even the most conscientious voters can't vote intelligently on so many judicial seats. In a survey of Cook County voters after the 1998 primary, half those polled said they based their judicial votes on "hardly any" or "no" information; five percent said their votes were based on a "great deal" of information. Voters in the primary were faced with choices in sixteen judicial races. In the coming general election, they'll have in addition the seventy-two retention judges to consider.

In Illinois editorial writers, law professors, and most of the bar groups have been pushing for merit for decades—the Illinois State Bar Association and the Chicago Bar Association first recommended it in 1952. Opposing them have been the party bosses, who deride merit selection as an elitist attempt to rob ordinary citizens of their voting power. And the party bosses always win.

Some minorities and women have also opposed merit on the grounds that it will make it harder for them to win judicial slots. But evidence suggests that minorities and women get judgeships at least as often by appointment as by election.

Merit selection was one of the chief reforms proposed by the commission established in the wake of the Greylord probe of judicial corruption in Cook County. That commission in 1985 took note of the "particularly corrosive effect" of campaign fund-raising by judges under the elective system. Donations to judicial candidates come primarily from lawyers, as the commission pointed out—lawyers likely to appear in front of the judges to whom they donate.

But the Greylord commission's merit selection plan went the way of all other merit proposals in Illinois. Thus while Greylord may have reduced the practice of lawyers slipping money to judges, either directly or through a deputy or clerk, it's still perfectly legal, and customary, for lawyers to pass money to judges through their campaign committees.

Illinois judicial candidates are prohibited from personally soliciting or accepting campaign contributions. If they want to raise money, they must establish committees run by others. This is supposed to insulate judges from their contributors. But in practice, it's a rare judicial candidate who doesn't closely monitor his campaign, if he doesn't actually manage it himself. The treasurer of Citizens to Elect Judge Daniel Michael Locallo is the judge's cousin, John Locallo. But Judge Locallo allows that John Locallo is mainly a figurehead. The judge himself is running his campaign, he says. He knows who gives to him and how much.

Locallo's committee will take in $21,850 for this retention bid. Most of this comes from criminal defense lawyers, some with cases pending in his courtroom. The checks aren't especially large—a few are for $500, most are for $300 or less; the lawyers are expected to give to other judges as well. Locallo allows that many lawyers donate to judges not because of their high regard for those judges but simply to better their odds in those courtrooms: "Let's just say they figure it won't hurt 'em." Of course, he'd never favor a lawyer just because he was a contributor, he says. But under a system in which judges are dependent on lawyers for campaign funds, he acknowledges, "the potential for influence is there."

One might wonder why some judicial candidates bother raising money at all—the retention judges, for instance, since they're usually shoo-ins. But in Cook County retention judges, and candidates running unopposed for vacant seats, typically raise money anyway, because they're expected to show their gratitude to the party responsible for their election. In Cook County that's usually the Democratic Party in the city and the Republican

Party in the suburbs. In the 1980s the Cook County Democratic Party defined gratitude precisely, requiring a specified "donation"—as much as $10,000 in some years—from each judicial candidate it endorsed. In 1993 the Illinois Supreme Court banned judges and judicial candidates from paying such assessments. But judges are still allowed to contribute voluntarily to political organizations through their campaign committees. The contributions are voluntary in the way that some confessions are—and candidates for the Cook County bench usually make the judicious choice. In Locallo's first campaign for a full circuit seat in 1992, his committee sent a total of nearly $6,000 to various Democratic ward and political committees. "If you're asking people to push your candidacy, people are going to expect you to contribute," Locallo says.

The Cook County Democratic Party has announced its support for all seventy-two retention candidates this year, including the eight judges who have been found wanting by at least two bar groups. Party chairman Thomas Lyons says the party won't "play God" by recommending that a judge be dumped. Perhaps the $40,000 donation sent to the Democratic Party by the retention judges, through their Committee for Retention of Judges in Cook County, plus all the money sent to individual Democratic ward organizations by individual judges, has something to do with this reluctance to "play God." The judges' retention committee also sent $20,000 to the Cook County Republican Central Committee in appreciation of that party's unwillingness to play God with any of the suburban judges.

There's another reason for the parties to support all the retention judges, the good and the bad alike. A Chicago political adage, "Don't back no losers," has a corollary: "Don't oppose no likely winners." Party leaders understand that retention judges almost always will be retained, with or without the support of the parties. One can't predict when a case that's important to the parties, or to one of their bigwigs, will come before a judge. The parties would just as soon be on good terms with the entire bench. As the infamous Boss Tweed of New York's Tammany Hall used to say, "It's good to know the law, but it's better to know the judge."

Locallo favored merit selection even before this campaign against him and even though he got his full circuit judgeship via election. Other than the people on the bar association evaluating committees, hardly anyone in the county knows anything about most judicial candidates, he says. He also thinks judges should be "insulated from political pressure"—a sentiment that hasn't diminished during this attempt to dump him "based on a decision in one case as opposed to my overall record."

• • •

LOCALLO ISN'T GETTING much work done in 302 the week before the election. He leaves the bench frequently to answer phone calls in his chambers. Many of the calls are from reporters. The judge hasn't been reluctant to express his views about the campaign against him. If the Carusos were "used to having things their way, I guess they were disappointed," he tells a *Tribune* reporter. On a black radio station he derides this attempt "to interfere with the independence of the judiciary," adding, "I will not be intimidated." On a TV newscast he says the Carusos are "cowards, just like their son was a coward, an eighteen-year-old beating up a thirteen-year-old." Locallo takes offense when a law professor suggests in the *Sun-Times* that it might be inappropriate for a judge to be making such comments. "I'd like to say to that idiot, 'Let's [threaten to] take your professorship away from you, even when you're doing the right job,'" Locallo tells me. "'Are you gonna just sit on your ass and do nothing?' If I'm gonna go down, I'm gonna go down fighting."

Also interrupting Locallo's work are the defense lawyers who stop by the courtroom to express their support for him. A lawyer tells Locallo he won't be able to make it to his fund-raising dinner later in the week, but he'll be sending a check to his campaign committee. The judge invites a few of the visiting attorneys back to his chambers for chats. The courtroom prosecutors and public defenders are growing weary of these disruptions and of the brownnosing. "'Hi, Judge—I just wanted to kiss your ass,'" PD Amy Thompson grumbles to herself after Locallo repairs to his chambers with a lawyer one morning.

Locallo gets some bad news shortly before the election. He learns that Jesse Jackson's PUSH/Rainbow Coalition is planning to support seventy-one of the seventy-two judges up for retention. It will urge voters to dump only one judge—Locallo. Jackson still objects to his approval of the plea deals.

But Locallo enlists the aid of two local African American criminal justice heavies: his mentor, Appellate Justice William Cousins, and former Appellate Justice Eugene Pincham. Cousins and Pincham contact Reverend Jackson on Locallo's behalf, and Jackson soon announces that PUSH/Rainbow will be supporting Locallo after all. Later, Locallo's campaign committee will send three checks to PUSH for a total of $1,200.

LOCALLO'S FUND-RAISER is held at Villa De Marco, an Italian restaurant a half mile east of the courthouse, on the evening of Thursday, October 29, five days before the election. Villa De Marco is a modest place but large enough to accommodate a crowd. It has hosted many fund-raisers for

26th Street judges as well as the holiday party the judges throw for court personnel each December.

By seven-thirty P.M. the restaurant is crammed with public defenders, private criminal attorneys, judges, and a few prosecutors, who fill their plates with chicken and pasta from the buffet table. After the attendees wolf down dinner, they head for the bar. Locallo works the crowd effortlessly. The liquor flows freely and the clamor grows. Then Michael Bolan, another 26th Street judge, whistles the gathering to order.

The noise abates as Judge James Obbish, a former prosecutor and a friend of Locallo's, welcomes everyone. With Locallo standing next to him, Obbish pokes fun at the probation sentences Locallo gave Jasas and Kwidzinski. Before driving here tonight from his home in a western suburb, Obbish says, he'd seen a kid in his neighborhood "who didn't belong, if you know what I mean." There are snickers from the crowd. "I got out of my car," Obbish continues. "Got out my baseball bat. And then I thought, 'I'm not doing that community service!' " Everyone roars, including Locallo. "Anybody who says it isn't a deterrent doesn't know what they're talking about," Obbish says. Then he turns to Locallo. "What the *hell* were you thinking?" There's more laughter.

"We all know what a great guy Danny is," Obbish says. "And we all know, more importantly, what a great judge he is. He did what he was supposed to do, and it's unfortunate that some people are trying to use it against him." Then, to loud cheers, he introduces Locallo to the crowd.

Locallo is brief. "It's been tough times for my wife and my family, and it's so gratifying the support you've given us. I know you're all behind me. Sometimes you're way behind me," he says, to chuckles. "Thank you for being here. Let's have a great time tonight, and we'll kick their ass on Tuesday."

Appellate Justice Cousins drops by later in the evening and, on Locallo's request, addresses the crowd. Locallo introduces the thin, silver-haired Cousins as "the best judge in the state of Illinois," and Cousins responds in kind, calling Locallo the best prosecutor to work in his courtroom when he was at 26th Street. Cousins relates the efforts he made to convince black political powerhouses that Locallo deserved their support. He told them "that Judge Locallo is one of the best human beings that I know," he says. At Cousins's side, Locallo jams his hands into his pants pockets and looks sheepishly at his shoes. "Dan may feel some unease, just like some defense counsel and prosecutors feel when they're not sure of the outcome of a trial," Cousins says. "But everything's gonna be all right."

ON TUESDAY, NOVEMBER 3, voters in the fourteenth precinct of Chicago's 25th Ward—the precinct in which the Caruso family resides—turn thumbs down on Locallo, with 111 nays and 82 yeas. But in almost every other precinct in the county, the verdict is different. Locallo coasts to retention with a 78 percent affirmative vote, well above the required 60 percent.

At nine P.M. on election day Locallo and his wife and two children drive from their home to the office of the Illinois Judges Association downtown. The mood in the spartan assembly room is buoyant. With half the vote reported, it looks as if not only Locallo but all seventy-two judges on the retention ballot will be retained. On a TV in a corner of the room, a newscaster is talking about the anti-Locallo campaign: "Apparently it didn't work."

Some judges were miffed at Locallo before the election. They feared that the campaign against him might drag some of them to defeat as well. But now Locallo is being treated as if he just quarterbacked his team to victory. The other judges are shaking his hand and slapping his back.

"I think all that great press you got energized the voters," Judge Thomas Hett says.

Locallo responds that the credit really should go to the Carusos. "Maybe we can all get cigars at their cigar shop."

He takes a call from a reporter. "This is a great day for the independence of the judiciary," the judge says into the phone.

The final results will show no judge up for retention getting less than 64 percent. All eight judges whose retention was opposed by two or more bar groups have survived. Judge Jeffrey Lawrence, who was opposed by all nine bar groups evaluating him, has received 66 percent. "We retained all our qualified judges," Chicago Bar Association president Leonard Schrager will say tomorrow. "Unfortunately, we also retained the unqualified ones."

Now, in the IJA office, Locallo makes it clear he has no conciliatory feelings regarding the Carusos just because he's won. "If they thought I was going to give them a break because I'm Italian, they misread me," he says. "If they thought I was going to be a shrinking violet because of their campaign, they totally misread Daniel Michael Locallo." His only regret about the Caruso case "is that I didn't give the sonovabitch ten."

The Bridgeport case may prove to be pivotal in the history of the courthouse, he says. He'd stood his ground despite enormous pressure, showing, to blacks in particular, "that nobody's above the law" in Cook County. "It was important to send a message to blacks who are saying, 'The system is against us, we can never get justice.' I don't think anybody can say that justice was not done in this case."

BUT MICHAEL KWIDZINSKI probably can.

In all of the stories about the Bridgeport beating before Caruso's trial, there'd been little debate about the innocence or guilt of the three defendants. Their guilt was assumed; the only questions concerned what prompted their attack and whether they'd get away with it. The usual public belief—that if the defendants hadn't done anything wrong they wouldn't have been charged—was only accentuated by the disappearance of one witness and the slaying of another.

And then that presumption of guilt was confirmed by Caruso's conviction and Jasas's and Kwidzinski's guilty pleas. Those attacking the plea deals and those defending them agreed on one point: Jasas and Kwidzinski got away with something. No one in the media entertained the possibility that the lack of evidence against Jasas and Kwidzinski might be due to their actual innocence. After all, they admitted their guilt—they pled guilty.

But at 26th Street, pleading guilty doesn't mean you are.

The evidence suggests that Jasas was indeed a second attacker. But it also suggests that Kwidzinski wasn't the third.

Caruso and Jasas were implicated by three of their friends: Thomas Simpson (the forgetful witness at Caruso's trial), Mike Cutler (the witness who was slain), and Richard DeSantis (the missing witness).

Kwidzinski, on the other hand, wasn't implicated by Simpson in either his statement at the police station or his grand jury testimony. And while Cutler implicated Kwidzinski in the statement he signed at the police station—a statement written up by a prosecutor—in his grand jury testimony Cutler incriminated only Caruso and Jasas.

DeSantis implicated Kwidzinski in his police station statement. But DeSantis had a motive for fingering others: so he wouldn't get charged himself. He'd certainly been a prime suspect. Two anonymous tipsters identified him as one of the attackers. William Jaramillo—the Hispanic youth who was with Lenard and Clevan at 33rd and Shields—identified DeSantis as one of the youths who joined Caruso and Jasas in chasing Lenard toward Princeton. And when detectives first asked DeSantis where he was on the night of the attack, he lied, saying he was at his girlfriend's. Only after the detectives confronted him with the fact that this alibi didn't check out did DeSantis admit to being on the scene. Eight hours later he signed the statement implicating Caruso, Jasas, and Kwidzinski.

The day after he signed his statement, DeSantis was summoned before the grand jury. By this time he had a lawyer with him. And when DeSantis was asked about the beating, he invoked his Fifth Amendment protection against self-incrimination.

Kwidzinski, questioned repeatedly at the station over a period of more than twenty-four hours, with no lawyer assisting him, consistently maintained he was on the scene but that he didn't play a role in the attack. The notes of one detective suggest that Kwidzinski was reluctant to implicate any of his friends, but that he ultimately acknowledged seeing Caruso initiate the attack at 33rd and Shields, and seeing Caruso and Jasas chasing Lenard down 33rd. He said he didn't see what happened around the corner on Princeton.

Detectives and prosecutors were under pressure to lodge charges quickly—Mayor Daley had assured reporters shortly after the story of the beating broke that police were handling the matter and would be making arrests. "The heat [pressure] was a factor," allowed Stanley Turner, the lead detective. Turner also allowed that the case against Kwidzinski rested solely on DeSantis and therefore was weaker than the cases against Caruso and Jasas. Nevertheless, prosecutors decided to charge Kwidzinski along with Caruso and Jasas. The press was alerted, the three defendants were marched into court, bonds were set, and Mayor Daley proclaimed that the culprits had been nabbed.

That Kwidzinski was charged as the third attacker must have been good news for another Bridgeport youth, sixteen-year-old James Guadagno. Guadagno had also been a suspect. An anonymous tipster implicated him, as did Jasas, who told detectives he saw Guadagno and another youth beat Lenard on Princeton. In addition, a cousin of Caruso's acknowledged driving Caruso from the scene of the beating—along with another youth named "Jimmie Dua," according to a detective's notes. Detectives wanted to question Guadagno, but they were unable to locate him the first two days of their investigation. The detectives weren't sure at this point how many attackers there were. The report they wrote after Caruso, Jasas, and Kwidzinski were charged seemed to suggest they believed Guadagno might have been a fourth attacker: it listed him as "wanted" and specified that the case would still be open "pending further arrests."

A day after Caruso, Jasas, and Kwidzinski were charged, Guadagno walked into the detectives' office, accompanied by his mother and a lawyer. Detective Turner says that when he asked Guadagno about the attack, Guadagno "broke down and started crying, and he nearly jumped into his mother's arms. And at that point the lawyer cut the conversation. He said, 'If you want to talk to him again, get a warrant for his arrest.' We didn't have enough to support a warrant."

But a day later the detectives got a new lead further implicating Guadagno. A tip led them to four young women—Bridgeport natives who were then college freshmen—who were at a party on the night of the attack along with Caruso, Jasas, Kwidzinski, Simpson, Cutler, and Guadagno. Questioned separately by detectives, all four women said they heard

Guadagno bragging about the role he played in the beating of a black boy near Armour Square Park earlier that evening. "I had this nigger on the ground, and I was kicking him in the head," Guadagno said, according to one of the women. Another woman said she heard him say, "I stomped this nigger in the head. I took care of the neighborhood." All four women repeated their accounts of what they heard to the grand jury.

One of the women, Guadagno's former girlfriend, Dina Short, told the grand jury she had a separate conversation with Guadagno at the party. She said Guadagno told her he was riding in Caruso's cousin's car, and on Princeton "he seen Frankie Caruso stomping on the black boy's head, and Victor Jasas was kicking him. He jumped out of the car and ran over to his friends, kicked the kid like once or twice in the butt, and then saw the kid was unconscious. And Frankie was stomping on his head, and he pulled Frankie off of him."

Two of the women told detectives that Kwidzinski, too, talked about the beating at the party—but only to say that he was there but didn't participate.

Detective Turner told me Guadagno wasn't charged because the statements of the four young women were inadmissible hearsay. But their statements were, in fact, admissible. Statements about another person's voluntary, self-incriminating remarks meet a hearsay exemption—they're considered more reliable since it's not in the speaker's interests to lie when making them.

Genson had tried to call Guadagno as a witness during Caruso's trial. But in a hearing outside the presence of the jury, Guadagno had taken the stand and invoked the Fifth. When Thomas Simpson had invoked the Fifth, Locallo had found "no basis" for his assertion that his testimony could have been self-incriminating. But Guadagno had such a basis, Locallo ruled, in declining to force the youth to testify. Genson then sought to have two of the women who'd overheard Guadagno's incriminating remarks at the party testify about those remarks. Locallo decided he'd allow that testimony. But he also ruled that if Genson called the two women, the state would be allowed to call Dina Short in response, to testify that Guadagno had implicated not only himself but also Caruso in his remarks about the beating. So Genson had decided not to call the two women.

Guadagno told me he had "not a clue" why anyone would claim they'd heard him say he'd beaten a black kid on the night of the attack. Then he declined to answer further questions, saying, "I definitely don't need to be in any book."

Guadagno may have been difficult to prosecute, given that the only other witness to implicate him directly was Jasas, and one defendant can't be forced to testify against another.

The more significant question is not why Guadagno wasn't charged, but why the charges against Kwidzinski weren't dropped—if not immediately after the authorities talked with these four women, then at least after detectives located Jeffrey Gordon three weeks later. Gordon, the neighbor who broke up the beating on Princeton, told detectives there were only three attackers. (His vague description of the three—white, young, short, with short hair—fits Caruso, Jasas, and Kwidzinski but also Guadagno, who's a dead ringer for Caruso.)

But by the time the detectives learned there were only three attackers, the state's attorney's office was in a tight corner. Prosecutors had already declared they'd charged the three offenders. When the defense lawyers claimed the wrong people were charged in a rush to justice, the state's attorney's office dismissed this as the usual defense propaganda. To then cut loose Kwidzinski, and perhaps charge Guadagno in his stead, would have generated endless assertions by Genson, and by Jasas's lawyers, that if the authorities were wrong about one of the attackers, they probably were wrong about the other two as well. Dropping the charges against Kwidzinski thus would have required immense political courage.

The day Caruso was sentenced, I told Detective Turner that sources close to Caruso and Jasas had conceded to me after Caruso's trial that those two were guilty of the attack—but that these sources also insisted that the third assailant was not Kwidzinski. "Kwidzinski wasn't as bad as the others," Turner allowed, "but he was an asshole, too. They were all assholes." But was Kwidzinski one of the offenders? I asked. Turner shrugged and said simply, "He was there."

THE GRAND JURY had functioned in its usual way in April 1997, when it was asked to consider the indictments of Caruso, Jasas, and Kwidzinski.

The Founding Fathers imported the grand jury system from England as a check on the power of prosecutors and other public officials. Under the Fifth Amendment, felony charges lodged by authorities can stand only if they are approved by a panel from the community. They can be approved only if the panel finds "probable cause" that the accused committed the charged offense—and the definition of probable cause is up to the panel. This Fifth Amendment protection applies only to federal cases. In most states, prosecutors can either seek an indictment from the grand jury or a finding of probable cause from a judge in a preliminary hearing. In Cook County, nearly half the felony cases result from grand jury indictment.

In America's early years, the willingness of grand juries to reject indictments earned them the label the "People's Panel." But as criminal law grew more complex, grand jurors became increasingly dependent on the prose-

cutors who brought proposed indictments to them. Soon it was the prosecutors who were running the show, with the grand jurors serving as their willing subordinates. Already in 1870 dissatisfaction with the grand jury led to
a push to abolish it at that year's Illinois Constitutional Convention. The
grand jury had "ceased to be any protection to the interests or the rights of
the people," one delegate said; another derided it as "utterly useless . . . an
engine of oppression and persecution." The delegates decided to eliminate
grand jury indictment in misdemeanor cases, but they kept it for felony
charges. A half century later, in his 1922 study of the Cook County Jail
and courts, George Kirchwey noted that in larger cities the grand jury was
"believed to have become little more than a machine for registering the
will of the State's Attorney," and that the record in Cook County "gives
one the uneasy feeling that the Grand Jury conceives its function to be the
finding of indictments instead of the protection of those unjustly accused."
Little seems to have changed in that regard; in the years 2000 through
2003, Cook County grand juries approved 1,769 indictments for every
indictment they rejected.

It's the same story elsewhere. In Arizona, a prosecutor said in 1974 that
if grand jurors were given a napkin, they'd sign it; the chief judge of the
New York Court of Appeals observed in 1985 that a good prosecutor could
persuade a grand jury to indict a ham sandwich. Some legal scholars have
said the state's control could be diminished by limiting the prosecutor's
role to proposing indictments and questioning witnesses, and having an independent lawyer available to consult with the jurors. This suggestion has
had as much success as other suggestions for decreasing a prosecutor's
power.

Grand jurors in Cook County serve for a month. Their sixteen members,
chosen by the presiding judge from the available pool, swear to "diligently
inquire" into the matters brought before them.

The grand jury room at 26th Street, on the courthouse's fourth floor, has
an air of neglected dignity. The walls are still decorated with the building's
original Egyptian frieze, but some of the paint is chipping away. The three
long crescent tables at which the jurors sit are a handsome dark oak, but
they're cracked and scarred. The ancient, grimy fan bolted to one wall is
still used some afternoons when the air-conditioning proves insufficient.
Witnesses sit front and center, facing the jurors, the prosecutor who does
the questioning, and the court reporter. In most cases there is only a single
witness—a police officer who summarizes the evidence, often in five minutes or less. The police officer is excused, and the prosecutor and the court
reporter leave the room to let the panel deliberate and vote in secrecy.
Deliberations are sometimes dispensed with in favor of an immediate vote

conducted by hand. A simple majority suffices for an indictment. The fore-person summons the prosecutor and court reporter back into the room and announces a "True Bill." The prosecutor presses a rubber stamp on an ink pad and stamps the indictment. The "True Bill" stamp in the grand jury room is usually damp, the "No Bill" stamp bone dry. The prosecutor brings in the next police officer for the next case.

Taped to the wall next to the entrance to the grand jury room is a memo from the supervisor of the grand jury for the state's attorney's office, James Tansey. Dated September 1997, the tattered message was still on the wall in 2004. It gives a pep talk to prosecutors who work with the grand jury. "The grand jury serves as the root of the state's attorney's family tree," the memo says. "When the silence of the courtroom is broken with the six-letter word 'Guilty,' we can all partake of the fruit. We planted the seed and nourished the charge."

Marcelle Porter, a south-side nurse, served on the March 1997 grand jury. Porter, then sixty-eight, described the prosecutor working with her grand jury as "pushy." She was disappointed by how easily the jurors, herself included, were persuaded to do his bidding. She said she's normally independent minded and that on several occasions during her month of service, when the evidence in a case seemed weak, she simply didn't vote. But other times, even when she wasn't sure a case merited indictment, she found her hand going up with everyone else's. "You feel like an extension of the prosecutor," she said.

In April 1997 prosecutor Lawrence O'Reilly asked the grand jury to indict Caruso, Jasas, and Kwidzinski for attempted murder, aggravated battery, and hate crime. O'Reilly presented a single witness—Detective Turner. (The previous month's grand jury had heard from seven witnesses regarding the Bridgeport case. But that was merely to get those witnesses on record. Prosecutors often bring witnesses to the grand jury to "lock in" their testimony, to make it harder for them to recant at trial.)

Detective Turner was succinct. He was in the grand jury room less than five minutes, judging from the five double-spaced pages of his testimony. He answered the eighteen leading questions put to him by O'Reilly with a total of twenty-two words.

Had Turner's investigation shown that Caruso, Jasas, and Kwidzinski were in the area of the beating? "Yes." Had it shown that those three individuals struck Lenard Clark in the head and body with their fists and feet? "Yes." Had it shown that they called Lenard a nigger during this beating? "That is correct." Had it shown that they intended to kill him? "That is correct."

Turner's investigation had yielded considerable evidence that Caruso and

Jasas had beaten Lenard, and that Caruso had called Lenard a nigger. There was very little evidence that Kwidzinski had beaten Lenard, and none that he called him a nigger. But Turner had testified before the grand jury on many occasions, and he knew he didn't have to draw such distinctions.

Had his investigation shown that these three individuals struck Clevan Nicholson in the head with a fist? "Yes." Had it shown that they called Clevan a nigger? "Yes." In fact, Turner's investigation had shown that only one person struck Clevan and called him a nigger—Caruso.

O'Reilly concluded the examination by directing Turner to tell the grand jurors the basis of his testimony. Here Turner could have recapped the investigation, could have mentioned the witnesses interviewed and summarized what they said, so the jurors had something, other than his word, on which to base the crucial decision they were being asked to make. Instead, Turner simply said, "I am the investigating detective."

Even prosecutor O'Reilly apparently wanted a bit more from Turner than that. He asked Turner if his testimony was based on the "statements of defendants and statements of witnesses?" Turner said it was.

Among the statements from witnesses were those of the four women who heard another individual—Guadagno—bragging about his role in the attack. There was also the sworn testimony from Simpson and Cutler before the previous month's grand jury, implicating Caruso and Jasas—but not Kwidzinski. There was DeSantis's statement against Kwidzinski—but the statements implicating DeSantis as well. Turner or O'Reilly could have alerted the jurors to all this so they could have made an informed decision. But an informed decision wasn't being sought.

A grand juror had a question for Turner: "Was there an eyewitness who identified these three subjects?"

"There were several eyewitnesses," Turner said.

"They identified these three people that you are charging?"

"Yes."

The grand jurors' diligent inquiry exhausted, Turner was excused. O'Reilly and the court reporter left the jurors alone to consider the proposed indictments. The foreperson soon summoned the prosecutor and the court reporter back into the room. "True Bill," the foreperson said, and O'Reilly stamped the indictment.

FELONY CHARGES exact a toll, often a heavy one, from defendants, even from those who eventually are cleared or are allowed to plead guilty to lesser charges and to avoid prison.

Kwidzinski had an attempted murder charge, and a possible prison term of six to thirty years, looming over him for a year and a half. He was vilified in the papers and on radio talk shows. Like his codefendants, he heard rumors that African American gangs had contracts out on him and that his family's home might be bombed. Even the "break" of a sentence he ultimately got required three hundred hours of community service.

His parents had a lawyer to pay and a son's fate to agonize about. Kwidzinski's parents are divorced. His father, a carpenter, also named Michael, "was the kind of guy who internalized everything," Kwidzinski's lawyer, Kevin Bolger, says. "He worried about everything about this case. He worried about what might happen to his son even if he won—how his life would be hurt just by him being accused of this in the news."

On July 31, 1998, sixteen months after Kwidzinski was charged and two months before he pled guilty, the elder Kwidzinski suffered a fatal heart attack. He was forty-seven. "He worried himself to death about this case," Bolger says.

BUT WHY WOULD Kwidzinski plead guilty if he was innocent and if the evidence against him was so feeble?

For the same reason many defendants at 26th Street do. As Bolger explains, once a person is facing felony charges, the issue no longer is whether he did the crime; it's how to limit the damage.

A wise defendant, with the help of his lawyer, thinks pragmatically, Bolger says. Kwidzinski's choice, when he was offered the plea deal, was a guarantee of no prison, with only a misdemeanor conviction, versus a chance, albeit slim, of conviction and prison if he insisted on trial. Sometimes trials bring surprises—surprises that turn the flimsiest cases into convictions, says Bolger, a former prosecutor. "Police lie, witnesses lie. It's a fact of life. So you get the best deal you can and you get out of there."

Locallo allows that pleading guilty can sometimes be a "very attractive scenario," even for the innocent, and that had he been in Kwidzinski's shoes—considering a possible six to thirty versus misdemeanor probation— he "probably would have jumped at" the plea offer, innocent or not.

Prosecutors are apt to make pleading guilty an especially attractive scenario for the innocent. The weaker the case against a defendant, the more likely his acquittal if the case goes to trial—and therefore the better the bargain offered by the state in its attempt to get the conviction. Kwidzinski was offered a better deal than Jasas—misdemeanor probation instead of felony probation—because the evidence against him was thinner than it was against Jasas. Never mind that the evidence was thinner because he likely was innocent.

One measure designed to guard against the prospect of innocent defendants pleading guilty is the requirement that a "factual basis" for the plea be cited during the formal plea. Judges aren't obligated to scrutinize every bit of evidence against a defendant to be certain he's guilty—guilty pleas wouldn't save much time if judges had to do that. The "factual basis" usually consists of a prosecutor's brief summary of what the state's key witnesses would say if called to testify. If such testimony would indeed support a guilty verdict, the judge will accept the plea.

But in their haste to bag a plea, judges at 26th Street sometimes accept a factual basis that's devoid of facts.

That's what happened when Kwidzinski and Jasas pled guilty to Locallo. For the factual basis, Mandeltort simply said the state and the defense were stipulating that Jasas and Kwidzinski had both been "legally responsible and accountable" for Caruso's actions when Caruso punched Lenard and Clevan at 33rd and Shields. But to be accountable for another offender's actions in Illinois, a person must solicit, aid, or attempt to aid that offender. If there was a witness who could have testified as to how Kwidzinski or Jasas had solicited, aided, or tried to aid Caruso at 33rd and Shields, Mandeltort didn't mention him. She didn't mention any witnesses. While the factual basis doesn't require much specificity, it requires more than a prosecutor asserting, and the defense lawyers agreeing, that the facts would show the defendant was guilty. That would be a meaningless exercise, redundant of the defendant's plea, and providing no protection against guilty pleas from the innocent.

But Locallo didn't press Mandeltort for more. Instead he perfunctorily asked the lawyers for Kwidzinski and Jasas if they'd stipulate that "if those witnesses were called that they would testify in the manner as discussed?"—an odd question, considering that Mandeltort didn't mention any witnesses testifying. Without hesitation, the defense lawyers stipulated. Locallo asked Jasas and Kwidzinski how they wanted to plead, and they said they wanted to plead guilty. Locallo immediately found their pleas to be "knowing and voluntary" and that there was a factual basis for them.

The factual basis "probably should have been more thorough," Locallo conceded later, when I read the transcript of the pleas to him.

"NOW . . . EVERYONE CHARGED in this case has been held responsible and found guilty," state's attorney Richard Devine proclaimed at a press conference shortly after the pleas were formalized. "Make no mistake, none of this was easy," Devine added, reminding reporters about the witness problems. "Many said it would not be surprising if the Cook County State's Attorney's Office got no conviction at all. . . . I am proud of our office's total efforts in this case."

Whenever a defendant pleads guilty, most parties are satisfied, even if the defendant happens to be innocent. It's a conviction for the prosecutor and a dispo for the judge, a fee for the private defense lawyer or one fewer case for the PD. The defendant is relieved he didn't get something worse.

In the Bridgeport case, thanks to the press's dutiful acceptance of the authorities' party line about the culprits, all that most Chicagoans would understand about Kwidzinski was that he'd gotten away with something. For those few who knew otherwise, who were familiar with what really happened the night of the beating, a cynicism about the courts perhaps would be born or confirmed. They'd come away from the case thinking not that "nobody's above the law," but that certain things aren't beneath the authorities.

Kwidzinski declined to talk at length to me about the case. But the morning he pled guilty, I talked with him briefly in the hallway outside the courtroom. I asked him what he learned from his experience. Referring to police and prosecutors, he said he learned "that these people will do anything to cover their asses."

Shortly after Locallo took the pleas, I summarized for the judge the facts he hadn't heard in the factual basis—the facts suggesting Kwidzinski's innocence. "Interesting," he said, without much interest.

Didn't it concern him that he might have taken a guilty plea from someone who wasn't? "Well, let's just say he *was* guilty," Locallo said. Then he laughed, and added, "I mean, he *pled* guilty."

Epilogue: A Promising Future

LOCALLO WAS AT WORK in his chambers one January afternoon in 1999 when two FBI agents stopped in and told him that someone might be trying to kill him.

An informant had reported this to the bureau, the agents said, and the FBI had also been notified of a conversation overheard in a Cook County Jail visiting area that seemed to corroborate the tip. Two mothers had been discussing their sons' cases. When one mother said her son was in front of Judge Locallo, the other responded that she'd heard there was a hit out on that judge.

Locallo was given around-the-clock protection. Chicago police escorted him to and from work, and Cook County sheriffs watched him inside the courthouse. The guard was lifted after two weeks. "We killed the other side," the judge said with a laugh. He said the FBI had gotten assurances from "upper-echelon" mobsters that he wasn't in any danger.

Locallo said he assumed that if there really ever had been a contract out on him, it was because of the stiff sentence he gave Caruso. But it was his understanding that outfit bosses sanctioned hits only for matters related to their "business," not for settling personal grievances. On the other hand, he felt sure that Mike Cutler, the witness in the Caruso case who was slain before trial, had been the victim of a hit. Locallo said the reputed threat on his life had worried his wife and kids more than him.

Early in 2000 the FBI contacted him again. The bureau had gotten another tip that he might be in jeopardy. The information was sketchier this time, and Locallo declined another special guard, asking only that police patrols near his house be increased.

. . .

THE MISSING WITNESS in the Bridgeport case, Richard DeSantis, sur-faced in November 1998, two months after the Caruso trial finished and one month after Jasas and Kwidzinski pled guilty. On a Friday morning in November he arrived at 26th Street with his parents and a lawyer and sur-rendered himself to authorities in a first-floor courtroom.

DeSantis, twenty, was charged with obstruction of justice. He faced one to three years. After he was taken to police headquarters to be finger-printed, state's attorney Richard Devine held a press conference at 26th Street. Devine said DeSantis had impaired an "important prosecution in this community," adding sternly, "You do not play around with the law and the criminal justice system." Ellen Mandeltort, who handled the other Bridgeport cases and would be handling DeSantis's, vowed to prosecute him "to the full extent of the law."

What Mandeltort didn't say was how hard that could be. The state needed to prove not only that DeSantis fled but also that his intent was to obstruct the prosecution in the Bridgeport case.

After numerous delays, during which media interest in the DeSantis case cooled, DeSantis pled guilty in June 2002 for a one-year sentence. This wasn't a slap on the wrist, Mandeltort told me. "He wanted probation; we said no. He had to go to prison."

But he spent no time there. With the standard day-for-day credit, DeSan-tis's one-year sentence translated to six months; and although he was on bond for most of the three and a half years his case was pending, he had spent six months in jail. Anyone sentenced to prison must be processed into the Illinois Department of Corrections' reception center in Joliet, even if they owe no time. So on June 21, 2002, DeSantis was bused to Joliet. He got home later that day.

State's attorney Devine called no press conference announcing the results of the DeSantis prosecution. He could hardly want more headlines about another light Bridgeport plea deal. Mandeltort and DeSantis's lawyer managed to consummate the deal without the courthouse reporters notic-ing; it escaped mention in the dailies. The case slipped away quietly, as DeSantis had in 1998.

THE MURDER OF witness Mike Cutler remains unsolved. Detectives investigating the killing concluded he was slain in the course of a robbery and not because he was a witness in the Bridgeport case. There's been almost universal unwillingness to accept that conclusion. The skeptics include state's attorney Devine, prosecutors Mandeltort and Robert Berlin, Detective Stanley Turner, and Judge Locallo. In January 2000 a *Dateline NBC* feature about the Bridgeport case—"Witness for the Prosecution"—

implied that Cutler was killed because of the testimony he was going to give. In May 2003, near the fifth anniversary of Cutler's death, the *Chicago Sun-Times* attributed the police department's dismissal of the "hit" theory to the influence of organized crime. "One can only speculate what phone calls were made, what favors called in, to squash" the police investigation, the paper said. The beating of Lenard Clark "was tragic to begin with—a terrible, racially motivated crime," the *Sun-Times* said. But Cutler's murder "was even worse—a young man, attending college, killed because he did the right thing and came forward after his friends committed an unspeakable act."

The *Sun-Times* observed that the killers took Cutler's high school class ring and quoted State Representative Jim Durkin, a former prosecutor, as saying that this was a "classic mob hit tactic. You tell them to bring back the class ring to make sure they got the right guy." But a police spokesperson told me it wasn't even clear that Cutler was wearing his class ring that night. The detectives investigating Cutler's murder had pointed out that Cutler was shot once in the chest, not several times in the head, as one might expect in a hired killing. The *Sun-Times* suggested, however, that perhaps the hit men were instructed to make it look like a robbery, though this seemed at odds with the paper's class ring theory.

The *Sun-Times* also reported in May 2003 that the FBI had opened its own investigation into Cutler's murder. But later that year, special agent Ross Rice, spokesperson for the Chicago FBI, told me the Cutler slaying was "being investigated by local authorities. It doesn't appear that there's anything we have jurisdiction over." I asked Rice if the FBI had ever opened an investigation into the killing, as the *Sun-Times* had claimed. "Generally we don't comment on what we are or aren't investigating," Rice said. "But I have to say that a lot of times there's a lot of misinformation in the media."

If the murder merely stemmed from a robbery, "then it was one heckuva coincidence," prosecutor Berlin told me late in 2003. But though it's a less dramatic story, a coincidence may have been what it was.

DURING CARUSO'S TRIAL, his uncle, union bigwig Bruno Caruso, told me that a prison term of any length would be a "death sentence" for his nephew, since black prisoners would target him because of the racial nature of the Bridgeport beating. But his nephew survived. Caruso began serving his term in the medium-security Sheridan Correctional Center. For the relatives and friends who wanted to visit him, this was a fortunate assignment: Sheridan is one of the closest prisons to Chicago, just fifty miles southwest of the city limits. Locallo sentenced Caruso to eight years, but the standard day-for-day credit reduced the time he owed to four years. A six-month "meritorious service" credit, granted routinely to inmates because of the overcrowding in the prison system, trimmed his time to three and a half years. A three-month credit for attending school while in prison cut it to three and a quarter.

Within two years of parole, inmates are eligible for work-release and day-release programs. (In the latter they attend school or counseling sessions.) It's hard to get into these programs—there are a small number of spots and a multitude of eligible inmates. Caruso applied early in 2000. That April he was transferred from Sheridan to a day-release facility in Urbana, from which he attended school. He spent the last year of his sentence at home in an electronic detention program. He was paroled in December 2001, having spent a year and a half in a penitentiary. His most serious transgression while locked up was bringing ten pounds of raw hamburger into his cell block and refusing to explain where he got it or what it was for, an offense that earned him ten days in segregation.

On January 18, 2000—the day after Martin Luther King Day—the front page of the *Sun-Times* featured a photo of Caruso, then twenty, and Lenard Clark, sixteen, standing together in a visiting area of the Sheridan prison, Caruso's arm resting on Lenard's back, and Lenard grinning. The accompanying story reported that Lenard had visited Caruso at Sheridan twice. The newspaper didn't say from whom it had obtained the photo. Lenard's mother declined to talk to the *Sun-Times* about her son's visits to Caruso. But Caruso family friend Dominic Di Frisco was willing to. Di Frisco was the public relations executive who Locallo said tried to persuade him in October 1998 to reduce Caruso's sentence. The photo of Caruso and Lenard showed a "historic thing—the fact that these two guys have come together and begun to heal," Di Frisco told the *Sun-Times*. It was a "sincere effort . . . tantamount to placing a floral tribute on the tomb of Martin Luther King."

Callers to a talk show on WVON, a radio station with a predominantly African American audience, dismissed the reconciliation as a sham. Interviewed by the show's host, Cliff Kelley, Locallo suggested that the affair was orchestrated by Di Frisco, whom he labeled a "spin doctor." *Sun-Times* gossip columnist Irv Kupcinet, who'd run a half-dozen laudatory items about the Carusos in his column since the attack, called Locallo's questioning of the reconciliation a "shocking violation of judicial conduct."

IN NOVEMBER 2003 Leslie McGee acknowledged to me in a phone interview that she lied in her confession about the circumstances that led her to shoot Jean François. McGee, who was in the Dwight Correctional

Center, said François wasn't really just a cabbie she never met. They'd been in a relationship for nine months, and she shot him when he told her he was leaving her, she said.

They had met in the neighborhood, and he quickly let her know he was interested in her, she said. She was fifteen when they started going out. He took her to movies, pool halls, and arcades, gave her money, and bought her jewelry. He yelled at her once or twice but never hit her, she said. He told her that he loved her. He didn't tell her he had a wife and three children.

She said she made up the story about François being a cabbie she didn't know because she thought it made her sound less guilty. "It was the first story I came up with," she said. "I couldn't go back and change that lie. One lie led to another." She said she didn't tell the truth to her lawyer, Marijane Placek, because she feared that Placek would inform the prosecutors.

She said François first told her he had a wife and kids, and that he wanted to go back to them, on the evening of the shooting. "I asked him about twenty times, 'Are you sure you're gonna leave me?' He said, 'I have no other choice.' I thought, If you're not gonna be with me, then you're not gonna be with anybody." She had a gun on her because she was working nights as a cocktail waitress and felt she needed it for protection, she said; it was a coincidence, she insisted, that she'd started carrying it just two days before François told her they had to end their affair.

McGee, who turned twenty-four in 2004, has gotten her GED and a college-level certificate in computer technology while in prison, and she's taken classes in cosmetology. She's also been in disciplinary segregation repeatedly for fights and other violations. After she's released in 2007 she plans to work in a beauty shop or to design clothes. "I've matured mentally," she said. "I'm more patient today. I feel I have a very, very promising future."

IN APRIL 2001 the Illinois Supreme Court affirmed Locallo's decision to deny Leroy Orange a hearing regarding his torture claims. The high court sent the case back to 26th Street for the new sentencing hearing Locallo had granted Orange. But that hearing was repeatedly delayed, and it ultimately became unnecessary because of a historic act by Illinois governor George Ryan.

In January 2000 Ryan had declared a moratorium on executions in Illinois, citing his "grave concerns" about the state's "shameful record" of sending innocent men to death row. Since Illinois restored capital punishment in 1977, almost as many condemned men had been freed (ten) as executed (thirteen). Ryan appointed a commission to study the system and suggest reforms.

Ryan, a Republican, had supported the death penalty throughout a long political career. Critics of the moratorium contended he was using the issue to deflect attention from a scandal of his own—revelations of corruption in the secretary of state's office he directed before becoming governor.

On January 10, 2003, three days before leaving office, Ryan pardoned four death row inmates who'd maintained they were tortured at Area 2. One of the inmates was Orange. Ryan said the four men had not only been wrongfully convicted, but they were in fact innocent—they'd confessed to murders they hadn't committed. The evidence he offered to back that assertion was mainly a synopsis of the defense's claims in each of the cases.

The next day Ryan commuted the sentences of Illinois's 167 other death row convicts to natural life, saying they had been condemned under an unfair system.

Ryan was venerated and vilified for the pardons and commutations. He was one of 165 nominees for the 2003 Nobel Peace Prize. But Cook County State's Attorney Devine called the pardons "outrageous and unconscionable," adding that the courts and not a governor "should decide the issues in these cases."

But when Ryan announced the pardons, he said he'd acted because the courts failed to: "I can see how rogue cops, twenty years ago, can run wild. What I can't understand is why the courts can't find a way to act in the interest of justice." Despite "overwhelming" evidence of torture at Area 2, Ryan said, Orange was denied his request for a hearing concerning the circumstances of his interrogation. "How does this happen?"

"Ryan is not a lawyer," Locallo later told me. "He has no understanding of the criminal justice system."

In December 2003 Ryan was indicted on federal corruption charges for allegedly steering contracts and leases to family and friends during his tenure as secretary of state. Those charges were still pending in January 2005.

Orange and the three other death row convicts pardoned by Ryan are now suing the City of Chicago, its police department, and the state's attorney's office for millions. In 2004 Orange received $161,000 unrelated to the lawsuit—he got the money through a law that allows those pardoned on the basis of innocence to be compensated by the state for their years in prison. But there were also problems for Orange in 2004. In February he was arrested near his South Side home and charged with selling crack cocaine. While on bond for that case, he was arrested again four months later for possession of cocaine. In January 2005 Orange pled guilty to possession in both cases and was sentenced to five years in prison.

Illinois has enacted several laws in the last two years intended to make wrongful convictions in capital cases less likely—including the videotaping of interrogations in homicide investigations.

In 2002 a special prosecutor began investigating whether Commander Jon Burge, or detectives working under him, had committed any crimes for which they could be prosecuted. "We believe something happened," the special prosecutor, Edward Egan—a former appellate justice and a former first assistant state's attorney—told the *Chicago Tribune* a year into his investigation. "You'd have to be a chump not to." But whether detectives committed crimes that could be proven in court was an "entirely different matter," Egan said. His probe was still continuing in January 2005.

Burge, who turned fifty-seven in 2004, is retired and living in Florida. Because he's never been convicted of any crime, he continues to receive a full police pension.

DAN YOUNG JR., the retarded man who confessed to participating in the 1990 sexual assault and murder of Kathy Morgan, continued serving his life sentence for that crime—until January 31, 2005, when the state dropped the case against Young and his codefendant, Harold Hill.

The state's attorney's office began reinvestigating the case in 2001 under pressure from the *Chicago Tribune* and from defense lawyer Kathleen Zellner. Zellner, who has represented numerous convicts who were later exonerated, had taken on Young's and Hill's cases after she learned they'd confessed to committing the Morgan murder with a man who was locked up at the time, a man who had also given a confession but who wasn't prosecuted.

DNA tests run on matter found on Morgan's fingernails had identified two genetic profiles, neither of them matching Young or Hill (or the third man who confessed). DNA tests of hairs recovered from Morgan's clothing, and of other crime-scene evidence, also excluded Young and Hill. Bite mark evidence used against Young at his trial was discredited as well.

In dropping the case against Young and Hill, prosecutors said they had not concluded the two were definitely innocent, only that dismissing the case was the proper action in view of the evidentiary discoveries. Hill remained in prison because he had three years left on an unrelated robbery sentence. Young went home, having been locked up for nearly thirteen years. The state's attorney's office and the Chicago Police Department each said it had no plans to investigate the detectives who obtained the confessions.

LARRY BATES, the cocaine addict who got a third probation from Locallo in June 1998—this time with mandatory inpatient drug treatment—waited in jail for three months before a treatment bed opened for him in a southside rehab center. His days in the center that fall consisted of "meetings,

meetings, meetings, meetings, meetings." He found some of the talk helpful, but he was growing anxious "to get back to dealing with reality," he
said one evening that November. He also said he didn't appreciate being
treated like a child. The counselors prodded the clients to speak up in the
meetings, but clients who said something a counselor disapproved of sometimes were directed to write a six-page essay as a "consequence."

When Bates completed his ninety days and was released early on a
December morning, he felt more than ready to go. "Halle*lu*jah!" and
"Praise the *Lord*!" he said upon leaving the center. He was brimming with
pride and optimism as he rode a bus back toward the west side. "I felt like
my being patient and persistent had paid off. I wanted to get back to living
as a human being who's about something, and who *has* something. I
wanted to get back to being responsible."

He found work as a machinist in a small factory. It paid minimum wage,
"but you gotta crawl before you can walk," he said then.

Two weeks after he left the rehab center he got married to Lillie Gross,
the mother of two of his children. Gross, a hospital nutritionist and a longtime friend from church, had been visiting Bates in jail and in the rehab
center. When he got out of the center "he seemed like the man I met twenty-
some years ago," Gross said. "I know he can relapse. But life is a chance. I'll
be there to support him even if he does fall back to his addiction."

The wedding was on a Saturday evening in the Inspirational Deliverance
Center, a west-side chapel. Bates wore a black tuxedo with a white bou-
tonniere pinned to his lapel, and a white bow tie. About seventy-five people
attended, the vast majority women and children. A friend of the couple
sang "Have I Told You Lately That I Love You." When the pastor told
Bates, "You may salute your bride," he gave Lillie a bashful peck. Then he
and Lillie quickstepped out of the chapel under the arched hands of their
bridesmaids and groomsmen and to the cheers of those in the pews.

When Bates would head home from work at the end of a day he'd
almost always encounter some of his drugging friends. They made it clear
he was more than welcome to join them again. "But I know what's gonna
happen to me if I get into that same type of lunacy. I'm gonna end up in
prison," Bates said in December 1998.

After several months at minimum wage, he began tiring of crawling,
but with his felony record he couldn't find anything better. He and Lillie
quarreled occasionally. His friends' overtures grew more enticing. By mid-
1999 he was into that lunacy again, selling drugs to pay for drugs. By early
2001 he was back at 26th Street, charged with two new drug-dealing
offenses. He pled guilty to both in February 2001 and headed to prison for
the first time, at age forty-seven, with a seven-and-a-half-year sentence.

Bates applied for work-release when he got to within two years of his parole date. But he was informed that the nature of his conviction—drug-dealing within a thousand feet of a park or school—made him ineligible. It also disqualified him from serving his last year at home on electronic detention.

As he neared his release date, May 2004, he tried to prepare himself mentally for being free again. As a fifty-year-old with multiple felony drug convictions, finding work would be a challenge, he understood. "It ain't gonna come as fast as I want, this I know. I'll have to go through a lotta turndowns. Since I've been here I've seen some thirty guys leave and come back," he said of his minimum-security prison in Taylorville.

Lillie picked him up on his release date and drove him back to Chicago. They've been living with her parents on the west side ever since.

As of late November 2004 Bates had stayed clear of further criminal problems. But his employment woes had persisted and that outlook remained gloomy. He'd worked sporadically—drywall and plumbing jobs, temporary service. He's filled out many applications but his criminal record kept him from landing anything permanent. "It's been a struggle but I haven't given up," he said that month.

It also was a battle to stay off cocaine. Down his block he could see young men making their sales. "It's hard to resist, I ain't gonna lie to you," he said. "It's a fight every day." When he wasn't working he kept himself busy— lifting weights, applying for jobs, visiting his children, and playing with his three grandchildren. He believed that if he walked down the street and bought a rock he'd be headed back to prison before long—and that the next sentence would probably be at least ten years. "Being a criminal and doing drugs ain't nothing but a downward plunge all the way," he said. "I just have to stay focused on what I have to do. I'm getting too old for this type of situation."

DESPITE DROPS in violent crime, Cook County keeps sending more inmates to prison—19,299 in 2003, up from 15,529 in 1997. Much of that 24 percent increase was attributable to a crackdown on parole violators. The largest proportion of newly sentenced prisoners, however, continues to be drug offenders. The shipments of new prisoners from Cook County are still 80 percent African American.

Both the jail and the courthouse at 26th Street are still swamped, mainly because of the drug cases. In 2002, with the jail population rising above eleven thousand, Cook County sheriff Michael Sheahan announced that he might have to house some inmates in tents. That didn't happen, but fifteen hundred inmates slept on floors on some nights. The glut of prisoners has put pressure on courthouse staff to dispose of cases even faster.

Police wagons still drop off prisoners at the rear door of the courthouse every day, but the prisoners are no longer carted from the basement to a first-floor courtroom for their bond hearings. Instead, the defendants are ushered one by one in front of a camera in a cramped office in the basement. On a small TV monitor they see the image of the judge who will set their bond. The judge is at his bench in a courtroom on the floor above; as soon as he sees the defendant on his monitor, and sometimes before, he commences rushing through the bond hearing script. Spectators in the courtroom gallery see a tiny TV image of their relative or friend, and the defendants in the basement don't see their loved ones at all. The defendants are "not distracted by who's in the courtroom, families present and so forth," a bond court judge observed after the system was introduced in 1999. An official in the public defender's office decried the "dehumanizing" system when it began. But a spokesperson for the sheriff's office crowed about the time saved by the innovation.

IN MARCH 1999 Locallo was transferred to a civil courtroom downtown. This was a little more than a month after the first purported threat on his life, but he said the transfer had nothing to do with that. The chief judge of the circuit court, Donald O'Connell, had asked him to make the switch to the Law Division, which handles personal injury and medical malpractice suits seeking $50,000 and up. "I don't get a rush out of those kind of cases. I like dealing with cases concerning personal liberty," Locallo said shortly before he left 26th Street. "But you don't turn the chief judge down." He also figured he might be improving his chances of moving up to the appellate court by broadening his judicial résumé.

His office after the transfer was in the Richard J. Daley Center, in the North Loop, Courtroom 1912. Think of the year the *Titanic* sank, he'd tell jurors. He had indeed risen in the court system—sixteen floors. His chambers were larger, and he'd gone from no natural light to sometimes too much: the office overheated on summer mornings from all the sun he got through his floor-to-ceiling windows. On the rare occasions when he paused in his work, he could see the sailboats on Lake Michigan.

The defendants here weren't dark-skinned men and women in tan uniforms, guarded by deputies; they were doctors, hospitals, corporations, and public agencies. As at 26th Street, the vast majority of civil cases were resolved without a trial. In a typical month, he'd settle fifteen to twenty-five cases in pretrial conferences and preside over just one or two trials. He enjoyed the give-and-take with the lawyers in the pretrial conferences and prided himself on his knack for generating settlements. The conferences were similar to plea bargaining, he found, except the haggling was over large sums of money instead of years in prison. Disposition tally sheets were sent to judges monthly here instead of weekly, a reflection of the lesser importance of dispos as compared with 26th Street. He stayed among the dispo leaders nevertheless.

In April 2004 Locallo blundered, and he was subsequently exiled to a courthouse in suburban Rolling Meadows. It was an extracurricular mistake. A presiding judge in a different division had taken, Locallo thought, way too long to dispose of a case. Locallo concocted twenty facetious reasons the judge had held onto the case so long, photocopied the list, and distributed it to some judges and lawyers. When the object of his lampoon got wind of it she voiced her displeasure to the chief judge, and Locallo was soon on his way to the suburbs, where he was relegated to hearing minor civil suits.

Locallo told me late in 2004 that he expected the chief judge to transfer him back downtown before long. "This is like work-release," he said. "The cases here are by no stretch complicated. There's not enough work. It's basically a waste of my talent. But that's the price you pay for literary license."

In November 2004 Locallo was retained again, along with the seventy other Cook County circuit judges on the retention ballot. The bar groups once again extolled him. "His fairness and integrity are unquestioned," the Chicago Council of Lawyers said. The CCL called him "exceptionally skillful" at running a courtroom and "exceptionally hard-working," and it expressed concern that "such a talented jurist is not assigned to a division where he would be able to preside over more complex matters."

Locallo turned fifty-two in October 2004. He hasn't run for the appellate court because there haven't been vacancies recently, but he still plans to. "I'm shooting for 2006—there might be some openings then," he told me late in 2004. "I still have the passion to get there but I will not consider myself a failure if I don't."

He missed his colleagues at 26th Street, but not much else about the place. He wanted to get back to doing the big lawsuits in the Daley Center; he'd found that assignment fulfilling and the environment pleasing. His work as a criminal court judge had been more important, though, he said: "Liberty is more precious than money. A lot of people can get by without much money, but it's pretty tough to be in a cage."

ACKNOWLEDGMENTS

SOURCES

NOTES

INDEX

ACKNOWLEDGMENTS

This project began with an Alicia Patterson Fellowship I was awarded in 1993 to report on urban criminal courts and the poor. The fellowship allowed me to take a leave from my job as a feature writer for the *Chicago Reader* to concentrate on this subject. My thanks to the Patterson foundation and its director at the time, Margaret Engel.

It was my great fortune that a judge for the Patterson competition that year was Robert A. Caro, the incomparable biographer and journalist. Caro thought I should write a book on the criminal courts, and he expressed faith in my ability to write an exceptional one. The confidence he has shown in me has been unwavering, and I will always be indebted to him for it.

Caro did more than suggest I write this book, however. He also connected me with Katherine Hourigan, managing editor at Knopf, who has been instrumental in the publication of all four of his books. Bob raved to me about Kathy's literary judgment and about the care she lavished on her projects. With her editing of this book I have seen firsthand what Bob described: despite her many other responsibilities, she has found time to shape the book with care and wisdom. She has also been my patient champion, relentless in her conviction, even as I flailed about for years before finding my focus, that I would ultimately succeed.

I appreciate the help of Kathy's assistant, Eric Bliss, production editor Kathleen Fridella, designer Iris Weinstein, production manager Marci Lewis, publicist Elizabeth Cochrane, and the legal counsel of Jon Fine.

My agent, David Black, believes that journalism is worth little if it isn't readable, and that it isn't readable unless it tells a story. His reminders of that improved the book. Thanks also to Joy Tutela at his agency.

Two colleagues at the *Reader*, John Conroy and Tori Marlan, read the book as it was developing, chapter by chapter. Their advice was indispensable, not only because they are superb writers, but also because they know the landscape well, having repeatedly shone lights into the shadows of the Cook County criminal justice system. Their criticism was precise, challenging, and yet kind, and their generosity with their time touched me.

I benefited from the expertise of two veteran 26th Street lawyers: private attorney Dan Coyne and Jeffrey Howard of the public defender's office, who helped me understand the workings of both the law and the courthouse. Vincent Boggan's knowledge of the law and the courthouse was also invaluable, particularly because he has seen things from a different perspective. A friend of many years, Vincent is doing time in the Menard Correctional Center. My conversations with him over the years have helped me understand a defendant's view of the criminal justice system.

The beat reporters in the courthouse in 1998—Terry Wilson of the *Chicago Tribune,* Lorraine Forte of the *Chicago Sun-Times,* and Karen Craven of the *City News Bureau*—shared their hard–earned insights and were delightful company throughout the year. Rob Warden's reporting on criminal justice in Cook County in the 1980s provided helpful background—particularly his outstanding coverage of the George Jones "street files" case and of Greylord. John Conroy's pioneering work on torture by Chicago detectives aided my understanding of Leroy Orange's case. The reporting of the *Tribune's* Maurice Possley and Steve Mills has also enlightened me.

THE LATE DR. DONALD RACKY hooked me on journalism when I was a freshman at Chicago's St. Rita High School and he was the inspirational advisor to the school newspaper. He cultivated in me a skepticism essential for any reporter, but particularly for a reporter who would one day write about the courts.

Robert A. Roth, president of the *Reader,* has been a steadfast supporter ever since he hired me twenty-three years ago. He backed this project wholeheartedly, even though it took me away from the *Reader* for years. I'm grateful to *Reader* editor Alison True for her patience as my leave from the paper grew ever longer. I also appreciate the friendship shown and guidance given me by Alison and others at the paper during my career, especially Mike Lenehan and Kitry Krause.

The writings of two prominent legal scholars have informed this book. One is the late David Bazelon, judge in the court of appeals in the District of Columbia for thirty-seven years. Judge Bazelon died in 1993, and I regret never having met this exceedingly compassionate person. I am proud to know he grew up in Chicago, and I hope this is a book he would have liked. The other scholar is law professor Richard Delgado, now on the faculty at the University of Pittsburgh School of Law, whose provocative essays are a reminder of the value of original thinking, even in—or especially in—the often rigid world of the law.

A word of thanks to the friends who helped sustain me during this endeavor, especially Robert Bowser, Dave Cella, Jack Demuth, Tori Marlan, Bernie Tadda, and Cass Wolfe. Now that I have actually finished they will have to find something else to kid me about. I have confidence in them.

My mother wanted to be a writer. She had a biting wit and a questioning mind; had she lived in a different era she would have been a tenacious reporter, and the public, if not some public officials, would have been better off for it. I wish she at least had lived to see this book. I am grateful to her and to my father for their nurturance, and to my brother, Mike, for fending off bullies and hardly picking on me.

My children, Natalie and Peter, have grown from youngsters to young adults during the course of this project. They make everything I do feel worthwhile.

This book would never even have been attempted if not for my beloved, Jane Neumann. As usual she was ahead of me, believing I was capable of writing it before I believed it, and sure of its importance. Nor could I have finished without her help. She gave me time when I needed time and prodded me when I required that. She has always been my first reader, an arrangement that would have ended long ago but for her keen editorial sense. She has suffered without complaint the squatters in our home—the piles of transcripts and boxes of case files clogging the corners for years. She has helped with innumerable book-related tasks while working fulltime to support the family. Her help with the book pales, however, next to the care and warmth she has blessed me with throughout this project, and throughout our life together.

I was a fixture in Courtroom 302 in 1998, watching the proceedings from the jury box or the gallery, and this book is based on what I saw and heard. I also conducted hundreds of interviews and spent countless hours studying records and trial transcripts to better understand what I witnessed in court.

I continued researching this book well after 1998. Over the succeeding years I talked repeatedly with principals in the cases covered here, until I felt I grasped what had happened both on the surface and beneath it.

Judge Locallo made me feel welcome in the courtroom from the start. In Illinois, as in most states, judges are prohibited from commenting publicly on pending cases. Locallo was happy to discuss cases with me after they concluded, however—sometimes moments after. We had thirty-two formal sitdown interviews, most of them lasting more than an hour, as well as many briefer conversations. We usually talked in his chambers late in the afternoon or in the evening. In subjecting himself to a year of scrutiny, he displayed his trademark courage and confidence. And he responded to my endless queries with infinite patience.

The fact that Locallo so clearly supported my venture seemed to persuade the other courtroom personnel that they ought to as well. Notwithstanding Locallo's cooperation, however, the other workers in 302 might have been chilly to a stranger—especially a stranger whose avowed purpose was to monitor them and write about what he saw. But I was shown more geniality than wariness. Seven prosecutors and six public defenders were assigned to the courtroom at some point during 1998. All of them talked with me at length. For their friendliness and the time they gave me, I am grateful to prosecutors Joe Alesia, Andrew Dalkin, Mark Ertler, Stan Gonsalves, Mike Nolan, Mark Ostrowski, and Frank Vazquez, and public defenders Diana Bidawid, Amy Campanelli, John Conniff, Bob Galhotra, Kathryn Lisco, and Amy Thompson.

The clerk in 302 during the first half of 1998, Duane Sundberg, acquainted me with his filing system early in the year, and often, after court had been recessed for the day, I sat alone in the courtroom, paging through files of pending cases. Locallo usually was at work in his chambers; we took turns being the last to leave the courtroom.

The clerk during the second half of 1998, Angela Villa, was equally helpful. The clerk's files provide a helpful but sketchy view of a case, since, in Illinois, police reports (other than the arrest report) are not included in them. Prosecutors and defense lawyers granted me access to the police reports and other documents I wanted to review.

Besides the lawyers assigned to 302, there were many other attorneys with cases in the courtroom in 1998—private lawyers, as well as prosecutors and public defenders in special units. When I sought help from these lawyers it was given almost without exception. Other attorneys familiar with 26th Street broadened my understanding of the courthouse. Thanks to those mentioned in the text, and also to Larry Axelrood, Darron Bowden, Cathryn Crawford, James Cutrone, Janine Hoft, John Murphy, Thomas Needham, Robert Nemzin, Kevin Smith, James Sorensen, Richard Steinken, and James Stola. I especially appreciated my discussions with Jack Carey, a witty, kindhearted public defender who supported this project enthusiastically but succumbed to cancer before he could see the result.

Judges and former judges who shared their viewpoints of the courthouse included Robert Bastone, Robert Bertucci, Richard Neville, and Joseph Urso; retired circuit judges Lou Garippo, Michael Getty, Thomas Hett, and Earl Strayhorn; retired appellate justices William Cousins and R. Eugene Pincham; and presiding judge Paul Biebel and his predecessor, current supreme court justice Thomas Fitzgerald. Thanks also to judges Ray Garza and James Varga for their insights about Locallo, who had been their colleague in the state's attorney's office.

At the heart of criminal court proceedings is not the judge, however, but the defendant, who is the reason for the whole exercise. Reporters' access to defendants is often blocked by defendants' lawyers while cases are pending, since statements to a reporter can hurt a defendant's case. Once the verdict is in, reporters tend to lose interest. As a result, the unfiltered perspective of defendants is frequently neglected. But I had time on my side. I talked several times with most of the defendants whose cases are described in this book—often in jail or prison interview rooms. For their willingness to discuss their experiences I am grateful to Larry Bates, Kevin Betts, Tony Cameron, De'Angelo Harris, Leslie McGee, Terrence Pouncy, and Dino Titone, and a host of other defendants whose cases I was not able to include in the book.

Joan Stockmal, a spokesperson for the Cook County sheriff's office, was instrumental in setting up interviews in the Cook County jail, and Nic Howell, a spokesperson for the Illinois Department of Corrections, arranged the interviews I conducted in four prisons.

Deputies Gil Guerrero and Laura Rhodes allowed me to interview some defendants through the bars of the courtroom lockups. The deputies' insight into the goings-on in the courtroom was particularly informed, given their knowledge of what was going on behind it. Their good humor also made the year more enjoyable.

The courtroom lockups are among the places in the courthouse that defendants in custody know all too well, and the general public and reporters rarely see. Another such place is the courthouse basement, the entree to the halls of justice for most defendants, as I related in the prologue. For allowing me to watch that baptism on several occasions I am indebted to the late Ed Hassel, who was in charge of courthouse security in 1998. Lieutenant Kenneth Promisco also facilitated those visits, as did Lieutenant John Hopkins and Sergeant London Thomas. Stockmal of the sheriff's office arranged for me to view the complex process by which inmates are moved daily from the jail to the courthouse for their court dates.

Innumerable spectators, witnesses, and relatives and friends of defendants or victims offered their views to me in the gallery, in the hallway outside the courtroom, and sometimes in their homes.

Jurors are often so worn down by their service that the last thing they want to do is rehash it. I appreciate that some were willing to do so nonetheless.

When I wasn't in Courtroom 302 in 1998, I was often in the clerk's office in the adjacent administration building. The clerk's office is on the fifth floor, whereas the county psychiatrists and psychologists are on the tenth floor; some clerks like to say that this means they're only half nuts. The clerks were fully helpful and pleasant as they located one old file after another for me—no easy task considering the hundreds of thousands of these files. My gratitude to Bill Marino, Peggy Anderson, Margaret Schadt, Debra Grinstead, Bobbi Krol, and Wes Bauer. Jack Cusack explained the process by which evidence is impounded, and Dennis McNamara provided statistical data. Really ancient files were tracked down by Phil Costello and Jeanie Child of the clerk's archives department, aided by Tom Sobun, the office's capable point man in the county's huge, dusty file warehouse not far from the courthouse. Mary Espejo and Bob Kushnir in the Daley Center downtown found the misdemeanor files I needed to see. Marcus Ferguson clarified the mysterious case-assignment process for me, and Ralph Ferro was a font of knowledge about bond court.

Wayne Johnson, in 1998 the Chicago Crime Commission's expert on the Chicago outfit, shared his expertise with me, and detective Scott Keenan of the Chicago police training division arranged for me to attend a training for detectives in interrogation methods in 1998.

Others who enriched my perspective by providing their own, or who got me information I needed, included Rhonda Schullo, probation liaison in Courtroom 302; Patrick Durkin, director of the Cook County boot camp; Charles Fasano, prison and jail program director for the John Howard Association; Melody Heaps, founder and president of Treatment Alternatives for Safe Communities; court reporters Paul Marzano and Thomas Manno; Michael Boehmer at the Cook County Medical Examiner's office; Bruce Olson of IDOC's planning and research department; criminal court administrator Peter Coolsen; James Jordan, law clerk to presiding judge Biebel; and Jerry Neal, the affable food service worker who carts meals to jurors.

Thanks also to spokespersons Pat Camden and Edward Alonzo (Chicago police), Sergio Molina and Dede Short (Illinois Department of Corrections), Bill Cunningham and Sally Daly (Cook County Sheriff), Mary Nolan and Carolyn Barry (Cook County Circuit Court Clerk), John Gorman (Coak County State's Attorney's Office) and Ross Rice (FBI).

I HAD TWO ENGAGING interviews with the dean of Chicago criminal lawyers, Harry Busch. Busch began practicing criminal law in the 1920s in the courthouse at Illinois and Dearborn, the predecessor to the current courthouse. He was in his mid to late nineties when I spoke with him in 1997—he was elusive about his precise age. He was living in a high-rise retirement home on the north side, near the lake. He interrupted himself at times during our conversations by saying "strike that."

Busch had been a prosecutor for four years in the late 1920s before he began a career as a defense lawyer—a career that lasted more than half a century, during which he represented many mobsters and public officials accused of corruption. The main changes during this time, he told me, were the growth in drug cases and in plea-bargaining, developments that displeased him. He was so opposed to narcotics that he never represented a defendant on a drug charge: "To me that would have been obnoxious." And he rarely sought plea deals for his clients; he preferred to try their cases before juries. "I was there to do a job, not to be another cog in the wheel," he said. The pleasure from crafting a plea deal could never match the pleasure he derived from winning a jury trial: "When you win one of those, you feel you're entitled to dance—and the music in your system is playing."

Busch claimed to be the first person to have set foot in the courthouse at 26th Street when it formally opened on April 1, 1929. He said that happened because he was then the prosecutor assigned to the chief judge's courtroom. He remembered the courthouse being "very clean" when it opened. "It didn't stay that way long," he said.

Our second interview was in February 1999. During that interview, Busch fielded a call from Supreme Court Justice Michael Bilandic. Bilandic had been mayor of Chicago before he was elected to the Supreme Court, and before he'd been mayor he'd been an alderman in Bridgeport. The day of this second interview happened to be the day before a mayoral election in Chicago. After Busch hung up, he told me Bilandic had wanted to know if he'd be working his precinct tomorrow. Busch had promised the justice he would go around his high-rise reminding people to vote.

Busch's mind and tongue were still sharp in this interview. He told me he didn't like the fact that some prosecutors claimed to be working on the side of the angels. "Oh c'mon, that's a lot of shit," he said. "They're on the side that's paying their salaries."

Busch died a year and a half later, in October 2000. His family said he was 97; according to the Illinois Attorney Registration and Disciplinary Commission, which said Busch was still licensed to practice law, he was 101.

THE NOTES THAT FOLLOW provide references to the books, law review articles, newspaper stories, and other sources that supplemented my research. The sources of direct quotes from interviews are identified in the text; when the source of paraphrased information is unclear, the source is identified in the notes.

NOTES

PROLOGUE: WELCOME TO COUNTY

3   *They sold cocaine:* Examples cited are from the prisoners' arrest reports.
    At the district station: Details of the booking procedure are from Chicago police spokesman Pat Camden.

4   *Thirty courtrooms:* In 1998. By 2004 there were thirty-two trial courtrooms in the building; two courtrooms formerly used for preliminary hearings had been converted to trial courtrooms.

11 *He lost the leg:* Interview with Walter Williams's brother, Henry Williams.

16 *He's fast:* The deputies' preference for a speedy judge in bond court is nothing new. In 1950, Northwestern University researcher Samuel Dash (who later would become chief counsel of the Senate Watergate Committee) spent five months watching proceedings in the Municipal Court of Chicago, including its felony branch, in which bonds were set and preliminary hearings conducted in felony cases. "A judge's popularity among the bailiffs" in the felony branch "depends almost entirely on his speed of action," Dash observed. "It is not unusual for the most conscientious judges who attempt to get all the facts of the case disclosed before the court to be extremely unpopular with the bailiffs and the targets of many a curse throughout the morning." Dash, "Cracks in the Foundation of Criminal Justice," *Illinois Law Review,* 1951, vol. 46, p. 388.

16 Gerstein v. Pugh: 420 U.S. 103

17 *The amount of the I-bond:* In 1998, judges were still setting I-bonds in various amounts. Shortly thereafter, they began setting them routinely at $10,000.

18 *"Poor and friendless":* George W. Kirchwey, *Reports Comprising the Survey of the Cook County Jail* (Calumet Publishing, 1922), pp. 23–24.

18 *Slickly choreographed:* This choreography is not a recent creation. "The bailiffs set up systems to insure the rapid presentation of defendants before the court," Dash wrote about the Municipal Court in 1950. "A defendant is held 'on deck' while one is before the bench and is shifted into place before the judge as soon as the prior defendant is snatched away." Dash, "Cracks in the Foundation of Criminal Justice," p. 388.

18 *Chester's lawyer:* Interview with his lawyer, Kent Brody.
19 *A medical examiner:* Cook County Medical Examiner case report, 471 Jan. 98, and interview with medical examiner Dr. Edmund Donoghue.
21 *"No man":* From an address to the Sunset Club of Chicago ("What Shall We Do with Our Criminals?"), March 27, 1890. Printed in *Live Questions* (Donahue & Henneberry, 1890), p. 308.
21 *Imprisonment of fifty thousand:* Altgeld referred to a report of the Bureau of Labor Statistics of Illinois about the number of convicts nationally in 1880. *Our Penal Machinery and Its Victims* (first published in 1884), reprinted in *Live Questions,* p. 156.
21 *A "maelstrom":* Ibid., p. 162.
21 *Nearly 1.5 million:* At year's end in 2003, there were 1,470,000 people under the jurisdiction of federal or state adult correctional authorities. Another 691,000 prisoners were in local jails. "Prisoners in 2003," Bureau of Justice Statistics, November 2004.
21 *"At every point":* Samuel Walker, *Popular Justice: A History of American Criminal Justice* (Oxford University Press, 1998), p. 8.

ONE · WHITE SALES

27 *No small task:* Details of the procedures for bringing inmates to the courthouse from Joan Stockmal, Cook County Jail public information officer.
31 *Virtually no blacks:* The proportion of blacks in Norwood Park increased fifteenfold between 1990 and 2000—from .06 percent to .9 percent, according to the U.S. Census Bureau.
31 *Superman cape:* Interview with Locallo's mother, Anna Mae Locallo.
32 *Bar associations have praised:* "Judge Locallo exemplifies the many qualities needed to be an excellent judge. He is intelligent, hardworking, fair, even-tempered and balanced in his judicial duties"—Chicago Bar Association, 1992. "Judge Locallo is widely acclaimed as having outstanding legal ability and judicial temperamant [and] . . . is considered to be fair and of high integrity"—Chicago Council of Lawyers, 1992.
32 *One a month:* In 2001, the forty felony trial judges in Cook County (counting its suburban courtrooms) presided over 395 jury trials; in 2002—the last full year for which such information was available—the forty judges presided over 344 jury trials. Data from the office of Paul Biebel, criminal court presiding judge in 2004.
35 *About three-quarters; just over half:* From 1994 to 2003, 76 percent of felony defendants in Cook County were convicted. Of those sentenced to prison or probation, 53 percent were sentenced to prison. My calculations from "Annual Report of the Illinois Courts: Statistical Summary," Administrative Office of the Illinois Courts, for years 1994 through 2003.
37 *More than four of every five:* In 2001, 81 percent of Cook County's felony cases were disposed of by guilty pleas; in 2002 and the first half of 2004, 85 percent, according to data from presiding judge Biebel. (There was "confusion" about the 2003 data, Biebel said.) These percentages include cases dismissed by the state in pretrial stages. Considering only cases resolved by pleas or trials, 86 percent of the cases were disposed of by pleas in 2001, 90 percent in 2002, and 91 percent in 2004.

38 *In fact, prosecutors:* "The trial judge shall not initiate plea discussions." Illinois Supreme Court Rule 402 (d) (1). "If a tentative plea agreement has been reached by the parties . . . the trial judge may permit, upon request of the parties, the disclosure to him of the tentative agreement. . . ." 402 (d) (2).

38 *The most populated:* In 1998, the nation's three largest jail jurisdictions were Los Angeles County, with an average daily population of 21,136 at midyear; New York City, with 17,680; and Cook County, with 9,321. "Prison and Jail Inmates at Midyear 1998," Bureau of Justice Statistics. But inmates in Los Angeles and New York are held in facilities spread over several sites, whereas all Cook County inmates are held at 26th and California.

38 *One percent:* From 2001 through the first half of 2004, 0.9 percent of the felony cases in Cook County were tried by juries, according to data from presiding judge Biebel.

39 *Fifteen jury trials:* Quarterly Reports, Criminal Division, Circuit Court of Cook County, 1997.

39 *Began sending its clerks into courtrooms:* In announcing its plan to monitor judges, the crime commission shrewdly suggested it was merely doing judges a favor. Judges had been chided publicly for allowing cases to "drag along for months" and for issuing continuances "on the slightest pretext," the commission noted; and some judges had been criticized for permitting their "social and political activities to interfere with an honest day's work on the bench." Judges were "helpless against such criticism and no doubt would welcome the active efforts of the Chicago Crime Commission to correct any untrue viewpoint held by the public." "In Support of the Judges," *Bulletin of the Chicago Crime Commission*, Oct. 6, 1920.

39 *A trial court judge who hesitates:* A. T. Andreas, *History of Chicago, from the Earliest Period to the Present Time* (A. T. Andreas Co., 1884–1886), vol. 2, p. 457.

39 *Surged to tenth:* Criminal Division disposition statistics, Dec. 29, 1997.

40 *That includes:* Criminal Division quarterly reports, 1997.

40 *Misdemeanor arrests were soaring:* "Trends and Issues 90," *Illinois Criminal Justice Information Authority*, 1990, p. 141.

40 *"What's next":* William Grady, "Approaching the bench head-on," *Chicago Tribune*, Dec. 30, 1993.

41 *Plea bargaining has been a staple:* Samuel Walker, *Popular Justice*, pp. 73–74.

41 *Abolition of plea bargaining: Courts,* National Advisory Commission on Criminal Justice Standards and Goals (1973), pp. 42–49.

42 *He's fit if:* 725 ILCS (Illinois Compiled Statutes) 5/104–10.

42 *In psychiatric hospitals:* With Cameron's permission, I reviewed his state mental health records at the Tinley Park Mental Health Center.

43 *Inmates usually get it:* Interview with Illinois Department of Corrections spokesperson Nic Howell. In addition, inmates usually get a six-month "meritorious service" credit, also designed to alleviate prison overcrowding, and they can trim another three months by attending school while incarcerated.

43 *"Truth-in-sentencing" law:* 730 ILCS 5/3-6-3.

43 *Cameron's 1986 conviction:* Transcript and records in that case (85CR-3534).

43 *It's up to prison officials:* For defendants found guilty but mentally ill, "The Department of Corrections shall provide such psychiatric, psychological, or other counseling and treatment for the defendant as it determines necessary." 730 ILCS 5/5-2-6 (b).

47   *U.S. Supreme Court: North Carolina v. Alford,* 400 U.S. 25 (1970).

47   *Critics:* John H. Langbein, "Torture and Plea Bargaining," *University of Chicago Law Review* (fall 1978), p. 15.

47   *But Supreme Court justices:* Speaking of plea-bargaining generally in a ruling a year after its *Alford* decision, Chief Justice Warren Burger observed that "if every criminal charge were subjected to a full-scale trial, the States and the Federal Government would need to multiply by many times the number of judges and court facilities." *Santobello v. New York,* 404 U.S. 257, 260 (1971).

TWO · A GROWTH INDUSTRY

49   *"Lamentable but true":* Hammett, "The New Cook County Criminal Court and Jail Buildings," *The Western Architect,* September 1929, p. 157.

50   *A decorative fountain:* Chicago Department of Transportation press release, May 13, 1998.

51   *The county's first courthouse; a larger one built; a courthouse exclusively for criminal cases:* Weston Goodspeed, *History of Cook County, Illinois* (Goodspeed Historical Association, 1909), p. 218.

51   *Officials predicted; "No other city":* "Citadel of justice," undated 1893 *Chicago Herald* article, on file with Commission on Chicago Landmarks.

51   *Kirchwey:* "The next generation is likely to witness a great advance in the development of preventive measure which may materially reduce the volume of crime," Kirchwey wrote hopefully. "The psychological and psychiatric study of the delinquent, which is now only in its infancy, may be expected to equip us with new methods of handling an increasingly large percentage of those who now find their way into jail." George Kirchwey, *Reports Comprising the Survey of the Cook County Jail* (Calumet Publishing, 1922), p. 56.

52   *Taxpayers finally approved: Chicago Tribune,* February 25, 1925.

52   *Hopelessly hooked:* Mark H. Haller, "Urban Crime and Criminal Justice: The Chicago Case," *Journal of American History,* 1970, p. 619.

52   *The first sites considered:* "Report of the Committee on New County Jail and Criminal Court Building," November 11, 1924.

52   *Cermak's real estate holdings:* "Cermak's folly still there after 40 years," *Chicago's American,* April 1, 1969.

52   *Courthouse opened:* "Judge rebels at new courts, halts a trial," *Chicago Daily News,* April 1, 1929. "New courts open in storm of protest," *Chicago Herald & Examiner,* April 2, 1929. "Judge finds his new court like a movie stage," *Chicago Tribune,* April 2, 1929.

53   *Object of the courthouse staffers' wrath:* "Cermak's folly still there after 40 years," *Chicago's American,* April 1, 1969.

53   *Air-conditioning:* "County approves courts renovations," *Chicago Tribune,* Aug. 21, 1973.

53   *Young lawyers:* "Concentrate courts in Loop, head of bar urges," *Chicago Tribune,* Sept. 3, 1963.

53   *Campaigned repeatedly:* "Ask criminal court shift to Loop area," *Chicago Tribune,* June 5, 1959; "Crime courts in Loop a hope—for future," ibid., Sept. 13, 1963; "Don't lose the chance to consolidate courts," *Chicago Daily News,* March 13, 1961.

53 *"Certain elements":* Chicago Tribune, Sept. 13, 1963.

53 *"Well-heeled tenants":* "Remote court location worsens crime problem," *Chicago Daily News,* Feb. 22, 1960.

54 *At the cornerstone ceremony:* Chicago Crime Commission, *Criminal Justice* (September–October 1927), p. 4.

54 *Overbooked:* "County jail: a study of frustration from the start," *Chicago Tribune,* Dec. 18, 1967.

54 *"Crime flourishes":* Challenge of Crime in a Free Society, President's Commission on Law Enforcement and Administration of Justice, 1967, p. 279.

54 *"Individual instances"; "not designed":* Ibid. p. 6.

54 *"To eliminate slums":* Ibid., p. 15.

54 *"Better candidates": Report of the National Advisory Commission on Civil Disorders,* 1968, p. 130.

54 *"Unprecedented levels":* Ibid., p. 2.

55 *"Incontestable": Courts,* National Advisory Commission on Criminal Justice Standards and Goals (1973), p. 1.

55 *"If New York"; no new prisons:* Ibid., p. 352.

55 *"Lock up":* "Remarks by Governor James R. Thompson on the Attorney General's Task Force on Violent Crime," *Northwestern School of Law Journal of Criminal Law & Criminology* (fall 1982), p. 867. (Thompson made his remarks in October 1981.)

55 *Six hundred state and fifty federal prisons:* "Justice Expenditure and Employment in the United States, 1999," Bureau of Justice Statistics, February 2002, p. 7.

55 *Huge expenditures:* State government spending on corrections rose from $6 billion in 1982 to $34 billion by 1999; federal corrections spending rose from $541 million to $4 billion in the same period. Ibid., p. 3.

55 *Has quadrupled:* In 1980 there were 502,000 inmates; "Prisoners in 1994," Bureau of Justice Statistics, August 1995. In 2003 there were 2,086,000 inmates; "Prisoners in 2003," Bureau of Justice Statistics, November 2004.

55 *It's not clear:* "Despite three decades of study and a nationwide quasi experiment of unprecedented scale, it is still uncertain how large an effect prisons have on the crime rate." William Spelman, "What Recent Studies Do (and Don't) Tell Us About Imprisonment and Crime," *University of Chicago Crime and Justice* (2000), p. 419.

55 *Waxed and waned:* The violent crime rate peaked in 1981, declined through 1986, rose again until 1993, and has since dropped dramatically. "Criminal Victimization, 2003," National Crime Victimization Study, Bureau of Justice Statistics, September 2004.

55 *Incarceration rate has risen every year:* "Prisoners in 2002," Bureau of Justice Statistics, July 2003; "Prisoners in 1994," Bureau of Justice Statistics, August 1995.

56 *Persistence of poverty:* Ted Robert Gurr, *Violence in America,* vol. 1. (Sage Publications, 1989), p. 15.

56 *The proportion of young males in the population:* James Alan Fox, "Demographics and U.S. Homicide," in *The Crime Drop in America* (Cambridge University Press, 2000).

56 *The prevalence of guns:* Franklin E. Zimring and Gordon Hawkins, *Crime Is Not the Problem: Lethal Violence in America* (Oxford University Press, 1997).

56 *The emergence of certain drugs:* Bruce Johnson, Andrew Golub, and Eloise Dunlap, "The Rise and Decline of Hard Drugs, Drug Markets, and Violence in Inner-City New York," in *The Crime Drop in America.*

56 *"The biggest growth industry":* "Courts undoing 49-year-old 'joke,'" *Chicago Sun-Times,* April 3, 1978.

56 *More than doubled; doubled again; leveled off:* Clerk of the Circuit Court of Cook County.

56 *For decades:* Details on the jail's growth and the cost of housing inmates are from Cook County Department of Corrections and from "Crowding at the Cook County Jail," Illinois Criminal Justice Information Authority, October 1989.

56 *Tractor Works:* "Tractor Works: 50-Year History, 1910–1960," undated article from the archives of Navistar International Corporation.

57 *But in 1969:* International Harvester Company press release, May 15, 1969.

57 *Illinois spent $100 million; more than a billion; furnishes two-thirds; Eighty percent:* Illinois Department of Corrections data.

57 *Whose population is 26 percent:* In the year 2000, according to the U.S. Census Bureau.

THREE · BAGGAGE

58 *Robbery of a toll collection driver:* "Indict two cops in coin heist," *Chicago Tribune,* Dec. 24, 1977; August Locallo interview.

61 *"Predisposed toward criminals":* "Rivals Phelan, Pincham trade bitter attacks," *Chicago Sun-Times,* March 14, 1990.

61 *"It is essential":* "Judges also have a duty to dissent," *Chicago Tribune,* March 28, 1990.

61 *Coasted:* Locallo—69,403; Republican Jeffrey Gunchick—41,143. *Chicago Tribune,* Nov. 5, 1992.

62 *Appeared before a Democratic Party subcommittee:* "County Dems launch judicial slating process," *Chicago Daily Law Bulletin,* Nov. 24, 1997; "Dems List Judicial Slate," *Chicago Lawyer,* Jan. 1998.

63 *Comiskey Park:* Since renamed U.S. Cellular Field.

64 *"Bunch of thugs":* "Teens deny hate attack," *Chicago Sun-Times,* March 25, 1997.

64 *"To join together":* "Mayor's message to city on race: 'There is no place in Chicago for hatred,'" *Chicago Sun-Times,* March 27, 1997.

64 *Raised $100,000:* "Breakfast may be wakeup call," *Chicago Tribune,* April 22, 1997.

64 *"We African-Americans":* William Hampton, *Chicago Defender,* April 28, 1997.

64 *"No justice":* "Hopes rise for teen a week after beating; victim stirs from his coma as 150 March in Bridgeport," *Chicago Tribune,* March 29, 1997.

65 *"Race chasm":* "Beating a blunt reminder of Chicago race chasm," *Los Angeles Times,* March 26, 1997.

65 *"Ugly side":* "Chicago neighborhood reveals an ugly side," *New York Times,* March 27, 1997.

65 *"A savage crime":* "Chicago's Last Hope," *Time,* April 7, 1997.

65 *"Savage":* Clinton's weekly radio address, March 29, 1997.

Notes to Pages 65–67 / 365

65 *Extended his best wishes:* "President calls Lenard's family in hospital," *Chicago Sun-Times,* March 31, 1997.

65 *Jesus's crucifixion:* "Beating topic of Clinton talk, Jackson rally," *Chicago Sun-Times,* March 30, 1997.

65 *Lenard was sent home; "Many kids":* "Clark in spotlight of old, new neighbors," *Chicago Tribune,* May 2, 1997.

65 *"Hang":* "Three suspects in Clark beating indicted; protesters at court in alleged hate crime," *Chicago Tribune,* April 24, 1997.

65 *"We ask":* "Three Bridgeport youths indicted," *Chicago Sun-Times,* April 24, 1997.

66 *Whites committed:* Twenty-three blacks and 15 whites were killed; 342 blacks and 178 whites were reported injured. Almost all of the fighting was interracial, but 154 blacks and 75 whites were arrested, and 81 blacks and 47 whites were indicted. Chicago Commission on Race Relations, *The Negro in Chicago: A Study of Race Relations and a Race Riot.* (University of Chicago Press, 1922), p. 35.

66 *Decades of beatings:* Arnold R. Hirsch, *Making the Second Ghetto: Race and Housing in Chicago, 1940–1960* (Cambridge University Press, 1983), pp. 40–99.

66 *Beatings and shootings of blacks by white cops:* Ibid. p. 50; Dempsey J. Travis, *An Autobiography of Black Politics* (Urban Research Press, 1987), pp. 285–89.

66 *"Considerable restraint":* "Hanrahan backs police," *Chicago Tribune,* Dec. 9, 1969.

66 *A federal grand jury: Report of the January 1970 Grand Jury,* U.S. District Court, Northern District of Illinois, pp. 104–6.

66 *County prosecutors dropped the charges:* Ibid., p. 111.

66 *None of the police officers:* Twelve policemen, along with Hanrahan and one of his assistants, were charged with conspiracy in the Panther raid, but they were all acquitted. "Hanrahan, 13 others freed in raid case," *Chicago Tribune,* October 26, 1972.

66 *A profusion:* John Conroy, *Unspeakable Acts, Ordinary People: The Dynamics of Torture* (Knopf, 2000).

66 *"Systematic":* "Special Project Conclusion Report," Office of Professional Standards, Chicago Police Department, Sept. 28, 1990. In 1999, Senior U.S. District Judge Milton Shadur declared it "common knowledge" that officers at the station had "regularly engaged in the physical abuse and torture of prisoners to extract confessions." *U.S. v. Maxwell,* 37 F. Supp. 1078, at 1094.

66 *Judges commented:* In a murder case, "If there were a colored man in the [jury] box he would soon be put out," Judge Hugo Pam said. Judge Charles Thomson said that if one was to ask a prosecutor why he dismissed a "colored" man from a jury, "I don't think he would give you any reason." Chicago Commission on Race Relations, *The Negro in Chicago,* p. 352.

67 *"Where a white man":* Ibid., p. 353.

67 *Reversed two: People v. Kirkendoll,* 415 Ill. 404 (1953); *People v. Crump,* 5 Ill. 2d 251 (1955).

67 *First used: Campbell v. the People,* 16 Ill. 16 (1854).

67 *Thanks mainly:* But it apparently wasn't only prosecutors who were keeping blacks off juries in earlier years. Responding to a survey in the late 1950s, the public defender's office here reported an arrangement a "number of years" before by prosecutors and defense lawyers "to excuse all negroes by agreement."

Jack Greenberg, *Race Relations and American Law* (Columbia University Press, 1959), pp. 406–7.

67   *"Case after case":* Appellate Justice William White, special concurring opinion in *People v. Bonilla,* 117 Ill. App. 3d 1041 (1983).

67   *Decision in 1986: Batson v. Kentucky,* 476 U.S. 79.

67   *Still try to skirt:* E.g., *People v. Morales,* 308 Ill. App. 3d 162 (1999), *People v. Randall,* 283 Ill. App. 3d 1019 (1996), *People v. Kindelan,* 213 Ill. App. 3d 548 (1991).

67   *All-white cast:* "2004 Diversity Survey," *Chicago Lawyer* (July 2004), pp. 12, 22.

67   *County prosecutors were unwilling; changes in federal law:* John Noonan, *Bribes* (Macmillan, 1984), pp. 584–601.

67   *Fixing:* James Tuohy and Rob Warden, *Greylord: Justice, Chicago Style* (Putnam, 1989).

68   *Poor and cloutless defendant:* "Government's Official Version of the Offense," *U.S. v. Maloney,* 91 CR 477.

68   *Roots in organized crime:* Four days after the attack, the city's black-owned newspaper, the *Chicago Defender,* noted that Caruso was the great-nephew of former first ward alderman Fred Roti. "Bridgeport attack outrages community," March 25, 1997. After twenty-two years as alderman, Roti had gone to prison in 1993 for federal corruption offenses. Newspaper stories in July 1997, about a probe of local labor unions, reported the alleged mob ties of Caruso's father. "Probe targets mob in laborers union," *Chicago Tribune,* July 14, 1997.

68   *"This case":* Nathaniel Howard, president, Chicago Chapter, MAD DADS (Men Against Destruction—Defending Against Drugs and Social Disorder), *Chicago Defender,* April 3, 1997.

69   *"The fastest white man":* Schwind interview.

70   *Eight mob bookies:* "Nab 8 mob bookies, close big race wire," *Chicago Tribune,* Dec. 16, 1967.

70   *Pled guilty: U.S. v. Victor Locallo,* 67 CR 693; "Six sentenced on racing charge," *Chicago Tribune,* Dec. 13, 1969.

FOUR · GOOD FACTS, BAD FACTS

72   *Three reporters:* For the *Chicago Tribune,* the *Chicago Sun-Times,* and the *City News Bureau,* a local wire service.

78   *Planting high-rises in ghettoes:* Martin Meyerson and Edward C. Banfield, *Politics, Planning and the Public Interest: The Case of Public Housing in Chicago* (Free Press, 1955); Devereux Bowly, *The Poorhouse: Subsidized Housing in Chicago* (Southern Illinois University Press, 1978), p. 112.

86   *Second-leading employer:* In August 2004, the leading employer, Graham Hospital, had 510 employees, Illinois River 369, according to the Canton Area Chamber of Commerce.

86   *Inside the prison:* As of June 30, 1998: Illinois Department of Corrections Planning and Research calculation for the author.

86   *Outside the prison:* Author's calculation from U.S. Census Bureau 2000 population estimates for Canton, and IDOC statistics for Illinois River.

86   *Designed to house; one of 1900:* IDOC data.

86 *The minimum $380,000:* At $20,000 a year, the approximate cost of housing an inmate in both the jail and Illinois prisons in the 1990s, according to the Cook County Department of Corrections and the IDOC.

FIVE · LUCK

100 *Police found:* "Body identified," *Chicago Sun-Times,* Jan. 18, 1995.

102 *Convicted of at least one charge:* My calculations from "Annual Report of the Illinois Courts: Statistical Summary," Administrative Office of Illinois Courts, for the years 1996 through 2003.

SIX · BUSTED AGAIN

110 *More than 320,000 drug offenders:* In state prisons—246,100; in federal prisons—78,501. "Prison and Jail Inmates at Midyear 2001," Bureau of Justice Statistics, April 2002.

110 *Well over $7 billion a year:* In 2001, the average annual operating cost per state inmate nationally was $22,650. "State Prison Expenditures, 2001," Bureau of Justice Statistics, June 2004. For federal inmates it was $23,001. "Federal Prison System—Salaries and Expenses, 1975–2003," Budget Trend Data, Justice Management Division, Department of Justice.

111 *Nearly one million drug probationers:* In 2003, just over 4 million adults were on probation in the U.S., and 25 percent of them had been convicted of a drug law violation. "Probation and Parole in the United States, 2003," Bureau of Justice Statistics, July 2004.

111 *Blacks are incarcerated; doubled; quintupled:* "Poor Prescription: The Costs of Imprisoning Drug Offenders in the United States," Justice Policy Institute, 2000

111 *A rerun of a 1950s campaign:* John Helmer, *Drugs and Minority Oppression* (Seabury Press, 1975), chapter five.

111 *Fearful that the scourge could spread:* "The most terrifying thing about the drug disease among the youth to parents and citizens who are worried about its rapid spread is that it happens to normal and average children—not only to subnormal children." Testimony of Congressman Sidney R. Yates to the U.S. House of Representatives, Subcommittee of the Committee on Ways and Means, April 1951. "Gentlemen: somewhere right at this minute a little boy like yours, or a little girl like mine, is getting a first taste of the needle." Testimony of Lois Higgins, Chicago Crime Prevention Bureau, ibid.

111 *Ghettoes were swelling:* Chicago's black population grew by 77 percent in the 1940s and by another 65 percent in the 1950s, climbing from 278,000 in 1940 to 813,000 by 1960. Hirsch, *Making the Second Ghetto,* pp. 16–17.

111 *Police began sweeping:* In 1946, Chicago police made only 550 drug arrests. In 1950, the department doubled the number of narcotics officers from six to twelve, and police made 3,712 drug arrests. By 1955, the bureau had sixty officers, and Chicago police were making more than 7,000 drug arrests a year. Testimony of Chicago Police Commissioner Timothy J. O'Connor to the U.S. Senate, Subcommittee on Narcotics of the Committee on the Judiciary, hearing in Chicago on "Illicit Narcotic Traffic," Nov. 21, 1955.

111 *Lawmakers greatly toughened:* Congress passed mandatory minimum sentences of two years for drug offenders in 1951; in 1956 Congress increased the penalty for a first conviction to five years for some drug offenses, and authorized juries to impose the death penalty for adults who sold heroin to minors. David F. Musto, *The American Disease,* (Oxford University Press, 1999), pp. 230–31.

111 *Officials acknowledged:* "The white race is responsible for the distribution of narcotics in America, and let's not kid ourselves," Cook County State's attorney John Gutknecht told the Subcommittee on Narcotics the day that Police Commissioner O'Connor testified. But data presented at the hearing indicated that 1 in 4,100 whites were arrested by Chicago police for drug crimes, compared with 1 in 71 blacks.

111 *Frank Lopez:* Case file in *People v. Lopez,* 51–1869; Supreme Court ruling, 10 Ill. 2d 237 (1957).

111 *A kinder attitude; treatment centers sprouted:* Musto, *The American Disease,* chapter 11; Michael Massing, *The Fix* (Simon & Schuster, 1998), p. 86.

111 *"White kids":* Myron Orfield Jr., "The Exclusionary Rule and Deterrence: An Empirical Study of Chicago Narcotics Officers," *University of Chicago Law Review* (Summer 1987), footnote 23.

111 *Began falling:* "Drug Use Trends," Office of National Drug Control Policy, October 2000.

112 *Unemployment rate for blacks:* "Selected Civilian Unemployment Rates, 1975–2002," U.S. Department of Labor, Bureau of Labor Statistics.

112 *Reagan:* "Drugs are bad, and we're going after them," the president said in his weekly radio address on Oct. 2, 1982. "We've taken down the surrender flag and run up the battle flag."

112 *Brightened the unemployment picture:* In 1982, the criminal justice system employed 1.27 million persons; by 2001, it employed more than 2.2 million. During that period, the number of police rose by 38 percent, the number of judicial and legal employees by 97 percent, and the number of corrections employees by 149 percent. "Justice Expenditure and Employment in the United States, 2001," Bureau of Justice Statistics, May 2004.

112 *A third; two and a half years:* "Felony Sentences in State Courts, 2000," Bureau of Justice Statistics, June 2003, pp. 2–3. The average prison sentence for federal drug offenders was more than twice as long (six years and four months), but only 7 percent of drug convictions are at the federal level. Ibid, p. 3.

112 *Addicts accused of nonviolent crimes:* 20 ILCS 301/40-10 (2004).

117 *The first court in the nation:* "Council activates anti-dope drive," *The Police Digest,* Chicago Police Department, August 1951.

117 *Weren't traffickers:* "Slaves to Drugs Unveiled in Court," Crime Prevention Bureau, 1951.

117 *The court disposed:* Alfred R. Lindesmith, *The Addict and the Law* (Indiana University Press, 1965), pp. 90–93.

117 *"Long, shabby":* "Dope: Congress Encourages the Traffic," *The Nation,* March 16, 1957.

117 *Drug night court program:* Judge Thomas Fitzgerald, *Chicago Bar Association Record,* May 1990; "Assessment of the Feasibility of Drug Night Courts," U.S. Department of Justice, Bureau of Justice Assistance, June 1993.

118   *"One of the smartest":* "The overload in narcotics court," *Chicago Tribune,* July 27, 1992.

118   *Crime magically swells:* After a special drug court was formed in Denver in 1995, the number of drug cases filed tripled in two years. Morris B. Hoffman, a Denver judge, later observed: "The very presence of the drug court, with its significantly increased capacity for processing cases, has caused police to make arrests in, and prosecutors to file, the kinds of ten- and twenty-dollar hand-to-hand drug cases that the system simply would not have bothered with before, certainly not as felonies." Hoffman noted that this "net-widening" effect is a "well-recognized phenomenon whenever law enforcement resources are targeted at designated kinds of cases." Hoffman, "The Drug Court Scandal," *North Carolina Law Review* (June 2000), p. 1437.

118   *Began arresting more of the addicts:* Both Judge Fitzgerald and the chief assistant state's attorney in the night court program told the Justice Department researchers that police had been arresting more people they caught with small amounts of drugs than they had before the courts opened.

119   *"Like opening":* Fry's written testimony to the Illinois Task Force on Crime and Corrections, Aug. 14, 1992.

119   *"Deludes the public":* "Making Room for Justice," *Chicago Crime Commission,* March 1996.

119   *Died in committee:* Interview with Chicago Bar Association lobbyist Larry Suffredin. The bill died because "there were a number of [legislators] who wanted to show they were strongly opposed to drugs," Suffredin said.

120   *No panacea:* "Addicts who successfully complete a treatment program but who cannot get work because they have no marketable skills or are uneducated will quickly return to drug dealing, crime, and addiction when returned to their communities." Melody M. Heaps and Dr. James A. Swartz, "Toward a Rational Drug Policy: Setting New Priorities," *The University of Chicago Legal Forum* (1994), p. 201.

121   *Minimum possible sentence:* Both times Gilliam was caught allegedly selling drugs, she was within a thousand feet of a school, making the crime a Class 1 felony, with a minimum term of four years.

121   *But for Prohibition:* "Volstead law expands jails, Cermak charges," *Chicago Tribune,* Sept. 16, 1927.

121   *The opposite effect:* Prohibition "led to a breakdown of law and order with the connivance of those in authority. The remedy was worse than the disease.... Prohibition cases clogged the courts, impeded true justice, and brought the performance of law into disrepute." Sean Dennis Cashman, *Prohibition, the Lie of the Land* (Free Press, 1981), pp. 2, 154. "The loot of Prohibition was enough to buy judges, state's attorneys, and whole police forces." Andrew Sinclair, *Prohibition, the Era of Excess* (Little, Brown, 1962), p. 230. In Chicago, the homicide rate leaped in the 1920s. But it's hard to know how much of this was attributable to Prohibition, and how much to changing demographics, to immigration patterns, or to the advent of the automobile. Leigh Bienen and Brandon Rottinghaus, "Learning from the Past, Living in the Present: Understanding Homicide in Chicago, 1870–1930," *Northwestern School of Law Journal of Criminal Law and Criminology* (spring/summer 2002), pp. 515, 530.

122   *Seven Austin officers:* "7 Chicago cops indicted in shakedowns," *Chicago Tri-bune,* Dec. 21, 1996. All seven were convicted. They received prison sentences ranging from 5 years to 115 years. "Austin cops sent to prison," *Chicago Tribune,* Oct. 19, 2001.

122   *"That even":* Gutknecht testimony to the U.S. Senate, Subcommittee on Narcotics of the Committee on the Judiciary, hearing in Chicago on "Illicit Narcotic Traffic," Nov. 21, 1955, p. 4295.

SEVEN · A REAL LAWYER

125   *Before the public defender's office was created:* William Scott Stewart, "A Criticism of the Public Defender System," *The John Marshall Law Quarterly* (June 1936), pp. 257–58.

125   *Officials troubled:* Charles Mishkin, "The Public Defender," *Chicago Bar Association Record* (February–March 1931), p. 98; *Report of the Judicial Advisory Council of the State of Illinois and the Judicial Advisory Council of Cook County,* 1931, pp. 25–28; Newman F. Baker, "The Public Defender's Work in Cook County," *Journal of Criminal Law and Criminology* (1935), pp. 5–9.

125   *How cases had been flowing; "using":* Philip J. Finnegan, "The Public Defender System in Cook County, Illinois," *United States Law Review* (1934), pp. 479–86.

125   *"A virtue":* Stewart, "A Criticism of the Public Defender System," p. 258.

125   *In 80 percent of the cases:* 2004 estimate for the author by supervisors in the office of the Cook County Public Defender.

127   *In the late nineteenth century:* Harris v. Illinois, 128 Ill. 585 (1889); Morgan v. Illinois, 136 Ill. 161 (1891).

127   *Reviewing courts and lawmakers:* In Patton v. U.S., 281 U.S. 276 (1930), the U.S. Supreme Court sanctioned bench trials in federal criminal cases. The Patton opinion lists the numerous cases upholding bench trials in state courts. By the mid-1930s, the bench trial option had been adopted "almost universally" in state courts. Albert W. Alschuler, "Plea Bargaining and Its History," *Columbia Law Review* (January 1979), p. 33. One of the early proponents of bench trials, journalist and lawyer Raymond Moley, saw them as an alternative to plea bargaining. But if bench trials reduced plea bargaining at all, they did so only briefly; by 1940, plea bargaining rates were as high or higher than they'd been in the 1920s. Ibid., p. 33.

127   *Bench trials were approved: People ex rel. Swanson, State's Attorney, v. Fisher,* 340 Ill. 250 (1930).

127   *"Rules of law":* Sir William Holdsworth, *A History of English Law* (Methuen & Co., 1922), 3rd edition, vol. 1, p. 349.

127   *Outnumbered jury trials:* The 1961 and 1985 ratios are my calculations from "Annual Report of the Illinois Courts," Administrative Office of the Illinois Courts, for those years. The 2003 ratio is an estimate from criminal court presiding judge Paul Biebel.

133   *The defendant was charged:* From Locallo's written opinion, May 10, 1989, in *People v. Bentley,* 88 MC1 36900801.

133   *During a bench trial:* "Trial hears testimony from speechless victim," *Chicago Sun-Times,* Oct. 19, 1995.

139   *26th Street Crew:* The elder DeSantis, also named Richard, was arrested in 1992 and charged with syndicate gambling. Police said DeSantis and another man

were taking bets on pro football games on cell phones in their cars, and that records in the cars indicated the men had handled $500,000 to $1 million in bets. Police said at the time that they suspected both men were members of the 26th Street Crew. "Two allegedly took $500,000 in bets," *Chicago Tribune*, Dec. 28, 1992. DeSantis later pled guilty to syndicated gambling, a felony, and was placed on probation and fined $1,000. Case file in *People v. DeSantis*, 93CR 503701.

139 *Prosecutors aren't worried:* "Mob ties to Clark witness," *Chicago Sun-Times*, July 2, 1998.

EIGHT · CHARLIE CHAN

141 *Cutler had been a year ahead:* The background on Cutler and my account of his slaying is based on interviews with his mother, Mary Kalinsky; with "Linda"; and with Chicago police spokesperson Sergeant Edward Alonzo.

142 *Detectives told reporters:* "Cops don't see link to Clark case in shooting death of witness," *Chicago Tribune*, May 18, 1998.

147 *Case law directs: People v. Ward*, 208 Ill. App. 3d 1073 (1991).

147 *"Miracle at 26th Street":* "Man defends himself in murder trial, wins," *Chicago Sun-Times*, July 16, 1994.

147 *A year later: People v. Hudson*, 95 CR 33003.

148 *A dollar-eighty a page:* In 1998; in 2002 the rate rose to $3.15.

NINE · PERSEVERATION

151 *One forced changes: Palmer, et al., v. City of Chicago, et al.*, 82 C 2349.

151 *The other: Jones v. City of Chicago, et al.*, 83 C 2430.

151 *"A frightening": Jones v. City of Chicago, et al.*, U.S. Court of Appeals for the Seventh Circuit, 856 F. 2d 985 (1988).

154 *Show-ups are generally considered:* Gary L. Wells, et al., "Eyewitness Identification Procedures: Recommendations for Lineups and Photospreads," *Law & Human Behavior* (1998), pp. 630–31.

155 *"Equivocal":* 7th Circuit (1988), p. 995.

155 *"Full of falsehoods":* Ibid., p. 990.

155 *"Student":* Bonita Brodt, *Chicago Tribune*, May 18, 1981.

158 Brady v. Maryland: 373 U.S. 83.

160 *Preparing witnesses:* Gershman, "Symposium: Effective Screening for Truth-Telling: Is It Possible? Witness Coaching by Prosecutors," *Cardozo Law Review*, (February 2002), p. 829.

164 *"That's my sister's"; "still hysterical":* "Witness, 11, hysterical at murder trial," *Chicago Tribune*, April 8, 1982.

165 *The state is accountable:* "The suppression by the prosecution of evidence favorable to an accused upon request violates due process . . . irrespective of the good faith or bad faith of the prosecution." *Brady v. Maryland*, 373 U.S. 83, at 87.

165 *"Deliberate misconduct"; "firm belief":* "Murder mistrial—police tactics come under scrutiny," *Chicago Tribune*, April 18, 1982.

166 *It prompted:* Testimony of William Kunkle, chief deputy state's attorney, Jan. 3, 1983, *Palmer v. Chicago*, 82 C 2349.

166 *Also compelled: Palmer v. Chicago*, 562 F. Supp. 1067, 1081 (1983).

166 *Prosecutors are generally immune: Imbler v. Pachtman*, 424 U.S. 409 (1976).

166 *The jurors fumed:* Rob Warden, "George Jones Gets Even," *Chicago Lawyer,* April 1987.

168 *Laverty got a disciplinary investigation:* "Cop faces discipline for court testimony," *Chicago Tribune,* May 7, 1982.

TEN · FREELY AND VOLUNTARILY

171 *Three disciplinary complaints:* Two of the charges were ultimately dismissed. The third became part of a complaint that eventually resulted in Washington's suspension from law practice for six months. *People v. Orange,* 168 Ill. 2d 138 (1995).

173 *Orange's disciplinary record:* Orange had committed only a "few minor" disciplinary violations in his fourteen years in prison, according to IDOC spokesperson Dede Short.

175 *Identified fifty criminal suspects:* "Special Project Conclusion Report," Office of Professional Standards, Chicago Police Department, Sept. 28, 1990.

175 *Military policeman:* Conroy, *Unspeakable Acts, Ordinary People,* pp. 61–62.

175 *The* Vigilante: John Carpenter, "Former cop accused of torture lies low in Florida," *Chicago Sun-Times,* Aug. 20, 2000.

175 *Andrew Wilson sued Burge: Wilson v. City of Chicago,* 86 C 2360; Conroy, *Unspeakable Acts, Ordinary People,* pp. 68–72.

176 *Deep Badge:* Interview with Wilson's attorney Flint Taylor.

176 *One letter:* Conroy, *Unspeakable Acts, Ordinary People,* pp. 158–59.

176 *Melvin Jones:* Wilson's lawyers had alleged that nine days before their client was abused, Burge had "electroshocked Melvin Jones on the genitals and thigh with a device in a wooden box and threatened him with a gun while he was handcuffed to a ring in the wall in an Area 2 interview room in an attempt to coerce a confession from him." In a May 15, 1995, response, the city admitted the statement's truth. *Wilson v. City of Chicago,* 86 C 2360.

177 *Gettleman assessed:* Conroy, *Unspeakable Acts, Ordinary People,* p. 235.

178 *Widespread; "poor and uninfluential"; "in some": Report on Lawlessness in Law Enforcement,* National Commission on Law Observance and Enforcement (1931), pp. 4, 159.

178 *"Electric monkey":* Ibid., p. 139.

178 *"It had":* Ernest J. Hopkins, *Our Lawless Police: A Study of the Unlawful Enforcement of the Law* (Viking Press, 1931), p. 220.

178 *"Thoroughly at home"; "Chicago telephone book"; "goldfish room": Report,* pp. 125–26.

178 *"Here's the best":* Ibid., p. 131. One police commisioner told the Wickersham Commission: "A policeman should be as free as a fireman to protect his community. Nobody ever thinks of hedging a fireman about with a lot of laws that favor the fire." Ibid., p. 179.

178 *"Tried the thumbscrews":* Ibid., p. 181.

178 *Psychological ploys:* Richard A. Leo, "From coercion to deception: the changing nature of police interrogation in America," *Crime, Law and Social Change* (1992), p. 35.

179 *Involuntarily given: Miranda v. Arizona,* 384 U.S. 436 (1966).

179 *If a defendant; "freely and voluntarily"; "general judicial tolerance": Our Lawless Police,* pp. 283–84.

179 *"Cops Protest"; "We are": Chicago Herald-Examiner,* date unspecified, quoted in *People v. Rogers,* 303 Ill. 578, 588 (1922).

180 *"At the expense"; high court directed:* Ibid., 590.

180 *Andrew Wilson: People v. Wilson,* 116 Ill. 2d 29 (1987).

180 *Gregory Banks: People v. Banks,* 192 Ill. App. 3d 986 (1989).

181 *The city paid him: Banks v. City of Chicago,* 91 C 6470 (U.S. District Court, Northern District of Illinois).

181 *Chicago police lie:* Myron Orfield, "Deterrence, Perjury, and the Heater Factor: An Exclusionary Rule in the Chicago Criminal Courts," *University of Colorado Law Review* (1992), p. 75.

183 Boyd v. United States: 116 U.S. 616.

ELEVEN · FATHER AND SON

185 *"Highly unlikely":* "Minister pushes for meeting with Clark, alleged attackers," *Chicago Defender,* July 7, 1997.

187 *Bruno Roti:* "Re: Bruno Roti," Chicago Crime Commission (CCC) memo, March 11, 1954.

187 *Democratic club; murders and bombings:* CCC memo.

187 *Series of arson fires; "sometimes paternal"; "give the go":* "Uncover plot to oust Negroes from 1st Ward," *Chicago Defender,* Sept. 7, 1946.

187 *When Bruno Roti died:* "Bruno Roti: Mystery mob boss," *Chicago Daily News,* July 10, 1958.

187 *Several of his six sons:* CCC memo.

187 *His son Fred: U.S. v. Marcy and Roti,* 90 CR 1045; "Roti found guilty on racketeering, bribery charges," *Chicago Tribune,* Jan. 15, 1993.

188 *Control of gambling:* Office of the Independent Hearing Officer, Laborers' International Union of North America, "In Re: Trusteeship Proceedings, Chicago District Council, Order and Memorandum" (Finding of Fact No. 26), Feb. 7, 1998; "List hoodlums ruling flow of graft," *Chicago Sun-Times,* Feb. 3, 1960.

188 *Arrested repeatedly:* Skid Caruso was one of the "1st ward hoodlums" who helped bring a $100,000–a-night crap game to Chicago from the suburbs in 1962, Chicago police said that year. The game operated in the 200 block of West Cermak Road. "Probe how dice game ran wide open," *Chicago Tribune,* Nov. 4, 1962. Earlier that same year, state's attorney's police had raided another large dice game across the street. When the police broke into the secret gambling room, the occupants attempted to flee through a freshly dug underground tunnel, but their escape was foiled when a fat gambler got wedged in the tunnel. Skid Caruso was among the eighteen arrested, and was one of the six charged with operating the game. A newspaper story about the raid made note of a "gallery of ancestral pictures flanking a family coat of arms" on a wall of the gambling room. "The coat of arms is of the Caruso family and an accompanying legend says the line was founded in 1026 by an Italian 'Cavalier of Fortune' in the service of Emperor Frederick II." In another corner of the gambling room was a glassed-in shrine with religious statues and holy pictures. *Chicago Sun-Times,* May 7, 1962.

188 *"Upper stratum": Juice Racketeers: Report on Criminal Usury in the Chicago Area,* Illinois Crime Investigating Commission, 1970, p. 128.

188 *Skid's son Frank:* "Frank [Toots] Caruso grew up within the organization with membership being passed from father to son like a family business," federal prosecutors maintained in 1996, in a filing in *U.S. v. LaMantia et. al.,* 93 CR 523. Caruso was not among the defendants in that case, but federal authorities had submitted FBI information about Caruso in support of a request to tap Caruso's phone during a gambling investigation.

188 *Several Chicago unions:* "In Re: Trusteeship Proceedings, Chicago District Council" (Findings of Fact Nos. 39 and 51), Feb. 7, 1998.

188 *Charles Bills:* "Union lifts curtain on mob in push to purge ranks," *Chicago Tribune,* Aug. 8, 1997.

188 *He and three Bridgeport friends: U.S. v. LaMantia et. al.,* 82 CR 871.

191 *Ice pick:* "Tapes show mob threat to 'cut heart' of 'gambler,' "*Chicago Sun-Times,* Sept. 7, 1983.

191 *"A lot of nonsense":* Transcript in *U.S. v. LaMantia et. al.,* Sept. 30, 1983.

TWELVE · DEFECTIVE PRODUCTS

193 *Treatment Alternatives for Safe Communities:* TASC stood for Treatment Alternatives to Street Crime when it was created in 1972. It later became Treatment Alternatives for Special Clients before it was renamed again in 1996. Interview with Melody Heaps, TASC founder and president.

197 *Coroner's jury ruled:* Coroner's Verdict, Inquest No. 290305, March 11, 1975.

199 *An hour and fifty-four minutes:* "Youth gets life term despite plea," *Chicago Sun-Times,* Sept. 22, 1982.

199 *"By about":* Cooney interview.

203 *"The retarded":* "Report of the Task Force on Law," *President's Panel on Mental Retardation, Task Force on Law,* 1963, p. 33.

203 *"Anecdotal accounts"; "more susceptible"; "great care":* Fred Inbau, John E. Reid, Joseph P. Buckley, and Brian C. Jayne, *Criminal Interrogation and Confessions* (Aspen Publishers, 2001), pp. 431–32.

204 *"Dramatic tones"; "a positive attitude":* Ibid., p. 404.

204 *"Heavy burden": Miranda v. Arizona,* 384 U.S. 436 (1966), at 475.

205 *A study:* Morgan Cloud, George B. Shepherd, Alison Nodvin Barkoff, and Justin V. Shur, "Words Without Meaning: The Constitution, Confessions, and Mentally Retarded Suspects," *University of Chicago Law Review* (spring 2002), p. 495.

205 *A checkered career:* Maurice Possley, Steve Mills, and Ken Armstrong, "Veteran detective's murder cases unravel," *Chicago Tribune,* Dec. 17, 2001.

205 *Boudreau helped pay:* Deposition of Kenneth Boudreau, June 20, 1996, in *Wiggins v. Burge, et al.,* 93 C 199.

206 *The rate of hospitalization:* David Mechanic and David A. Rochefort, "Deinstitutionalization: An Appraisal of Reform," *Annual Review of Sociology* (Annual Reviews, Inc., 1990), vol. 16, issue 1, p. 301.

206 *The money promised:* Ralph Slovenko, "The Transinstitutionalization of the Mentally Ill," *Ohio Northern Law Review* (2003), p. 641.

206 *Sixteen percent:* "Mental Health and Treatment of Inmates and Probationers," Special Report, Bureau of Justice Statistics, July 1999.

206 *That would equal 333,000:* Sixteen percent times the inmate population at midyear 2003, which was 2,079,000, according to the Bureau of Justice Statistics.

206 *The number of patients:* "Highlights of Organized Mental Health Services in 2000 and Major National and State Trends," Substance Abuse and Mental Health Services Administration.

206 *A widespread public belief:* In one telephone survey, 89 percent of the respondents agreed that "the insanity plea is a loophole that allows too many guilty people to go free." V. P. Hans, "An Analysis of Public Attitudes Toward the Insanity Defense," *Criminology,* 4(2) (1986), pp. 393–415. In another study, 209 University of Wyoming students were asked to guess how many felony defendants invoked an insanity plea in a given two-year period in Wyoming. As a group, the students guessed 37 percent. In fact, less that one-half of one percent of the defendants had entered the plea. Richard A. Pasewark and Deborah Seidenzahl, "Opinions Concerning the Insanity Plea and Criminality Among Mental Patients," *Bulletin of the American Academy of Psychiatry and Law,* 7(2) (1979), pp. 199–202.

206 *Eight-state study:* L. A. Callahan, H. J. Steadman, M. A. McGreevy, and P. C. Robbins, "The Volume and Characteristics of Insanity Defense Pleas," *Bulletin of the American Academy of Psychiatry and Law* (1991), pp. 331–38.

206 *In Cook County:* According to Paul Biebel, criminal court presiding judge.

206 *More time in custody:* Grant H. Morris, "Placed in Purgatory: Conditional Release of Insanity Acquittees," *Arizona Law Review* (fall 1997), p. 1061.

206 *Guilty but mentally ill:* Mark A. Woodmansee, "The Guilty but Mentally Ill Verdict: Political Expediency at the Expense of Moral Principle," *Notre Dame Journal of Law, Ethics & Public Policy* (1996), p. 341.

207 *They kill themselves:* Charles Lloyd, *Suicide and Self-Injury in Prison* (Home Office Research Study, London, 1990).

207 *Mentally retarded prisoners: Ruiz v. Estelle, 503 F. Supp. 1265* (1980).

THIRTEEN · FIXES

212 *He once scolded a jury:* "He just sat on the bench up there and shouted at the top of his voice," one juror told a *Tribune* reporter. Maloney said he was only shouting at the public defender for interrupting him. The transcript showed that Maloney had told the jurors, "How you arrived at this verdict is beyond me." The juror said that because of the way the judge had treated the jury, she'd lie if necessary to avoid future jury service. "A shocking verdict and jolting response," *Chicago Tribune,* May 13, 1986.

213 *Operation Greylord: Chicago Sun-Times* reporter Art Petacque disclosed in August 1983 that an ongoing investigation of the Cook County courts would soon result in indictments. The first indictments were announced that December. Tuohy and Warden, *Greylord,* pp. 139–40. "Greylord" was a "sarcastic reference to the dignity of the English lord chancellors, who wear wigs, and the lack of dignity in the Chicago courts." Ibid., p. 45.

214 *"Not germane": People v. Titone,* 151 Ill. 2d 19 (1992).

214 *Maloney, by then retired: U.S. v. Maloney,* 91 CR 477; "Ex-judge Maloney guilty of fixing murder cases," *Chicago Sun-Times,* April 17, 1993.

214 *Another 26th Street judge:* "Rukn convictions set aside; corruption of judge is cited," *Chicago Tribune,* Sept. 19, 1996.

217 *Roth not only fixed cases: U.S. v. Roth,* 85 CR 763; 860 F. 2d 1382 (1988).

218 *Stopped investigating Lane:* Tuohy and Warden, *Greylord,* p. 132.

219 *Convictions in the 1980s and 1990s:* Most of the convictions were a result of Greylord, but Maloney and two other judges were convicted after a second federal probe in the late 1980s and early 1990s, Operation Gambat. "Gambat" was derived from "gambling attorney;" federal prosecutors' chief witness, Robert Cooley, was an outfit attorney with gambling debts.

219 *In a 1990 survey:* "Report on the Operations of the Criminal Division of the Circuit Court of Cook County," Chicago Crime Commission, October 1990. Maloney also got poor marks in knowledge of the law and impartiality, and in his willingness to avoid personal or political favors.

220 *"Distinct possibility":* Seventh Circuit appellate judge Ilana Rovner, concurring in part and dissenting in part in *Bracy v. Schomig,* 286 F. 3d 406, at 426 (2002).

220 *Local prosecutors weren't about to expose:* "Not only outright corruption and not only the dictates of a political machine but also restraints imposed by friendship, political indebtedness, and political fear worked to discourage local prosecutors from pursuing local grafters." Noonan, *Bribes,* pp. 600–1.

220 *Federal laws passed in the 1970s:* Especially the Racketeering Influenced and Corrupt Organization Act (RICO), enacted in 1970 to help federal prosecutors fight organized crime. The use of RICO against local corruption was a "facet of the larger tendency to federalize provincial preserves," Noonan argues. It can't be known if corruption increased in the 1970s and 1980s, but Noonan doubts it did. "What was clear was that corruption was being investigated and punished on a scale unknown before"—because the feds had gotten involved. *Bribes,* pp. 584–601.

220 *The first judge in the nation:* Tuohy and Warden, *Greylord,* p. 36.

220 *On the first day; "I love": U.S. v. Roth,* 860 F. 2d 1382, 1383.

220 *Olson pled guilty:* "Judge Olson gets 12-year sentence," *Chicago Tribune,* March 22, 1986.

220 *"Never fixed a murder":* Maloney wasn't the only judge at 26th Street who did that. In 1977, Judge Frank Wilson acquitted reputed mob hitman Harry Aleman of the 1972 shotgun murder of a Teamster's steward, despite the testimony of two eyewitnesses. An informant later told authorities he'd bought the verdict from Judge Wilson with $10,000 of mob money. In 1990, shortly after Wilson learned that the acquittal was being investigated, he shot himself to death. Prosecutors later sought to retry Aleman, and his lawyers cited the Fifth Amendment protection against double-jeopardy in their attempt to block that effort. But the Illinois Appellate Court held that because of the fix, Aleman hadn't been in "jeopardy" the first time he was tried. He was convicted in 1997 and sentenced to one hundred to three hundred years. The lawyer who first represented Aleman in the case was Maloney, although by the time of his first trial Aleman had a different lawyer. Maurice Possley and Rick Kogan, *Everybody Pays: Two Men, One Murder, and the Price of Truth* (Putnam, 2001).

220 *"Selling the prosecutor":* This ploy has existed for at least a half century: Samuel Dash wrote about it in 1951 in his study of the federal branch of the Municipal Court of Cook County. It was well known that prosecutors in that branch were usually willing to reduce felony charges to misdemeanors to get guilty pleas, Dash wrote, but defense lawyers would warn clients—especially

young first offenders—that they were facing a long prison term. "The attorneys inform the defendant that they know the judge and the prosecutor and with a little money can buy them off and get them to accept a plea of guilty to a misdemeanor. The frightened defendant doesn't care how he is saved, so long as he is saved. Somehow he raises the money his lawyer demands. The lawyer pays no money to the judge or prosecutor, but pockets the money." After the defendant is allowed to plead guilty to a misdemeanor and is given probation, he "informs his friends that his lawyer is a 'sharp operator' and that the judges and prosecutors can be bought off." Dash, "Cracks in the Foundation of Criminal Justice," p. 395.

221 *"Mafia factotum"; "racketeer"; "ruthless"; "depraved": Bracy v. Schomig,* 286 F. 3d 406 (2002).

224 *Salaries of circuit judges:* Administrative Office of the Illinois Courts.

224 *Bribing clerks: U.S. v. Wolfson,* 83 CR 976. Dean Wolfson was a defense lawyer who in 1985 was sentenced to seven and a half years in federal prison for racketeering and mail fraud, charges stemming from Greylord. In 1994, when Wolfson asked a judge to end his probation early, prosecutors submitted a thirty-three-page filing detailing how he bribed clerks and had them steer cases to corrupt judges. "Government's Response to Defendant's Motion for Early Termination of Probation," *U.S. v. Wolfson,* August 30, 1994.

224 *A commission:* "A Report on the Felony Courts," *Special Commission on the Administration of Justice in Cook County,* 1987, p. 17.

224 *No audit:* According to Paul Biebel, the presiding judge in 2004.

226 *Anthony Spilotro:* William F. Roemer Jr., *The Enforcer* (Donald I. Fine, 1994).

226 *Members of Titone's family:* Dino Titone interview.

226 *Wasn't unwise for Spilotro:* "Spilotro not guilty in murders," *Chicago Tribune,* Oct. 28, 1983. Spilotro didn't have to spend time in jail while his case was pending, having posted $100,000 bail; nor was he confined to Illinois, as Maloney allowed him to travel to Las Vegas over the objections of prosecutors. ("Judge approves Spilotro travel to Las Vegas," *Chicago Tribune,* March 19, 1983.) At Maloney's sentencing in 1994, federal prosecutors offered testimony from an outfit turncoat that the Spilotro acquittal was fixed. But one of the assistant state's attorneys who'd prosecuted Spilotro testified that the evidence in the case had been so weak that he'd have been "very, very surprised" if Maloney had convicted Spilotro. ("As a lawyer, Maloney paid off judges, admitted mobster says," *Chicago Tribune,* July 21, 1994.)

226 *Mob leaders:* Roemer, *War of the Godfathers* (Donald I. Fine, 1990), p. 289.

227 *A ruling upheld: Bracy v. Schomig,* 286 F. 2d 406 (2002).

227 *"It is a sad day": Bracy v. Schomig,* 248 F. 3d 604 (2001).

228 *"There are doubtless"; "appalling"; "not written for easy cases": Bracy v. Gramley,* 81 F. 3d 684 (1996).

229 *"Overbearing conduct": People v. Blue,* 189 Ill. 2d 99 (2000).

FOURTEEN · A SENSITIVE AREA

233 *"A mysterious 'black box'":* "Cop 'black box' torture charged," *Chicago Tribune,* Feb. 9, 1984.

FIFTEEN · WHAT REALLY HAPPENED

242 *In recent years:* Saundra Westervelt, *Shifting the Blame: How Victimization Became a Criminal Defense* (Rutgers University Press, 1998), pp. 65–80.

244 *The world's first such court:* David Tanenhaus, *Policing the Child: Juvenile Justice in Chicago, 1870–1925* (University of Chicago Ph.D. thesis, 1997); David Rothman, *Conscience and Convenience* (Little, Brown, 1980), pp. 205–36.

244 *Similar courts:* Within five years, ten states had juvenile justice procedures; by 1920, all but three states had juvenile courts. Ibid., p. 215.

244 *"The problem":* Julian Mack, "The Juvenile Court," *Harvard Law Review* (1909–10), pp. 119–20.

244 *But even in the earliest years:* Tanenhaus, "The evolution of transfer out of the juvenile court," *The Changing Borders of Juvenile Justice* (University of Chicago Press, 2000), pp. 13–43.

244 *Across the nation:* Daniel E. Traver, "The Wrong Answer to a Serious Problem: A Story of School Shootings, Politics and Automatic Transfer," *Loyola University Chicago Law Journal* (winter 2000); David S. Tanenhaus and Steven A. Drizin, "'Owing to the Extreme Youth of the Accused': The Changing Legal Response to Juvenile Homicide," *Northwestern School of Law Journal of Criminal Law and Criminology* (spring/summer 2002), p. 641.

244 *Increases the recidivism:* David L. Myers, *Excluding Violent Youths from Juvenile Court: The Effectiveness of Legislative Waiver* (LFC Scholarly Pub., LLC, 2001); Donna M. Bishop, et al., "The Transfer of Juveniles to Criminal Court: Does It Make a Difference?" (*Crime & Delinquency*, 1996), p. 183.

244 *Perhaps:* F. P. Reddington and A. D. Sapp, "Juveniles in Adult Prisons: Problems and Prospects," *Journal of Crime & Justice* (1997).

249 *PTSD became:* Westervelt, *Shifting the Blame*, pp. 130–31.

249 *"Development":* Diagnostic and Statistical Manual of Mental Disorders, fourth edition (American Psychiatric Association, 1994), pp. 424–29.

249 *First used as a criminal defense:* Westervelt, *Shifting the Blame*, pp. 129–36.

249 *They wrote an article:* Larry Heinrich, Hon. Michael S. Jordan, and Marijane Placek, "Perspectives on the Battered Woman Syndrome: It's Time to Modify Illinois Law," *Illinois Bar Journal* (February 1994).

250 *According to the National Center:* Julia Whealin, "Child Sexual Abuse: A National Center for PTSD Fact Sheet," http://www.ncptsd.org (visited Dec. 12, 2004).

259 *In reality:* Interview with IDOC spokesperson Sergio Molina.

SIXTEEN · PREJUDICE

261 Batson v. Kentucky: 476 U.S. 79.

261 *Great Britain did so:* Judith Heinz, "Peremptory challenges in criminal cases: a comparison of regulation in the United States, England, and Canada," *Loyola of Los Angeles International & Comparative Law Journal* (November 1993), p. 201.

261 *"Charade": People v. Randall,* 283 Ill. App. 3d 1019.

262 *Not a single black male:* No agency collects racial data on Cook County jurors. But in 2000, the *Chicago Reporter,* an investigative monthly, studied census tract information of jurors who reported for duty during the first six months of that

year. The magazine found that men from black neighborhoods were "far less likely" to be picked for juries than men from white neighborhoods and women of any race or ethnicity. "The color of justice on Cook County juries," *Chicago Reporter,* April 2001.

267 *"It may fairly": State v. Chapple,* 135 Ariz. 281 (1983).

268 *Prosecutors are required: People v. Godina,* 223 Ill. App. 3d 205 (1991).

270 *Martha DiCaro:* "Hood's son acquitted in girl's death," *Chicago Tribune,* April 11, 1981; "Killing unexplained; family asks, 'Why?'" Bonita Brodt, *Chicago Tribune,* April 26, 1981.

275 *He's convinced:* Comments that Clevan made at a press conference two weeks after the attack seem to lend support to Turner's contention that more than one youth attacked Clevan and Lenard at 33rd and Shields. One white youth "hit me across my head and the other had hit Lenard," Clevan was quoted as saying. Chinta Strausberg, "Other Bridgeport victim relives incident," *Chicago Defender,* April 7, 1997.

277 *A judge may bar testimony: People v. Illgen.* 145 Ill. 2d 353, 365 (1991).

278 *"At least an associate":* "In Re: Trusteeship Proceedings, Chicago District Council" (Finding of Fact No. 65), Feb. 7, 1998.

283 *With the intensive-care photo:* Interviews with Atif Sheikh and two jurors who wished to remain anonymous.

EIGHTEEN · COMPASSION

289 *$51 a day:* Cook County Department of Corrections estimate.

292 *Locallo received good news:* "Lawyer groups unite in opposing divorce court judge's retention," *Chicago Tribune,* Oct. 13, 1998.

293 *Judges have been retained:* Larry Aspin, William K. Hall, Jean Bax, and Celeste Montoya, "Thirty Years of Judicial Retention Elections: An Update," *Social Science Journal* (2000), p. 1.

293 *Retention rates are even higher:* From 1964 through 1994, the retention rate was 99.2 percent in the nine states other than Illinois that have retention elections. Ibid.

294 *"Perfectly reasonable":* "Justice for Lenard Clark," *Chicago Tribune,* Sept. 22, 1998.

294 *"Justice has been served":* "Wounds to heal," *Chicago Sun-Times,* Sept. 23, 1998.

294 *"Send a strong message":* Ibid.

294 *"Fully accountable":* "For Clark jurors, an agonizing decision," *Chicago Tribune,* Sept. 20, 1998.

294 *Illinois law generally dictates:* It did in 1998. A 2003 amendment (P.A. 93-160) makes it easier for judges to issue consecutive sentences.

294 *"Substantial change":* 730 ILCS 5/5-8-4 (a) (1998).

302 *Davis will resign:* "NAACP prez resigns, denies being ousted," *Chicago Defender,* Oct. 21, 1998.

303 *"Environmental disasters":* Testimony of deputy corporation counsel Susan Lichtenstein, Dec. 22, 1993, *U.S. v. Wolf,* 92 CR 737.

304 *Wolf later pointed out: U.S. v. Wolf,* 90 F. 3d 191 (1996).

NINETEEN · POLITICS

311   *"Justice was not served":* "Punishment in Clark case must fit crime, Rev. Jackson says," *Chicago Defender,* Oct. 22, 1998.

311   *Robert Shaw:* "NAACP prez resigns, denies being ousted," *Chicago Defender,* Oct. 21, 1998.

311   *"The justice system"; "We all know":* "Outcry at Clark sentence," *Chicago Defender,* Oct. 21, 1998.

311   *"Let off":* "Probation for savage racial beating," *Independent,* Oct. 20, 1998.

311   *"I'm gonna":* Jack Higgins, *Chicago Sun-Times,* Oct. 21, 1998.

311   *In tears; "for continued":* " 'Why didn't they go to jail?' mom asks," *Chicago Tribune,* Oct. 21, 1998.

312   *Junior-middleweight boxer:* "Different career paths for Jankovich, LaRosa," *Chicago Sun-Times,* March 26, 1998.

320   *A large ad: Chicago Defender,* Oct. 24, 1998.

320   *Humanitarian award:* "Gator hails award given to Caruso Sr.," *Chicago Defender,* Oct. 15, 1998; "Clark beating shatters fragile racial alliance," *Chicago Reporter,* April 1999.

320   *"By all accounts":* "A judge under siege," *Chicago Sun-Times,* Oct. 27, 1998.

320   *"Travesty of justice":* "Judge owed justice in face of Caruso allies' attack," Steve Neal, *Chicago Sun-Times,* Nov. 2, 1998.

320   *"He's fair":* "Judges up for election walking a delicate tightrope," *Chicago Tribune,* Oct. 23, 1998.

320   *Leaders of bar groups:* Letters supporting Locallo were written by the president of the Cook County Bar Association, the judicial liaison of the Illinois State Bar Association, the chairman of the board of the Chicago Crime Commission, the president of the Chicago chapter of the Federal Bar Association, and the chairman of the Illinois Committee for Judicial Independence of the American Judicature Society. *Chicago Sun-Times,* Nov. 2, 1998, p. 32.

321   *"Vindictive":* "A judge under siege," *Chicago Sun-Times,* Oct. 27, 1998.

321   *In other democracies:* Steven P. Croley, "The Majoritarian Difficulty: Elective Judiciaries and the Rule of Law," *University of Chicago Law Review* (spring 1995), p. 691.

321   *In the nineteenth century:* Ibid., p. 716.

321   *In fifteen states:* Alaska, Arizona, California, Colorado, Florida, Indiana, Iowa, Kansas, Maryland, Missouri, Nebraska, Oklahoma, South Dakota, Utah, and Wyoming. Ibid., p. 726.

321   *"Hardly any":* Chicago Bar Association's *Judicial Voters Survey,* reported in "Some candidates come out swinging but ballot loses punch," *Chicago Lawyer,* November 1998.

321   *Pushing for merit for decades:* Rubin G. Cohn, *To Judge with Justice: History and Politics of Illinois Judicial Reform* (University of Illinois Press, 1973).

322   *Minorities and women get judgeships:* "The Majoritarian Difficulty," pp. 784–86.

322   *Merit selection was one of the chief reforms; "particularly corrosive":* "Report on Judicial Selection," Special Commission on the Administration of Justice in Cook County, October 1985.

322   *Illinois judicial candidates are prohibited:* Code of Judicial Conduct, Rule 67, Canon 7 (B) (2), Illinois Supreme Court Rules.

322 *Locallo's committee:* Campaign disclosure records, Illinois State Board of Elections (ISBE).

323 *In the 1980s:* Marlene Arnold Nicholson and Norman Nicholson, "Funding Judicial Campaigns in Illinois," *Judicature* (May–June 1994), p. 298.

323 *In 1993:* Code of Judicial Conduct, Rule 67, Canon 7, A (1) (d), Illinois Supreme Court Rules.

323 *But judges are still allowed:* Code of Judicial Conduct, Rule 67, Canon 7, B (1) (a) (iii).

323 *In Locallo's first campaign:* Campaign disclosure records, ISBE.

323 *"Play God":* "Voters decide county judiciary worth keeping," *Chicago Tribune,* Nov. 5, 1998.

323 *Perhaps the $40,000; $20,000:* Campaign disclosure records, ISBE.

324 *"Used to"; "to interfere"; "I will not":* "Judge stands by Clark rulings," *Chicago Tribune,* Oct. 24, 1998.

324 *"Cowards":* WMAQ-TV, 10 P.M. news, Nov. 2, 1998.

324 *Law professor suggests:* "Clark trial judge defends himself with media blitz," *Chicago Sun-Times,* Oct. 24, 1998.

324 *Three checks to PUSH:* Two checks for $500 each were issued to PUSH by Locallo's committee on Oct. 31, 1998, and another for $200 on Dec. 5, 1998. Campaign disclosure records, ISBE.

326 *Thumbs down; in almost every other precinct:* Chicago Board of Elections; Cook County Clerk.

326 *"We retained":* "Voters decide county judiciary worth keeping," *Chicago Tribune,* Nov. 5, 1998.

327 *Two anonymous tipsters:* My account of the police investigation is based on the reports and handwritten notes of the investigating detectives, my interviews with Detective Turner, and transcripts of testimony before the grand jury.

327 *He invoked:* Grand jury transcript, March 25, 1997.

329 *"He seen Frankie":* Grand jury transcript, March 27, 1997.

330 *Nearly half:* In the years 2000 through 2003, 46 percent of the felony cases were indictments, according to data from presiding judge Paul Biebel.

330 *"People's Panel":* Richard D. Younger, *The People's Panel: The Grand Jury in the United States, 1634–1941* (Brown University Press, 1963).

330 *As criminal law grew more complex:* Susan W. Brenner, "The Voice of the Community: A Case for Grand Jury Independence," *Virginia Journal of Social Policy and the Law* (fall 1995), p. 67.

331 *Already in 1870; "ceased to be"; "utterly useless":* Debates and Proceedings of the Constitutional Convention of the State of Illinois (E. L. Merritt & Bro., 1870), at 1434 and 1438.

331 *"Believed"; "gives":* Kirchwey, *Reports Comprising the Survey of the Cook County Jail,* pp. 45–46.

331 *Approved 1,769 indictments:* According to data from presiding judge Biebel.

331 *Napkin:* "Grand jury called tool of the prosecutor," *Arizona Daily Star,* Feb. 10, 1974.

331 *Ham sandwich:* The New York judge was Sol Wachtler. "Do we need grand juries?" *New York Times,* Feb. 18, 1985.

331 *Legal scholars:* Brenner, "The Voice of the Community." One state—Hawaii—has an independent grand jury counsel. Ibid., p. 94.

332 *Eighteen leading questions:* Grand jury transcript, April 17, 1997.

334 *Prosecutors are apt:* Albert Alschuler, "The Prosecutor's Role in Plea Bargaining," *University of Chicago Law Review* (1968), p. 60.

335 *"Factual basis":* "The purpose of the rule is to allow the trial court to insure that defendant is not pleading guilty to a crime which his acts and mental state do not support." *People v. Dilger,* 125 Ill. App. 3d 277 (1984).

335 *To be accountable:* 720 ILCS 5/5-2 (c).

335 *Requires more:* Judges must determine in the factual basis "that the acts alleged to have been committed by the defendant constitute the offense to which defendant is pleading guilty . . . to prevent the possibility of defendant pleading guilty to a crime beyond the confines of his acts." *People v. Billops,* 16 Ill. App. 3d 892 (1974).

EPILOGUE: A PROMISING FUTURE

338 *"Important prosecution"; "to the full extent":* Devine press conference, Nov. 20, 1998.

338 *DeSantis was bused:* Interview with IDOC spokesperson Sergio Molina.

338 *The skeptics:* The circumstances surrounding Cutler's murder "remain suspicious," Devine told a reporter in 2003. "Who killed Michael Cutler?" *Chicago Sun-Times,* May 11, 2003. Mandeltort, Berlin, Turner, and Locallo expressed their doubts in interviews with me.

338 *Dateline NBC feature:* "Witness for the Prosecution," Jan. 14, 2000.

339 *"One can":* "It's about time someone got serious about Cutler probe," *Chicago Sun-Times,* May 13, 2003.

339 *"Classic mob hit":* "Who killed Michael Cutler?"

339 *But a police spokesperson:* Interview with Sergeant Edward Alonzo.

340 *Hard to get into; Caruso applied; ten pounds of raw hamburger:* Molina interview.

340 *The accompanying story; "historic thing":* "Clark visits his attacker," *Chicago Sun-Times,* Jan. 18, 2000.

340 *Callers:* "We had every caller say that it was phony, a setup, a gimmick. Nobody thought this was a good idea," said the host of the talk show, Cliff Kelley. "Lenard Clark, attacker reportedly now friends," *Chicago Sun-Times,* Jan. 19, 2000.

340 *"Spin doctor":* "Judge Locallo tells of death threats in Caruso trial," *Chicago Defender,* Jan. 20, 2000.

340 *"Shocking violation":* "Kup's Column," *Chicago Sun-Times,* Jan. 21, 2000.

341 *Illinois Supreme Court affirmed: People v. Orange,* 195 Ill. 2d 437 (2001).

341 *"Grave concerns"; "shameful record":* Ryan statement to reporters, Jan. 31, 2000.

342 *Deflect attention:* "Our family feels that Gov. Ryan is using the issue of the death penalty to divert attention from his own political scandals," said a letter published in the *Tribune,* signed by Ruth A. Adcock and "the Brewer family," surviving relatives of the victims of a triple homicide in downstate Illinois. Adcock and the Brewer family wanted the man who was on death row for the triple homicide executed. *Chicago Tribune,* Feb. 9, 2000. Letter-writer Todd Janus likened Ryan's moratorium to President Bill Clinton's bombing of a Sudan pharmaceutical

plant, with which, Janus said, Clinton "diverted attention . . . from his lying under oath and obstruction of justice." *Chicago Tribune*, Oct. 28, 2002.

342 *Ryan pardoned four:* The speech announcing the pardons was given at the DePaul University College of Law.

342 *Commuted the sentences:* Ryan announced the commutations at the Northwestern University School of Law.

342 *One of 165 nominees:* "Oddsmaker puts Ryan at 12–1 for winning Nobel," *Chicago Sun-Times*, Oct. 9, 2003. The prize went to Iranian human rights activist Shirin Ebadi.

342 *"Outrageous and unconscionable":* Devine added that it was a "shocking disgrace and insult to the victims' families and our idea of justice that these violent convicted murderers will be free to roam the streets, while every day the victims' families continue to mourn the loss of their loved ones." Statement to reporters, Jan. 10, 2003.

342 *Now suing:* "Ex-inmate sues, charges torture," *Chicago Tribune*, Jan. 11, 2004.

342 *Orange received $161,000:* Interview with one of his lawyers, Cathryn Crawford.

342 *In February he was arrested; arrested again:* "Inmate freed by Ryan racks up 2nd arrest," *Chicago Sun-Times*, June 18, 2004.

343 *"We believe":* "Probers believe brutality claims," *Chicago Tribune*, May 21, 2003.

343 *Had taken on Young's and Hill's cases:* Interview with Zellner.

343 *In dropping the case:* "12 years behind bars, now justice at last," *Chicago Tribune*, Feb. 1, 2005.

345 *Cook County keeps sending:* IDOC data.

345 *Crackdown on parole violators:* In 2003, 3,623 Cook County parolees were returned to prison for technical violations—such as failing drug tests or missing meetings with parole officers—compared with only 566 in 1996, according to the IDOC.

345 *Largest proportion:* In 2002, 42 percent of the prisoners admitted to Illinois penitentiaries had been convicted of drug crimes, 31 percent of property crimes, and 24 percent of violent crimes. "2002 Statistical Presentation," IDOC.

345 *Still 80 percent:* Ten percent of the prisoners sent from Cook County in 2003 were Hispanic and 9 percent were white, according to the IDOC.

345 *Inmates in tents:* "Tents ready for possible jail overflow," *Chicago Tribune*, April 17, 2002.

345 *Fifteen hundred inmates:* "Justice is pushing inmates to the floor," *Arlington Heights Daily Herald*, June 23, 2002.

346 *"Not distracted"; "dehumanizing"; time saved:* Joy Bergmann, "Court TV," *Chicago Reader*, March 26, 1999.

INDEX